The History & Artistry of
NATIONAL
Resonator Instruments
by Bob Brozman
with Dr. John Dopyera Jr.,
Richard A. Smith & Gary Atkinson

Library of Congress Catalog Card Number:
93-70855

ISBN 0-931759-70-6
SAN 683-8022

National is a Registered Trademark of National Reso-Phonic Guitars Inc.
871 Via Esteban, #C - San Luis Obispo, CA 93401

Duolian is a registered trademark of the Gibson Guitar Corp.

Cover Art **- Scott McDougall**
712 N. 62nd St Seattle,WA 98103

Layout **- Bob Brozman & Ron Middlebrook**
Production **- Ron Middlebrook**

Special thanks to John Seivert
for the photos

Contents

PREFACE.....3

CHAPTER 1
DAD, Some Personal Reflections......5
  by Dr. John Dopyera, Jr.

CHAPTER 2
The Early History of National......19
  by Richard Smith and Bob Brozman
The Tri-cone Guitar......21
Forming The National Corporation......27
Disagreements At National......29
Dobro Versus National......31
National's Factory......33
The Early 1930's......36
National and Dobro Merge......38
National - Dobro Moves To Chicago......42
The Search For Amplification......48
  by Gary Atkinson
Metal Instrument Production Time Line......50

CHAPTER 3
National's Array of Instruments and Models......51
       Style 1......53
       Style 2......55
       Style 3......61
       Style 4......66
       Style 97......74
       Style 35......78
       Style M-3 Hawaii......82

CHAPTER 4
Single Resonator Instrument Styles......83
Style O......85
Don Guitars......89
Style N......90
Triolian Models......90
Duolian......96
National/Supro "Collegian" Models......97
Wood Bodied Resonator Guitars......97
National Guitar Models from a Musician's Perspective......100

CHAPTER 5
Construction Details of Metal Resonator Instruments......103
Necks and Headstocks......103
Fingerboards......105
Metal Bodies......107
Tricone Resonator System......108
Single Resonator System......109
Coverplates......110
Tailpieces......112
Parts Lists......113

CHAPTER 6
Hawaiian Recording Artists Using Nationals......115
       Sol Hoopii......115
       The Tau Moe Family......121
       Sam Ku West......129
       King Bennie Nawahi......131
       Jim and Bob, The Genial Hawaiians......133
       David Kane......134
       Various classic photos of Hawaiian musicians......135

CHAPTER 7
Blues and Jazz Artists Using Nationals......142
       Tampa Red......142
       Son House......145
       Booker White......146
       Bo Carter......148
       Blind Boy Fuller......149
       Walter Vincent......150
       Peetie Wheatstraw......152
       Scrapper Blackwell......153
       Bumble Bee Slim......154
       Oscar Aleman......155
       Black Ace......156
       The "Mike" McKendrick Brothers......159
       Various Jazz Artists With Nationals......193
Nationals On The Street......197
  by Gary Atkinson

CHAPTER 8
Advertisements and Catalogs......200

CHAPTER 9
Set-up and Maintainance of Nationals......241
Bridge Saddle......242
Neck Attachment and Angle Considerations......242
Tuning Gears......243
Resonator and Body Rattles......243
Maintaining Plated and Painted Body Finishes......245
Proper Shipment and Case Storage......246

CHAPTER 10
The Future of National......247

APPENDIX A
National Serial Numbers......253
General Grouping of National Serial Numbers......253
The Tricone Serial Numbers......254
Silver Ukuleles......256
Silver Mandolins......257
Silver Tenor and Plectrum Guitars......258
S-Prefix Style O Guitars......258
X-Series Silver "Don" Guitars......259
Triolian Guitars......260
Duolian Serial Numbers......261
1936-1941 Letter-Prefix Serial Numbers......262
Wood Body Nationals......263
NATIONAL SERIAL NUMBER LIST......264

APPENDIX B
The National Company, A Chronology......280
From 10-12-1926 to 1942

APPENDIX C
Hawaiian Artist Discography......290

PREFACE

I had been playing guitar for 8 years, when, in 1968, I stumbled across a National guitar. As a result, my life has changed irrevocably. I never played a regular acoustic guitar again. It took very little time to realize that I would someday be earning my living playing Nationals. I have been using these remarkable instruments exclusively since then. I began as an itinerant street musician in the early 1970's. I haven't held a day job since--moving first into clubs, colleges, festivals, and finally over the last decade, records and worldwide touring. I owe it all to the National. Every time I open one of my road cases I get stunned momentarily by the look of the National inside, just as I did when I first saw one at the impressionable age of 14. The look of these instruments conjures up an optimistic vision of the future through the minds of the 1920's and 1930's.

I've learned a lot about the playing of music and the creation and alteration of sounds--all taught to me by the interesting sonic characteristics of the National. The various musics I've been attracted to over the years have always featured Nationals. In fact, it was the hunt for recordings of Nationals that led me through 1920's and 1930's blues, Hawaiian and jazz music. The powerful tonal response of resonator instruments has taught me much about techniques for controlling and manipulating dynamics and tone.

In 1984, I received a letter from John Dopyera, Jr. who is the son of the inventor of the National. In this letter John stated "Dad has all your records, and is a big fan of yours--you really should get in touch with him. He is in a private nursing home without much contact from musical friends." I had assumed that John, Sr. had passed away, so I was very surprised to receive the letter. Since the National had long meant so much to me, I was greatly honored that the inventor was a fan of mine. I called John, Sr. immediately and we had a long conversation about his masterpiece invention, the National guitar.

I began visiting John in Grants Pass, Oregon several times a year. During these visits we passed the time in various ways. Naturally, I conducted several formal interviews concerning the specifics of the National story from the invention to the eventual departure of John from the company. I also was able to learn from John many construction and set-up details that otherwise would have been lost to history. John's strong dual sense of musical tonal quality and mechanical inventiveness was still vibrant.

We also spent time playing music together. In his 90's, John could still play violin, mandolin, and Hawaiian guitar. It gave him great pleasure to play on my National instruments, since he had long ago given away or lost any Nationals he had. John stated quite clearly on several occasions that tonally and esthetically, his greatest invention was the metal tricone National. He was quite bitter about having his ideas and patents appropriated by George Beauchamp, particularly with regard to to the single cone resonator. In this book, with the factual evidence I have gathered, I will show how this actually happened, and thus clearly establish John Dopyera as the inventor of the National, and George as the man who created the National company. The instruments never would have been made without the interaction of these two men.

An interesting side issue is the statement by John that the Dobro was "second best" to the National in sound. He further stated that the only reason Dobros were constructed of wood was because he and his brothers could not afford the machine and stamping tools to work in metal.

My last few visits with John were rather sad, since he was almost completely bedridden and very depressed about his health. Sometimes I would play the old tunes quietly while he sang or hummed the melodies from his bed. It was heartbreaking to see this great man sitting alone in a nursing home, without receiving any of the recognition he deserved. I made many attempts while John was alive to bring him recognition through articles in Guitar Player and Frets, as well as dedicating some of my albums to him. This book represents the culmination of these efforts. It is a labor of love, as well as an intended monument to the man who created these unique 20th century American instruments.

The author and the inventor at the author's home, 1985

When I began to write this book in 1988, I thought it would take six months, or maybe a year, when wedged in between tours and recording projects. Little did I know what it would require to tell the complete story. Even as I was putting the finishing touches on this work, new variations of Nationals would continue to appear. The huge variety of instruments and models produced in so short a time by National never fails to astound me. Because of this, all chapter files will be kept open for future revised editions. It will not surprise me to hear of more instruments turning up which are not shown in this book. No story concerning events that happened fifty years ago can ever be complete, but the volume you are reading is by far the most extensive work ever written concerning National.

This is the story of a family of uniquely American instruments--which left their indelible stamp on blues, Hawaiian and jazz music. It is also a human story of invention, competition, enthusiasm, glory and desperation. The blending of Old World craftsmanship and modern factory work set the stage for an entirely new generation of guitar companies such as Rickenbacher and Fender-- companies that freed themselves from the traditional ways of making guitars. In some cases these later instruments were disastrous both musically and esthetically. National still had enough of the Old World in it to maintain quality standards in both tone and design.

Perhaps readers will wonder why this book stops at World War II when many instruments were made with the National name well into the 1960's. The answer is that the post-war Nationals were made by different people catering to a new, different market, with a radically different sense of visual design. Additionally, the production of metal-bodied National resonator guitars ceased in 1941. The post-war Nationals bear little resemblance to the prewar instruments. The 1920's California Nationals are like fine art. The 1930's Nationals begin to approach popular art. The late 1930's Chicago Nationals were well on their way towards approaching the cheaper look of Harmony, Kay, and other Chicago makers. The postwar instruments go all the way and beyond--into the strange pastel kitchen dinette colors of the 1950's. Somewhere out there is a person who loves that period and those instruments with the same intensity that I feel for the pre-war Nationals. The book on postwar Nationals should be written by that person. The same is true for the subject of Dobro guitars, John's Dopyera's second best invention. The call is out for a Dobro-lover to write a much-needed Dobro book. I'm not that person either. I am strictly a "NATIONAL" man.

I have, however, included a brief chapter about the new National Reso-phonic company, simply because I feel that builders Don Young and MacGregor Gaines have their hearts in the right place regarding the continuation of the old time National tradition. They have done numerous fine restorations to original old Nationals. Now they are building new Nationals and are deeply committed to preserving the sound, craftsmanship and esthetic of the old models while forging ahead with new designs, as John Dopyera continued to do until his passing.

The fact that so many of the old Nationals are still in service today is a testament to their quality, durability, fascinating tone and undeniable visual appeal. Barring any radical changes in civilization-as-we-know-it, Nationals will continue to be played well into the next century by new generations of resonator enthusiasts. It is hoped that this book will enhance the reader's enjoyment of the instruments.

I wish to offer my heartfelt thanks to Dr. John Dopyera, Jr. for the contibution of his chapter on the family background and life story of his father, as well as supplying rare family photographs. John has spent several years as the guardian of the Dopyera legacy, and has created museum exhibits in the past, with plans for future large events. Our meetings and many phone conversations brought to life the shadowy facts behind the John Dopyera, Sr. legend. Dr. Dopyera's recent travels to a newly open Czechoslovakia have revealed family records that indicate the Dopyera family were violinmakers going back to the 16th Century. His father brought that tradition into the American 20th century.

Richard Smith is the other person without whom this book would not have been complete. The guitar-playing public already owes him thanks for his Rickenbacher book as well as numerous other articles pertaining to Fenders and other vintage instruments. In researching the Rickenbacher book, Richard contacted Al Frost, who was involved in National and and knew the principal men involved with Rickenbacher. Mr. Frost still had in his possession over five hundred pages of the complete minutes of all National Board of Directors meetings from the beginning in 1927 until the late 1930's. Many legal documents were also included. These documents, and much discussion between Richard and myself, enabled us to answer many troubling questions, solve myriad controversies, explode various myths, and to give credit where due. Our collaboration on the company history has made the book more of a colorful human story than might be expected. Deep in the echoes of these instruments lie the passions of the men who made them.

Numerous musicians, dealers, and collectors contributed information for the Appendix on serial numbers. They are acknowledged at the end of the serial number listing. The code of the National serial numbers has now been cracked-- thanks to the many people who responded to the call for these numbers. Players will now be able to ascertain the dates their National instruments were made within a few months. For the first time, reasonably accurate production totals are available in print. Special mention must be given to a few people who contributed large batches of numbers: Walter Carter, of Gruhn Guitars, who compiled numbers from past sales records, provided about 200 numbers and descriptions. Dave Crocker, owner of Fly By Night Music, sent in dozens of serial numbers and helped me locate several important instruments, including the George Beauchamp custom guitar, which otherwise would not have seen publication in this book. Mark Makin, long-time British National collector, compiled about 200 hundred numbers of instruments in the U.K. and Europe. The fortunes of long-distance phone companies went up considerably as we exchanged serial numbers and spent hours discussing the meaning of significant new numbers we'd found. Gary Atkinson, also of England, who contributed The Search For Amplification, at the end of Chapter 2 and the section of Chapter 7 on street musicians, also contributed a lot of time in deep discussion of many aspects of the book.

Ron Middlebrook, the publisher of this work, is to be thanked for spending two years calling periodically to persuade me to undertake the project, and for two more years patiently spent awaiting the finished manuscript. His guidance and experience helped me turn a body of knowledge into the tangible object you now hold.

Special thanks to Catherine MacDuffee Brozman for her endless patience in months of editing, rough layout, and long discussions on the finer subtleties of the convoluted subjects contained in this volume.

Bob Brozman, 1992

DAD
SOME PERSONAL REFLECTIONS
by John E. Dopyera, Jr.

Dad was born in Strazia, Austro-Hungary, on July 6, 1893. He was the fourth child in a family of ten and was the eldest son. He had three older sisters. When Dad was about three years of age, the family moved to Dolna Krupa where Grandfather Dopyera became the village miller. Aside from the political implications of living within a monarchy where local government was rooted in the aristocracy and in the church, Dad's memories of his childhood seemed to be very positive.

A nightingale singing all night long also left a lasting impression on dad. He often spoke of this. He said that in the springtime in mating season the nightingale sang throughout the night. Because it sang all night its throat would become raw. When Dad looked out at it one morning, sure enough, there was blood coming from its throat.

As the eldest son Dad very early on worked with his father in the mill. Dad often commented that most of his skills as a craftsperson were developed working with his

Wedding picture of Josef and Katherine Dopyera. (1880's)

Grandmother Katherine and six of her children, prior to immigrating to the U.S.

Dad remembered that the mill stream had many trout and that he was always impressed with his younger brother, Rudy's abilities to catch these fish. He even one day caught a fish in his hands. Rudy was in a tree extending over the stream and spotted a trout in the water below. He jumped from the limb and successfully grabbed the fish and threw it out to the stream bank.

father. He also learned five languages as he had to speak with customers who came to the mill who spoke Czech, German, Hungarian, Polish, and Russian.

Dad spoke often about the cutting of the mill stone and the need to repair it. Apparently an inexperienced helper left the stones grinding against each other without grain between them. The cutting edge of the mill stones became dull and Grandfather Dopjera had to dissemble them and resharpen them. The lasting impression for Dad was the need for using tools and equipment properly.

Grandfather, Josef Dopjera appeared to have many talents including that of avocational violin maker. Dad learned his violin making skills from his father and in fact had made two violins under his father's tutelage before the age of 14 when the family emigrated to America.

All of the ten children were born in the "old country." Stephanie, Erma, and Laura, then Dad. Rudy and Louis came next then two sets of boy-girl twins, Robert and Valeria and Gabriella and Emil. Laura, Gabriella, and Robert are still living.

I know very little about Grandfather and Grandmother Dopyera except that Grandfather was born in Care', Austro-Hungary and that Grandmother was Catherine Sonnenfeld. A church document indicates they were married in 1887. Family lore has it that Grandfather Dopyera was reluctant to emigrate but was aware that war (World War I) was looming on the horizon and didn't want his sons to have to serve in the Duke's Army. The family left for America in 1908.

Typical of immigrant families of the era the eldest child often preceded the family to become familiar with the new country. Dad's two older sisters, Stephanie and Erma, "came over" in 1905 or 1906, lived in New York and Laura came over shortly thereafter. Stephanie met her future husband, a young German immigrant while working as a domestic in New York City. They moved out to the west coast and wrote for Erma to join them. Erma met her future husband, on her train trip out. He was a skilled carpenter, headed out to San Francisco to get work repairing damage caused by the 1906 San Francisco earthquake. Thus, family "representatives" of the Dopjera family were on the West Coast. Laura returned to the "old country" and accompanied the rest of the family in their crossing. Unlike most central European families that ended up in Pennsylvania, Ohio, or Chicago, the Dopyeras went almost directly to southern California. Family lore attributes the family location to the San Francisco earthquake.

Dad never talked much about the boat trip over but from what he did say it appeared that it was a difficult experience. The family came over in steerage, below decks. They had to supply their own sleeping gear and food. The trip took about three weeks.

Church in Dolna Krupa from postcard.

School in Dolna Krupa.

Work crew at Pacific Sash and Door. (Los Angeles) c. 1909 John (sitting) and Rudy Dopyera. (standing far right)

6

Top: After a successful hunting trip, John, center,
with brother Louis to his left, and a friend.
Right: John Dopyera, c. 1910-11 in U.S.
Bottom: Slavic gathering at Dopyera home, Los Angeles,
c. 1913-1914. John (second from left) next to Rudy.

John Dopyera in one of his many shops.

other ethnic groups toward Slovak immigrants. The Dopyera family appears to have been the third Slovak family to arrive in Los Angeles and as new "kids on the block" got the brunt of slurs and bullying so common in settings where other ethnic groups were already well-established. Dad appeared to be more sensitive to these put-downs than others as he remembered it still when he was quite old as a very painful experience. His life-long affection for Rudy, his next younger brother, seems in part to stem from the fact that Rudy on more than one occasion came to his defense when some bully was picking on him.

It is evident from the family pictures that the Dopyeras soon became involved in the broadly defined Slavic community. Russians, Ukrainians, and Serbs seemed abundantly present at the gatherings and in later years Dad's older sister Laura became an official in the National Slovak League of America.

Another characteristic of the Dopyera family evident from early pictures is involvement with music. Grandfather played violin as did Dad. Rudy played bass, and brothers, Louis, Bob, and Emil played viola. The pictures give no evidence of the sister's involvement with music.

Sometime during the teens, Dad, with his father, started a general cabinet making and repair shop in which they also repaired musical instruments. A second family base had by that time been established in Taft. The family members seemed to move back and forth between Los Angeles and Taft, taking the Ridge Route, now called Grapevine. One of Dad's horror stories concerns driving the Ridge route during a heavy wind storm. Apparently when they got to Los Angeles and got out of their car, they became aware that most of the paint on the car had been sand blasted away.

During those days Dad enjoyed hunting, hiking, camping. He spoke of hunting with friends in the Monterey peninsula, Yosemite, San Bernadino and Mojave deserts. He also talked about a trip to Death Valley. He also attended many Vaudeville shows, both for the music and the stand-up comics.

Fortunately the Dopyeras were healthy and made it through immigration with no problems. I don't know if they stayed in New York for a period of time or whether they left directly for the west coast. When they did depart, they boarded a boat for Galveston, Texas and from there took a train across the New Mexico and Arizona Indian territories.

Grandfather Dopyera, Dad, and shortly thereafter, Rudy almost immediately took jobs as skilled craftspersons at Pacific Sash and Door in Los Angeles. They worked ten hour days for a daily wage of $2.50 each and, with this income, supported the family.

Aside from a number of telling photographs, I know little of Dad's early days in southern California. I do know that many of the expectations about the land of golden opportunity fell short, in large part because of discrimination of

Unknown man in homemade car in front of John Dopjera's (1st) cabinet shop, Los Angeles or Taft, California.

John Dopyera and his father in one of John's shops.

During the early twenties Dad and Rudy started manufacturing banjos. How many they made and sold, I do not know. It was during this time, however, that an incident occurred that was to change the shape of acoustic instrument development and manufacturing. Dad told me that one day a vaudeville guitar player named George Beauchamp stopped by his shop to talk about a problem he was having. As Dad described it, Mr. Beauchamp indicated that his acoustic guitar was unable to produce enough volume to compete with other instruments in the vaudeville orchestra. (Ten years later this problem was "resolved" with the production of electric guitars.) What else went on in their conversations remains unknown. What developed, however, was the idea of placing aluminum resonators into the guitar body to amplify the sound played on the guitar.

Dad told me that he spent several months experimenting with dozens and dozens of aluminum alloys as well as shapes of spinning blocks before he produced resonators that worked. I especially remember him telling me that he was told by spinners that aluminum as thin as he was working with could never be spun, that it would rip or tear in the process. Dad was working with aluminum between .005" and .008" thick.

The first resonators were the six inch resonators for the triplate. Three resonators were placed inside the well of the guitar and each of the three collected sound from different combinations of the six strings. The result of the experiment produced the all-metal German-silver Hawaiian guitar.

The influenza epidemic at the end of World War I hit Dad very hard. He went into a weakened state and was hospitalized for six months. Dad's memories of this episode produced some of his worse nightmares. I suspect these memories are related to the strong negative attitudes he developed about the medical profession which lasted throughout his life and which motivated him to seek non-medical methods for sustaining health.

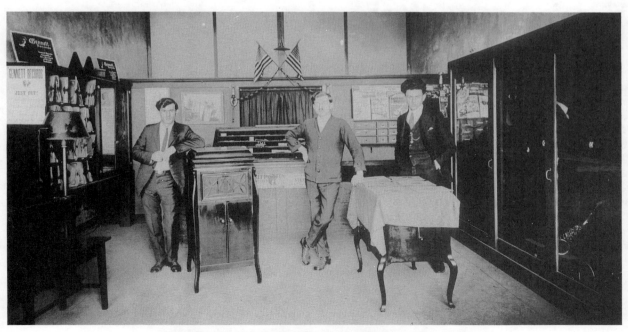

John Dopyera (center) with brothers Rudy (to his right)
and Emil (left) in retail music store possibly in Porterville.

John Dopyera portrait, 1927.

The partnership of Dad and George Beauchamp apparently was not destined to endure. While Dad did not spend a lot of his life putting down others, his few cryptic comments to me as I was growing up suggested that Mr. Beauchamp partied considerably and was not always as accountable as he might have been regarding company finances. A 1928 Popular Science Magazine shows a picture of George Beauchamp holding a National Silver Triplate. The printed material indicates that he, George Beauchamp, was the inventor. I'm sure that the appearance of such a statement would not have enhanced the working relationship between Dad and his partner. Whatever the reasons, Dad suddenly in 1929 resigned as shop foreman of the company and returned all of his stock to the wife of the third partner, Ted Kleinmeyer. This early history of the National is described in other chapters. The company continued on for several more years after Dad's departure.

The development of the DOBRO guitar came about as a direct consequence of Dad's resignation from National. As part of his contribution to the National partnership, Dad had turned over his patents on the National resonator. Subsequent to his departure from National Dad and Rudy began working on a different version of a resonator. The National resonators consisted of cones -- that is, they had a convex shape with a form called a "biscuit" which held the bridge on top. The

Proof against Warping; the Metal Guitar and Its Inventor

ALL-METAL GUITAR PRODUCES LOUD, SWEET TONE

Besides being proof against warping and checking, an all-metal guitar devised by a Los Angeles inventor is said to possess great volume, making it adaptable to more efficient use in an orchestra, and yet maintains the sweet tone of the wooden instrument. German silver was the material used in manufacturing the guitar shown in the accompanying illustration.

Apparently sufficient enthusiasm came about from these early efforts that Dad and Beauchamp decided to start a company and begin manufacturing the instruments in quantity. Dad (and Rudy as well) were apparently very skilled in conceptualizing manufacturing processes. Not only did Dad design the manufacturing flow in the National (and later DOBRO) shops, he also built many of the assembly jigs used in the plant. I'm told that he also served an (informal) quality control function in personally examining each instrument that left the production line. His standards were high and if it wasn't right, he sent it back, thus, putting his popularity in jeopardy at times.

It seems clear, historically, that the major buyers initially were the Hawaiian-steel guitar players--Sol Hoopii, for one. Exactly how many triplates were manufactured is unknown, but based on the research by the author of this book, it is probably safe to say less than 8,000 were made from 1927 to the end of their production in 1941.

George Beauchamp posing in a 1928 Popular Science photo as the inventor of the National.

Dopyera family portrait (July 4, 1926) in Los Angeles. Possibly 40th wedding anniversary for Josef and Katherine. Back row: John, Stephanie, Rudy; Middle row: Emil and Gabriella (twins), Valeria and Robert (twins); Front row: Erma; Seated: Josef and Katherine, Laura and Louis.

John Dopyera and Elizabeth Vera Candee, wedding picture (1927).

DOBRO resonator instead of being convex was concave and the bridge was placed in the center of the aluminum "spider-web" arrangement. Because Dad was concerned that National would sue him for patent rights, he placed the patent in Rudy's name (National sued, anyway, for patent infringement-- but lost). DOBRO was chosen as the name for this new style resonator and guitar apparently for somewhat "mystical" reasons. DOBRO had five letters and there were five Dopyera brothers. DOBRO was a contraction of Dopyera Brothers and DOBRO also means "good" in Slavic languages.

Dad's brother, Louis, had invested in the National and he also invested, along with brother Bob, in the DOBRO. Apparently with the onset of the depression, the National Company began to have financial difficulties and Louis bought them out. He also managed to own more than 50% of the stock in the DOBRO Corporation and after several years of manufacturing in Los Angeles, he decided that the company should move to Chicago. He, along with Vic Smith, foreman, and Al Frost moved the operation there, with some ties left in California. Gradually the whole business shifted to Chicago, manufacturing a wide variety of guitars until they could no longer get materials due to the advent of World War II.

At this point, I will leave the history of the DOBRO and other facets of the broader Dopyera family history and will focus on some personal reflections about Dad, his personality and the events I personally knew about from the 1930s onward.

Dad married my mother, Elizabeth Vena Candee, in 1927. He got to know my mother, according to family lore, through knowing Grandmother Candee first. Subsequent to Dad's illness during his late twenties, he began to explore non-medical aspects of health and along with his explorations he discovered Christian Science. Grandmother Candee was a Christian Science practitioner. Dad claimed that he was cured of his difficulties through his association with her. Somewhere along the line through his contact with Grandmother Candee, he met my mother. My mother, aside from being a good cook and a good traditional Christian, also played piano. An early picture of Dad and Mom shows Mom playing piano and Dad, the violin.

My brother, Joseph was born in August of 1928 and I, a year later in August of 1929. We were obviously too young to be very aware of the tumult going on during this period with Dad's departure from National and the startup of the DOBRO company. I do remember going to the DOBRO factory with my mother on many occasions to pick up my father after work. I can still picture the racks of freshly produced guitars waiting to be boxed and shipped and I can still smell the paint that came out of the lacquer room. These kinds of impressions fade slowly and maybe never disappear at all.

I have clear memories too of Dad going off to work in one or the other of several small shops he owned and worked in during the thirties. One was on Normandy Street, another on Hoover, and then in the late thirties, a guitar shop on Florence Avenue called the Guitar House. Dad obviously enjoyed construction. He was involved in the construction of every house or house/shop combination he lived in until he was close to ninety and lived in a nursing home.

He had obviously learned informal teaching skills quite well. Dad taught me to use tools at a very early age. By age seven, I was using a band-saw and other adult tools. Although I did not follow in my father's craft of musical instrument production, I acquired skills and confidence in the use of tools which I have used throughout my life.

John Dopyera and his unique aluminum resophonic violin, completed in 1938. Photograph probably taken in the 1960's.

I have several strong memories of Dad during my childhood days in Los Angles as always trying things out, both in the shops and elsewhere. He was frequently involved in developing experimental instruments, doing custom work for clients. He was inventive in every day situations as well. There was one situation in which he saw a rat in the garage. It jumped into a guitar shipping carton which contained guitar parts. Dad immediately put the cover on it and tied it closed. He then took the box out to the driveway, had Mom drive the car closeby and then made a small hole in the carton. He then connected a hose between the hole and the car exhaust, thus fumigating the poor rat.

Dad was also always exploring ideas. He was very curious. He joined the Masons and the Rosecrucians. He "read" widely. He was a health food faddist before anyone knew there was such a thing as a health food. He read and talked about the advice of Stanford Kingsley Klaunch, Bernard McFadden, Adelle Davis. He would go off to meetings and lectures and bring back exotic foods like mangoes, pomegranates, Halvah. Throughout his life, he was preoccupied with diet and with observing the effect of what he ate on his health. He was a good cook, creating wonderful potato pancakes, strudels, poppy seed pastries, honey cakes. He also liked gardening. We moved to 77th Street in Los Angeles in 1934 and he planted citrus trees, grape arbors, and had elevated strawberry beds. Eating delicious fresh fruit and berries that he had grown himself seemed to give him great pleasure.

Although he was always frail, weighing only about 105-110 pounds during most of his adult life, there was seemingly nothing seriously wrong with his health. He always had a concern about his diet, however, and fussed when we ate what he called "dyspepsia" foods like ice cream, cake, and cookies. He did take care of himself by taking what we teasingly called "Dad's vitamins, potions, pellets, and pills."

Our family frequently enjoyed picnics and beach outings on weekends. We had wonderful times packing up and driving off to the strand at Rainbow Pier at Long Beach from our house on 43rd Street and later, on 77th Street. We enjoyed walking on the strand, listening to concerts by George Philip Sousa's band and drinking apple cider purchased from vendors there. Ocean beaches still symbolize happy times to me.

One of my childhood memories of Grandfather Josef is of him sitting quietly in an easy chair smoking a pipe. Some family pictures also portray him in this posture. Although Grandmother Dopyera learned English, Grandfather never did. Dad was very saddened when Grandfather Josef died in 1937. Dad and his brothers constructed an elaborate "mill" motif of flowers for the funeral. Most of the conversation on that occasion was in Slavic so I have no knowledge of the content of the tributes which were paid to Grandfather Josef by Dad and his brothers and sisters.

During 1937-1938 three events occurred which were significant for our family. Hitler invaded Czechoslovakia, Grandfather died, and a great aunt on my mother's side of the family also died. This latter loss lead to a journey cross country which drew us away from Los Angeles. My mother inherited much of my great aunt's estate and she, therefore, needed to go to Springville, New York to take care of those matters. Evidently Dad felt free enough at that time to take a break and so a 1939 Buick was purchased and our family (which by this time also included my sister Anne, born 1934) drove together from Los Angeles to New York State and back. We were gone for three months -- June, July, and August of 1940. There were, of course, no Interstates and it took close to a month to make the trip cross country. We took the southern route out and the northern route back. Mother drove all the way since, for some unknown reason, Dad gave up driving prior to that point in time.

On the way back to California, we drove to Grants Pass, Oregon. Dad's brothers, Rudy and Ed, had moved there shortly before. Uncle Rudy had purchased 120 acres on Eight Dollar Mountain. Uncle Ed, Aunt Rose, and Cousin Rosemarie also lived close by in Kirby, Oregon. The fact that Ed and Rudy were in southern Oregon plus the possibility of war lead my parents to decide to move there as well.

We returned to Los Angeles so that Dad could straighten out business affairs and in August of 1941 we moved north. The three pieces of property owned in Los Angeles were sold for insignificant amounts of money. We arrived in Oregon in time for we children to attend school. When the war started in December, Dad and Mom felt they had made a good decision. We had a large garden and my mother canned extensively. We had a cow and raised chickens, ducks, geese. With our own eggs, milk and produce, we were able to be much more self-sufficient than in the city. Although we were very poor, the war scarcities did not particularly affect daily life for our family. The acreage we acquired bordered on an irrigation ditch and Dad had the idea that it would be possible to have a mill on this ditch. His boyhood memories of the village where his father was the miller evidently served as a model which he, in fantasy at least, wanted to recreate.

Dad almost immediately acquired a rental shop in Grants Pass for $35 a month in which he did various repairs for musical instruments and did other kinds of building and repair work as well as some retail sales. A second rental shop burned and he then built a new building to house his endeavors. I was old enough at age 13 to be part of this construction effort.

Our life in Grants Pass was very different than in Los Angeles but there were many parallels. There were many family get-togethers with Uncle Rudy and Uncle Ed and Aunt Rose. Uncle Rudy, at that time, had a lady friend named Mrs. Clara Young. We children were fascinated by her as she had a second hand store which had lots of novelties, including a stuffed two-headed lamb. She joined us on our outings. Sometimes other family members came to visit from California. Grandmother Dopyera came and stayed with Rudy for an extended period. There were hikes, picnics, visits to Deer Creek for fishing. Other friends of my father's such as Mr. Bruno, the local violin teacher (from whom I had a couple of very unsuccessful lessons) and Homer Goff and their families often went on picnics with us. The fourth of July picnics were especially memorable as they coincided with cherry picking. Oregon's sweet cherries were a great hit with dad, as well as with the rest of us.

Dad's curiosity about non-conventional health care continued throughout his life. He frequently visited chiropractors and osteopaths. Various health publications arrived by mail. There was much talk of the dietary recommendations of Leroy Cordell and Gaylord Hauser. The health food sage, Stanford Kingsley Claunch, came up to Oregon and visited us. I remember that we took him on a fishing trip down the Rogue River. Dad started the first health food store in Grants Pass, Oregon in 1947.

Josef Dopyera working on violin in son John Dopyera's shop in Taft, Calif.

Dad also continued to be curious about mystical matters. He continued affiliation, or at least communication with, the Rosecrucians, the Masons, and other diverse groups. Mom and we children attended the local Baptist church but dad did not. He also was less conventional politically than most of his contemporaries. He was interested in the Technocracy movement and meetings of that group were important for him while living in Grants Pass. Basically, I would describe dad politically as a social democrat. He had strong humanitarian concerns. I think that he was always outspoken about his views. He evidently believed what he was told when he came to the United States about its being a land of "free speech." Although he was out-spoken about "social evils" such as war, poverty, tyranny and the misuse of power, there was never any doubt that he was intensely patriotic and loyal to the United States.

As a child, I remember that my mother and father's relationship was relatively placid although perhaps storms were brewing. During the time we lived in Los Angeles and Dad had a fairly regular income, his role as family provider was never an issue. If there were major disagreements between them, we as children were not aware of them, with the possible exception of family gatherings when my mother felt excluded because of the family members speaking Slavic to each other. However, after we moved to Oregon, income was always an issue, despite the relative self-sufficiency of rural living.

As a teenager, I probably became less aware of Dad's activities and preoccupations. There was a poor match for me with some of the demands in high school and I dropped out of school, as my brother had before me, before finishing. I don't recall that this created any particular concern within the family. When I, in July of 1948, announced to the family that I had joined the Air Force, however, there was a short but bitter verbal attack on my father by my mother. She blamed him for my decision and recounted his many failings as a husband and father.

Later that year, my father returned to California, divorcing my mother and leaving her and my sister, Anne (then 16) in Grants Pass. I was in the Air Force and had little communication with Dad. He seldom responded to the letters I wrote. I believe he was embarrassed about his writing, especially his spelling. His formal education was very limited, perhaps an equivalent of third grade, and although he read widely, he lacked in ability to write, other than phonetically.

My mother wrote that investigators had come to Grants Pass inquiring about my father's activities and, about this time, while in the service, I was questioned about the kind of meetings my father attended and was asked what languages I personally spoke. These episodes were evidently just one of the aberrations of that time period's equivalence of witch hunting for "pinko" suspects. Nothing ever came of it.

I visited my father during a couple of my leaves when he was living in El Monte, California. He had remarried and seemed very satisfied with his new life. His wife, Eva, was pleasant and I enjoyed my visits. He and brother Rudy, who had also moved from Oregon, had built a new building on Concert Street which housed a shop, retail business, and living quarters. Dad supplied musical instruments, especially violins, to the local school district. By this time, Uncle Ed, Uncle Rudy, and Aunt Gabriella had rented shop space in Long Beach within which they were again producing resophonic guitars. I visited them there, was warmly received, and observed, with mixed feelings, the dickering and bickering which it seems had always been a part of these endeavors.

In subsequent years, I was discharged from the Air Force, received a high school equivalency, graduated from Reed College, married, had three daughters, received a Ph.D. from Syracuse (N.Y.) University, and pursued a professional career as a psychologist. My visits to my dad and other west coast family members were infrequent. During these years, Dad and Eva moved to Escondido, CA and he constructed yet another shop within which he did a retail and repair business with musical instruments and continued the innovative development which was always a part of his endeavors. His wife, Eva, died suddenly of a heart attack in 1964. Fortunately, he had many good friends in Escondido and an active life which he greatly enjoyed as long as his health and age permitted.

In 1974, due to my own relocation to California, I had opportunities for closer contact and appreciated being able to experience the kind of life that he had developed for himself. He lived in the back of the building he had built there. It was cozy and cheerful, full of books and magazines, and instruments in and out of cases. He loved cats, and one in particular, a large yellow tabby, was a companion for many years. Every day he would call his cat in a way that none of us had ever been able to replicate and the cat would come running to be fed and get petted. The back yard had fruit trees he had planted and which produced for him the fruit that he so liked to eat. He ate out frequently with his friends. There was a health food supermarket with the "goodies" he most enjoyed nearby. He frequently was invited to gatherings in which he and others had a small orchestra; he played violin, of course. He had a "treatment" once a week at the chiropractor. He did physical stretching exercises daily and was doing eye exercises for his vision. He talked, as he always had, about diet a great deal. It was one of his characteristics to classify his old friends or acquaintances about whom he spoke according to nationality, the languages spoken, and their diet. If their dietary habits had been in conflict with his own, he very often ended his portrayal of what they ate with a telling shrug and the comment, "And where are they now?" One could only conclude that, due to their poor diet, they had expired long ago. He talked of a wonderful visit to a health spa and of his trip to Hawaii. He dreamed and schemed about his new inventions such as a special rod he had developed which would greatly improve the necks of guitars. He told of a 1973 trip he had made across the country to talk to officials at the Martin Company as well as other guitar manufacturers about this invention. It was evidently unsuccessful. Although this was an unresolved aspect of his life, there were few other discrepancies. The front of the building housed his shop and it, like all of his previous shops, was a great center of productivity and a great clutter. He could always reach and find just what he needed and was able to move from the innumerable projects he had simultaneously underway even though it seemed, on the surface, to be a jumble. He discarded little and what he had included wonderful tools, including some of those which had come from Czechoslovakia with his father, woods of all kinds, forms for experimental instruments, and a great many other kinds of materials. The sign on the front said Fiddle Fret Shop.

While living in Escondido, Dad enjoyed some of the attention which came his way as a result of his earlier endeavors. Many people who had never met him before called or stopped by his shop to visit with him and ask him questions about their instruments, how they should solve a "buzz" or "rattle" problem in a resonator or straighten a neck. Dad gave freely of his time and knowledge. It was during this time that Beverly King, editor of the DOBRO NUT (later RESOPHONIC ECHOES and now COUNTRY HERITAGE) invited Dad to respond to questions for a questions and answers column in her publication.

L to R: Emil, John, and Rudy during the 1970's.

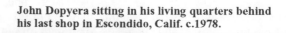

John Dopyera sitting in his living quarters behind
his last shop in Escondido, Calif. c.1978.

John and his yellow tabby cat in the 1970's.

As Dad began to age and it became clear to my brother, sister, and I that a time would come when he would need some assistance, we talked with him about this. He very much wanted to maintain his independence and not be a burden on us. We worked out an arrangement with him that as long as he could comfortably sustain himself financially and physically, we wouldn't "interfere" with his life. During the late 1970s, some of his experiences were becoming "touch and go." He was very generous and was known to make a hand-out to virtually any "cause" that came knocking on his door. Unfortunately, some people who passed themselves off as friends began to take advantage of his generosity. We know that one "friend" took him for well over $5000 and when my brother, Joe, confronted this person, asking her to return the money, she sneered at him, saying, "Your dad is an old sucker and I took him and so what!"

As the years went on it became more and more difficult for dad to manage for himself in Escondido. When his brother Rudy, however, became ill, he went to live with dad and somehow dad cared for him until Rudy's death in 1978. They had always been very close. Despite his apparent gregariousness, Dad was a very shy and gentle person. My guess is that his strong relationship with his brother Rudy was that they complemented each other. Rudy was Dad's extreme opposite. An excellent craftsperson, much appreciated by dad, Rudy was "rough" and brash. Dad and Rudy must have spent thousands and thousands of hours during their lifetimes arguing, experimenting, and solving problems. Rudy's death must have created a tremendous void for Dad. My brother, Joe, died after a very brief illness the same year. Dad was greatly shaken by these losses. My sister Anne, who continued to live in southern Oregon, visited, put things in order from time to time, and attempted to arrange for outside help. These were difficult times. By 1980, it became impossible and dad, at age 86, went back to Oregon to stay. Anne and I sorted with trepidation through the clutter and richness of the life accumulations of our Uncle Rudy and our father. Finally, effects related to the development of the resophonic instruments went into storage for eventual relocation and museum display. Dad, at age 89, went to Grants Pass where the remainder of his life, to age 94, was spent with various kinds of care arranged by sister Anne. He died January 3, 1988.

John Dopyera, 1986, at age 92 explaining his latest idea in resonator inventions.

It is my personal sense that Dad never completely acclimated to "modern" life. He seemed always to be somewhat dismayed at what he saw in the world around him and I suspect that this contributed to his intensity about life. Considering that his lifetime spanned the period from small village feudal life in Austro-Hungary to the fast-moving high-tech milieu of southern California, this is perhaps not surprising.

As I reflect on the characteristics which were central to his life, I recall his intensity, his innovativeness, his interest in solving problems, his perseverance, his sense of humor and his love of telling his stories, his need to be independent, his sense of loyalty, his concern for his food and his health. He was slight, thin, and wiry. He was dapper and fastidious. His life strengths came from his love of precision and his tenaciousness. He was often moralistic and self-righteous. These qualities undoubtedly did not endear him to some of his associates.

Although he is known as the inventor of the resophonic system, his own primary identity was with violins. He thought of himself as a violinist and a violin maker. Even though in objective terms, his major contribution was with guitars, he also had at least three patents relating to violins and several violin-related innovations that he never patented. His successes were well-mixed with disappointments. The rewards he gained from his work on the NATIONAL and DOBRO resophonic guitars were not financial. He realized few financial benefits. His rewards were ample, however, in what mattered to him most -- the appreciation of those who enjoyed using and listening to these instruments. In that regard, he was very successful.

John, still playing Hawaiian guitar in 1986.

Photographs Courtesy of Dr. John Dopyera, Jr.

John Dopyera Jr., John Dopyera, and the author, 1986

George Beauchamp, (left), Al Beauchamp, and Slim Hopper
in the mid 1920's, as the Boys from Dixie.

CHAPTER 2

The Early History of National
by Richard Smith and Bob Brozman

GEORGE D. BEAUCHAMP

All businesses have characters. However, the instrument manufacturing industry seems to have more than its fair share because it attracts musicians--characters almost by definition. George D. Beauchamp (pronounced Beechum) was a musician who became involved with manufacturing during a time of rapidly changing technologies, the mid-1920s. He was one of the primary participants in National's early history and played a central but controversial role. Al Frost, who eventually became a partner in the Valco Manufacturing Company, once called him "the mysterious Mr.Beauchamp." Solving the mystery surrounding George's contribution to National is not simple. For one reason, he died in 1940 long before people would recognize what he and his partners had accomplished. When writers started pursuing the National guitar's history, George wasn't around to tell his side of the story.

Part of the confusion about Beauchamp has its roots in an emotionally charged conflict that arose in the late 1920s between him, the Dopyeras and other National stockholders. The depth of resentment and anger in these disagreements--likened by some to the Hatfield-McCoy Feud--not only colored the story but heightened the controversy surrounding George. We've tried to clarify the nature of the controversy and bring in opinions from different sides. In addition, we've tried to use hard facts to temper statements made by family members after years of acrimony. But sorting the facts has not been easy. Different people viewed George Beauchamp and his work with the company almost like a Rorschach test. Everyone had their own opinion. (The writers here even disagree on certain points.)

Over the years Beauchamp made hundreds of friends in the music and entertainment field. During his tenure at National, he made a few enemies too. John Dopyera felt that George stole ideas and patents from him. John was furious when he saw a 1927 Popular Science magazine photo of George with a caption describing him as the National's inventor. Yet George's son, Nolan Beauchamp, maintained that his dad was a victim of the Dopyeras. He said: "[George] brought life into National with his heart and soul, and the little life savings he had. He inspired and created National and then the Dopyeras stabbed him in the back." We found no evidence in hundreds of pages of patent and business papers that George actually invested money in National, although he was one of its first stockholders. As for back stabbing, you can determine the value of the stories on each side of the dispute.

Shaking the emotion out of the accounts, some facts about George Beauchamp do emerge. Foremost, he was a catalyst for John Dopyera's radical ideas and walked into the inventor's life at an opportune moment. Born in Texas, George took violin lessons as a boy, giving him a firm musical background. In the early 1920s he took steel guitar lessons. He started playing professionally around 1923, touring the vaudeville circuit in 1924 and 1925. Those who knew him, even John Dopyera, acknowledged George's talent. He was a fine musician. His booking agent was the prestigious William Morris Agency. George, his brother Al and a friend named Slim Hopper called their trio The Boys from Dixie. When Slim and George performed as a duo, they called the act Grasshopper and George. Emil Dopyera stated that George also worked part-time as a house painter in the mid-1920s--an occupation that many musicians are too familiar with.

Los Angeles, quickly becoming the entertainment capital of the world, was a wonderful place to be a musician in the 1920s. In its exciting environment and warm climate, George and his group practiced their instruments during afternoons at Griffith Park. George was an entertainer with a good sense of humor rather than a serious singer. Carl Barth, John Dopyera's nephew, remembers the funny lyrics to George's ditties. With the popularity of Hawaiian music, George usually played steel guitar in vaudeville. His first instrument was a flat-top Martin with a high nut, though he had wanted a louder guitar since starting vaudeville.

Like many musicians, Beauchamp lived a hard life. He was a heavy drinker and a tireless workaholic. Nolan once wrote that his dad was as wild as the West Texas plains. Doc Kauffman, Leo Fender's first partner, remembered visiting Beauchamp's house in the 1930s one morning around ten o'clock. Doc found George asleep in his car on the driveway, having landed there the night before either too drunk or too tired to go inside. When Doc tapped on the car, a startled Beauchamp jumped up and threw an empty wine jug through a closed side window. Doc, probably more startled than Beauchamp with all the broken glass flying around, jumped back until he saw George laughing. To him it was just a joke. In a dry deadpan, Beauchamp said, "Boy, my son does a great job cleaning these windows."

George also worked in a duo with Hopper, known as the Grasshopper and George.

Beauchamp jumped up and threw an empty wine jug through a closed side window. Doc, probably more startled than Beauchamp with all the broken glass flying around, jumped back until he saw George laughing. To him it was just a joke. In a dry deadpan, Beauchamp said, "Boy, my son does a great job cleaning these windows."

But Beauchamp also had a serious side and passionate interests. Around 1925 he began a determined search for a louder, improved guitar. He was not alone. Frustrated by the pitiful state of guitar technology, most orchestra guitarists longed to be heard over the louder brass and reed instruments. They imagined an instrument loud enough to cut through an orchestra like a banjo, yet one that would retain the sweetness so characteristic of the acoustic guitar. Band leaders generally considered the guitar a rhythm instrument, so, guitarists were given very few solos in band arrangements. Nevertheless, by the mid 1920s virtuoso guitar soloists started to emerge thus making the guitar more and more popular. The banjo was by far the most popular stringed instrument in the early and mid 1920s. That is, until Eddie Lang and a few other pioneer recording artists inspired thousands of banjo players to take up the guitar almost overnight. All these aspiring players needed louder, more affordable instruments.

TOWARDS A LOUDER GUITAR

Many would-be inventors in America and Europe had similar ideas about how to make guitars louder. By the 1920s there were at least two plausible means: mechanical amplification and electrical amplification. Attempts to mechanically amplify guitars started in the late Nineteenth century. An English patent from 1860 hints at a primitive version of a resonator guitar, but represented a failed attempt. Later efforts to mechanically amplify stringed instruments were inspired by the technology of Edison and Victrola phonographs. The principle component of these early non-electric phonographs was a pickup head that transmitted sound from the stylus to a small mica disc. The disc acted like a banjo skin or the paper in a kazoo. It amplified the sound. A long horn acted like a megaphone, directing the sound to the listener's hear.

Around 1910, the English company Stroh created violins based on this principle, using a larger (spun or stamped) conical disc of thin aluminum and an external horn. These bizarre-looking violins enjoyed limited popularity. The Stroh company also reportedly produced a small quantity of guitars, both standard and Hawaiian, and mandolins. The tone of the violin models was rather thin and reedy, though it did project well enough to be recorded by early recording machines. Other examples of early mechanically amplified instruments included the Shovelene, invented by Joseph Ferretti. Dubbed a combination of the violin and cornet, *Musical Merchandise* magazine pictured it in May 1927.

In vaudeville, Beauchamp had seen a violin with a phonograph-like horn coming out of its body. Such instruments did not catch on but were probably fairly well-known in the trade, as evidenced by the pictures found in old publications. As part novelty, Beauchamp wanted someone to build him a guitar with an amplifying horn. No one knows if he knew that Stroh probably already made such a steel guitar. Los Angeles was not a remote outpost, but still out of the musical manufacturing mainstream centered in Chicago, New York and Europe. Traditionally, outsiders usually have the radical ideas that change industries. At this point, none of George's ideas were that earth shaking. Yet he was on the right track.

George in 1930, from the National catalog.

Besides the horn amplified guitars, during his vaudeville years, Beauchamp became interested in the idea of electric instruments. Forward looking inventors had imagined electric instruments as early as the late 1800s. Serious work on electric guitars began in the 1920s when Hawaiian and standard guitar gained widespread popularity and when advances in sound amplification made a true electric guitar seem possible. After his stay at National, George would go on to invent the first practical electric guitars with string driven pickups. But the sorry state of amplifier and microphone technology in the mid 1920s doomed his earliest efforts. George would wait until 1931 and his collaboration with Adolph Rickenbacher to continue.

Meanwhile, Beauchamp pursued a mechanically amplified Hawaiian guitar, that is, one that would use some kind of horn or resonator. He apparently contacted several local people in the guitar and violin business, settling on the Dopyera brothers. John Dopyera's shop at 50th and Broadway was fairly close to Beauchamp's Los Angeles home. He probably did not know John Dopyera very well. Nevertheless, at this point John, unlike George, had already established himself as a recognized inventor. John recalled that at eight years old, back in Czechoslovakia, he had invented an improvement to his father's flour-grinding mill. He held several patents starting at age nineteen and was busy applying for more. These early patents represented solutions to problems brought to him and included an improved shipping crate and a machine for making picture frames. By the mid 1920s John and his brother Rudy had designed improved banjos that they built in their shop. Their efforts eventually led to several banjo related patents.

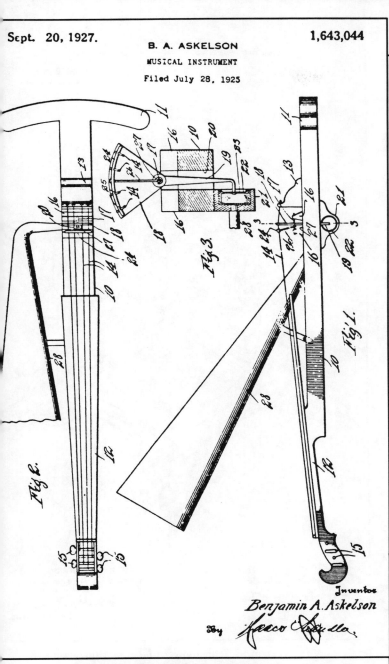

Akelson's 1925 application for a patent on a primitive Stroh-type resonating violin.

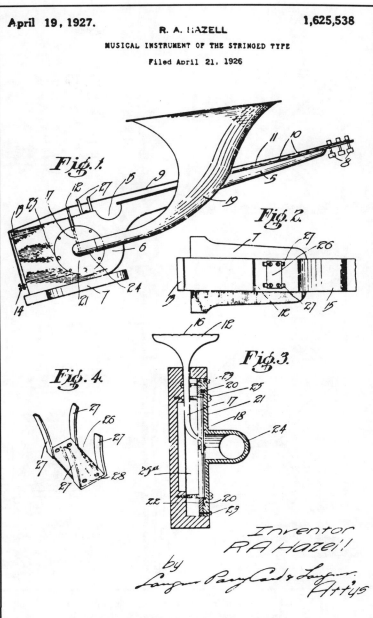

Hazell's 1926 application for a similar instrument.

John realized as the popularity of banjos began to decrease in the mid 1920s that he needed a new direction. He had chosen to make a living with musical instruments and had a strong sense for what would sell. According to Carl Barth, who did most of the resonator-spinning at National, John had been talking about a resonator guitar at least since 1923 when his shop was in Taft, California. He had already considered making guitars by the time Beauchamp showed up with a rough plan for his new guitar. Against John's better judgement--he knew George's idea wouldn't work before it was made--the Dopyeras built a Hawaiian guitar for George following his suggestions. It sat on a stand and had a wild looking walnut body with a Victrola horn attached to the bottom. According to Adolph Rickenbacher's later account, Beauchamp played this instrument in vaudeville for a short period. It looked swell. But as John had foreseen, it sounded terrible.

THE TRI-CONE GUITAR

After John built the first guitar, George had another idea, inspired by a phonograph or another instrument he had seen. Nolan Beauchamp recalls that his father took the reproduction head off their Victrola. George gave the disc to Dopyera and suggested he apply the same principle to a guitar. The order of these events is not one hundred percent certain, and this suggestion may have occurred prior to the building of the walnut guitar. Moreover, as we've already noted, other inventors already had similar ideas. But no one had made the necessary advances to convert a failed attempt into a commercial success as John Dopyera would soon do. The distinguishing mark between tinkerers and true inventors like John Dopyera was commercial success. In John's case, he was on the verge of shaking up the whole guitar industry.

Using the mica disc as a starting point, he started to experiment with discs made out of a variety of other materials, including paper, pressed fibre, glass, tin and other sheet metals. John found that conical shaped ninety-eight percent aluminum resonators, looking similar to small loud speakers and crafted with the proper thickness and hardness, worked the best. The resonators were wafer thin, like the mica discs in the Victrola reproduction heads, but conical rather than flat. John said that he turned a lathe originally used to make banjos hoops into a spinning lathe. His nephews, at first Paul and then Carl Barth, spun the resonator discs. Paul Barth later told Nolan Beauchamp that he had learned the

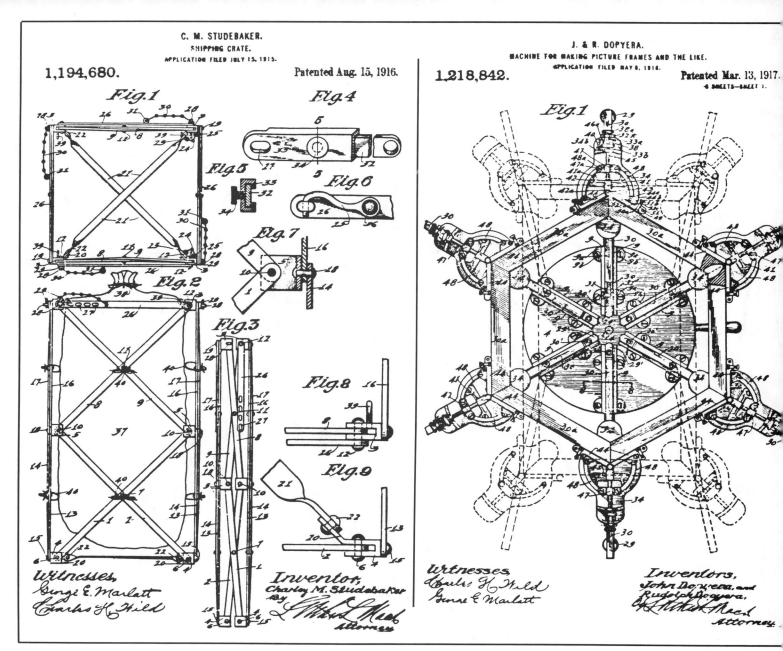

The following text accompanies the patent drawings:

Top left drawing:

C. M. STUDEBAKER.
SHIPPING CRATE.
APPLICATION FILED JULY 15, 1915.

1,194,680.

Patented Aug. 15, 1916.

Fig.1 *Fig.4* *Fig.5* *Fig.6* *Fig.2* *Fig.7* *Fig.3* *Fig.8* *Fig.9*

Witnesses,
George E. Marlett
Charles H. Field

Inventor,
Charley M. Studebaker
By
Attorney

Top right drawing:

J. & R. DOPYERA.
MACHINE FOR MAKING PICTURE FRAMES AND THE LIKE.
APPLICATION FILED MAY 8, 1916.

1,218,842.

Patented Mar. 13, 1917.
4 SHEETS—SHEET 1.

Fig.1

Witnesses,
Charles H. Field
George E. Marlett

Inventors,
John Dopyera, and
Rudolph Dopyera,
By
Attorney

A 1916 patent for an improved shipping crate.
John Dopyera is listed as one of the inventors.

A 1917 patent by John Dopyera for a machine used in
making picture frames. John was obviously a man with
a good imagination regarding factory techniques.

metal spinning technique working for a Los Angeles jewelry concern. John's tri-cone patent reads in part:...the diaphragms are in fact so thin that they may be readily flexed or indented by pressure of the finger thereon. Diaphragms of such character are therefore more easily vibrated and more readily communicate the vibrations to the body of the instrument than when constructed of wood, which of necessity be substantially thicker than aluminum in order to provide sufficient rigidity and strength.

John attached his resonators to a cast aluminum bridge that had an inserted wooden saddle. According to his patent, he chose aluminum because he wanted a material that transmitted the sound to the cones without losing any sound through vibrations from the bridge itself. The aluminum resonators amplified the bridge's vibrations the same way the small mica disc in a Victrola reproducing head amplified the needle's vibration. He installed this assembly into a metal guitar body. Dopyera tried using from one to four resonators in his tests, concluding that the best combination was three. He did not, however, rule out the use of a single resonator for increased volume. His decision to use three cones was

dictated by his desire to match the increased volume with the best possible musical tone. (Part of John's later problems with George stem from a weakness in the wording of his tri-cone patent. By saying that three cones were preferable, his patent failed to protect the overall resonator concept. This enabled George to subsequently receive patents for the single-cone National.)

After some tinkering and adjustments, the prototype was ready. It got the nickname tri-cone or tri-plate because of the three speaker-like cones John placed under its bridge. John described the moment he and Rudy first strung up the prototype, apparently Beauchamp was not present: "The tone of the tri-plate flowed like a river. I went home and told my wife, 'Jesus, we got a hell of a something here!'"

During much of his lifetime, Dopyera insisted that the idea for a disc or diaphragm type resonator was his alone, something he had thought about long before meeting Beauchamp. Later in life John scoffed at the suggestion that Beauchamp had made any significant contributions to the tri-cone's invention. However, two years after producing the first tri-cone, when John stormed out of the company, he assigned

22

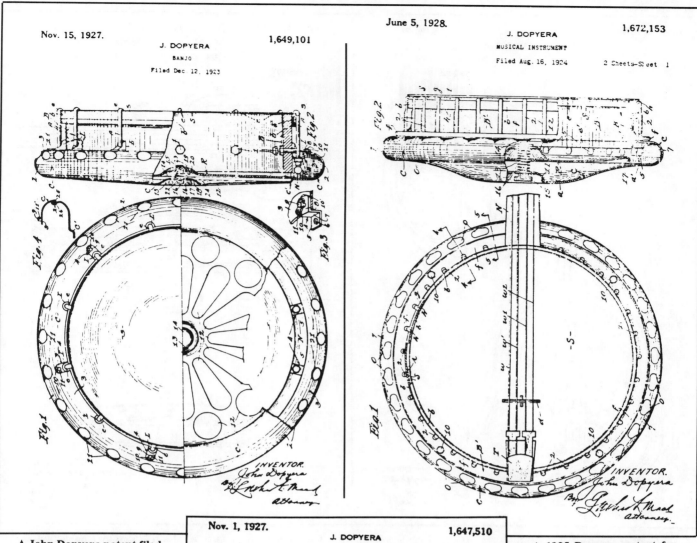

Nov. 15, 1927.

J. DOPYERA
BANJO
Filed Dec. 12, 1923

1,649,101

June 5, 1928.

J. DOPYERA
MUSICAL INSTRUMENT
Filed Aug. 16, 1924   2 Sheets-Sheet 1

1,672,153

A John Dopyera patent filed in 1923 for a banjo improvement.

A 1925 Dopyera patent for banjo resonator improvements.

A mid-1920's Dopyera brothers banjo, based on John's banjo patents.

Nov. 1, 1927.

J. DOPYERA
VIOLIN
Filed Dec. 12, 1923

1,647,510

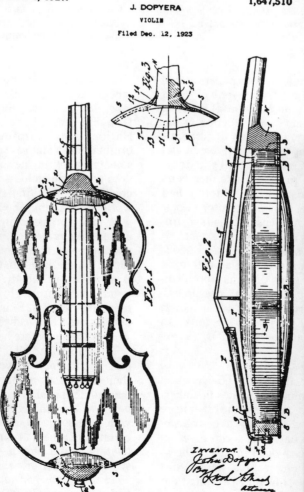

A 1923 Dopyera patent for an improved neck attachment for violins.

Detail of neck, showing a National logo that precedes the design used when the National company was formed.

23

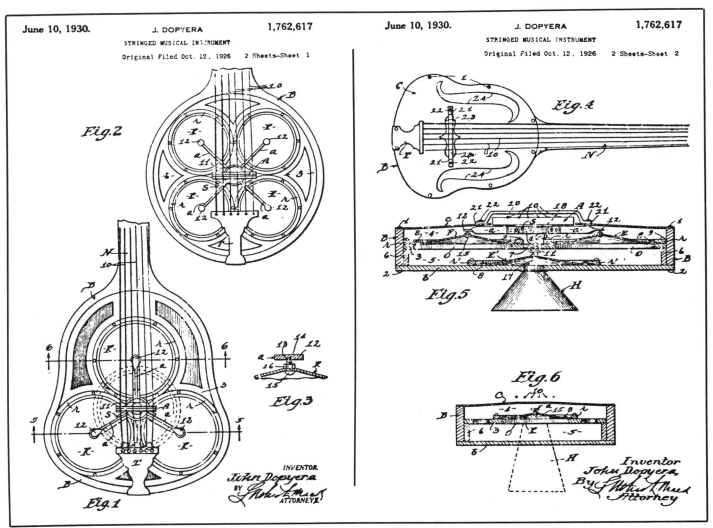

Further illustrations from the 1926 patent, which is quite different than the final National tricone patent.

This patent, filed October 12, 1926, shows an actual resonator instrument, with projecting horn, presumably like the walnut instrument made for George by John.

his patent to the National stockholders. The papers stated that Beauchamp, Paul Barth and Ted Kleinmeyer had "each contributed his time and efforts and substantial sums of money in and about the development and perfection of the said invention." Unfortunately for John, this document's language left some doubt in assigning credit where credit was due. It obscured each party's place in National's history. Likely, John had not read the fine print because there's no doubt that he, with the help of his brother Rudolph, had made the first tri-cone guitar. True, they made it for George because he needed a louder guitar. And custom-made instruments usually follow the customer's needs to some extent.

But the tri-cone was John's invention. His previous patents proved that he was much more than a craftsman working to the customer's specifications. He was a problem-solver and inventor--a man who applied original ideas to create new solutions. Though Carl Barth was just a teenager at the time, he was as close as any person living today to John's and George's work at National in the 1920s. He expressed his views as follows:

"When people are working together, I think it's very common for there to be a dispute about who did how much in putting an invention together. One mind stimulates the other. A person can mention one thing that can cause the other to be able to make one step more. Then when it's all over you say this is what we want. Now, you go back and try to give out the credit and that's a difficult thing to do. I must say, however, that though George studied electronics, he was not mechanically minded. In fact, I almost never saw him at the shop or the factory. "

Whatever the individual, small contributions of others, the process that John followed illustrates the meticulous, deliberate way most inventors achieve breakthroughs. Dopyera didn't have a flash of genius, bringing forth Nationals like turning on a light bulb. He took several original ideas and several old ideas, recombining them into something entirely new. The fact that he used some old ideas does not diminish his accomplishments but demonstrates his creativity. John's first source of inspiration was simply the world around him. The mid to late 1920s were exciting times with many breakthroughs in music and entertainment technology like radio, talking movies, microphones and electric phonographs. Every month *Musical Merchandise* magazine reprinted the latest patent abstracts, including patents by B.A. Askelson and R.A. Hazell. Both of their new instruments used amplifying diaphragms and horns like those found in Victrolas. Being a violin repairman and operating a music store, John had probably seen these and Stroh-type instruments long before he met Beauchamp.

John had also seen the old-style phonographs stepping into the modern world. He once talked of walking to his shop every morning past stores that sold Victrolas. One day they all disappeared from the windows, indicating something new was happening. Sure enough, new electric phonographs with cone-shaped loudspeakers came out just days later. John claimed that he had already developed his speaker-like resonators by the time he saw the new machines sold on his street. Whether or not stores sold fully electric phonos by 1926, Bell Labs had successfully demonstrated loudspeakers with paper cones in 1925. Bell's loud speaker invention pre-

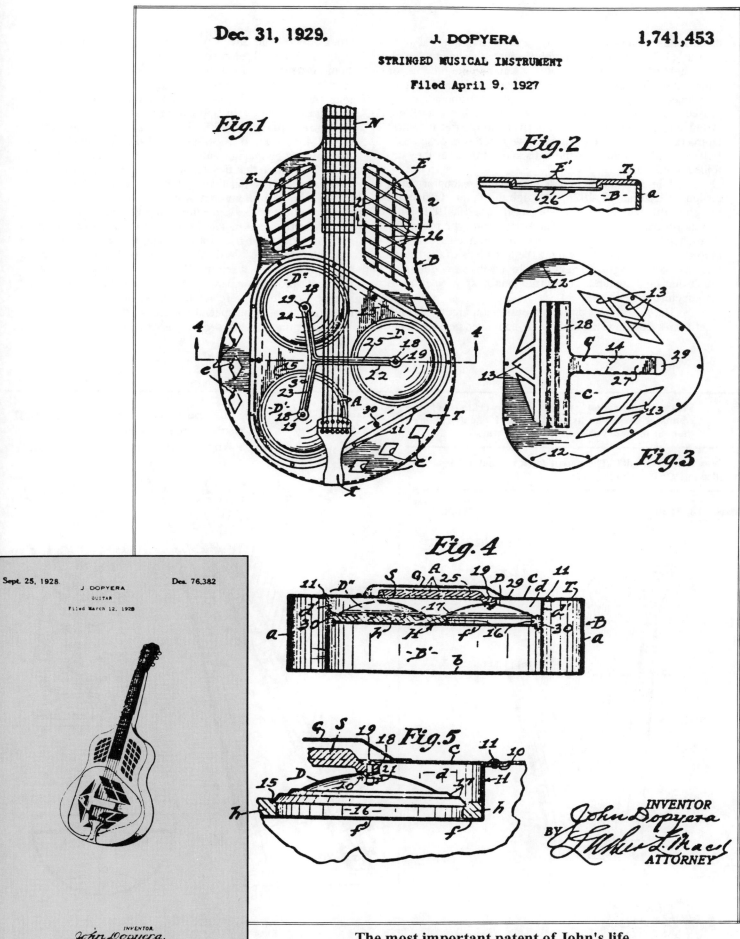

Dec. 31, 1929.

J. DOPYERA

1,741,453

STRINGED MUSICAL INSTRUMENT

Filed April 9, 1927

Fig.1

Fig.2

Fig.3

Fig.4

Fig.5

INVENTOR
John Dopyera
BY Luther L. Mace
ATTORNEY

Sept. 25, 1928.

J DOPYERA
GUITAR
Filed March 12, 1928

Dea. 76,382

INVENTOR
John Dopyera,
BY Luther L. Mace
ATTORNEY

The 1928 design patent showing the final visual form of the tricone guitar.

The most important patent of John's life. This tricone patent was filed April 9, 1927, and is very close to the finished product, though the T-bar and body shape are slightly different.

dated John's by a year, and Dopyera didn't live in a vacuum. He was a brilliant man filled with inventor's curiosity. He already held patents and undoubtedly watched the progress of others as published in the *Patent Gazette*. Inventors failing to keep an eye over their shoulder for the competition are easily passed. Leo Fender, a prolific inventor like John, took detailed photographs of his competitor's amplifier circuits. Dopyera, at the very least, must have noted subconsciously Bell's well publicized breakthroughs in electronics as they unfolded in the 1920s.

John first sought to patent a tri-cone resonator guitar design on October 12, 1926, although the Patent Office did not grant this patent, #1,762,617, until June 10, 1930. This design probably represented the early prototype made for Beauchamp. It had the three resonators concentrically arranged with respect to the bridge. The three legs of the bridge were the same length. Beauchamp loved the new guitar so much that he suggested going into business with John to manufacture it.

But the original prototype design apparently did not meet John's exacting standards as he continued perfecting an-

other design, the one National would manufacture. This guitar still used three resonators, but Dopyera repositioned them in the guitar. Like the first version, the bridge on the new design had three legs. Each leg attached to the top of a cone, but one leg was longer. It had an orangewood saddle to contact the strings. John applied for a patent on the improved tri-cone April 9, 1927. This design became patent #1,741,453, granted December 31, 1929. The tri-cone was also covered by Design Patent #76,382, granted September 25, 1928. Notice that the Patent Office took less time with these later applications than with the original.

Once John was satisfied with the design and the patent application, he and Rudy started to make the tri-cone guitars in their shop. The brothers called the new guitars Nationals, the name used for their banjos. John Dopyera once estimated that they built about forty instruments before a bigger factory was a reality. However, this period of the instrument's production, late 1926 and early 1927, remains the haziest. How many were actually hand-built? No one knows for sure, but based on special features of these very early tri-cones and the number seen in recent years, John's figure seems correct.

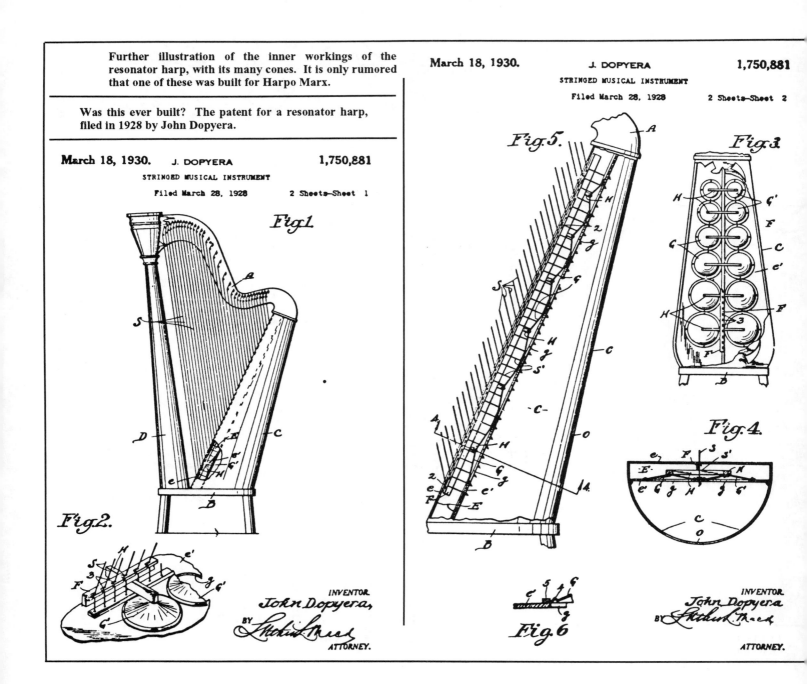

Further illustration of the inner workings of the resonator harp, with its many cones. It is only rumored that one of these was built for Harpo Marx.

Was this ever built? The patent for a resonator harp, filed in 1928 by John Dopyera.

FORMING THE NATIONAL CORPORATION

We do know that George Beauchamp got really fired up, beginning a search for investors and capital to build a larger factory. He took a National prototype and the Sol Hoopii Hawaiian Trio to a wild, lavish party held by his cousin-in-law Ted E. Kleinmeyer. Kleinmeyer was in his early twenties and had just inherited a million dollars (equal to about $15,000,000 today). He often hosted impressive parties. Sol Hoopii was the leading steel player in California and would soon make his name known worldwide using a National. Teddy paid Sol $500 to perform that night. To Kleinmeyer's guests, some of Los Angeles' wealthiest citizens, good entertainment was no surprise. But at this gathering, the new guitar with Sol at the helm doubly thrilled everyone. When George approached Kleinmeyer with the idea of starting a new company to make the guitar, the awe-struck millionaire then and there gave Beauchamp a check for $12,500. It was more than enough to start organizing substantial production of the new metal-bodied guitars and to form the National String Instrument Company.

No one knows the exact date factory production of the National guitars began, but the best estimate is the summer and fall of 1927. Beauchamp hired his friend Sol's trio to introduce the guitars at the Western Music Trades Convention in San Francisco. The August 27, 1927 issue of The *Music Trades* showed Sol in his familiar pose embracing his beloved tri-cone. By fall the Chicago Musical Instrument Company (CMI), one of the country's biggest distributors, had become National's exclusive distributor in the central states. CMI's ads started appearing in music magazines. One ad from December 1927 boasted that National Silver Guitars were the fastest selling "Big" item since the saxophone: "Hawaiian and Spanish Models for immediate delivery. Tenor Model soon."

National's partners decided to form a corporation that could issue stock and raise capital to expand the factory further. The State of California certified the National String Instrument Corporation on January 26, 1928. The Dopyera brothers sold the trademark National name (they had registered it August 16, 1926) to the corporation in exchange for common stock. Besides Ted Kleinmeyer, Paul Barth, George Beauchamp and John Dopyera, the original members of the new organization included Murray Ferguson. Ted Kleinmeyer was president while George Beauchamp was secretary/treasurer. George signed the minutes for the board of director's first meeting on February 29, 1928.

At a July 16, 1928 meeting, the directors unanimously resolved to divide the executive management of the company into three departments. The first department's head was the general manager. His job covered business relations, the sales force and the office employees. In addition, the board granted him "General Supervisory power of the complete business." The second department's head was the factory superintendent. His job was to oversee all work of manufacture and raw material and to supervise all factory workmen. The third department's head was the assistant factory superintendent. His responsibility was to supervise the stockroom and the shipping department.

Art meets business in 1928–a company letterhead for a stock sale certificate.

CAPITAL STOCK $500,000.

10,000 SHARES PREFERRED PAR VALUE $10.00
40,000 SHARES COMMON $10.00 PER SHARE

National String Instrument Corporation

INCORPORATED UNDER LAWS OF THE STATE OF CALIFORNIA

FACTORY AND OFFICE, 1855 WEST 64TH ST., LOS ANGELES, CALIF.

Present subscription price $30.00 for 2 shares of Preferred with 1 share of Common.

Purchase Agreement For Stock

An actual stock certificate for 17 shares of National stock, sold to Adolph Rickenbacher in 1928.

At the same July 1928 meeting John Dopyera moved and Paul Barth seconded that the directors appoint George Beauchamp general manager. The board vote was unanimous. Likewise, the directors unanimously appointed John Dopyera as factory superintendent and Paul Barth as assistant factory superintendent. George's salary was $55 per week. John's was $50, and Paul's was $48. The new company, still fueled for the most part by Teddy's cash, got off the ground in a big way. Acting as general manager, George hired some of the most experienced and competent craftsmen available, including several members of his own family and several members of the Dopyera family. He purchased expensive equipment for the factory located the year before near Adolph Rickenbacher's metal stamping shop. The address was 1855 West 64th Street, Los Angeles, California.

The original National instrument line included Spanish and Hawaiian style tri-cones. At first the different models ranged only from the plain, non-engraved Style 1 to the rose pattern engraved Style 2. The company also made four-string tenor guitars, a mandolin and a uke. All of these earliest models employed John Dopyera's tri-cone resonator system. After the first few hundred instruments, two more ornately engraved models were introduced. John and his wife designed the beautifully engraved Style 3 model called Lily-of-the-Valley. Beauchamp designed the engraving pattern for the even more elaborate top-of-the-line Style 4 Artist's Model. This design was called the Chrysanthemum pattern. Both the Style 3 and Style 4 models had several types of hand engraved cuts and were priced close to Martin's fanciest models. In later years, John Dopyera would claim that the Style 4 had "too much engraving, that hurt the tone." No doubt part of this comment reflected John's personal feelings about George, though it seems at least with Spanish-neck tri-cones that the non-engraved models have the deepest tonal qualities.

ADOLPH RICKENBACHER

Adolph Rickenbacher (usually spelled Rickenbacker after World War II) was born in Switzerland in 1892. Apparently, as a child his parents died and other relatives brought him to America. One of his distant cousins was World War I flying ace Eddie Rickenbacker. Before moving to Los Angeles in 1918, Adolph lived first in Columbus, Ohio and then in Chicago, Illinois. He and two partners formed the Rickenbacher Manufacturing Company in 1925 and two years later incorporated the business. Beauchamp met Rickenbacher through Ted Kleinmeyer, who knew him from another manufacturing venture. Adolph was a likeable and generous guy from most reports. He was also a shrewd and hard businessman who did things his own way.

By the time he had met Beauchamp and had joined forces with the guitar operation, Rickenbacher was a highly skilled production engineer and machinist. He was proficient in a wide variety of manufacturing techniques using both metals and plastics. In addition, Rick had business experience and money to invest. He owned thirty-four shares of National's preferred stock and seventeen shares of its common stock from June 1928 to July 1933. The company gave him the title of engineer on the back of the 1930 catalog. Rickenbacher Mfg. manufactured the metal bodies for the Nationals with one of the largest deep drawing presses on the West Coast. The shop was able to produce as many as fifty guitars a day. That was enough production capacity to challenge the major Eastern and Mid-West guitar manufacturing companies.

A. RICKENBACKER
ENGINEER

The 1930 catalog photo of Adolph Rickenbacher.

DISAGREEMENTS AT NATIONAL

By late 1928 business at National was booming. Nearly every major steel guitar recording artist and performer played a tri-cone. The overnight success was euphoric. On weekends some stockholders sailed to Catalina Island or just past the twelve mile limit for wild gambling and drinking parties. The newly prosperous guitar makers partied on land with musicians, movie stars and the Los Angeles elite. The money and illegal booze attracted girls for sure. According to the rumors, some of the management had affairs with various National secretaries. To sum things up, the Roaring '20s with all the decadent trimmings surrounded National those first years. National was not all business by any means. That world looked fun to almost everyone except John Dopyera.

For John, the honeymoon at National was over by late 1928. He had quickly become disgruntled with George Beauchamp and his band of merry stock holders. Part of John's problem with the others was a deep-seated personality conflict. Dopyera, walking the fine line between frugality and penny pinching, complained that the factory wasted, among other things, sand paper. He was right, but the others couldn't care less. While most of John's co-workers nipped on Green River, a flavored syrup laced with bootleg whiskey, John drank carrot juice and ate a banana every day for lunch.

George and John were at the center of National's first bitter conflicts. Carl Barth says that the two had no noticeable animosity towards each other. Still, they were stamped from different sheets of metal. They had completely different backgrounds and life experiences leading to entirely different expectations about how the company should proceed. John thought that Beauchamp threw away money with his experiments. In the 1970s, Dopyera pointed to the failure of the Bakelite neck Beauchamp had tried to introduce on National Triolians. George was collaborating with Adolph Rickenbacher who used the early plastic to make Kleen-B-Tween toothbrush handles. In 1935, George and Adolph would successfully introduce Rickenbacher electric guitars made with a seemingly stronger Bakelite formula. Nevertheless, the material was never ideal for guitars, as customers with defective-necked Nationals had already discovered. Beauchamp's vision of the Bakelite neck did fail on Nationals, and John did say, "I told you so." But Dopyera's resentment ran much deeper than bickering over details. In the few short years since their meeting, he had grown to distrust George with a passion. John believed he embodied National. In 1973 he called himself the "main spoke of the wheel," adding that he, in fact, had all the good ideas. In his view, his fellow stock holders headed by Beauchamp couldn't invent anything useful, much less run a company or a factory. Nothing qualified Beauchamp the hard drinking guitar player to make decisions that affected John and the future of his work.

Apparently, John and George's biggest dispute concerned development of a single-cone guitar. By the end of 1928, National had the machinery and manpower to turn out hundreds of guitars per week. But the company had a limited line of instruments. The elaborate tri-cone guitars were expensive and soon demand for them would drop as the market among professionals became saturated. The West Coast firm needed a simpler, more affordable design to augment what it offered music stores. In his early experiments with guitars John Dopyera had ruled out a single-cone design, probably because he could not make one that pleased a perfectionist's ear. He stated in a patent application for the tri-cone: "It is preferable to use three and never less (sic) than three resonators."

According to George's son Nolan Beauchamp, his father invented the economical and highly popular single resonator design. To be sure, George Beauchamp's name is on the single-cone patent, filed on March 3, 1929, three months after John's abrupt departure. Still, in patenting the single-cone National, Beauchamp was following through with work started by Dopyera, work that included a single-cone mandolin and ukulele. The cognitive leap from National's mandolin and uke to the single-cone guitar was obvious, leading Al Frost to ask how George even got a patent on the invention. No one knows where John's work ended and George's work began. Some people have suggested that Beauchamp simply patented Dopyera's discarded ideas. To some extent, he probably did. Nevertheless, George should be given credit for seeing the design's commercial potential. It not only became a good seller, saving the company during the Great Depression, but a sizeable part of the National legacy. George Beauchamp, not John Dopyera, made the single-cone National guitars a reality.

Whatever the single-cone guitars would do for sales, the final straw for Dopyera was finding out that Beauchamp had claimed the patent for it. (Besides Dopyera, Paul Barth would later claim partial credit for the design, too.) Dopyera, who the others usually pushed around quite easily, felt victimized and betrayed. The big issue here was probably money because John later said he thought little of the National single-cone guitars. He wasn't particularly proud of them.

John quit National in January of 1929. At a special meeting on January 17th, National's board discussed the circumstance: Dopyera had left his position in an emotional outburst. Showing their loyalties at the time, the remaining board members gave Beauchamp a vote of confidence. John, the odd man out, resigned as an officer, director and stockholder on February 19, 1929, assigning his stock interest to Ted Kleinmeyer. Harry Watson took John's responsibilities as shop superintendent. On March 3, 1929 National's board of directors had filled the vacancy left by Dopyera with Charles Farr, an attorney. Paul Barth became vice-president while Beauchamp became secretary.

Another Beauchamp version of a single cone with three peaks. This was never produced.

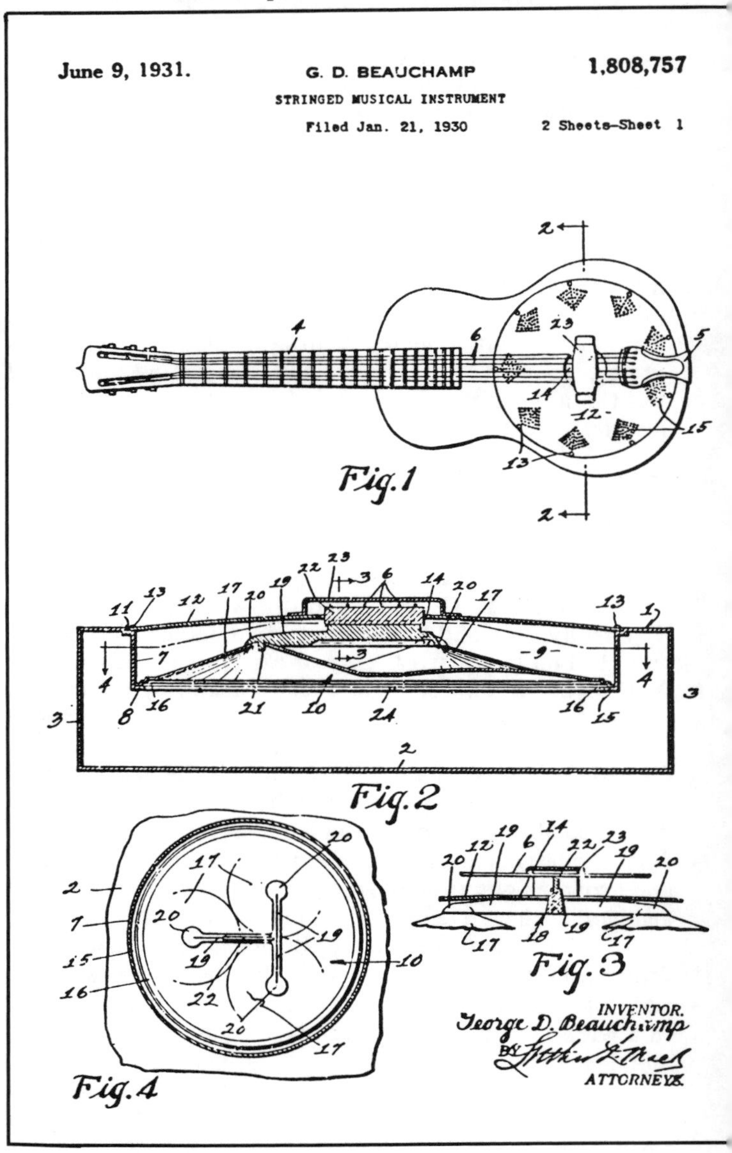

June 9, 1931.   G. D. BEAUCHAMP   1,808,757
STRINGED MUSICAL INSTRUMENT
Filed Jan. 21, 1930   2 Sheets—Sheet 1

Fig.1

Fig.2

Fig.3

Fig.4

INVENTOR.
George D. Beauchamp
BY
ATTORNEYS

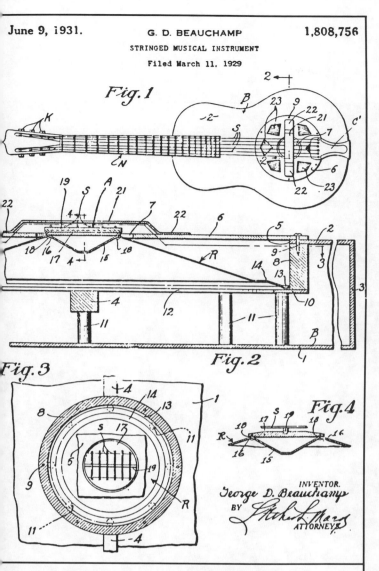

G. D. BEAUCHAMP
STRINGED MUSICAL INSTRUMENT
Filed March 11, 1929

1,808,756

Fig.1

Fig.2

Fig.3

Fig.4

INVENTOR.
George D. Beauchamp
BY
ATTORNEYS

Beauchamp's patent drawing of the single cone guitar which went into production.

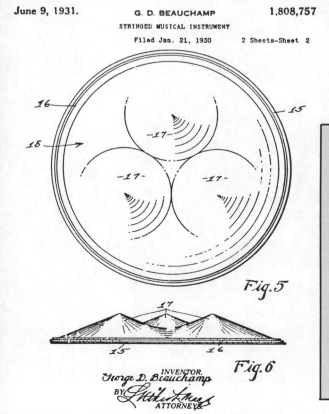

June 9, 1931.

G. D. BEAUCHAMP
STRINGED MUSICAL INSTRUMENT
Filed Jan. 21, 1930   2 Sheets-Sheet 2

1,808,757

Fig.5

Fig.6

INVENTOR.
George D. Beauchamp
BY
ATTORNEYS

Details of the strange resonator system of the never-produced guitar. It looks like a cross between a single and triple resonator system.

DOBRO VERSUS NATIONAL

One has to conclude that Dopyera had walked out in total disgust and refused to return without giving the matter too much thought. Running from the adversity, he inexplicably signed away his patent rights to the others. Perhaps he thought the company would fail without him. More significant though, John had confidence in a new project he'd already begun at home, the creation of another single-cone resonator guitar called the Dobro. John said many times that he worked on the Dobro guitar while still employed at National. On June 6, 1929 the Dopyeras' filed a patent application for the new guitar under Rudy's name to eliminate any chance that National or Beauchamp would claim this invention. The brothers formed the Dobro Manufacturing Company, later called the Dobro Corporation, Limited, to make the guitars.

Beauchamp reacted to the Dopyeras' new company with propaganda ploys that would have made some tricky politicians proud. What could have been good clean competition between the two companies became a war, so to speak. George believed, rather incredibly, that the Dobro design violated his patent on the single-cone guitar. Trying to scare Dobro's new accounts, he started telling anyone who would listen. Since the two companies had many of the same customers, George could do the Dopyeras great damage. In George's defense, he did have a family to feed and a business to save during the most difficult economic times of this century. But then again, so did John Dopyera.

The Dopyeras' reaction to Beauchamp anti-Dobro campaign was predictable. They started legal action: the best defense is a good offense. Minutes for National's January 3, 1930 board meeting mention a lawsuit for $25,000 in damages. A year later, January 1, 1931, a newspaper in Los Angeles announced another action for $2,000,000. The court threw out the first two counts of this suit, but gave Dobro the right to amend and reinstate part of the first count. It did, asking for $225,000 in damages. But rather than cripple or destroy National, a better solution for the Dopyeras' problem became apparent. They realized a chance to regain control of National, the company John and Rudy had started years before meeting Beauchamp. Remember that National began with banjos in the early 1920s. It had expanded into guitar making on the strength of John's ideas, not just Kleinmeyer's money or Beauchamp's hard work. Now National barred the Dopyera brothers access to the company's books while Beauchamp actively tried to put Dobro out of business. To John and Rudy, Beauchamp's belligerence was more than a simple slap in the face.

Ask $2,000,000 Damages In Patent Suit Dispute

Charging the plaintiffs were improperly telling prospective purchasers they were liable to patent infringement suits, the Dobro Corporation, manufacturers of guitars, have filed suit for $2,000,000 damages in Superior court against the National String Instrument Corporation. The two musical manufacturers were principals in a federal suit over rights to make certain musical instrument parts.

Newspaper article announcing Dobro's intent to litigate.

31

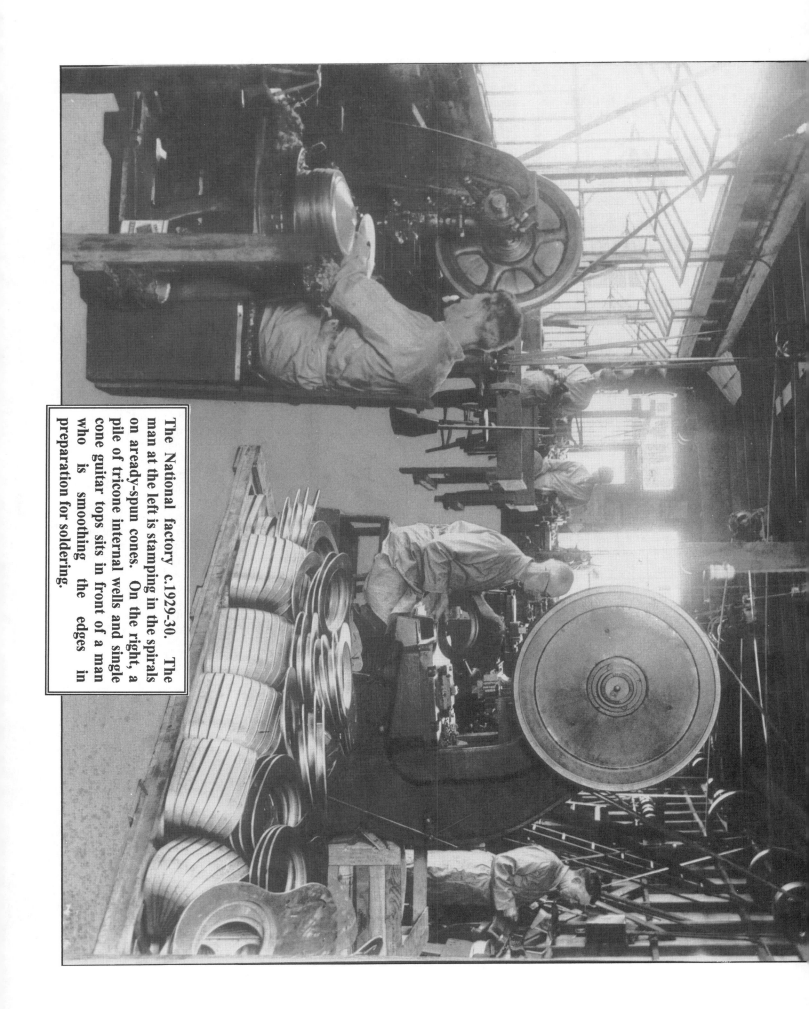

The National factory c.1929-30. The man at the left is stamping in the spirals on aready-spun cones. On the right, a pile of tricone internal wells and single cone guitar tops sits in front of a man who is smoothing the edges in preparation for soldering.

Several documents about the National/Dobro legal hassles have emerged. Although the complete story remains veiled, a court deposition about George Beauchamp, filed on March 30, 1931, sheds light on the Dopyeras' grievances. An unknown writer, presumably an instrument dealer, had visited National's factory where he had met Beauchamp. He told the visitor that Dobros infringed on National patents and that National had won a lawsuit with Dobro. Of course, those claims were completely false. Beauchamp had made the same declarations to other dealers that the writer knew. The dealer went to National again and observed that Beauchamp changed the details of his stories and made statements he could not back up. Yet as a result of Beauchamp's yarns, many instrument distributors and dealers had either cancelled Dobro orders or avoided its products altogether. Why? If a court had ruled that Dobro was infringing on National's patents, the company could have legally seized all Dobros out of stores and warehouses.

Apparently, Beauchamp tried to make his customers believe that the unique spider/bridge setup found in Dobros originated at National. At a later meeting reported by the music dealer in the court deposition, George claimed that he had perfected and completed the design six months to a year before the Dopyeras had left National. Beauchamp even offered a letter of assurance attesting to the "truth" of the these "facts." Amazingly, Beauchamp also bragged that he had originated Nationals, perfected all the patents and financed the company. To prove his point to the music dealer, George went to his safe and removed National's patent papers. Beauchamp showed the visitor these papers and the agreement that transferred all John's patents to National.

By showing the patents, Beauchamp had contradicted his earlier claims--the patents named John Dopyera as inventor. At this point the fellow who gave the deposition asked for the letter George had promised. But George objected to any written statement claiming that Dobro directly infringed on National's patents. The dealer became perplexed because Beauchamp was first to make that very claim. George said, "Dobro would give $10,000 for a letter of this nature." Indeed, with that letter the Dopyeras could have easily prevailed in court as Beauchamp realized. On the next day the writer again tried to get a letter from National, but neither Beauchamp and nor sales representative Jack Levy, who had joined in George's charade, would commit themselves in writing.

The deposition continued by describing a later phone conversation that the writer had with Jack Levy. He said that he thought the litigation between the two companies concerned the "single-cone patent that National bought from Dopyera." (The patent that George had allegedly filed behind John's back.) In this conversation, Levy conveniently acted surprised that the litigation pertained to the Dobro's spider/bridge construction. The writer also described a visit to Paul Barth's home. Barth truthfully stated that no one at National had worked on the spider/bridge while the Dopyeras were at National.

George's wild assertions had gotten National into a legal mess and revealed a side of his character that the Dopyeras never forgave. John's brother Emil wrote an open letter to the music industry published in the April 1932 *Musical Merchandise* magazine. He said: "Keep our business clean...While Dobro has kept its house in order, there is evidence that considerable `spring cleaning' is necessary among our competitors." He didn't mention National or Beauchamp by name, but to anyone familiar with the guitar industry the inference rang like the sound of a tri-cone. The Dopyeras were not angels, as evidenced in business dealings

among themselves. But that was family. The Dopyeras never considered George Beauchamp one of the brothers.

NATIONAL'S FACTORY

In 1928 Carl Barth was fourteen years old. He began working part-time on Saturdays and summer vacations at the new National factory. Because of his age, he was neither part of the decision making process nor party to the imbroglios between National's stockholders. National provided Carl with a good part-time job that lasted into the mid 1930s. Unlike his older brother Paul, who would make a career in guitar manufacturing, Carl left National after finishing school. He worked most of his adult life at Douglas Aircraft in the engineering department. Retired, he lives in Southern California.

National's factory as Carl remembers was well lit and airy. The workers had electric power tools, up to date planers, joiners and shapers. The instruments were made from scratch, from the ground up. Except companies that made small items like tuners, Rickenbacher's shop did the only outside manufacturing for National. Of course, Rick stamped the metal bodies. Carl says that when they came over to National, Rickenbacher had wrapped the metal around the

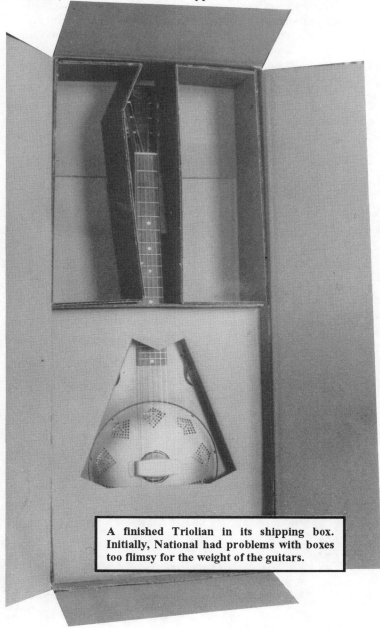

A finished Triolian in its shipping box. Initially, National had problems with boxes too flimsy for the weight of the guitars.

33

stamping, securing it with clamps. The flanges from the bottom were drawn in one piece. The top had a downward flange that went down inside the body, and workers at National soldered the two together. National's employees did all the metal cutting and assembly work.

National had a fine wood shop. Besides spinning resonators, Carl made the biscuits for single-cone guitars, the small round disk that sat on the resonator. He says, "That was done on a big mill with a fly cutter. Then I'd cut a slot on a saw." The wood arrived uncut or in large boards from the lumber yard. For example, the ebony for the better fingerboards arrived as small logs. A worker would rough saw it on a very large band saw and then put it through a planer. From that stage, the craftsmen cut fingerboards.

About fifteen or twenty people worked at the first Los Angeles factory during the peak production. Two people did nothing but final assembly. There was a partition in the factory that separated their room from the wood working machinery, dust and noise. The assemblers kept the door closed all the time. The engravers worked in another building behind the main plant. One full time painter did all the painting, lacquer in those days, in the main factory. Two secretaries, the sales representative and Beauchamp worked in the office. Two workers just did soldering and filing, a particularly rough job because the nature of solder. Their irons rested over a torch. When they dipped the irons to clean the tips, it produced a permeating, acrid smoke. But the solderers worked in a large room with a high ceiling and good ventilation. After soldering, they would file around the guitar edges, first with coarse files and then with finer files.

Despite the rather pleasant setting, by factory standards, vicious accidents did happen. Carl's father, Martin, who had been a building contractor in Taft, California before moving to Los Angeles, lost a finger using a shaper on a Spanish guitar neck. The jig broke, and his hand went into the high speed, razor sharp blade. Carl says that Rudolph had made the jig. While it should have held up, it did break, making everyone that much more alert to possible mishaps.

Dozens of Hawaiian and Spanish tricone bodies stacked on the factory floor like so much cordwood.

Imagine if you could take your pick....racks of nearly finished guitars, awaiting final assembly and polishing. Shown are tricones, tenors, plectrums and many other models too fuzzy to see. Wouldn't it be fun to spend a day there?

PAUL BARTH

At sixteen, Paul Barth dropped out of school to go to work. Never worldly or highly educated, he had a rare natural ability solving mechanical problems and working with machines. Still a teenager in the mid 1920s, Paul moved to Los Angeles and lived in John's shop at 50th and Broadway. John exposed Paul to instrument building, the trade he would pursue until his untimely death from a heart attack in 1973. Barth was a mild mannered twenty year old when the National Corporation got off the ground in 1928. Quiet and unassertive, the others found ways to take advantage of him. He didn't care for sales, but thrived on the factory and manufacturing side of the business. Paul was never one of the wild ones, despite the bad role models that surrounded him. Though drinking never became a problem, Beauchamp and his group did exposed him to it. Carl remembers Paul at an early age showing off a bottle of bootleg in his glove compartment.

Paul worked at the National factory until at least 1934. When George got the electric guitar business rolling at Rickenbacher, it took of couple of years for the company to grow, he hired Paul. George must have liked Paul and appreciated his skills to have included him in both National and Rickenbacher's Electro String. After Beauchamp left Rickenbacher in 1940, Paul took over its manufacturing, shifting to wartime production and back. He stayed until 1956, several years after Adolph had sold the company to F.C. Hall. From there, Paul designed guitars, first for Magnatone and then for a company in Riverside, California called Bartell.

Paul Barth, from the 1930 catalog.

HARRY WATSON

Harry Watson, a fine mechanic and craftsman, had replaced John Dopyera as shop superintendent. Born in England, he once served in the British navy. Carl Barth remembers Watson as rather ingenious, but very crude. He made toy models of dogs about an inch and a half long, cast out of a soft metal. One was turning to look at the other. Carl explains: "Well, as you're looking at them you think those are really cute looking little dogs. Then he'd put them in the mating position, and they'd fit perfectly." Harry Watson also made the neck and body for Beauchamp's prototype electric guitar. He was a handy guy to have around. However, Carl says that Watson had a mean streak. He had learned to fight in the navy. Although tall and lean, Watson was still muscular. Once in National's office, he punched Paul Barth, breaking a tooth. About this incident, Carl Barth says: "There must have been a little alcohol that floated around the place...A guy would have to be off his rocker to punch my brother who was such a mild-mannered character. He would never do anything that would warrant a fight." Watson's action made Carl's father very upset. Tears came to his eyes when he told Carl what had happened.

Carl remembers another story involving Watson. He and Beauchamp had been in the Mexican border town of Tijuana drinking heavily. As if they weren't already having fun, they got into a fist fight with each other. For some reason, it was broken up and left unfinished. The next morning Barth came to work at the factory and waited outside with the other employees for someone with a shop key. Up drove Watson. He said: "Stick around for the show. Beauchamp's coming, and we're going to have a fight. [We're going to] finish our fight here." Beauchamp, who could hardly measure up to Watson's height and reach, didn't show up. But Carl did see George a day or two later with a scarred up face and swollen eye. Watson had caught up with him somewhere else and had trounced him.

The tempestuous Harry Watson, from the 1930 catalog.

TED KLEINMEYER

Another character at National was Ted Kleinmeyer, once characterized by Nolan Beauchamp as a "spendthrift and playboy." Married to George Beauchamp's cousin, Cynthia Mitchell, Teddy had inherited a million dollars at age twenty-one and was trying to spend it all before age thirty. He would inherit another million then. Eventually he squandered all his inheritance. Before that, Ted was both trouble and a lot of fun. Likeable Teddy Kleinmeyer was a Roaring '20s version of the consummate party animal. His connections at City Hall gave him a police siren for his Lincoln so he could speed around Los Angeles with impunity. He bought expensive gifts like automobiles, radios and phonographs for his relatives and friends. Being successful at losing money faster than he made it, Ted started to hound Beauchamp for cash advances from National's till. Nolan Beauchamp said that George's fault was the inability to just say no—especially to his friends. However, when business conditions got bad and the money was gone, George had no choice.

Eventually Kleinmeyer would go to jail for writing bad checks. One newspaper called him "Poor little rich boy." After he got out of jail, he turned thirty and inherited another million dollars. Pursuing the rich man's life, he bought a polo pony ranch at the end of Vermont Avenue in Los Angeles. Unable to keep the ranch profitable, he went broke again. Kleinmeyer had divorced Cynthia, but his ex-father-in-law took him in anyway. When the elder Mitchell died in an auto accident, Teddy, forced to fend for himself, took a job as a school custodian in Temple City, California. Nolan Beauchamp said that Kleinmeyer died a poor alcoholic.

TED E. KLEINMEYER
PRESIDENT

THE EARLY 1930s

During January of 1930, George filed a curious patent application for a second style single-cone National. It looked like an attempt to cross a single-cone with a tri-cone. Apparently, the guitar was never put into production. Another discarded idea at National was an all aluminum guitar prototype George presented to the board in August. Of course, George's first Rickenbacher would be cast aluminum, and Dobro would also make a guitar out of the light-weight metal. On May 30 National introduced, priced at $85, the Style O guitars without sandblasted scenes. By July the company shaved the price to $62.50. In September Music Merchandise magazine announced that the guitar had the Hawaiian scenes that would become its trademark.

The depression slowed business, but orders kept coming. National stayed in business during the Depression making a luxury item for the same reason the movie industry was so successful: recreation and entertainment were the only real escapes from the economic reality. The company added distributors such as Sears and explored setting up exclusive distribution to South and Central America. With the Dobro lawsuit looming, the company started cutting back on expenses. In July 1930 Harry Watson resigned as the factory superintendent, and the position remained unfilled for two years. The factory still operated half day on Saturdays for a good part of the early 1930s. Workers got their checks on Fridays or Saturdays at noon. But the checks weren't always there. Carl Barth says: "We call it a cash flow problem now. We had another name for it then."

Carl Barth remembers that Sears sent people out to the factory to examine the production process. Sears didn't manufacture anything, but the giant mail order retailer had people who would evaluate tools, machinery and production techniques. They also looked at the solvency of the company. Apparently, Sears broke some companies that thought it would send a large volume of orders. If the retailer changed its plans, the manufacturer would be left with a huge unsold inventory. Sears wanted National to use less screws to hold the cover plates down, thus cutting material and labor costs. (All screw holes had to be tapped by hand.) Sears production experts also cut the number of lacquer coats on each instrument it bought from National. All in all, Sears and National had a good relationship during these years.

In the fall of 1931, Beauchamp, Paul Barth, Adolph Rickenbacher and C.L. Farr started organizing support for a new project, George's development of a fully electric guitar. They formed a company called the Ro-Pat-In Corporation on October 15, 1931. (No one remembers the significance of the name.) Ro-Pat-In became Electro String Instrument Corporation, makers of the Rickenbacher Electro guitars. The electric guitar would have little relevance to National for about two years. Nevertheless, the Rickenbacher Electro guitar that Beauchamp invented is widely considered the first modern electric guitar. Beauchamp probably chose to develop his guitar with Rickenbacher because of his increasingly perilous position at National.

**From riches to rags—twice in one lifetime.
Ted Kleinmeyer from the 1930 catalog.**

On November 10, 1931, the National board of directors removed Beauchamp and Barth from their management posts at the company. Unfortunately, the minutes from the November meeting did not explain the reasons but did show that Kleinmeyer, Ferguson and a newer member, Glenn E. Harger, voted against George and Paul. C.L. Farr and Beauchamp abstained. The minutes further stated that Barth and Beauchamp were given their checks in full, to and including November 14, 1931. Perhaps the board fired George and Paul in response to the new electric guitar venture. However, the firing probably resulted from earlier differences in opinion about the company's management, more specifically, George's irresponsible actions leading up to the Dobro lawsuit. The board was trying to distance itself from Beauchamp. Yet, at the January 4, 1932 meeting, the board gave George a chrome plated Style O guitar engraved with the #3 Silver Guitar pattern and the name Geo. D. Beauchamp. The board had fired George because it had to. It turned around to honor him because the members still liked him and recognized the work he had done to make National what it was.

After firing George, National was in the midst of several different power plays and switches between stockholders that would last for the next two years. For one thing, Louis Dopyera became a stock holder and started attending board meetings. C.L. Farr resigned on March 31st. Paul Barth replaced him. In June 1932, Ted Kleinmeyer drove up to Taft, California and sold his controlling interest in National stock to Louis Dopyera. It's unclear when Louis first obtained National stock, but with the June stock transaction he took controlling interest and was elected board president. On July 11, 1932, Murray Ferguson resigned to make room on the board for Jack Levy.

After Kleinmeyer was out of the picture in the summer of 1932, the directors hired Paul Barth to fill the vacant factory superintendent position. George, now working full-time with Adolph Rickenbacher, no longer had a position at National's factory but continued to participate on the board until January 1934. Indeed, Ro-Pat-In (Rickenbacher's Electro String) and National had business connections and overlaps for several years. For example, National's sales representative Jack Levy was one of Ro-Pat-In's first reps. Also, Rickenbacher Mfg. continued to make dies and stamped parts for both National and Dobro.

Every struggling company needs some drama. As if the family feud between the Dopyeras and Beauchamp's pranksters was not enough, there entered a real-life embezzler. Glenn E. Harger was one of the minor stock holders that joined National in 1931. He became the corporation's secretary, complete with full banking and check writing privileges. His handling of this position was less than legal, and he helped himself to an unspecified amount of money. On May 6, 1933 his peers discovered him. It's unclear whether the stockholders fired Harger or if he quit. In any event, the others hurried to remove his name at the bank. The corporate minutes described the evidence as "apparent shortages in the accounts of former secretary Harger." The board appointed Jack Levy as temporary secretary.

National sent a notice to Harger demanding an explanation of the irregularities, but the company took no legal action. Louis Dopyera did ask to have an accountant close the books each month. It seems odd that this decision was made so late in the company's history. Even the best managed companies employ thieves. But the Harger episode suggests that the changes in National's board and the belt tightening had created a management vacuum. No one was properly minding the office or the factory.

C. L. FARR
DIRECTOR

C.L. Farr, board member in the early 1930's.

National's big problem--the legal dispute with Dobro--had not gone away. The board charged Martin Barth with the task of creating a better feeling between the two companies, to carry the olive branch over to Dobro. The stockholders wanted an out-of- court settlement. In July of 1933, Barth reported the failure of his peace mission. Beauchamp moved to appoint Louis Dopyera to try the same thing, negotiate an end to the litigation. Then in the summer of 1933, the Chicago Musical Instrument Company (CMI), tried to take over National. In July Louis Dopyera called a special stockholders meeting to discuss "certain rumors and mis-statements made to various stockholders... for the purpose of obtaining options to purchase their stock."

CMI tried to wrestle control of National through Jack Levy. The Chicago based company had much to gain by owning National. As a major distributor, controlling the manufacturing would have meant higher profits on every sale. Louis Dopyera had the most to lose and fought the takeover. For him, the overriding issue was settling the crippling law suit with his brothers at Dobro. During August and September, several attempts were made to remove and replace board members. The stockholders disputed who owned how much stock and called an accountant to reconcile the stock ledger and the stock certificate book. In what must have been acrimonious sessions, the members fought over the legality of meetings. Farr, the attorney, pointed out that some of the stock was involved in court cases, for example, Ted Kleinmeyer's divorce. The fear of more litigation prevented some important votes about the fate of the company.

GLENN E HARGER
ASST. SECRETARY

Glenn Harger, who proved to be the wrong man to handle the company's money.

As soon as the Dopyeras settled with National, George Beauchamp, who had sided with Levy and CMI during their takeover attempts, left National's board and presumably sold his stock in the company. Yet the wrangling was not over. Paul Barth had a legal action against Louis Dopyera in Superior Court. Who knows what it concerned, possibly a dispute over stock ownership. Jack Levy was still sitting on the board and still objecting to the deal with Dobro. The new board for 1934 consisted of Levy, Auble, Louis Dopyera, Hughett and Edith Schumaker, who would soon resign and be replaced by Martin Barth. Meanwhile, National had a patent infringement lawsuit brewing with the Schierson Brothers, still another Los Angeles guitar maker.

The Dobro-National settlement had given the Dopyeras de facto control of both companies. On December 22, 1934 National board members Hughett and Auble resigned. Emil E. Dopyera and Maurice Sparling were added with Emil becoming secretary and Sparling becoming vice-president. Since Emil was Dobro's president and general manager, his membership on National's board pointed to the actual merger of the two companies. In March of 1935 National and Dobro announced that they would operate under the same roof at 6920 McKinley Avenue, Los Angeles in a building owned by Robert Dopyera. Emil Dopyera stated in an article in Music Merchandise magazine: "When in Los Angeles, we invite dealers and jobbers to visit the Dobro-National factory where hospitality prevails."

NATIONAL AND DOBRO MERGE

In September, Louis Dopyera reported that his mission to create harmony with Dobro was favorable. By November 1933, National's board finally had a settlement in the works. Dobro wanted $5000 cash plus stock. National's counter offer was to give the other company $2000 cash and nine hundred newly-issued shares of stock. The settlement gave the Dopyeras, when counting Louis, a majority interest in National and set the stage for a merger. National valued the settlement at $11,000, giving $9000 value to the nine hundred shares of stock that had an actual worth of about $1800. Obviously, giving stock to Dobro was preferably to paying $5000 cash.

In December, the board held a lengthy discussion on the settlement with Dobro. Two camps had emerged: Louis Dopyera with his supporters and the Jack Levy-CMI group. Dopyera had the most votes and prevailed with the compromise plan acceptable to the other Dopyeras. On December 8, 1933, Dobro dropped their suit against National. By December 21, a permit was granted to issue the new shares of National stock to the Dobro Corporation. Jack Levy objected in writing to the entire agreement but was overruled. In early January, Louis called for a motion that would end Levy's services as a sales representative. Levy objected that the present board had "not been acting long enough to know just how things are handled." Levy was spared, temporarily, as no one made the motion to let him go.

JACK LEVY
SALES REPRESENTATIVE

Jack Levy was involved as head of sales from 1928 to 1934 or 1935. He also represented Chicago Musical Instruments, a powerful company. This occasionally presented conflicts of interest.

On July 1st the merger became official: National became National-Dobro, and the Dobro company was dissolved. National-Dobro, a formidable force stronger than the sum of its weakened parts, pushed to consolidate its power in the industry. As reported in National's corporate minutes on September 26, 1934, the firm's lawyers had gathered evidence showing that the Schierson Brothers' resonator guitars infringed on Beauchamp's single-cone patent. We know very little about the Schiersons' operation except that it produced Vol-U-Tone electric guitars and Hollywood brand resonator guitars--the instruments in question. The court papers described three Schierson guitars using systems similar to National's, but with the cones turned upside down. If not for the lawsuit, the guitars would have been lost in obscurity like so many 1930s also-rans. Hollywood guitars had little comercial impact compared with Nationals or Dobros and sounded inferior. Nonetheless, lawyers convinced the board members that they needed to protect themselves and their patents. Despite a popular misconception to the contrary, a patent carries little weight until a court adjudicates it. Al Frost, speaking from his years of experience in the guitar industry, once said, "A patent is not really a license to manufacture, but a license to fight in the courts." Few patent cases actually went to court because of the expenses involved. (Good lawyers have always been expensive.) In the 1930s, a lot of bluffing and false representation about patents--like Beauchamp's campaign against Dobro--went on between companies. Some companies made fantastic claims, as Beauchamp had, and suffered no consequences.

In part, patent holders avoided legal fights because a patent was then open to examination and challenge in court. Judges doing their job would take a close look at an invention, usually a closer look than the patent office's. The outcome could be positive, with the patent upheld and strengthened. But on the other hand, considering convincing evidence, a judge might determine the patent to be prior art and therefore invalid. Then the patent was useless. So, taking a patent to court in an infringement case was risky.

We must assume that National's patent attorneys had much confidence in Beauchamp's patent, at least against the Schiersons. Indeed, National-Dobro prevailed in March of 1937. In his ruling, District Judge McCormick pointed out that although the Schierson guitars looked unlike the Nationals, they incorporated the "same mode of operation." The Schiersons not only lost the case but National acquired all the tools used to make Hollywood guitars, including a template for the resonators. Carl Barth still has it sitting on his garage work bench.

THE RISE OF ELECTRIC INSTRUMENTS

In the 1930s, like today, businesses that invented and sold technology had to make themselves obsolete before their competitors did. National's tri-cone had solved a problem for guitarists, making the company a leader in its field. The single-cone guitars consolidated that lead, with the only real challenges coming from Dobro and the Schiersons. The idea was to stay a step ahead of the pack, and National had succeeded. But the success of National's resonator guitars planted the seeds of the resonator's obsolescence. The

MORE PEOPLE PURCHASED

AND STILL MORE INQUIRED

FOR NATIONAL AND DOBRO AMPLIFYING STRINGED INSTRUMENTS IN 1934-1935 THAN EVER BEFORE.

A FACT ━━━━━

━━━━━ INDICATING THAT THE FASTEST SELLING GUITARS IN 1935-36 WILL BE THE NATIONAL-DOBRO AMPLIFYING AND ELECTRIC GUITARS ━━━━

REVELATION OF NEW MODELS. SUIT 545. STEVENS HARRY GERSTIN TO GREET YOU

NATIONAL - DOBRO CORP.

Los Angeles — Chicago — New York

March 1935 trade magazine ad. The merger of National and Dobro created a powerful entity capable of gaining a sizable share of the market.

pursuit of a louder guitar ultimately led to pickups and amplifiers, the stuff of electric guitars.

The bleak business climate after the 1929 stock market crash lead to austerity and cutbacks in all industries. National's days of excess, indulgence and expensive experimenting had ended by 1930. While National's stock disputes, law suits and infighting further weakened the company's competitive clout, the guitar industry was rapidly advancing the technology of electric instruments. It was a new field and still far from profitable. Nevertheless, forward thinking companies and individuals knew electric instruments were the wave of the future.

True electric guitars followed at least two well known historical scientific advances: the development of the vacuum tube by Lee De Forest in 1906 and the later development of a useful amplifier in 1913 by Western Electric engineer H. D. Arnold. AT&T and Western Electric scientists did virtually all the pioneering work in tube amplifiers, first developed for long distance telephone and radio. In 1925 AT&T and Western Electric combined to form an organization called Bell Laboratories, a company that eventually held patents for nearly every circuit used in electric guitar amplifiers. All public address system and hi-fi amplifiers, not to mention electric guitar amps, in the early days were manufactured under licenses from the Bell system.

However, Bell scientists didn't invent electric guitars. They had more important and profitable things to do - everyone used phones while relatively few people played guitar. Big corporations in America would wait until the 1960s after all the pioneering had been done to discover musical instrument manufacturing. That left the dirty work leading to practical electric guitars to musicians or their friends. The low-tech nature of the research like dissecting microphones and winding coils guaranteed that many musicians became tinkerers. For better, but mostly for worse, they experimented and created their own personal electric instruments. Few of the tinkerers understood the scientific principles involved. For them, progress was by trial and error. Among the few scientists trying to make louder instruments were engineers at Miessner Inventions, Inc. They would even-

tually patent a piano pickup that foreshadowed practical electric guitars. But in the 1920s Miessner concentrated almost entirely on developing electronic pianos and organs.

After the introduction of high fidelity sound equipment by Bell Labs in 1925, many players and inventors experimented with microphones trying to perfect their use in guitars. Electrically amplified guitars interested National's founders early on. George Beauchamp had become familiar with microphones used in vaudeville theaters. By early 1926 he had put together his own public address system that used what his son Nolan Beauchamp remembered as a Langvin amplifier with two horns on goose neck stands. George used one microphone for the guitar and vocals. Soon he had taken a microphone apart, attempting to attach the carbon button to the top of his Martin. Then, of course, he met John Dopyera and put aside experiments with electric guitars.

But Beauchamp didn't forget the electric guitar. The first well known electric guitars, though hardly modern or practical, came around 1928 from Hank Kuhrmeyer and the Stromberg-Voisinet company. They appeared in the 1929 CMI catalog, the same publication that featured National's first Triolian. Beauchamp and his crew at National must have seen these guitars. In a 1936 ad National stated: "Many new models of electric guitars are being offered to the trade today are almost duplicates of models [tested at our own cost and] discarded by our experimental department...as far back as 1928." By today's standards the Stromberg-Voisinet instruments were not true electrics because the pickup amplified body or bridge vibrations rather than string vibrations. True electric guitars translated the string's vibration directly into an electrical impulse then sent to an amplifier.

Beauchamp took night courses in electronics about the same time he left National. Carl Barth remembers that in the early 1930s his brother did too, at the National Automobile School in Los Angeles. Paul Barth helped Beauchamp in his home experiments with electric guitars. After Beauchamp left National and started at Rickenbacher, it took some time for National to start an electric guitar project. In another part of town Dobro wasted no time. Vic Smith told his story on several occasions, how he and fellow

1935 trade magazine ad which makes reference to National's rejection
of previous experimental electrics before offering its own electric.

Dobro employees experimented with magnetic pickups and pole pieces in the early 1930s. The musician/inventor responsible for Dobro's patented electric guitar designs was Arthur J. Stimson. He had performed on early radio in the Pacific Northwest with an electric guitar he had made. Coming to Los Angeles to promote his ideas, he had connected with the Dopyeras. Victor Severy, who Al Frost called an electrical genius, also worked with the Dopyeras on electric instruments.

Vic Smith often claimed that Dobro sold electrics before Rickenbacher. However, there are no documents, patent records or advertising to support his assertion. All the written records point the other way. George and Adolph were selling an electric guitar equipped with a modern string-driven pickup by August 1932. Vic Smith has argued that this so-called horseshoe pickup was an obsolete design. However, Paul McCartney, recording with the Beatles in the 1960s, would disagree. He played a Rickenbacher bass equipped with a pickup almost identical to the pickup developed by Beauchamp in the early 1930s. Sometime in 1933 Dobro had an electric on the market, but unlike the Rickenbacher it made little or no historical impact. Nonetheless, Dobro was doing research that would pay off in a couple of years.

With Beauchamp gone, Paul Barth was the only one at National known to champion the electric guitar. On June 16, 1933 a Mr. Kirkoff and a Mr. Hoter showed an electric pickup to National's board members. Today, no one remembers who these would be guitar makers were. Then in May of 1934, one of the strangest twists to the National story occurred. Adolph Rickenbacher, apparently on George Beauchamp's behalf, offered National George's electric guitar design for a ten per cent royalty fee. Rickenbacher was at best a reluctant partner in the electric guitar business. Later in life he would portray himself as the "father of the electric guitar." That's what it said on his business card. He even did little talks on the subject for school children.

However, Carl Barth says that the card should have read "The guy with the money that financed the father of the electric guitar, George Beauchamp." Rickenbacher made his money with the tool and die company. For him, making electric guitars was just a side venture and a liability in the early days. Anyway, National set Rick's offer aside because it had its own electrics on the way and didn't need Beauchamp's guitar. Who developed National's first electrics? No one seems to know for sure, but most likely Paul Barth had a hand in their creation. The company did produce an electric in Los Angeles by 1934 before the merger with Dobro. Al Frost called it the shovel: "One of my first jobs was to file burrs from the castings where flashing edges were rough." On the first National electrics, an adjustable unit attached from the rear. The back plate was then covered with felt to prevent the guitar from slipping from the lap. Al remembered that the hollow bodies were either sand cast or slush cast. Early advertising shows this Hawaiian model and an acoustic/electric Spanish model.

The biggest single event in the development of National and Dobro electrics was the merger of the two companies. While acoustic resonator guitars made up a large part of National-Dobro's 1935 catalog, the company increasingly concentrated on the development of electric instruments. Out of the newly combined efforts came some of best electrics of the 1930s. Producing electric guitars changed the whole character of National-Dobro's enterprise. For one thing, electric

National-Dobro Corp. Opens Chicago Offices

E. E. Dopyera, Gen. Mgr. of National-Dobro Corp. At Right: The New Visual Electric Reed Tuner

Harry Gerstin, Sales Manager of the Company

ANNOUNCEMENT has been made to the trade that the National-Dobro Corp., of Los Angeles, has opened eastern headquarters at 901 West VanBuren St., in Chicago, where business offices as well as assembling and warehousing facilities will be maintained to look after the eastern trade of this concern. This concern manufactures stringed instruments and specializes in electric guitars.

This corporation has also announced a new product, an electrical device for accurate tuning. This will tune harmo...

small table with a series of light panels mounted perpendicularly and directly in front. On this table is a delicate electric grinding machine, with which the operator may remove from the tuning points the smallest particle. The reed is attached to a resonator chamber of the same actual dimensions as that in the instrument. The operator establishes the note or frequency desired by dialing and manipulating a button which causes the reed to sound. This button lights a window in the unit, showing a band of light. The correct position of the ...

February 1936 article formally announcing National-Dobro's move to Chicaco. Emil (Ed) Dopyera's and sales manager Harry Gerstein's photos accompany the article. Also shown is a new device for tuning accordion reeds with electronic calibration. It is not known how many were made, though the article reads that these were to be built in Los Angeles.

steel guitars required less craftsmanship. The bodies and pickups were simple to make. The trick was making it all sound good through an amplifier. Al Frost remembered: "The old pickup coils were always dunked in tar or shellac to keep the competition from checking the number of turns, wire sizes, etc. We finally found copper wire as thin as human hair gave best results, number 44 as I recall..." Amplifier production borrowed the assembly line techniques of radio manufacturers. Once the designs and circuits were set, making the units became quite routine.

National-Dobro had a good wood shop, but it was not on a par with Gibson's, Kay's or Regal's. One style of guitar both National and Dobro had conceded to others was the traditional wooden-bodied acoustic. When Spanish electrics first became popular, most players wanted an acoustic equipped with an electric pickup as opposed to the solid bodies introduced by Rickenbacher. Why? Band leaders preferred the acoustic sound for rhythm playing and the amplified sound for solo work. To get work, most pro guitarists needed both sounds. Gibson and Epiphone acoustic-electrics were highly regarded in the late 1930s. National's top of the line electric guitars fell somewhere behind the leaders in prestige. National-Dobro lost its vanguard position in the guitar industry and the romance of the early days. However, it also consolidated its financial position by focusing on the student market and low-priced instruments. In 1935 the firm sold more than $600,000 in musical instruments through retail dealers.

For modern musicians of the 1930s, sentimentality played an insignificant role in the decision to play electric guitars or not. Few purists would hang onto the old sound of the tri-cone or Dobro once they heard good electric guitars. The pragmatic musicians who turned to National resonator guitars in the late 1920s were the first to champion the early electrics in the mid-1930s. Nationals resonator guitars were loud, but electrics were even louder. In this context, the

National resonator guitars were a blip on the screen of music history, a transitional invention that bridged the whisper of wood guitars to the blare of electrics.

NATIONAL-DOBRO MOVES TO CHICAGO

A sure sign that National-Dobro had lost its flair as a radical outsider, a position the early National company had carved for itself, was its move to the hub of musical instrument manufacturing, Chicago. The company began its move in January 1936; the actual drive took place in February during the dead of a harsh winter that had almost completely frozen Lake Michigan. Al Frost remembered motoring across the country in a Graham Paige car over a frozen Mississippi River. He was with Vic Smith, his wife, Emil Dopyera and sales manager Harry Gerstin. At that point in history, Chicago's location held many advantages. Harmony, Kay and Regal had large factories there. Many large musical instrument distributors and parts manufacturers called Chicago home as well. The city also hosted a large music trade show every summer. In addition, many major electronic firms that made tubes and transformers had factories in Illinois. National-Dobro's future was electric guitars. From a manufacturing point of view, moving close to suppliers and distributors made a lot of sense.

But another reason loomed in the veterans' thoughts. "Moving back east was a way of cutting clear from the [personal and business] problems out here," says Carl Barth. Moving to Chicago was a rebirth. National-Dobro took offices on the third and fourth floor of the old Addressograph building on Peoria and Van Buren. (One published address was 901 West Van Buren Street. Another address appeared on mid 1930s catalogs, 400 South Peoria Street. Yet another location was on Normandy Street.) A press release in January 1936 described the initial Chicago operation as a "branch office and stockroom." The transfer of manufacturing went in stages; until World War II, the company continued production in both Los Angeles and Chicago. Resonator parts still came from the McKinley factory, and Rickenbacher still stamped metal bodies. Vic Smith remembered that the old Dobro factory made amps for a short period.

Almost all the employees in Chicago were new to the company. John and Rudy Dopyera stayed in California where John worked on his resonator violin and other projects. Emil came to Chicago, but only stayed about a year. Soon the company moved to the ground floor of the Addressograph building and installed some heavy machinery. Some of the Chicago guitar manufacturers were better equipped to make certain products than others, and a sense of community had developed. Although there was plenty of competition, the factories cooperated and built things for each other. Regal had a close relationship with Dobro since their licensing agreement in January 1933. Harmony and Kay had made many of the wood bodies for National when the company had been in Los Angeles. These arrangements continued into the late 1930s. Apparently, a company called Chicago Electric made National-Dobro amps for a while in the mid 1930s. Thereafter, the Los Angeles transplants assembled all their own.

National-Dobro expanded into all areas of electric stringed instruments. Much of National-Dobro's business came from mail order companies such as Sears, Montgomery-Wards and Spiegel. By the late 1930s, National-Dobro supplied these firms more electric Hawaiian guitars and amplifiers than resonator guitars. Furthermore, National-Dobro sold pickups to other companies for their guitars. For older model resonator Nationals, late 1930s catalogs showed a conversion plate with a pickup that replaced the resonator. The copy stated, "Units are not sold separately, but conversions are made at the factory by National technicians only." Expanding into the growing music studio business, where children took private and group guitar lessons, the company introduced the discount line called Supro. In March of 1936 the first Supro electric steel and amplifier sets sold for $99.50.

National-Dobro made many advanced electric instruments, some way ahead of their time. An early pickup design had humbucking features. In July 1936 National-Dobro introduced the Violectric, an electric violin. It was not the first, but a strong contender. In amplifiers, National-Dobro had units with top-mounted controls like the later Fender amps. This feature became an industry standard. Of course, after World War II, patent records show one of the first compensated bridges came from National-Dobro's successor Valco.

In August 1941 CMI announced that it had purchased for exclusive wholesale distribution the entire production of National amplifying and electric guitars. Then Japan pushed the United States into World War II, prompting Congress to charge the newly formed War Production Board with the task of converting peace-time industries into defense industries. National-Dobro had no choice in the matter because the government ordered a halt to guitar manufacturing (General Limitation Order No. L-37). To do the war-related work, Vic Smith, Al Frost and Louis Dopyera bought out the remaining stock holders to form the Valco (standing for Vic, Al and Louis) Manufacturing Corporation. In the process National-Dobro was dissolved, as announced in an October 1943 article in Music Merchandise magazine.

Louis Dopyera, who Vic Smith once described as the "money man," bought a building on Chicago's west side. The address was 4700 West Walton Street. Valco made parts for airplanes throughout the war. After the war, the company made a few prewar style resonator guitars from leftover parts. Valco established and maintained its important position in the electric guitar industry until the mid 1960s. Al Frost, who eventually ran Valco's sales and manufacturing, became a highly respected leader in the music industry.

So, the resonator era that had started in the Roaring '20s and endured the Great Depression ended with World War II. After the war, National resonator guitars sat in attics and pawnshops. There was little recognition of their aesthetic or intrinsic value. However, in the last three decades the prewar National resonator guitar has become a symbol for American ingenuity, design, style and taste. These instruments had body parts stamped out like automobile fenders but were assembled with the care of violin makers. Nationals have a unique place in history. They bridged the gap between Old World and New World instrument making, embellishing the American musical experience from Hawaiian music and blues to country and jazz.

The strange factory-converted "Silvo" electrics used regular metal National bodies, with a circular plate containing bridge, pickup and controls, which went inplace of the acoustic resonator. Owners of resonator guitars could send their instruments back to the factory for this conversion.

National used some extra tenor guitar bodies, circular "Silvo" electric conversion plates, and square wood necks to add a Silvo Hawaiian guitar to the line. Probably not as popular as the more modern lap steels below, which were available at the same time.

National "Chicagoan" lap steel, c. 1939, in blond wood.

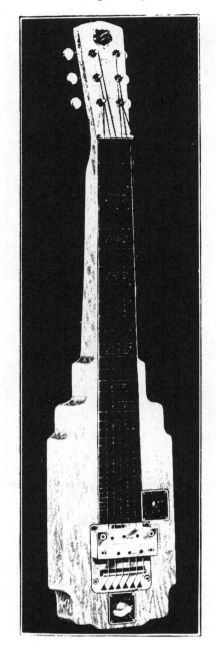

Deco-inspired National "New Yorker" lap steel, black and white celluloid-covered body. Many slight variations of this model were produced over the years, well after WW II.

Double-8-string Grand Console model, late 1930's. A modern machine for modern times. Compare these esthetics to the late 1920's instruments shown in this volume.

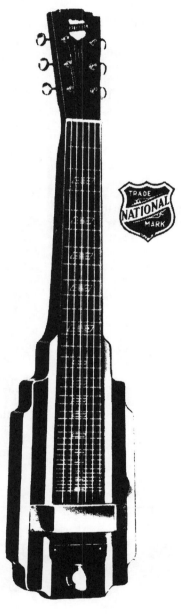

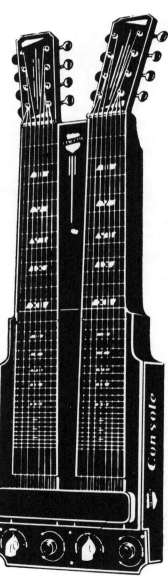

No band is complete without an electric banjo, and National was there in 1937-38 to fill that need. Presumably these are rare today, as are other electric banjos of the 1930's made by Gibson, Rickenbacker, etc.

National made a limited number of electric violins, and hot jazz fiddler Stuff Smith used and promoted them. Probably National bought finished violins elsewhere and installed the pickups at the factory. The tone is not easily confused with Stradivarius.

National electric mandolin, 1937. National electrified nearly every stringed instrument, except ukulele.

The "New Yorker" electric Spanish model was similar to the Chicagoan, but featured a sunburst finish and deco pickguard.

Two pickup instruments were very advanced for the 1930's. This model had a larger body than the New Yorker and the Chicagoan. Many collectors call this the Memphis Minnie model, as it is similar to the one she is photographed holding. This model underwent various slight changes over the 1936-1941 period. It is the strong opinion of this writer that, while National electrics were advanced for their day, they are far less interesting esthetically than the metal resonator guitars that gave the company its start.

1937 National "Chicagoan" electric Spanish guitar. Note pickup similar to Gibson "Charlie Christian" type. The lack of f-holes, looking strangely eyeless, was an advanced idea for its day, presaging more modern feedback-free archtop electrics.

THE SEARCH FOR AMPLIFICATION

by Gary Atkinson

The resonator system, which John Dopyera introduced to the National guitar, was a success both as an invention and as a commercial product. However, the question of how to amplify an instrument in the years before the advent of the electric pickup was not a new one and it would be wrong to assume that the mass production and worldwide sales of the National were the result of a unique experiment. To a great extent, the Dopyeras' and their colleagues were in the right place at the right time.

Seventy years before John Dopyera filed the first patent for his resonator system - the search for amplification had begun. Issued as patent number 2071 on 13 August, 1866, a device invented by Henry Bell would 'impart a fine tone' improvements to violins, violas and violincellos and quitars'. Bell, a British inventor, had discovered that the sound of the instruments could be enhanced by introducing a rectangular plate, curved transversely and made of crystal or glass, into the instrument body.

The plate would be placed parallel to the back and front of the instrument, with the convex surface turned towards the back. The size of the plate would depend on the size and type of the instrument, as the length and width would need to extend along practically the whole internal length and narrowest width.

As with the National resonators, the convexed plate would be suspended part way into the depth of the body and held in place by blocks fixed to the inner walls at the top and bottom of the body.

The blocks, which were covered by chamois leather, were positioned in pairs, gripping each side of the plate. Less specifically, the patent states that at some place the plate has a hole in it through which 'the sounding post should pass without contact'.

Whether or not this early attempt to improve the tonal quality of stringed instruments succeeded to the point of becoming a purchasable item is unknown, but extremely doubtful. Nevertheless, by the mid 19th century, volume was becoming an issue for stringed instruments. There were musicians who were no longer content to rely on the basic, traditional construction of their instruments to give them what they wanted.

Later, in 1884, patent number 11229 was published for J F Miller on August 13. With a reference to banjos, Miller introduced a concaved soundboard made of sheet metal into the body of the instrument.

Placed at the back of the body, the convex side of the disc faces the parchment diaphragm. The curve of the disc was shallow, rising from the back to only a third of the depth of the body. The rim of the body was provided with apertures which were fitted with metallic trumpet shaped tubes.

This was a serious attempt to amplify a stringed instrument and some of the characteristics used in this design can still be found in banjos today.

Judging by the many patents for the improvement of instruments during the 19th century, it would appear that wind instruments, violins and keyboards were receiving the most attention, with only rare references made to the guitar. This may have been because of the relative simplicity of the

mechanics and construction of the guitar. Other than making minor refinements to existing components, little more could have been done to develop the instrument , other than aesthetically or in the area of amplification. Another reason may have been a reflection of the comparatively small popularity of the instrument. This was certainly true of the latter half of the 19th century, where it is unusual to see any references to the guitar amongst the hundreds of musical instrument patents which were granted. Henry Bell's specific mention of the instrument was certainly quite conspicuous.

With John Dopyera's resonator in mind, the next invention is extraordinary. For the purpose of amplifying the guitar in particular, patent number 19130 was issued on 25 November, 1890 to H Dixon.

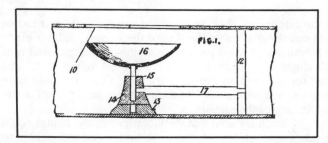

In this case a 'resonator bowl', the same size in diameter as the sound hole of the guitar, is placed upright just inside the body of the instrument. Positioned directly underneath the sound hole, the resonator is mounted from the centre of the convexed surface to the back of the guitar by a thin rod. The rod is connected to the back by a raised socket. Connecting this rod at a junction halfway down its length, at a ninety degree angle, is a second rod.

Extending along the body of the guitar, stopping approximately at the centre of the body, the rod is then connected by a third, again at a right angle to the second rod. The third rod connects with the internal walls of the front and back of the guitar.

The sound vibrations would be caught by the 'resonator bowl' where they would be amplified and transmitted by the rods back to the walls of the guitar body, thus achieving maximum results.

Again, whether or not this invention ever saw light of day is unknown. As for the successful results of the invention - who knows? It would be interesting to know how things sounded with the 'resonator bowl' and its stand only, discarding the second and third rods. The following attempt to amplify a stringed instrument takes the principle of the conical resonator further.

For 'violins and like instruments; mandolins and guitars' J M A Stroh was granted patent number 9418 on 4 May, 1899. The instrument used as an example was a violin. The neck was conventional, after that the traditional body which was used as a sound box has been completely discarded. In its place there is a banjo-like diaphragm made either of wood or parchment, mounted on a wooden frame.

Rather than the strings passing over the centre of the diaphragm, the diaphragm is positioned off centre, to the bass side of the bridge, so that the strings pass over the side

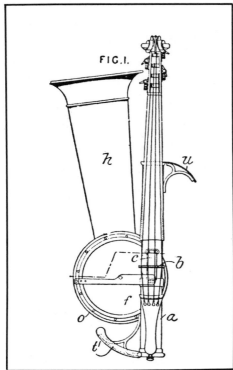

FIG.I.

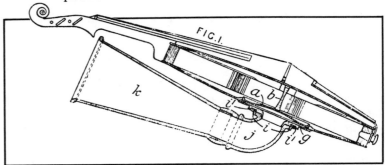

FIG.I.

On 1 June, 1912, patent number 12898 was granted to J McMillan and G McMillan, which was quite definite in its title of 'Sound Magnifying Appliances'. All previous patents were titled by the instruments applicable to the invention, as is the case with the majority of musical patents.

of the diaphragm. The centre of the diaphragm is just to one side and slightly below the line of the bridge. A horn made of aluminum or wood projects from the diaphragm, and runs at a slight angle from, and at a lower level to, the neck. The need for the neck to project forward and at the same time keep away from the neck probably determined the off centre positioning of the diaphragm.

Stroh realized that the vibrations of the strings could be taken most effectively from the bridge and transmitted to another point where they could be amplified. In this case, the sound vibrations travel from the bridge down to a block on which the bridge rests. An arm projects from the block carrying the vibrations to the centre of the diaphragm. The back of the diaphragm's frame is closed except for a hole through which sound travels and is projected through a 'tubular resonator or horn'.

On 16 February, 1901, Stroh added patent number 3393 in relation to his previous patent. This concentrated on the diaphragm. The outer diameter remains as a flat surface or, it is suggested, that it can be corrugated. The patent introduces a cone into the centre of the diaphragm, with the apex of the cone making a connection with the vibrating attachment.

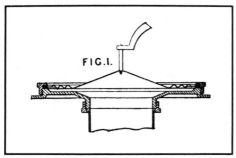

FIG.I.

Unfortunately, the type of material used to make the cone is not specified in the patent notes. It would be another 30 years before a bridge attachment would be connected onto the top of a single resonator.

Stroh's patent was successful enough to see commercial production, certainly in the form of a single and four string violin. However, it is uncertain if other instruments, such as mandolins or guitars, as mentioned in the patent were also produced.

For the purpose of this patent a violin is again used as an example. A diaphragm is fitted into the back wall of the instrument, with the convexed surface projecting into the body. Resting on the apex of the diaphragm is a thin sound post which extends vertically to the inner wall of the front of the instrument. The post does not connect directly underneath the bridge but slightly to one side of it, going towards the tailpiece. As with the Stroh violin, a horn attachment is used to project the sound but in this case it is connected over the resonator. The horn is connected to the diaphragm by a ninety degree elbow joint, and extends from underneath the instrument to a leg just short of where the neck and headstock meet. The elbow piece and horn can be rotated to direct the sound in any direction.

Taking the National into consideration, three comments made in the McMillans' patent notes are significant. Firstly, it is suggested that the horn and elbow piece could be removed completely and replaced by a 'resonator with an aperture in it'. Secondly, for the first time metal is recommended as a material to be used for the manufacture of the resonator, and thirdly, as with the selling points of the National, the McMillans recognized and noted that 'the instrument described is stated to be specially suitable for making gramophone or similar records.

Although this device was some way off John Dopyera's more refined, simpler but highly successful resonator system, this link in the resonator principle was a strong one. It was certainly strong enough to cause some concern 25 years later in the District County Court of San Diego, California.

As part of the infringement case brought against the guitar manufacturers Shireson Brothers of Los Angeles by George Beauchamp on Thursday 18 February, 1937, several previous patents had to be considered.

The Shireson Brothers were being challenged because of their wooden guitars. District Judge McCormick was told of five patents excluding Beauchamp's two single cone resonator patents of June 1931 and the Shiresons' resonator patent of 1932. Three of the patents were those of John Dopyera, one belonged to the French inventor Donboli and the fifth was that of J and G McMillan. Only one patent had any effect on the case which the Examiner had to make reference to and that was the McMillans' upon which one of the Beauchamp's original patent claim was rejected.

After the McMillans had their patent published it would be another fourteen years before John Dopyera, assignor to George D Beauchamp, T E Klienmeyer and Paul Barth, filed a patent for another resonator instrument which would open the first pages of the story of the National Steel Guitar.

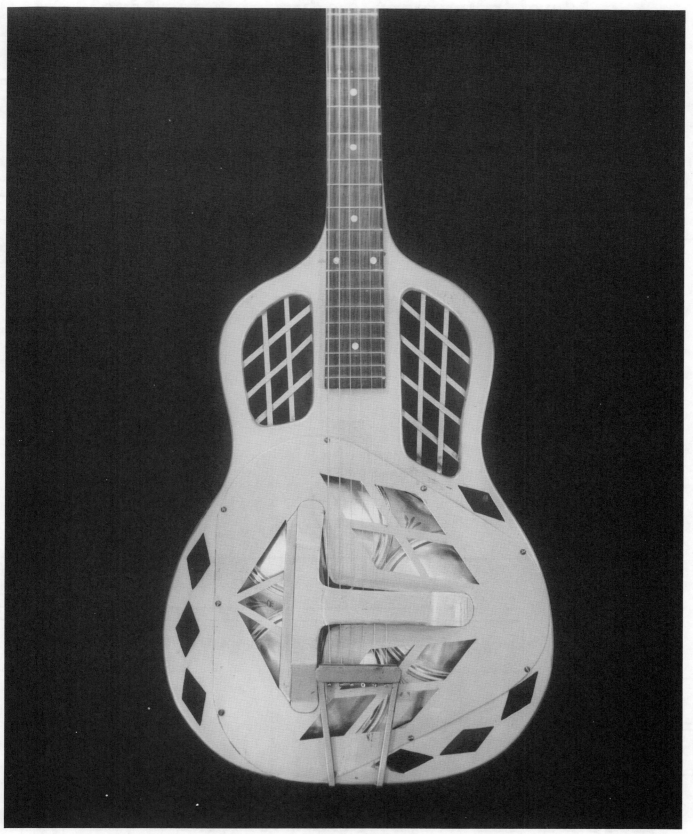

A 1927 National triplate, serial #102, possibly the third one made. Note odd shape of the upper grilles, with their hand-soldered strips which are actually woven into place. (Factory instruments have stamped upper grilles.) This instrument is somewhat more crude than #133, shown in the Style 2 section. Both are handmade pre-factory instruments. The diamond holes in the top are a signpost of these first 40 or so handmade tricones. The holes on #102 are larger than on #133.

Metal Instrument Production Time Line

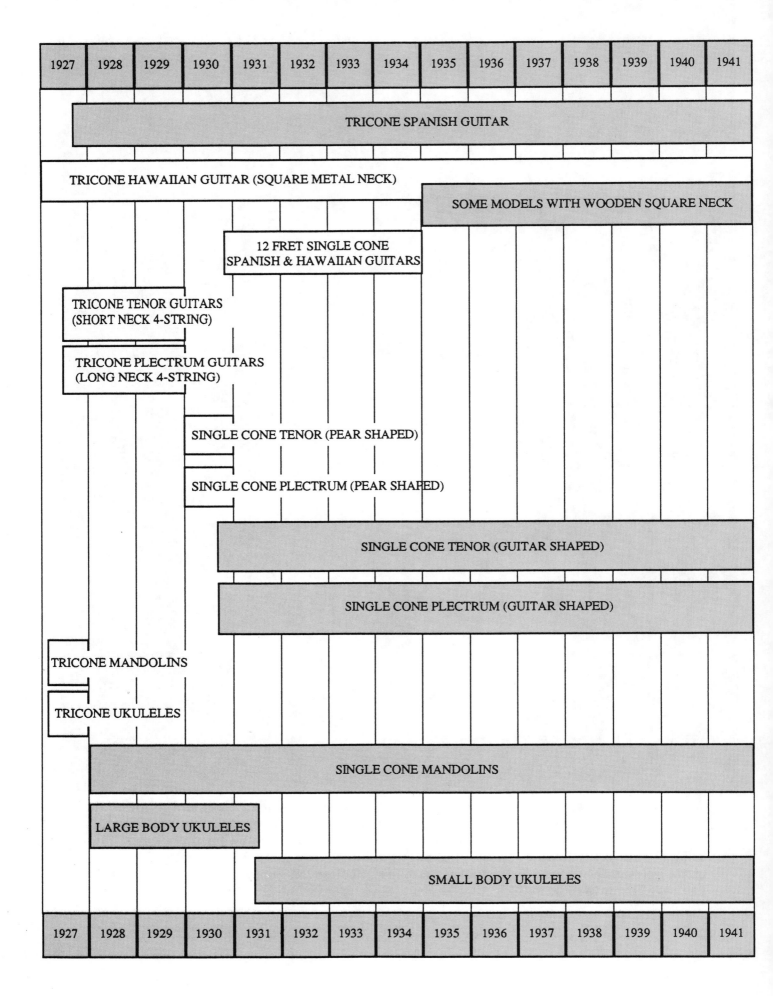

1927	1928	1929	1930	1931	1932	1933	1934	1935	1936	1937	1938	1939	1940	1941

TRICONE SPANISH GUITAR

TRICONE HAWAIIAN GUITAR (SQUARE METAL NECK)

SOME MODELS WITH WOODEN SQUARE NECK

12 FRET SINGLE CONE
SPANISH & HAWAIIAN GUITARS

TRICONE TENOR GUITARS
(SHORT NECK 4-STRING)

TRICONE PLECTRUM GUITARS
(LONG NECK 4-STRING)

SINGLE CONE TENOR (PEAR SHAPED)

SINGLE CONE PLECTRUM (PEAR SHAPED)

SINGLE CONE TENOR (GUITAR SHAPED)

SINGLE CONE PLECTRUM (GUITAR SHAPED)

TRICONE MANDOLINS

TRICONE UKULELES

SINGLE CONE MANDOLINS

LARGE BODY UKULELES

SMALL BODY UKULELES

1927	1928	1929	1930	1931	1932	1933	1934	1935	1936	1937	1938	1939	1940	1941

CHAPTER 3

NATIONAL'S ARRAY
OF
INSTRUMENTS AND MODELS

In the short life of the National company, an amazing variety and number of models were made. When one considers the various difficulties encountered by National, and the general business conditions of the Depression, this bewildering array of models represents a remarkable accomplishment. Some models were in production for the entire 1927-1941 period, and others lasted only briefly. At a peak production of nearly 50 instruments per day, literally thousands must have been made. Certain models are found fairly often, while others are quite rare or even unknown. It is difficult to calculate the exact numbers produced of each model, however the relative amounts of each model can be deduced from the number of surviving examples.

Categorizing and identifying the many varieties of Nationals has been a long and confusing process. Assembling a complete collection of every instrument, model, and variations within each model would be nearly impossible, requiring well over a hundred different items. In this chapter we shall see as many of these as possible, making the identification of Nationals easier for the owners and players of these amazing instruments.

In identifying a particular instrument as to year and model, it is important to remember the basic general types of construction National used. The items one must consider are:

---

1. **RESONATOR:**
Three-cone or single-cone
2. **BODY:**
German silver, brass, steel, or wood
3. **GUITAR BODIES:**
Neck joins at 12-fret or 14-fret
4. **GUITAR NECKS:**
Hawaiian (square) or Spanish (round)
5. **HEADSTOCKS:**
Slotted (1927-1935) or solid (1936-41)

When the above items are ascertained, exact identification of model and vintage is made easier. Serial numbers can help, especially on the 1927-1934 instruments (when the numbers followed a fairly logical sequence), but they cannot always be relied on to identify the model. The construction details and various changes to instrument parts will be described in Chapter 5. The serial number system will be discussed fully in the serial number appendix.

The huge range of instruments made by Nationals can also be placed in five time-categories that correlate with the major historical periods of the company:

1. Prototypes, false starts, and earliest produced
2. Models of the John Dopyera era 1928-1929
3. Models of the Depression years 1929-1935
4. Models of the Chicago era 1935-1941

National created an entire line of stringed instruments in addition to guitars. Again, it is an amazing variety for such a short-lived phenomenon. Between late 1927 and 1941, National produced the following instruments:

METAL BODY INSTRUMENTS
(dates are inclusive)

1. **Tricone Spanish guitars   1927 1941**

2. **Tricone Hawaiian guitars (square metal neck) 1927-41**

3. **12-fret single-cone Spanish & Hawaiian guitars '30-34**

4. **14-fret single-cone Spanish & Hawaiian guitars '35-41**

5. **Tricone tenor guitars (short-neck 4-string) 1927-1929**

6. **Tricone plectrum guitars (long neck 4-string) 1927-30**

7. **Single cone tenor guitars (pear-shaped)   1928-29**

8. **Single cone plectrum guitars (pear-shaped)   1928-29**

9. **Single-cone tenor guitars (small guitar shape) '30-41**

10. **Single-cone plectrum guitars (small guitar shape) " "**

11. **Tricone mandolins/ukes   1928**

12. **Single cone mandolins   1928-1941**

13. **Large body ukuleles   1928-1931**

14. **Small body ukuleles   1931-1941**

When one considers that all of the above instruments were made in several styles of ornamentation which varied over the years, it can be seen why so many individual instruments would be needed for a complete collection.

Wood body Nationals were also made at various times, including: very early tricone prototypes; early "Triolian" single cone guitars, 12 and 14 fret flat-top resonator guitars--mostly low-priced with bodies made by Kay or Harmony, and a late 30's archtop resonator guitar. Generally the bodies were made from 1/4" thick woods, so that the sound was still primarily resophonic. There were at least seven production wood-bodied models:

1. the first triolian single cone guitars, painted

2. the 12-fret "El Trovador", mahogany, 1932-33 only

3. the 12-fret "Estrallita", replacing the El Trovador

4. the "Rosita", a low-cost 14-fret model, after 1934

5. the "Trojan", a slightly better 14-fret model, 34-40

6. the "Havana," a post-1937 larger bodied model at $50

7. the "Aragon", a late 30s large, $175 archtop model of high quality with a gigantic sound.

All of these are described and illustrated in this book, as are all of the metal body instruments, in various models.

    Regardless of whether the instruments were Hawaiian or Spanish guitars, tenor guitars, plectrum guitars, mandolins, or ukuleles, NATIONAL USED ONLY ONE SERIES OF "STYLE NUMBERS" TO INDICATE MATERIALS AND ORNAMENTATION. All styles were nickel-plated, except Triolians, Duolians, and wood body models. All styles except Duolians have ivory celluloid fingerboard binding. As with any vintage guitar or any other collectible item, the more ornate and expensive the original item was, the more rare and sought-after it will be today.

    National also made a few custom one-of-a-kind instruments. Most were standard engraved models with an artist's name added to the body in engraving, though a few were truly custom, such as the sterling silver mandolin shown on the front cover of this book. There also was a special tricone made with palm trees etched on the body right through the plating (illustrated in this book). One can only speculate as to the numbers of other unique custom National instruments in existence.

    Original prices on National guitars ranged from student to professional, and were comparable with other makers. Guitar prices were as follows:

1928-1941	1935-1941
DUOLIAN: $ 32.50-35.00	
TRIOLIAN: $ 45.00-47.50	**DON #1: $ 80.OO**
STYLE O: $ 62.50-65.00	**STYLE 97: $ 97.50**
STYLE 1: $125.00	**DON #2: $110.00**
STYLE 2: $145.00	**DON #3: $125.00**
STYLE 3: $165.00	**STYLE 35: $135.00**
STYLE 4: $195.00	**STYLE 4: $195.00**

    Prices stayed remarkably consistent throughout National's entire history, with most models staying unchanged in price over the 13 years. This would never occur today, when most guitar companies raise prices each year.

    To lend perspective to the value of a dollar in the 1930's, a Martin D-18 cost $55, a D-28 was $100, and a top-of-the-line D-45 went for $200. Inflation from the Depression years to today is approximately 1500%. For National buyers, the real bargain was the Style O, at half the cost of a tricone. In fact, as shown in Chapter 2, it was the single cone models that saved National from the ravages of the Depression. The tricones were aimed at professionals, and once that market was saturated, and with the onset of the Depression, sales of tricones became an increasingly smaller part of National's business.

    The smaller instruments (tenor/plectrum, mandolin, and uke) were priced slightly lower than the guitars, in some cases. The price difference was larger on the more expensive styles than on the less expensive styles. This probably reflects the hourly labor costs of hand engraving. The following table of multiple-instrument models shows this:

styles	3	2	1	0	97	triolian
INSRUMENT						
Guitar:	$165.	$145.	$125.	$65.	$97.	$45.
Plectrum:	120.	100.	80.	65.	97.	42.
Tenor:	115.	95.	75.	65.	97.	37.
Mandolin:	95.	80.	65.	65.	97.	45.
Ukulele:	85.	80.	55.	40.	---	25.

    This table clearly shows where the good values were. Probably the least value for the money was the Style 97 mandolin, at two dollars more than the elaborately engraved Style 3 mandolin, which additionally had a higher quality neck and fingerboard than the Style 97. Perhaps the fact that the entire line of Style 97 instruments was priced at $97.00 contributed to their current rarity. This may also be true of Style O plectrums, tenors, mandolins, and ukes. National's ukulele prices were relatively high--the Martin 5K, a top-of-the-line pearl-inlayed uke, sold for a mere $50.00. It is also interesting to note that the Triolian mandolin cost more than the larger Triolian tenor/plectrum models. Generally, all styles of National guitars are more common than the corresponding plectrums, tenors, mandolins, and ukuleles.

Instruments from the golden production years:
Left: 1929 Style 4 Hawaiian #1173
Right: 1932 Style 3 Hawaiian #2568

DESCRIPTIONS OF CATALOGUED NATIONAL STYLE NUMBERS FOR TRICONE AND OTHER "SILVER" INSTRUMENTS:

STYLE 1:

no engraving

•

German silver body

•

Pearl-dot position markers

•

National decal on headstock

•

Ebony fingerboard, (rosewood below # 380)

•

Mahogany neck on guitars, maple on all others

•

Hawaiian model has integral square metal neck

•

This style applies to all Hawaiian and Spanish tricone guitars, single-cone tenor and plectrum guitars, mandolins, large ukes and small ukes. There were only slight changes made in this model from 1928-1941. Most Style 1 models were made before the mid-1930s. By 1935 an engraved "wiggle" was added as a border to all body surfaces of the tricone guitars. Style 1 was phased out as an available style for ukuleles, mandolins and tenor/plectrums. Priced at $125, style 1 was the best-selling German silver instrument. Certainly most tricone guitars seen today are this model. Curiously, of the Spanish (round) neck tricone guitars, the Style 1 models seem to have the best sound. Some people have contended that the body-engraving on the higher- priced models somehow interferes with the sound slightly. However, the subtleties involved are highly subjective.

The entire German silver series of tricone instruments was priced for professional players, and until late 1929 Style 1 was the least expensive National guitar model available. Style 1 was effectively replaced by the more ornate but less expensive style 97 by the late 1930's. There are certain Art Deco afficionados who contend that only the plain Style 1 Nationals are true examples of pure Art Deco design, and that the engraving on the higher models looks old- fashioned in comparison to the bodies. The author agrees that the style 1 tricone is a pure example of industrial, functional Art Deco design. There is, on the other hand, an undeniable attractiveness to the engraved models, which strongly evokes the feeling of "old world craftsmanship meeting modern technology."

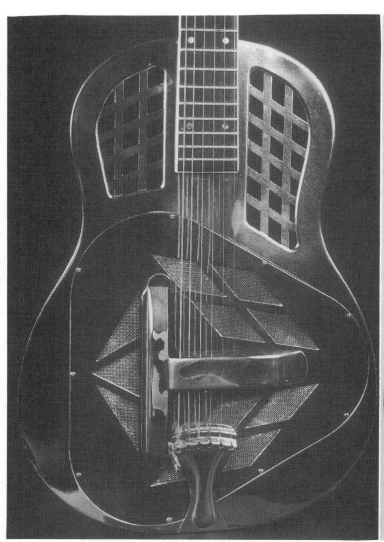

1928 Style 1 Tricone Spanish guitar, #0731.

1934 Style 1 Tricone Hawaiian, with "wiggle" border.

1928 Style 1 Ukulele, #143, with early screen-hole coverplate, and concentric-ring-stamped cone.

STYLE <u>2</u>:

Pearl-dot position markers

•

Hand engraved with a wild rose design

•

Integral metal neck on Hawaiian model

•

Adiitional roses on the coverplate (1927-28)

•

Ebony fingerboard (rosewood below c.#400)

•

German silver body, engraved 2-line borders

•

Decal sometimes on ebony overlay (all others)

•

Mahogany neck on guitars, maple on all others

•

National decal on mahogany headstock (guitars)

•

Style 2 applies to Hawaiian and Spanish tricone guitars, tricone and single-cone tenor and plectrum guitars, mandolins, and both large and small ukes. It was made from 1927-1939 with no changes other than that those Style 2 tricones numbered below approximately #400 had additional wild roses engraved on the triangular cover plate. Most were made before the mid-1930's, and, at $145, sold nearly as well as the style 1 series, particularly during the earliest days of National, approximately serial number 1000 and below. For the first few months of National's existence, style 2 was the only engraved model, and therefore was the top of the line. Many photographs of Hawaiian musicians of the late 1920s show these artists holding Style 2 tricones. The rose pattern engraving on the very earliest (1927) Style 2 instruments has more fine detail work than the engraving on the subsequent production instruments.

Hawaiian guitar #133. One of the first style 2 tricones, totally handmade in John and Rudy Dopyera's shop, in 1927. All cut-outs are by hand, and the smooth right-angle edges of the upper grilles were pounded into shape by Rudy, using hammers.

Rear view of #133.

Detail of body—note hand-soldered strips in upper grilles, but not interwoven like #102.

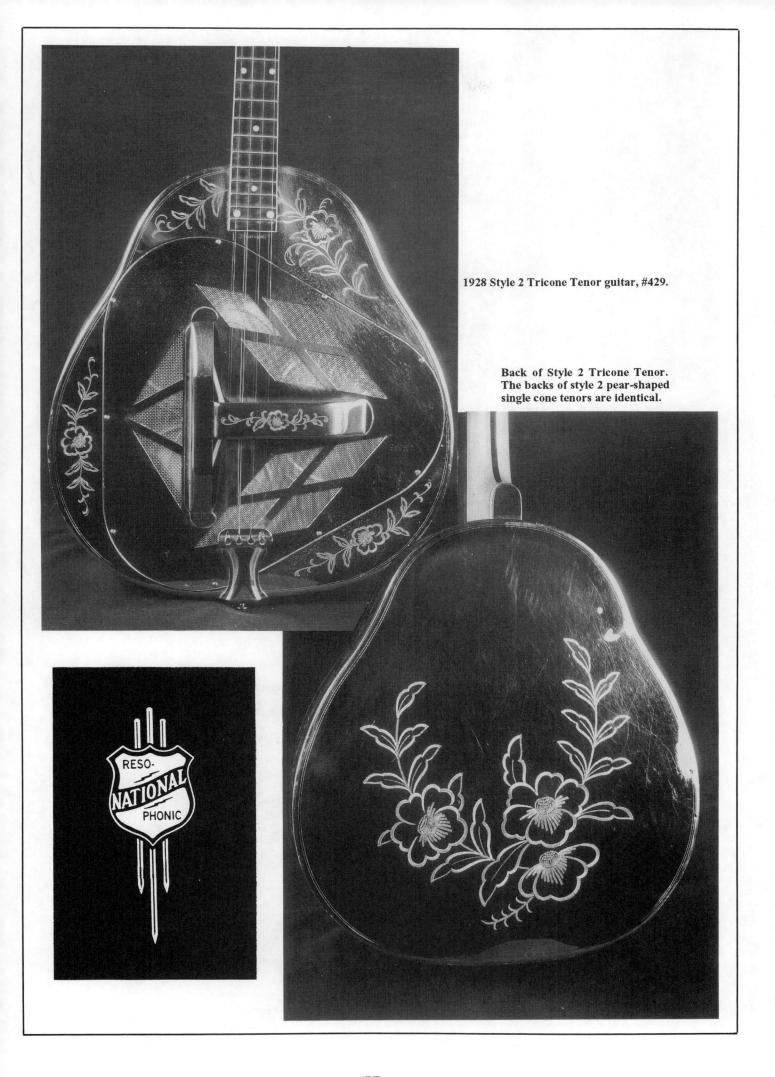

1928 Style 2 Tricone Tenor guitar, #429.

Back of Style 2 Tricone Tenor. The backs of style 2 pear-shaped single cone tenors are identical.

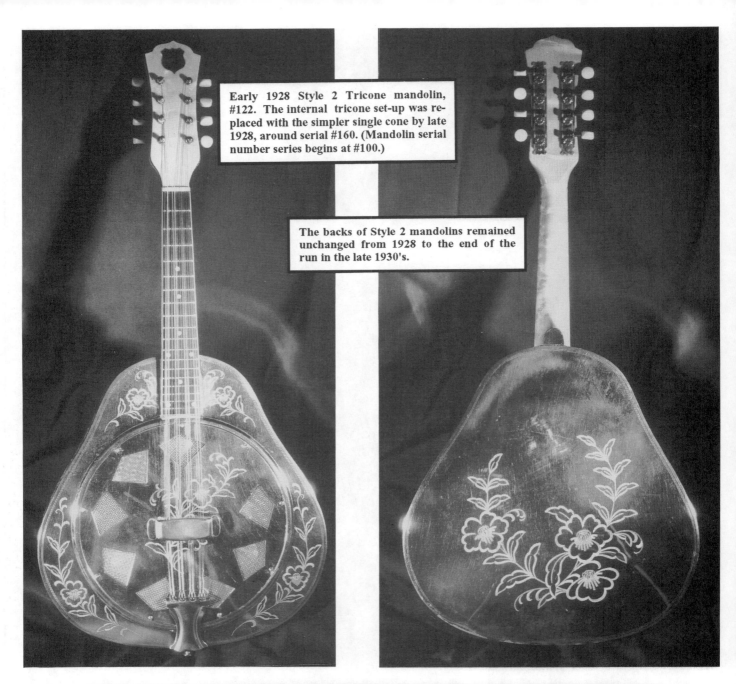

Early 1928 Style 2 Tricone mandolin, #122. The internal tricone set-up was replaced with the simpler single cone by late 1928, around serial #160. (Mandolin serial number series begins at #100.)

The backs of Style 2 mandolins remained unchanged from 1928 to the end of the run in the late 1930's.

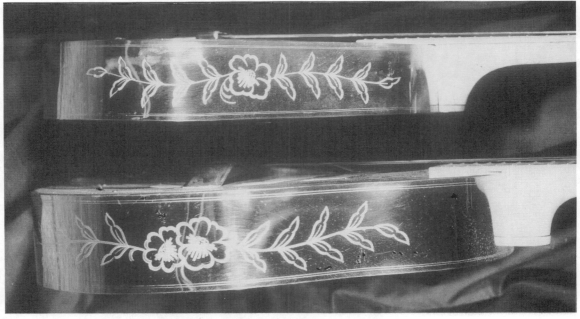

Side views of Style 2 mandolin (top) and tenor guitar.

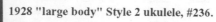
1928 "large body" Style 2 ukulele, #236.

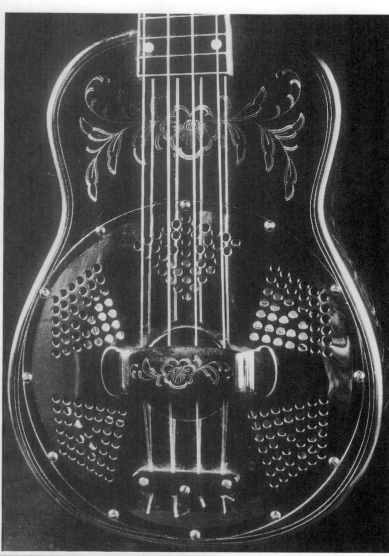

1931 "small body" style 2 ukulele, #312. Coverplates and cones are identical.

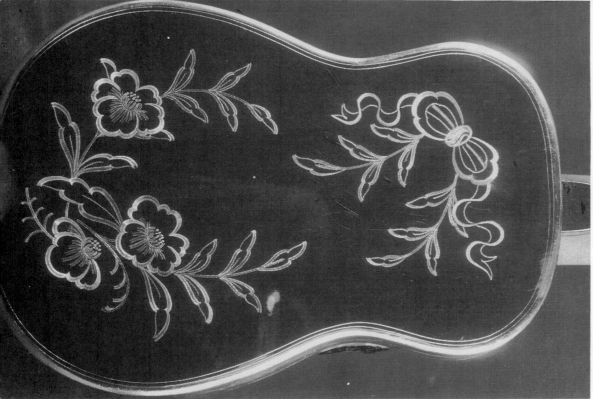

Back engraving of #236, a miniature of the guitar.

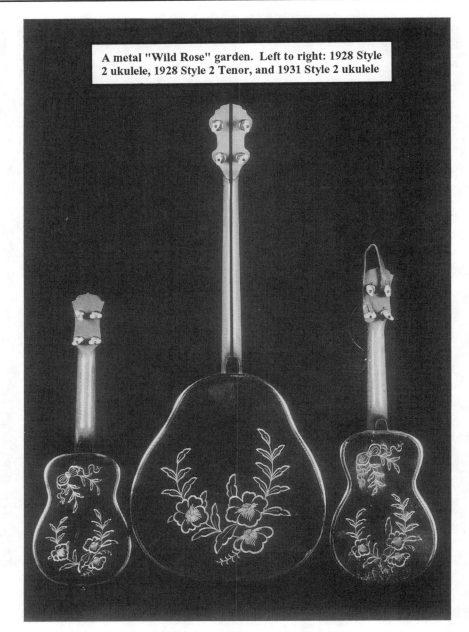

A metal "Wild Rose" garden. Left to right: 1928 Style 2 ukulele, 1928 Style 2 Tenor, and 1931 Style 2 ukulele

Detail of ukulele coverplate handrest.

STYLE 3:

**Elaborate lily-of-the-valley engraving
(5 different variations over the years)**

•

German silver body, engraved 2-line borders

•

Ebony fingerboard, fancy square pearl inlays

•

Engraved pearl National logo in ebony overlay on headstock

•

**Pearloid overlay with engraved logo
(normally a Style 4 feature) sometimes used instead.**

•

Hawaiian guitar has integral square metal neck

Style 3 applies to Hawaiian and Spanish tricone guitars, tricone and single-cone tenor and plectrum guitars, mandolins, and both large & small ukes. This beautiful style was the top-of-the-line model for all the above instruments except tricone guitars and Hawaiian guitars (see style 4). The engraving detail is exquisite, and the lily-of-the-valley motif was designed by John Dopyera and his wife. Made from 1928-1941, five variations were produced. While the actual pattern of the engraving was consistent, the positioning of the fronds of lilies was changed on the guitar top as follows:

A: 3 separate fronds on coverplate c.#400-500
(see Jim & Bob photo, Chapter 6)
B: no lilies on coverplate, fronds descending
C: no lilies on coverplate, fronds ascending
D: 3 half-fronds on cover attach to rest of top engraving
(around serial #2400-2500)
E: whole pattern flows over top, thru cover, 1933-41
(after serial #c.2500, only seen on Hawaiian models)

A Style 3 ukulele, 1931-1939.

Late 1930 Style 3 Spanish Tricone guitar, #S 46. The engraving pattern is Variation C.

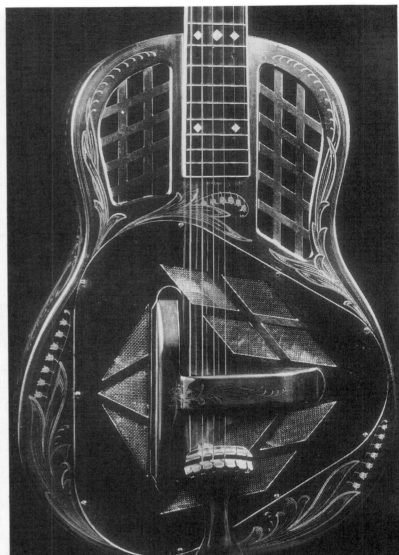

1928 Style 3 Spanish Tricone, #0675, variation C.

Early 1930 Style 3 Hawaiian, #2438, Variation D engraving, very short-lived pattern.

Back of neck, #2438, unusual extra frond of

The pattern changed again in weeks. 1930 Style 3 Hawaiian guitar, variation E--the "flow-through" pattern.

Standard engraving on the neck near the body on all Style 3 Hawaiian guitars.

The pattern for the sides on all Style 3 guitars was generally identical to this one.

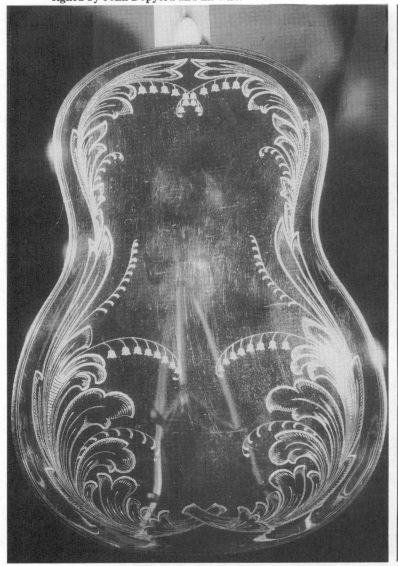

Back of roundneck tricone #S 46. This pattern was designed by John Dopyera and his wife.

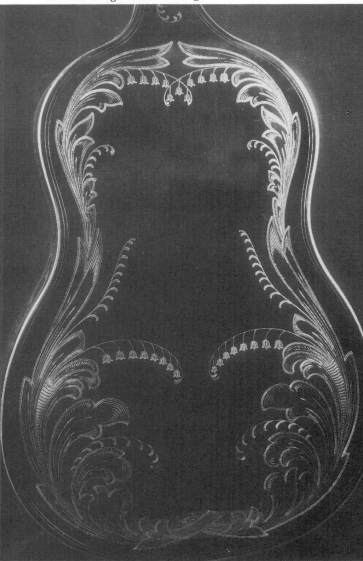

Back of squareneck tricone #2568. This beautiful design remained unchanged from 1928 to 1941, and outlasted all other designs in the catalog.

Left: 1938 Style 3 Mandolin, #A 6273, raised-center coverplate. Right: rare 1929 pear-shaped single cone Style 3 tenor guitar, #633. About 250 were made with this body style, but most were Style 1's and 2's.

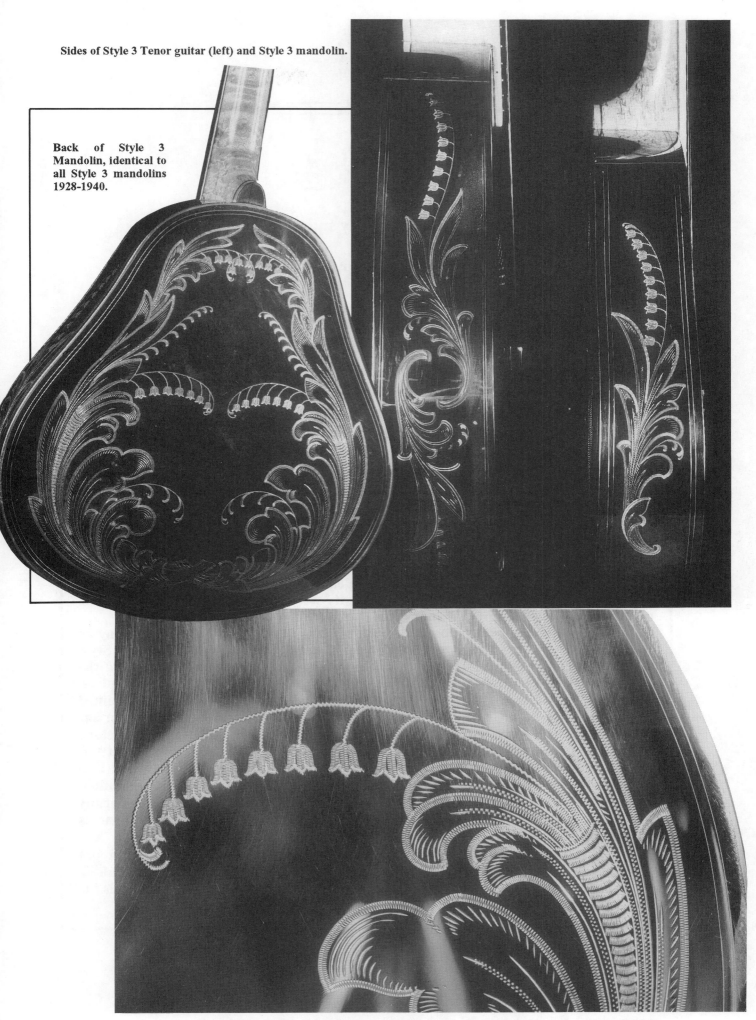

Sides of Style 3 Tenor guitar (left) and Style 3 mandolin.

Back of Style 3 Mandolin, identical to all Style 3 mandolins 1928-1940.

The artistic quality of engraving work at National was remarkably and consistently high. A single branch of lily-of-the-valley flowers, incised into German silver with steel tools.

STYLE 4:

Ebony fingerboard, fancy square pearl inlays
•
German silver body, engraved 2-line borders
•
Highly elaborate chrysanthemum engraving,
(2 main variations)
•
Hawaiian model has integral square metal neck
•
Engraved pearloid headstock overlay Engraved pearl logo on
ebony overlay (normally a Style 3 feature) sometimes used instead
•

Style 4 was the absolute top of the line model for National, and was used only on Hawaiian and Spanish tricone guitars ONLY. Introduced in 1928 at $195, this flagship model is quite rare today. The original advertising made references to purchases of this model by "royal families worldwide." The lavish chrysanthemum pattern was reportedly designed by George Beauchamp.

Many different types of engraving cuts were made to create the elaborate decoration of these beautiful instruments.

The flowerless pattern on the Style 4 guitar #0141 shown in this book may be the first attempt at creating a top-line design. Certainly it is the earliest known Style 4 guitar. The earliest models shown in the catalog, on string packages and on the company letterhead had separate fronds of chrysanthemums on the cover plate. This was soon changed to a flow-through-the-cover-plate design which remained unchanged from 1928-1940. The work of at least three different engraving men has been seen on style 4 instruments. Examples are illustrated in the photographs below.

The periods of the three engravers are: 1927-32, 1932- c.1936, and 1936-1941. The engraver of the first five years was a Mr. Williams. It is amazing how many he was able to engrave and how quickly he could do the job with consistent perfection. Most Style 4 tricones date from the 1928-1932 period, since tricone sales generally diminished after that. The last few Style 4 guitars had an added plexiglas pickguard.

There are 2 known Style 4 instruments that were not guitars and not catalogued: a tricone tenor guitar (#12) custom engraved style 4, and the unique radio-presentation mandolin made in l929 which has style 4 engraving as a basis for its even more elaborate design.

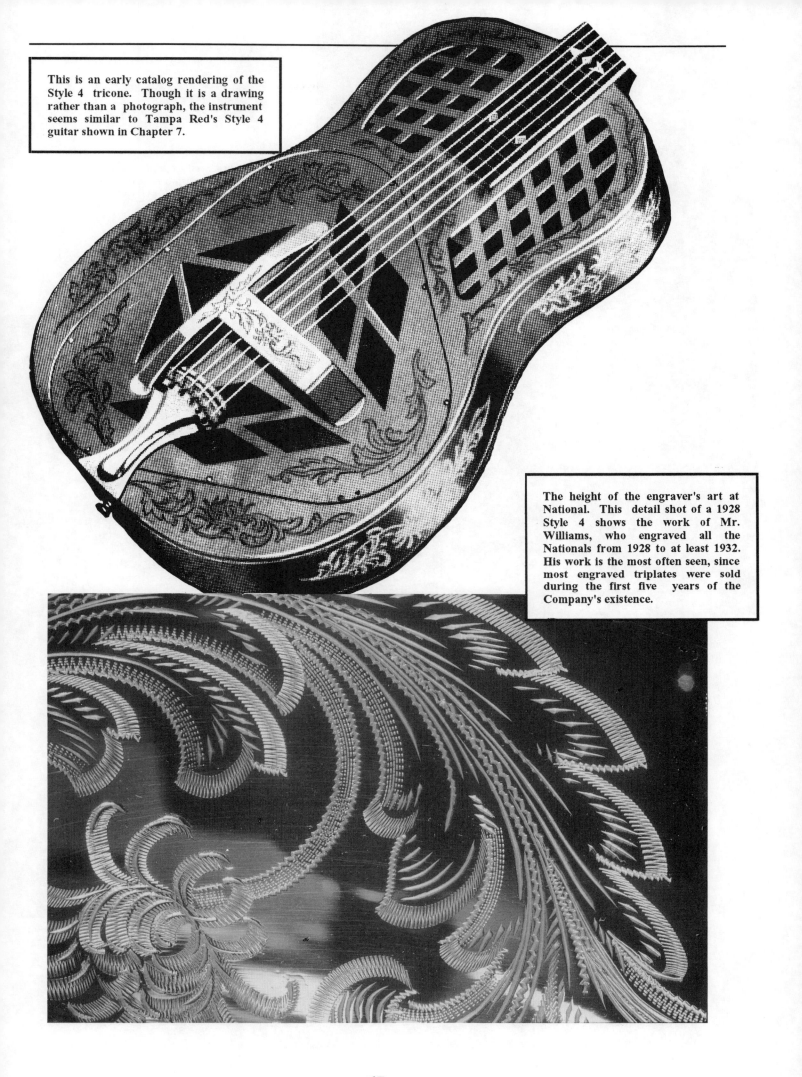

This is an early catalog rendering of the Style 4 tricone. Though it is a drawing rather than a photograph, the instrument seems similar to Tampa Red's Style 4 guitar shown in Chapter 7.

The height of the engraver's art at National. This detail shot of a 1928 Style 4 shows the work of Mr. Williams, who engraved all the Nationals from 1928 to at least 1932. His work is the most often seen, since most engraved triplates were sold during the first five years of the Company's existence.

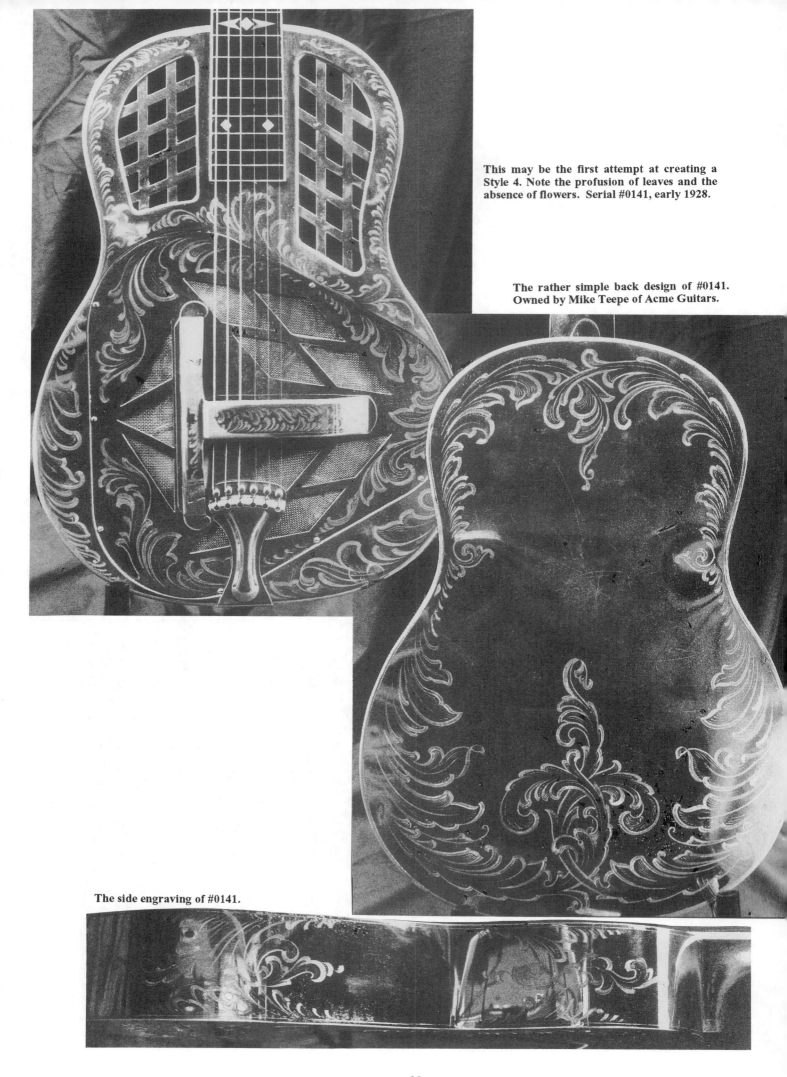

This may be the first attempt at creating a Style 4. Note the profusion of leaves and the absence of flowers. Serial #0141, early 1928.

The rather simple back design of #0141. Owned by Mike Teepe of Acme Guitars.

The side engraving of #0141.

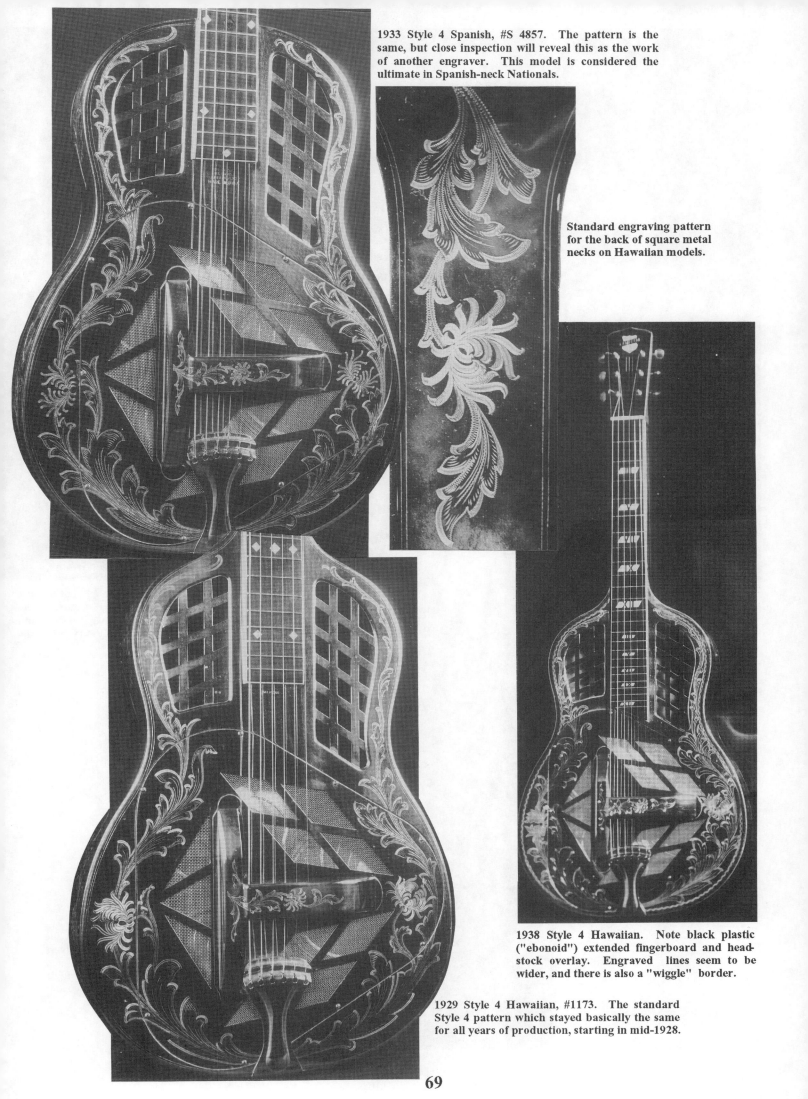

1933 Style 4 Spanish, #S 4857. The pattern is the same, but close inspection will reveal this as the work of another engraver. This model is considered the ultimate in Spanish-neck Nationals.

Standard engraving pattern for the back of square metal necks on Hawaiian models.

1938 Style 4 Hawaiian. Note black plastic ("ebonoid") extended fingerboard and headstock overlay. Engraved lines seem to be wider, and there is also a "wiggle" border.

1929 Style 4 Hawaiian, #1173. The standard Style 4 pattern which stayed basically the same for all years of production, starting in mid-1928.

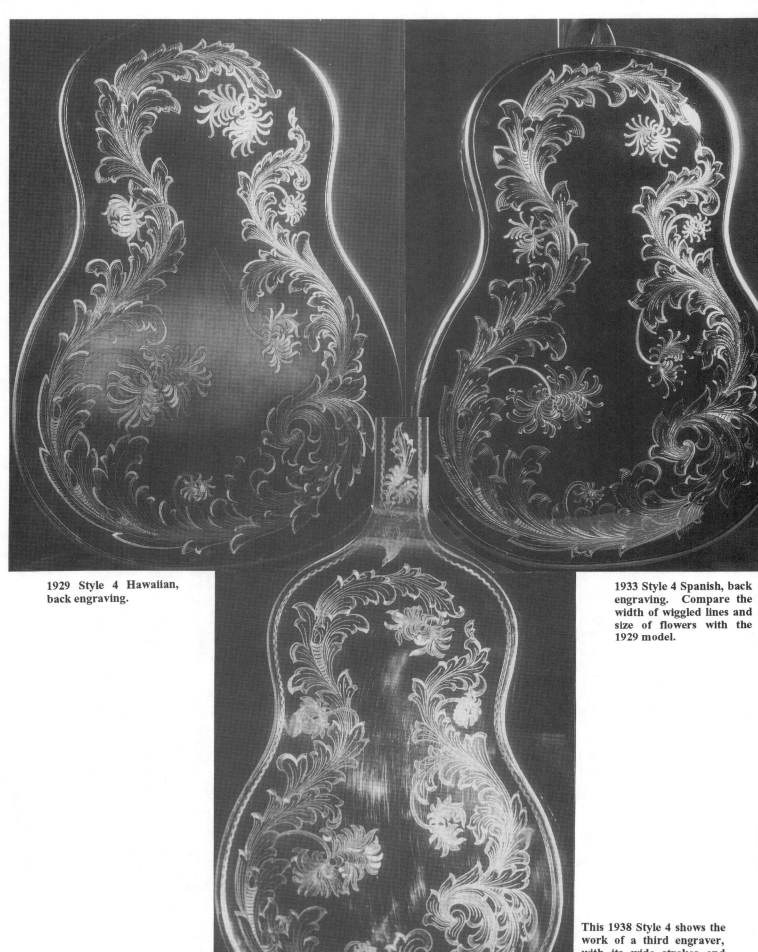

1929 Style 4 Hawaiian, back engraving.

1933 Style 4 Spanish, back engraving. Compare the width of wiggled lines and size of flowers with the 1929 model.

This 1938 Style 4 shows the work of a third engraver, with its wide strokes and deeper cuts. Note wiggle border, not seen on earlier models.

1933 Style 4 engraving detail. Note the several different types of cuts. It is unknown how long each instrument took to engrave. National charged 75 dollars more for a style 4 than for the plain style 1.

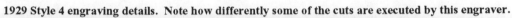

1929 Style 4 engraving details. Note how differently some of the cuts are executed by this engraver.

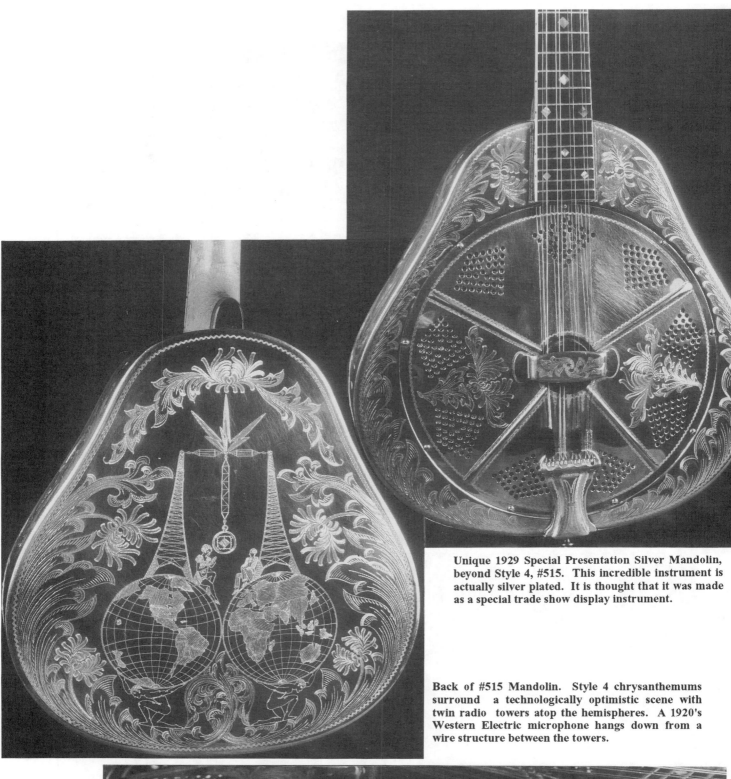

Unique 1929 Special Presentation Silver Mandolin, beyond Style 4, #515. This incredible instrument is actually silver plated. It is thought that it was made as a special trade show display instrument.

Back of #515 Mandolin. Style 4 chrysanthemums surround a technologically optimistic scene with twin radio towers atop the hemispheres. A 1920's Western Electric microphone hangs down from a wire structure between the towers.

Side view of special mandolin. Engraved more densely than the guitars.

A unique feature of this instrument is the addition of screens underneath the drilled holes in the coverplate. A wiggle line surrounds the fingerboard, coverplate ribs, and coverplate perimeter.

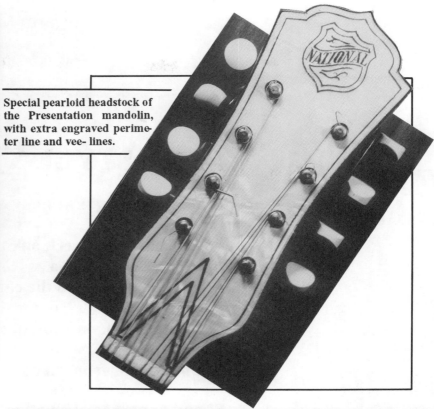

Special pearloid headstock of the Presentation mandolin, with extra engraved perimeter line and vee-lines.

The global perspective, in metal, complete with 1929 political borders. The finest example of National engraving in existence, and a unique design.

Detail of handrest engraving (2 times actual size).

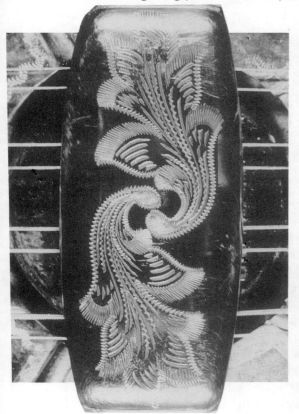

STYLE 97:

Brass tricone guitar body (nickel plated)

•

Dark mahogany neck on Spanish models

•

Slotted headstock on the earliest (1935-36)

•

Solid headstock on subsequent instruments

•

"Ebonoid" fingerboard on Hawaiian guitars.

•

Ebony fingerboard on all others, pearl dots

•

Brass single-cone tenor, mandolin, bodies
(no single-cone Style 97 guitars)

•

Hawaiian model has square wood neck, not metal

•

Dark-stained maple square neck on Hawaiian guitar

•

Moderne black and white celluloid headstock overlay

•

Sandblasted scene of female surfrider in Hawaiian setting, etched
portions then colored with airbrushed enamel

•

The rare style 97 was made in small quanities from 1936 to 1940. It was offered as the first tricone guitar priced at under $100. This was made possible by the lower cost of brass, and, with all the color ornamentation, this guitar was a real bargain compared to the Style #1 (plain) at $125.

This design was also used for guitar-shaped single-cone tenor and plectrum guitars and mandolins. These smaller instruments were not as much of a bargain as the guitars, as seen earlier in this chapter.

Keeping in mind that by 1936-1940 National's business was declining as players switched from resonator to electrics, these are very rare guitars today, and the tenors, plectrums and mandolins are rarer still. Very few examples exist.

Interestingly, this unique use of brass in a tricone body yielded a different tone than the German silver bodies, not as many overtones, and very even response across the range of notes. These tonal characteristics make the round neck model 97 a great jazz guitar. The Hawaiian models are not quite as resonant as the Hawaiian tricones of German silver, but still have a great warm tone.

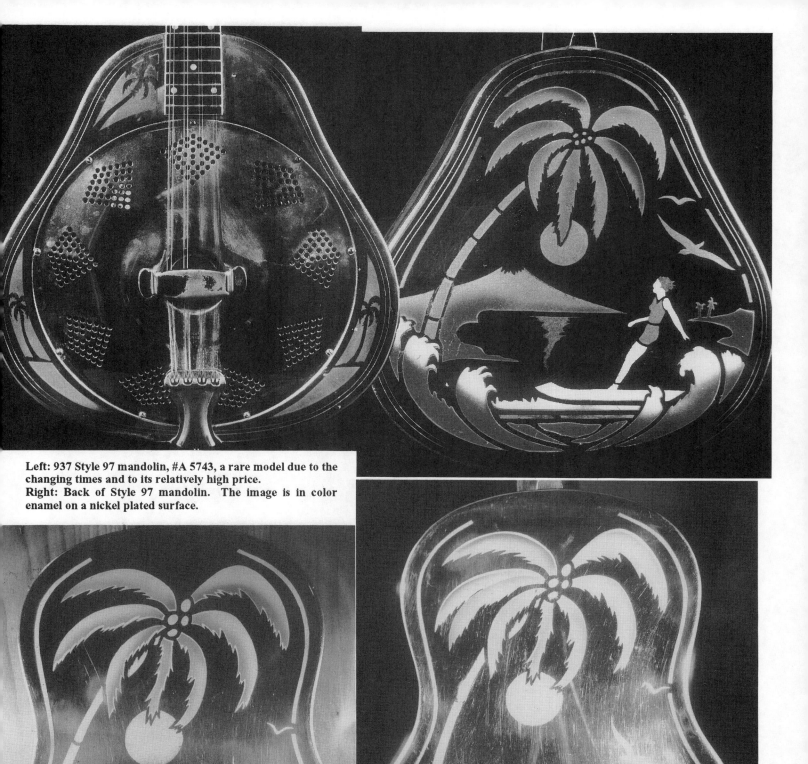

Left: 937 Style 97 mandolin, #A 5743, a rare model due to the changing times and to its relatively high price.
Right: Back of Style 97 mandolin. The image is in color enamel on a nickel plated surface.

Left: Surf's up! 1936 Style 97 Tricone Hawaiian guitar back, #B 1901. This is the standard image for this model.
Right: Oops! Someone slipped and put in an extra palm leaf on the back of this 1938 Style 97 Spanish guitar, #A 6448.

**Front of 1936 Style 97 Hawaiian, with long 'ebonoid'
fingerboard and modernistic Roman numeral markers.**

Style 97 side pattern.

Detail of female surfrider.   Detail of front lower bout.

77

STYLE 35:

Maple neck on Spanish model

•

Ebony fingerboard on Spanish model

•

Brass tricone guitar only (nickel plated)

•

Engraved "wiggle" borders on all surfaces

•

"Ebonoid" fingerboard on Hawaiian model.

•

Integral metal square neck on Hawaiian model

•

Moderne black and white celluloid headstock overlay

•

Sandblasted scene of "minstrel" motif, etched portions then colored with airbrushed enamel colors

•

Style 35 was made ONLY in tricone Spanish and Hawaiian GUITAR models. The brass construction enabled National to price this model at $135, ten dollars less than a Style 2. However, like the style 97 instruments, this model was produced towards the end of National's lifespan, from 1936-1940, and hence very few were sold.

Musicians were more interested in the new electric instruments, and resonator guitars were becoming passe. The Hawaiian model is very rare, and the Spanish model is even scarcer. At least one Hawaiian model has been seen with the etched portions of the design left uncolored, as the color feature was dropped from the design towards the end of the Model 35's production run.

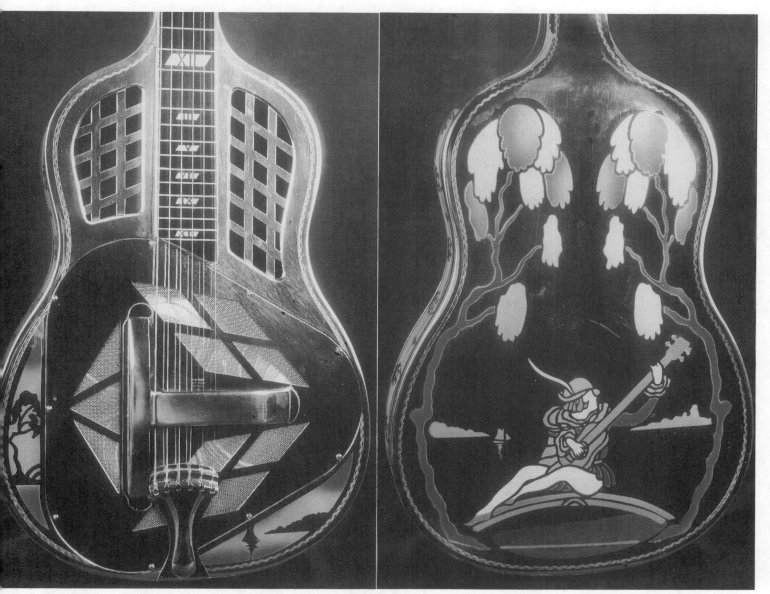

Style 35 Tricone, Hawaiian, #A 5743, just 3 instruments away from the mandolin shown a few pages back. This rare model was the only other color-and-silver tricone made by National, though some have been seen without color. Extended ebonoid fingerboard is somewhat different than the Style 97 fingerboard.

The back of the Style 35 shows a slightly foppish minstrel playing a resonator lute-like thing under a pair of cartoon-ish trees. This design pushed the limits of taste into new territory for National. Perhaps as the novelty of resonator instruments began to wear off in the mid-1930's, the company thought that more novel visual designs would sell. The model's rarity attests to the weakness of that premise. However, the colors are stunning (see color pages) and these instruments sound as good as any tricones.

The sides of the Style 35 were etched without colors and repeat the bridge-and-trees motif of the back.

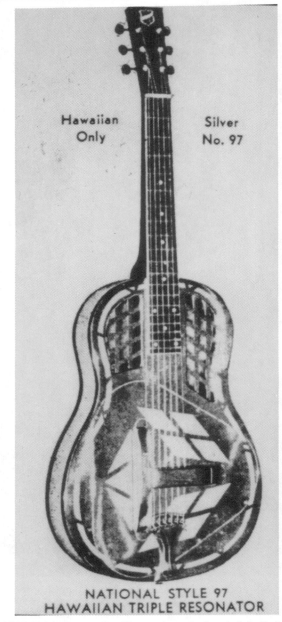

Hawaiian
Only

Silver
No. 97

**NATIONAL STYLE 97
HAWAIIAN TRIPLE RESONATOR**

1935-1936 era catalog illustration of what is labelled a
Style 97 guitar. Perhaps a very early version of the
model, however none have been seen in recent years.
Note spartan style O type square headstock. Standard
97's have the peaked tricone headstock

Another strange model,
never catalogued. This tricone's serial number, #A
2950, and its solid head-
stock would place it around
1937. An extremely rare
model, with only two, possibly three, in existence, all
with wooden squarenecks.

OTHER ETCHED
TRICONE GUITARS:

Two illustrations are shown here of
two unusual designs. The catalog cutting
refers to this as a Model 97. Perhaps it
was an early experimental design for the
model. Until an example is located, one
can only speculate as to what was on the
back.

The photographs of the other etched tricone shows a highly abstract "exploding palm tree" design. Three or four examples of this guitar have been mentioned by collectors, but it appears never to
have been designated with a model name. No mention of this model is made in any printed catalog or
advertising. It could be another experimental version of a budget-priced tricone. The wooden square
neck is finished in a muted charcoal grey metallic laquer, reminiscent of fine mid-1930's auto finishes.
While production of the model 97 spans the years 1936-1940, the solid headstock, arced National logo
and the serial number of this strange guitar place it in 1938. The headstock overlay is a silver-grey
pearloid with a dense "grain," a type seen on no other National instruments.

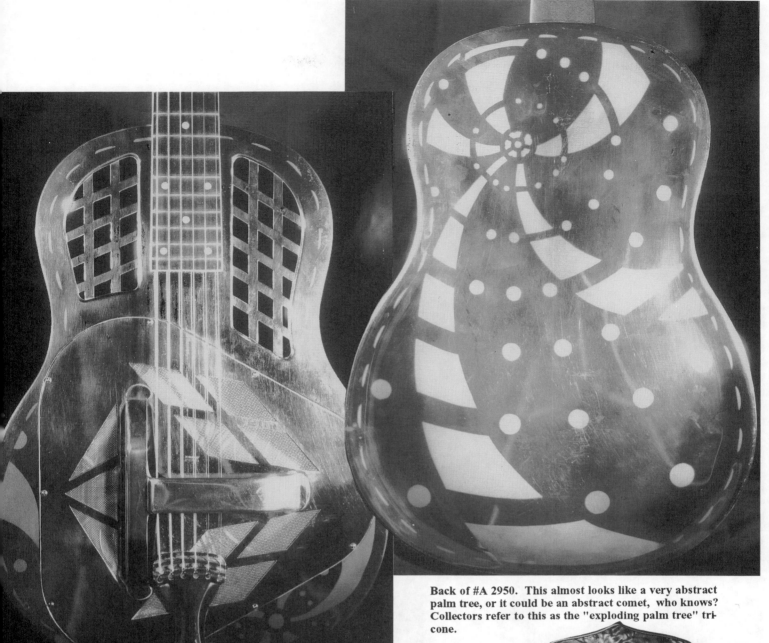

Back of #A 2950. This almost looks like a very abstract palm tree, or it could be an abstract comet, who knows? Collectors refer to this as the "exploding palm tree" tricone.

Front of body of #A 2950. Standard wooden fingerboard, and apparently meaningless designs etched into the top. Note "stitched" border etching.

The highly unusual dark silver-grey pearloid headstock overlay with engraved National lettering.

More abstract designs fill the sides, with the stitched border repeated.

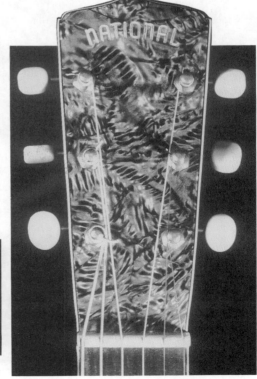

Unique custom tricone, #S 1602, from 1931. The etching goes through the plating revealing the brass in the etched portions. Unusual square headstock.

Back of #S 1602, with unique palms design. Predates catalogued brass (not German silver) tricones by four years. A custom order or an experimental design?

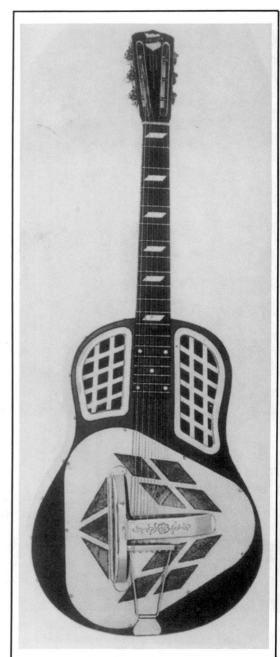

A partially WOOD tricone. Probably assembled during World War II or even later, from leftover parts. Wooden back and top, with metal sides, grille-pieces, and coverplate, which appears installed crookedly. A mystery guitar.

STYLE "M-3 HAWAII": Available with a wooden squareneck only, this was a wartime budget model tricone with brass body and a painted wood grain finish in a rather grim yellow tone. An inexpensive basswood neck was fitted, with a metal National logo plate on the headstock. The rosewood fingerboard was unbound. This model was advertised in 1941 only. The sound of these tricones is generally as good as any plated model. The spartan esthetic of this model evokes an image of wartime "blackout" model automobiles, with their painted rather than chromed trim pieces.

CHAPTER 4

SINGLE RESONATOR INSTRUMENT STYLES

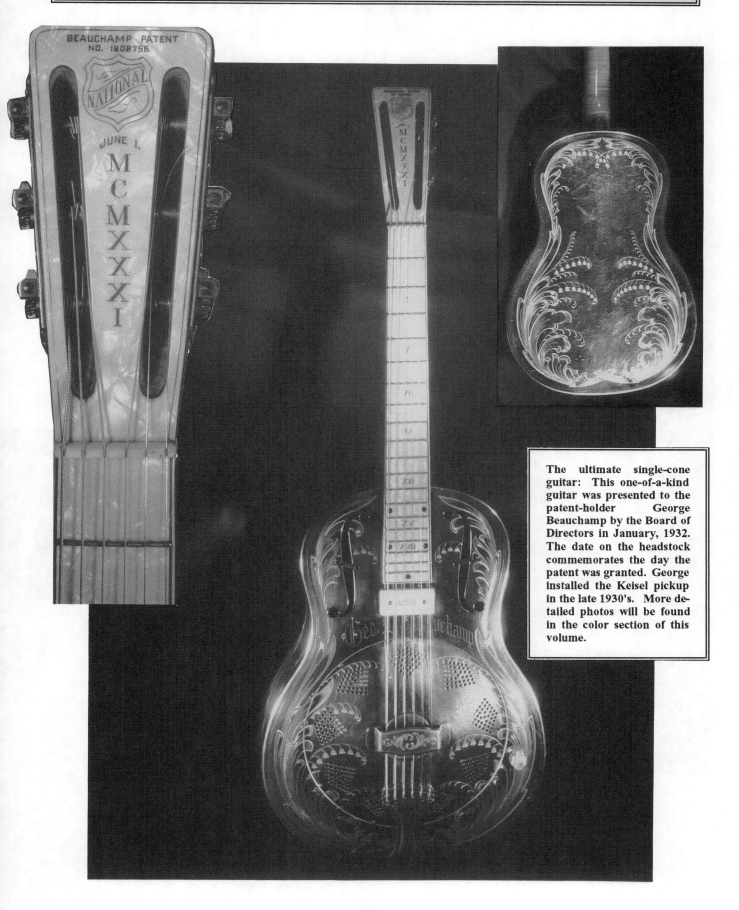

The ultimate single-cone guitar: This one-of-a-kind guitar was presented to the patent-holder George Beauchamp by the Board of Directors in January, 1932. The date on the headstock commemorates the day the patent was granted. George installed the Keisel pickup in the late 1930's. More detailed photos will be found in the color section of this volume.

Rear design of Variation 1 Style O's of 1930.

1930 Style O Guitar, Variation 1 of a series of classics

Variation 2, rear design, 1930-1931.

84

Bell-brass (nickel-plated) Single-cone body
First several hundred are steel body

Sandblasted Hawaiian scenes on body

Maple neck, black-to-clear sunburst finish
Some mahogany necks after 1936

"Ebonized" (dyed black) maple fingerboard

Pearl-dot position markers, amount varies
Slotted parallelograms after 1938

National decal on headstock 1930-1935
Arced NATIONAL logo in wood overlay 1936-1937
Black & white "deco" celluloid overlay 1939-40
Large head, black overlay, metal logo 1940-41

Guitars: 12-fret 1930-1934, 14-fret l935-1941

Guitars: Flat-cut F-holes 1930-1933

Guitars: Rolled-in F-holes 1933-1941

Hawaiian version 1933-41 has square wood neck

Style O applies ONLY to guitars with single-cone brass bodies, single cone GUITAR-shaped tenor and plectrum guitars, mandolins, and small body ukes. Style O does not apply to tricone instruments--it ALWAYS indicates brass body, single cone, and Hawaiian scene etching. The only exceptions are the earliest steel body guitars. Style O guitars are fairly common today.

Incredibly, there were at least eight variations of Style O guitars from its inception in July 1930 to the last models of 1941. The 12-fret models include five variations, and the 14-fret models were changed 3 times from 1935-1940.

The accompanying photographs of these models will make it easier to understand the following capsule descriptions of the variations: (Serial #'s are approximate and CHANGED FEATURES are capitalized) More instruments need to be found to pinpoint the exact serial number of each change, but the following numbers at variation change-points are accurate to within + or - 25 guitars. Some regular tricones are S-numbered, so that about 95% of the S-series are Style O's.

GENERAL VARIATIONS OF STYLE O GUITARS:

1. 12-FRET Steel OR Brass body, 2 palm trunks, many clouds and stars, etched border, plain cover plate, flat-cut F-holes (#'s S-1 to S-575) (July 1930 to c. 1931) (Some of the earliest may have lightning bolts and other abstract designs)
2. Brass, 2 palm trunks with fuzzy center, FEW clouds and stars, etched border, plain cover plate, flat-cut F-holes (#'s S-580 to S-1900) (1931)
3. Brass, 2 palm trunks with fuzzy center, few clouds and stars, NO etched border, plain cover plate, flat-cut F-holes (#'s S-1901 to S-3410) (1931-1932)
4. Brass, 1 palm trunk with CLEAR center, MORE clouds and stars than variations #2 & #3, LESS than variation #1, FOUR EMBOSSED RADIATING LINES ON COVER PLATE, flat-cut F-holes (#'s S-3420 to S-4500) (1932-1933)

5. Brass, 1 palm trunk and clouds and stars as in variation #4, coverplate as in variation #4, ROLLED-IN F-HOLES (#'s S-4501 to c. S-5400) (1933-1934)
6. Brass, 14-FRET body, NEW simpler Hawaiian scene, cover plate same as variations #4 & #5, rolled-in F-holes, slotted headstock, sometimes NEW "CHICKEN FEET COVER PLATE (c.1935-36)
7. Similar to variation #6, but NEW "CHICKEN FEET" COVER PLATE, Hawaiian scene is REVERSED AND FURTHER SIMPLIFIED, and small SOLID headstock WITH ARCED NATIONAL LOGO(c.1936-1937). 1939 MODELS HAVE BLACK AND WHITE HEADSTOCK, DECO LOGO. Many of these have pickguards.
8. Same as variation #7, but pickguard added, LARGE UNGAINLY HEADSTOCK with METAL National logo plate, LARGE PARALLELOGRAM FRETBOARD INLAYS. Palm tree etching now also on the SIDES. (1940-1941)

NOTE: VARIATIONS 6 & 7 SOMETIMES TURN UP WITH EITHER COVERPLATE, DEPENDING ON PARTS ON HAND.

Variation 3, rear design, same as Var. 2 without border.

Top Left: Variation 3, #S 3412, the highest numbered of this type.
Top Right: Variation 4, #S 3829, w/ coverplate ribs, and new etch.
Bottom Left: Variation 5, #S 5079, with new rolled f-holes.
Bottom Right: Back design of Var. 4 and 5 are identical and clear.

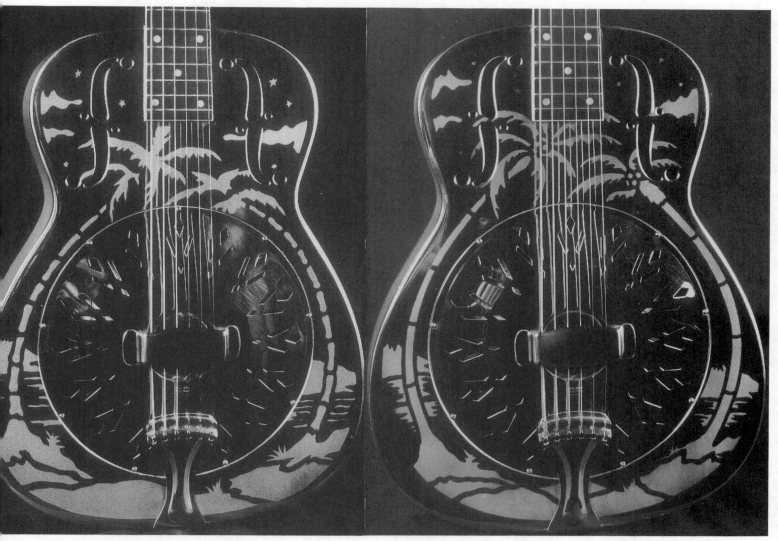

The first 14-fret Style 0, variation 6. New body size, new cover-plate and new tropical scenes. Sometimes found with older 4-rib coverplate. This example is from 1935, serial # 2344, from the series following the S- numbers.

The revamped 14-fret Style O, #A 6228, from 1937. New, simpler etching design front and back, and solid headstock. The last of seven different tropical scenes.

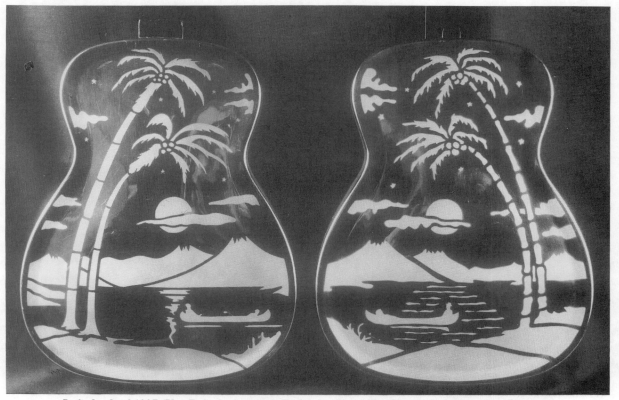

Left: back of 1937 (Var.7) Style O guitar. Right: back of 1936 (Var.6) Style O guitar. Designs are reversed in addition to the 1937 simplification. A complementary pair of idyllic scenes.

Modernistic geometric engraving adorns the back of this 1935 Don #2 guitar, # X 88. The most elaborate Don, the #3, had more conventional floral engraving.

Side engraving follows the same modern theme on the Don

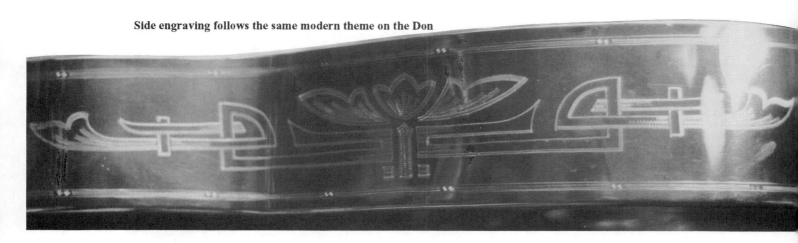

"DON" GUITARS:

3 Guitar models made 1934-1936

German silver 14-fret single-cone guitars ONLY

#1 Plain, with engraved borders on edges

#2 deco design, geometric engraving

#3 floral engraved, central engraving on back

High quality necks, fancy ebony fingerboards

Fancy square pearl inlays on #2 & #3

Pearloid headstock overlay on #2 & #3

Coverplate handrest engraved with "Don"

These unusual guitars were only briefly produced, perhaps only one or two batches. They were priced almost as high as the tricones, and again one must wonder why they brought out this model at a time of declining resonator popularity. These were definitely the highest quality single resonator guitars that National made. The name "Don" engraved on the coverplate has caused speculation about custom instruments made for a fellow named Don, but the name is meant to be evocative of the Spanish theme found in several mid-to late 1930s National model names.

Front view of Don #2 guitar, with ribbed coverplate.

Dons and Style N guitars were the only single-cone square headstock models with pearloid overlays.

1933-34 Catalog illustration of the rare Style N guitar, the 12-fret father of the Don models.

Large Single Resonator

Features of the Style N: Solid black fingerboard with genuine celluloid binding, pearl celluloid bound scroll, natural mahogany neck, steel reinforced, brilliantly plated body of a non-deteriorating metal.

Can be furnished for Hawaiian playing . . . by special order.

Style N. Spanish (Without case)............ **$75.00**

STYLE N SILVER

$75.00

STYLE N:

This scarce model appeared in the 1930 catalog and in a 1934 supplement, and may be thought of as a 12 fret ancester of the Don models. It was scarce because it was heavily outsold by the cheaper, more decorative Style O. Style N was a plain German silver 12-fret single cone guitar style only, and built with tricone materials and quality, priced at $85. The square headstock featured a white pearloid overlay, and the body was constructed out of three pieces like a tricone. Very soon after the 1930 catalog was issued, the $65 brass-bodied Style O was announced. With its Hawaiian ornamentation and lower price, the Style O quickly gained popularity and the Style N was only occasionally ordered and made until it was replaced by the Don in September 1934.

TRIOLIAN MODELS:

The name Triolian has often confused people who assume that this was the name given to tricone instruments. The Triolian originated as an experimental lower-priced guitar, which still was to employ a tricone system. It had a wood body, but only the first 12 protoypes actually did have a tricone set-up under a small round coverplate. (Possibly the ukulele coverplate was used.) The earliest production models had one large resonator, set into a wood body. The body had crudely sawn f-holes and the entire instrument was finished with a multi-hued laquer known as Polychrome. The first guitars of this type had a flower bouquet decal over the base colors of tan, pink and purple--similar to misty sunset colors. The very earliest of these first guitars had no spiral stamped into the cone. (Originality of the cone may be determined in this case by the presence of four small nails affixing the biscuit to the cone.) They have no serial numbers, and a coverplate with screens. These guitars were the first National single cone models.

The visual appearance of the early wood-body Triolian was changed after a few dozen were made. Theflower-bouquet guitars were superceded by several dozen un-numbered guitars of wood with the same screened-hole coverplate. These guitars were finished with a yellow- tan base with red and blue airbrushed highlights. There were added decorative images of Hawaiian scenes with a hula dancer, screen-printed over the base laquer. Tenor guitars were also built, with screen-hole coverplates and a male surfrider scene. By mid 1929, a drilled-hole coverplate was adopted, and the guitars began to receive serial numbers begining at 1000. About 600 were made, most with Hula girl design (some surfers) and drilled-hole coverplates.

The highest (at this writing) known numbered wood-body Triolian is #1626. It is identical in construction to the hula-girl models, but has stenciled palm tree designs which presage the metal polychrome Triolians which immediately followed.

In late 1929 the metal-bodied Triolian was produced with the same color finish but with a crude stencilled Hawaiian scene in black, with an orange sun. The necks and fingerboards were maple, finished in a clear laquer with red and blue highlights. Serialized from 0100 to somewhere in the 0200's, they were the first metal bodied Triolians. Subsequently, at least 1,500 guitars with this body were made with Bakelite necks. These necks were unstable, and a source of dealer complaints. They should be avoided as a player's instrument. Many of these were sent back to the factory for

The prototype Triolian, with its wood body and tricone set-up hidden under a ukulele-sized screen coverplate.

wood necks, and therefore new serial numbers, since all Triolians were number-stamped at the headstock.

Sometime in 1930, the serial numbers were changed to reflect the two colors which became available. The existing Triolians with the stencilled scene and highlights were now called Polychrome and given P-series serial numbers. The red and blue highlights were more faint, leaving a pea-green finish. The other color was a "walnut" brown-to-cream sunburst and these guitars were given W-series numbers. These two series are far more common than the earlier Triolians. At least 2,400 Polychrome Triolians and 3,400 Walnut models were made by 1935.

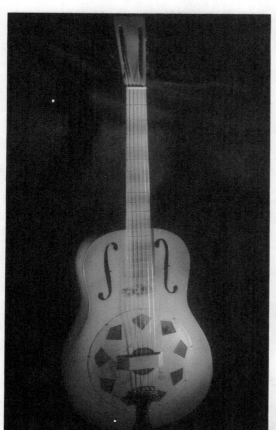

The Triolian guitar timeline:

1928:
Prototype was a 12-fret wood-body, with round cover plate over three-cone set-up. Twelve were made.

1928-1929:
Multi-hued painted 12-fret wood body single-cone guitars, f-holes, decal on back shows anemone bouquet, changed to Hawaiian hula girl. Earliest examples have screens on coverplate holes, followed by standard drilled coverplate. Opaque neck and fingerboard finish same as body. Last few have stencilled palm trees.

1929-1930:
12-fret steel body Triolian with multi-hued paint and stencilled scene. Neck and fingerboard finish is clear with faint red and blue highlights.

1930-1934:
12-fret steel body single-cone, painted sunburst brown or pea green, usually with crudely stencilled Hawaiian scene in black paint, maple neck, bound fingerboard of ebonized maple with pearl dots, rolled-in F-holes after 1933. Rolled in f-hole models are the rarest of 12 fret guitars.

1935-1936:
Same as above, but steel body now 14-frets clear, headstock changed from slotted to solid in 1936.

1937-1941:
Same as above, but finish changed to simulated rosewood grain, cream and brown celluloid pickguard added, last batch has extra large headstock.

The first production wood Triolian, wood body with single cone under a standard size but handmade coverplate with screens and crude handrest.

A bouquet of anemones grace the back which is airbrushed in numerous atmospheric pinks, blues and purples. These two different guitars show a variation in airbrushing. The subsequent "hula girl" wood Triolian is depicted in the color section.

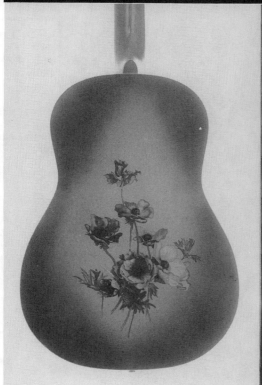
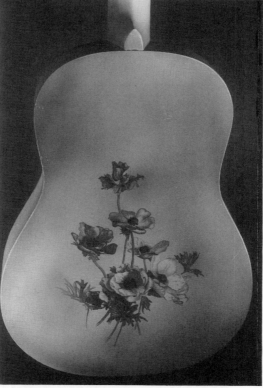

An example of the first production metal single cone: Polychrome Triolian #0186, three piece body.

Back of metal Polychrome, showing stencilled scene, rather crudely executed. No two are exactly alike. Colors and stencil positions vary.

1931 photo of a member of the Ballard Chefs Jug band with transitional pear-shaped single-cone Polychrome Triolian Tenor guitar. Full photo of band in Chap. 7.

Left: Front of early 1930's small-body Polychrome ukulele.

Palms grace the back of this Polychrome uke.

Triolians were given their own decal logo. The word continues to mystify people who don't know its origins.

Walnut sunburst Triolian, # 2574 W, with "hooks" coverplate attachment, dark brown sunburst, 1931-1932.

The first type of 14-fret Triolian continued the walnut sunburst and the ribbed coverplate. #3244 W, 934-35.

Lighter brown Walnut sunburst Triolian, #527 W, 1930.

Triolian mandolin, #560 W, rib coverplate, 1932. This mandolin and the #2639 W guitar were bought new and used by a brother act, Don and Bus Schmidt.

1932-33 darker Walnut sunburst Triolian, #2639 W, with ribbed coverplate.

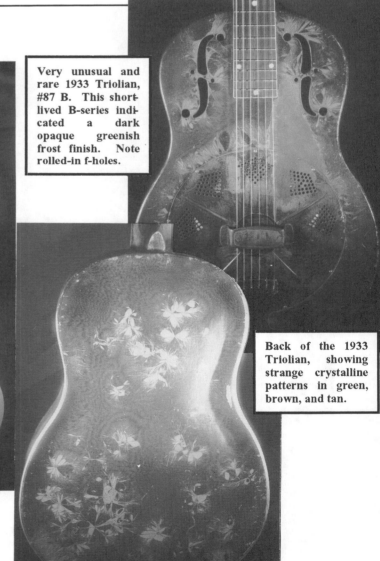

Very unusual and rare 1933 Triolian, #87 B. This short-lived B-series indicated a dark opaque greenish frost finish. Note rolled-in f-holes.

Back of the 1933 Triolian, showing strange crystalline patterns in green, brown, and tan.

1931 Polychrome tenor guitar with guitar shape, #2028P.

The Triolian series was probably National's best selling line, an excellent value at $45. The steel bodies made these instruments cheaper to build, and they are generally quite loud, if slightly harsh. The painted finishes were quite long-lasting, though they did chip on impact. Perhaps the most durable of the finishes was the simulated rosewood grain finish, though the idea of a metal guitar painted to look like wood seems a little strange in retrospect. This finish, however was in keeping with the then-current trend of wood-graining sheet metal stoves, heaters, and interior car trim pieces.

The standard (post-1930) Triolian style was applied to Spanish and Hawaiian guitars (no tricones), both guitar-shaped and pear-shaped single cone tenor and plectrum guitars, mandolins, and both large and small ukuleles. All these instruments were available in Walnut and in Polychrome finishes. The decal on most Triolians reads Triolian where the standard decal reads National. This long-lived series of guitars and mandolins was very popular among blues and hillbilly musicians.

Late 1930's Triolians had a very "designed" look, with "rosewood" grained paint job, known as piano-finish. Note arched finger-board and modern pickguard.

The Lone Cowboy, Y.U. Buffington, c.1931-32, with what appears to be an early B-finish Triolian with "hooks" coverplate.

Matching pickguard and headstock adorn this 1938 Triolian, # C 2479.

DUOLIAN:

Steel body single-cone guitars and Hawaiian guitars only

Unbound dyed maple fingerboard, with pearl or ivoroid dots

Slightly thinner gauge steel body

Crystalline paint finish 1931-1937

Mahogany-grain paint finish 1938-40

12-fret body 1931-1934

12 fret with Flat-cut f-holes 1931-1933
12 " Rolled in f-holes 1933-34 (rarest type)

14-fret body 1935-1940 all rolled-in f-holes

Pickguard added 1938-1940

Necks usually mahogany, some maple 1931-1935
Necks usually basswood, 1936-1940

Hawaiian necks on 14-fret body are mahogany

12-fret headstock usually stamped "National Duolian, sometimes a decal on later 12 frets.

14-fret headstock usually has National Duolian decal, sometimes stamped on early 14 frets.

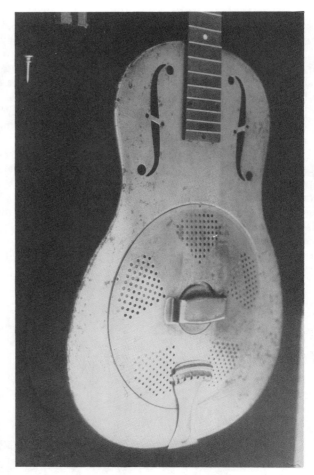

1931 Sears model Duolian, with large sieve coverplate.

This bottom-of-the-line model was also popular among blues and hillbilly musicians, and was advertised heavily in catalogs such as Sears. No other instruments besides guitars (and a few Hawaiian guitars) were made in the Duolian style. At $32.50 each, National sold thousands, which certainly helped them survive the Depression. Again, this was a tremendous value for a resonator instrument with equivalent sound and durability to the more expensive Nationals. Even Sears marketed an unlabeled Duolian at $29. These Sears models had a different coverplate, with substantially larger drilled areas.

Until the late 1930s, all Duolians had a "frosted duco" finish--a strange crystalline paint finish. This paint dried differently on every guitar, leaving varying random patterns in shades of gold to green. Several patents from the 1928 to 1936 era exist for this strange paint formula. The range of finishes was fairly wide over time, gradually changing in terms of color (silver to gold to green to brown to black). The depth and size of the crystal formations in the finishes varied considerably over time as well. Many Duolians survive today, and curiously, many are the 1935-40 era 14-fret models, perhaps proof that less affluent players were slower to switch to electric instruments. Also, electricity had not yet reached many rural areas in the 1930s.

1933 Duolian # C 7005, with rolled-in f-holes.

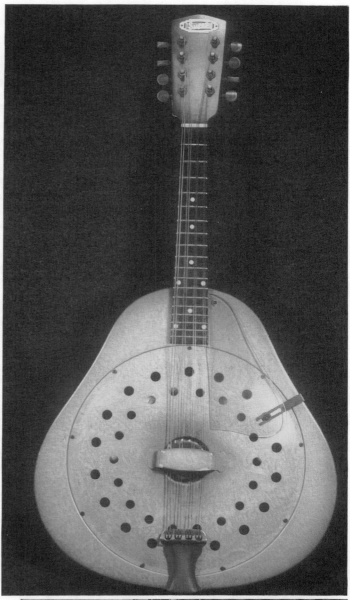

1939 Supro Collegian mandolin #C 4593, made in Chicago. Note Supro-style coverplate and finish. Pickguard and tuning buttons are clear celluloid.

NATIONAL/SUPRO "COLLEGIAN" MODELS:

In the late 1930s, National introduced a rock-bottom budget "student" model range, priced below the Duolian. Still retaining all the acoustic and structural qualities of Nationals, this model was essentially a Duolian with a simpler (and presumably cheaper-to-make) coverplate. The cover plate was punched with two concentric rings of holes, 18 holes in each ring. The bodies were finished in a yellowish wood-grain paint. There were Collegian guitars (Spanish and Hawaiian), tenor guitars, mandolins, and ukuleles made. These instruments were marketed under the National name as well as with a Supro label--there are no other differences.

WOOD BODIED RESONATOR GUITARS:

There were several wooden-bodied single-cone guitars made by National, or at least with all metal parts made by National. National developed body-manufacturing arrangements with Kay, Harmony, and in the late 1930s, even Gibson. The idea was for National to buy guitar bodies and necks from other makers, install the resonator and coverplate assembly, the tailpiece, tuners and National decal, and to make final adjustments. This proved to be much cheaper for National than creating a wood-body manufacturing section of their factory. National was able to buy these bodies from Harmony and Kay at prices from $5.00 to $10.00, add $5.00 worth of metal parts, and sell the finished product at prices ranging from $29.00 to $55.00. These guitars sold in quantities rivalling the metal guitars, and probably helped National survive in the rough business climate of the Depression.

The earliest Triolian guitars, described above, were also made with wooden bodies, though all parts including wood were made by National. They were manufactured only in 1928 and early 1929. Triolians were changed to metal bodies sometime in early 1930. For two years, no wooden Nationals were made at all until the introduction of the 12-fret Kay-bodied El Trovador model in February 1932, priced at $50.

The El Trovador was definitely the highest quality wood-body single-cone guitar ever made with the National name. The model name was obviously intended to evoke a Spanish theme, paving the way for other such "exotically" named products from National, and other companies. Examples such as the Fender Coronado or the Chrysler Cordoba come to mind.

The rare 1933 El Trovador, mahogany veneered 12-fret body by Kay, #K 387. Ribbed coverplate as seen on Style 0, Triolian and Duolian guitars of the period.

Kay made the bodies for the El Trovador, charging the National company $7.00 each. These guitar bodies were slightly larger all around than the standard 00 (grand concert) size of all other National guitars. The proportions were also somewhat different than standard, with a more narrow waist and longer upper bouts. They were made with 1/4" thick laminated mahogany with beautiful dark grain and finish. F-holes similar in style and positioning to the Style O or Triolian/Duolians were drilled and routed through the upper bouts. Necks were of high quality and made of mahogany, with a slim, slightly V-ed profile. Headstocks were of the slotted type, with a thin rosewood overlay to which the decal was affixed. The maple fingerboards were dyed black, with four inlayed pearl-dot position markers.

El Trovadors have very thick ivoroid binding around the top and back edges, with additional black and white lines along the sides as well as around the top and back. As with some ivoroid-bound National fingerboards, the "grain" of the ivoroid runs perpendicular to the binding strip, rather than the normal parallel grain. There is an added ring of white- black-white celluloid inlayed into the top around the circumference of the coverplate. The coverplates on El Trovadors are standard nickelled Style O or Triolian type. This model has its own unique National decal with the words "El Trovador" and "made in U.S.A." on it. The overall shape of the decal is identical to other National decals, with a black and gold color scheme, without the added red ink of the standard type.

The sound of the best of these models is quite clear, bright, and just about equal in volume and depth to any metal single-cone. The El Trovadors have superior sound to he later Trojan, Estrallita, and Rosita models with Harmony bodies, and have higher quality materials and workmanship. Many of the later Harmony-bodied Nationals are constructed with cheap birch or basswood plywood, both with less density than the mahogany-ply El Trovador, and consequently these instruments have a mushy sound in comparison. Unfortunately, since the El Trovador was only made briefly during the worst of the Depression, from February 1932 to December 1933, the model is very rare today. Probably 95% of the wood-body Nationals seen today are the less desirable Trojans, Rositas, and Estrallitas. Rosita models are distinguished by strange "cathedral" openings in the top, rather than f-holes.

In the late 1930s, National introduced two more wood body single cone guitars, the "Havana and the "Aragon." The "Havana" was a larger flat-top model with a single resonator offered at $50. The top was of spruce, with two large awkward-looking f-holes and a nickeled coverplate for the standard single resonator. The backs had a pressed arch, and the bodies were made by Kay. Very few have been seen.

The remarkable Aragon model was something of an anomaly for several reasons. First, the logic of introducing a very expensive resonator archtop guitar at a time when professional jazz guitarists were either confirmed Gibson- ites or playing electric seemes odd. Secondly, the construction of this model, with its fairly thin arched top, goes against the normal National principle of a non-vibrating top. In all other National designs, the resonator produces the sound, while the body material merely holds it in place and reflects the sound. John Dopyera felt that a flexible top which could vibrate would pull sound away from the resonator--which is why Nationals were designed in metal in the first place.

However, this rare guitar was a definite success, from an acoustic standpoint. The Aragon was the largest-bodied National ever made, at a 18" width. (Standard National body width is 14".) As a result, the treble and cutting power of this model equals any metal National, while the bass notes boom

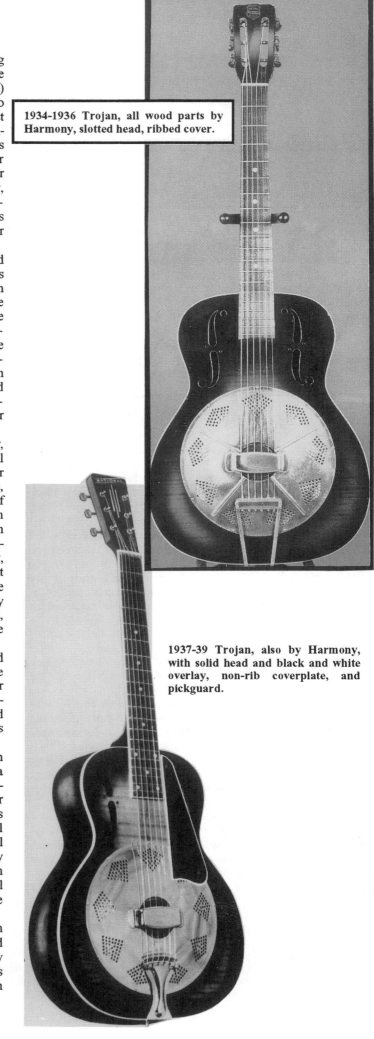

1934-1936 Trojan, all wood parts by Harmony, slotted head, ribbed cover.

1937-39 Trojan, also by Harmony, with solid head and black and white overlay, non-rib coverplate, and pickguard.

out so loudly that one begins to look around the room for hidden wires! Unfortunately, though the body is well- made, the proportions are somewhat ugly--making this guitar ideal for radio work.

The bodies were made by National by Kay or Harmony in Chicago and feature a sunburst finish over the arched spruce top and curly maple sides and back. The back is also arched. The body is bound with multiple black and white celluloid, and the edges of the f-holes are also bound in white. The fingerboard is inlayed with paralellograms of white pearl and colorful Japan pearl, and the headstock is inlayed with these materials with an Art Deco National logo. Two types of coverplates have been seen on this model, both defying Euclidian geometry, to fit the arched top. One is a unique slotted coverplate, the other has simple drilled holes, similar to the National/Supro Collegian models.

The catalog description reads like bad poetry:"Greater resonance and "timber" (sic), "Cushion-comfort frets", "shades away to a dreamy rhythm...." And let's not forget "special pure tone strings".

WHEN CULTURES COLLIDE: 1932 Aloha Hawaiian guitar, one of twelve made in SHANGHAI, CHINA by a local tinsmith, who apparently had access to a National coverplate and possibly a cone. This photo was taken in 1932 by Tau Moe, a Hawaiian musician on tour in China (see Chapter 6). Desperately sought by the author, though all twelve were probably melted down for farm implements during the Cultural Revolution.

1940-41 Aragon. Some, such as this one had Supro type coverplates. According to John Dopyera, about half of the original wood coverplates broke during manufacture necessitating the Supro cover. See the catalog chapter for an illustration of the other coverplate. Comparing the relative sizes of the coverplate and the body itself gives an indication of this guitar's hugeness.

NATIONAL GUITAR MODELS FROM A MUSICIAN'S PERSPECTIVE

The various types of instruments produced by National provide the musician with a wide range of tonal qualities, suitable for many styles of music and playing technique. Some models are more useful and appropriate for certain styles than others. While the comments that follow certainly fall into the realm of subjective opinion, they will serve as a general guide to help the player select the right type of National for his/her music.

The most important factors to consider in thinking about different types of Nationals are:

Resonator system (single or triple)

body material (German silver, brass, steel, or wood)

body length (12 or 14 fret)

neck material and profile (mahogany or maple, round or Vee profile) (for Spanish guitar).

Let us consider the metal-body guitars: We will assume that the guitars being discussed are set up properly for optimum tone and playability. (Set-up and maintainance will be covered in a later chapter.) The two major guitar types available are tricones and single cones. There are strong differences in their respective sounds.

THE TRICONES:

The tricone design was always the personal favorite of John Dopyera, who has said, "The tricone guitar flowed like a river." These guitars, whether Spanish or Hawaiian, have a lovely clear tone with a long sustain and a long, smooth decay. Natural and artificial harmonics ring through with amazing volume and clarity of tone. The sustain of extremely high notes is vastly superior to any other acoustic instruments and is measurably better than the single cone models in this regard. Many tricones will have a somewhat thin sound unless the neck angle is correct and the cones are set up properly. Normally, the sound is surprisingly rich and warm. On the best of these instruments, the entire body seems to radiate. Since the cones were hand-spun, no two tricones sound exactly the same. Differences in each cone depend on who did the spinning, and how hard the spinning tool was pressed against the lathe. Also, since the three cones resonate together, it is possible to have a better or worse "match" of cones in the set of three.

Generally, tricones are preferable for any music involving slide, whether bottleneck or lap style. Their smooth sustain and resonance in open tunings make them an unbeatable acoustic bottleneck guitar. Among lap players there are two preference groups. Almost all Bluegrass players prefer the Dobro sound to the tricone sound, but all Hawaiian players have always preferred tricones. The twangier tone of a Dobro suits country music better, while the liquid, more sophisticated tone of a tricone is best for Hawaiian, blues, jazz, and swing playing. Tricones have generally been played in open tunings, and not many tricone players used standard tuning. The 1930s jazz guitarist Oscar Aleman is a notable exception. Tricones are deeply resonant in open tunings and the resonance caused by the interaction of the indiviual strings contributes to the "reverb" sound. There are tones and sounds possible on a tricone which cannot be made on any other type of guitar, resophonic or otherwise.

It must be noted that the body metal (German Silver) of most tricones probably contributes to their tonal characteristics. The few brass-bodies tricones that have been seen have a somewhat different sound and because of the slightly decreased resonance yielded by this body metal, they do sound quite good for jazz in standard tuning.

THE SINGLE CONES:

The single resonator Nationals have a more strident tone than the tricones, with a louder initial attack but with a considerably shorter decay. The difference becomes most apparent when comparing this guitar's slide sounds in the highest ranges to the same range on a tricone. The single cone will sound more like playing slide on a banjo. In fact, a banjo sound, with its strong punch and quick decay, is like an exaggerated version of the single cone tonal tendencies. Plenty of recording artists have used the single cone Nationals over these years, including many bottle-neck blues players. The tonal qualities of the single cones sound great in standard tuning, for ragtime, blues, and early jazz. The short decay makes rapid-fire picking and chord changing come out very clearly. These guitars have 110% response, and cutting power with laser-beam penetration. Generally they are very slightly louder than tricones, and have a less sophisticated, less complex tone. Players must learn to really control the beginnings and, more importantly, the ends of notes, to avoid the harsh clanging that can build up quickly in these guitars. Therefore, lots of left and right hand damping is necessary to get a clean, professional sound.

Single cone bodies were made of either steel or yellow brass. A few German silver Don models were also produced. The tone differences caused by these body metals seems more pronounced on single cone guitars than on tricones. The steel bodied Triolians, Duolians, and earliest Style O guitars have a distinctly harsher "bluesier" sound with more "reverb" than the brass-bodied Style O guitars. The brass guitars seem better for ragtime, blues-ragtime and early jazz, while the steel bodied models seem more appropriate for Delta blues in open tunings or standard tuning, keys of A or E.

WOOD BODY NATIONALS:

Of the seven varieties of wood-bodied single cone guitars, it could be said that three basic types of tone are found. One type of tone will be produced by wood-body early Triolians and by El Trovadors. These two 12-fret models sound surprisingly similar to the metal body single cone guitars--loud and punchy with short decay--but with slightly warmer bass tone from the body wood. The Trojans, Estrallitas, Havanas and Rositas, with their cheaper lighter plywood, usually have a rather mushy sound and not as much clarity and volume. These four Harmony-bodied guitar models are virtually identical in tone, and probably are the least desirable Nationals in terms of good sound quality. The late 30's archtop Aragon, as mentioned before, is in a class by itself, with its giant bass response added to a treble which rivals the metal body Nationals.

12 FRET VS 14 FRET NECKS AND BODIES:

Another general area of concern to the player of these instruments is the length of the bodies. All tricone necks meet the body at the 12th fret. However on single cone guitars, National created a 14-fret neck in the mid 30s by shortening the body--not lengthening the neck. Consequently, the bodies of 14-fret guitars are shorter than the 12-fret bodies, and more squat in shape. This writer prefers the 12- fret body both for its more graceful, esthetically pleasing shape, and for the deeper tone of this longer body. The shorter 14-fret bodies tend to have a more compact sound due both the smaller body cavity and the greater stiffness of the metal on a smaller body. While it is true that most modern players prefer a 14-fret neck, most frets can still be comfortably reached on the 12 fret models.

When National switched to the 14-fret neck, they also changed the profile and feel of the neck, and later changed the type of wood used. The 12-fret necks are usually wide, with a rounded profile, while the 14-fret necks are quite triangular in profile. Most 12-fret single cone guitars had maple necks, early (1935-6) 14-fret necks were mahogany, and late (1937-41) 14-fret necks were made of lighter, cheaper basswood. In terms of durability, the earlier the manufacturing date of the guitar, the less chance of neck warpage exists. The basswood necks are the most likely to warp and, in fact, many left the factory with an added 1/4" layer laminated under the fingerboard for strength. Many players find the triangular necks to be uncomfortable, yet others who find the round-profile necks to be too big seem to like the triangular profile. This writer prefers the rounded type, yet does not have especially large hands. Of course, most guitars of this vintage have larger, wider necks than modern guitars with their rock n' roll-influenced slim, narrow necks.

OTHER PLAYING CONSIDERATIONS:

There is no question that National resonator instruments respond best when fingerpicks or at least a flatpick is used. For reasons of sound and the health of your resonator, picks are strongly recommended over bare-finger playing. The energy of each note is condensed at each beat by the attack of the pick to a more precise and penetrating point. Resonator rattles can be caused by the considerably larger string travel that bare fingers produce. You get at least twice the "volume/per amount of string movement" with picks than without. This can be seen easily on the bass strings. Another advantage of picks is that the player can make better use of the vast tonal range found along the string length by picking at different points along it.

National guitars, with their tremendous volume, resonance and sustain require the player to adapt his/her technique. More right and left hand damping is needed, to insure against unwanted resonances. The player must also have increased awareness of dynamics because the volume range of a typical National is three to five times greater than an ordinary acoustic guitar. The great projection that is a characteristic of Nationals has long made them ideal instruments for street performers. This volume and cutting power may make one unwelcome at jam sessions unless restraint, empathy and good taste are excercised. However, if you have something of value to say musically, a National will help you say it with crisp command and powerful authority.

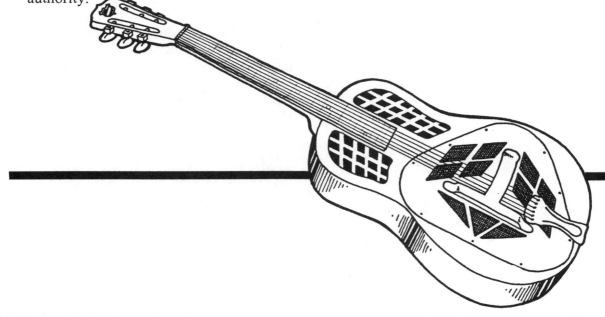

CHAPTER 5

CONSTRUCTION DETAILS
OF NATIONAL METAL RESONATOR INSTRUMENTS

NECKS AND HEADSTOCKS

The types of wood used by National to make necks were fairly standard in the industry: mahogany, eastern rock maple, and, in the Chicago era, basswood. Tricone guitar necks were generally mahogany, except style 35, which was maple. Tricone tenor and plectrum guitar necks were usually made of maple, often with a stripe of rosewood down the center. The very first few had walnut necks with a cherrywood stripe. German silver mandolins (style 1,2, & 3) were made with maple necks, the more expensive models having more figured grain. Some necks were birdseye maple, and some were more like curly maple. Ukuleles featured both mahogany and maple necks, somewhat randomly.

Tricone guitar and Hawaiian guitar headstocks had their own design, a classic that still looks good today. The simple peaked shape reflects the design of the National shield logo. All tricone guitar headstocks were slotted until 1936. Styles 1 and 2 had a National decal on the mahogany headstock. Style 3 generally had an engraved mother-of-pearl National shield logo set into an ebony headstock overlay. Style 4 generally had an overlay of mother-of-toilet-seat, engraved with a bordering line and a National shield logo. Quite often style 3 and 4 guitars show up with either headstock. Since the fingerboards of style 3 & 4 were also identical, National must have frequently used whatever neck was ready at the time of assembly. Tuning gears were three-on-a-strip, with cream-colored celluloid buttons. The strip was generally stamped with decorative "engraving."

It is interesting to note that when mother-of-toilet-seat was a brand-new material (mid-1920's), it was only used on the most expensive instruments--by the late 1930s, it was only used on cheap instruments, by most companies. Even today this material is evocative of cheapness, so its use on the expensive style 3 & 4 tricones is an ironic sidelight.

During 1929, the tops of the tricone headstocks were cut differently. Normally, the top edge was cut at a right angle to the slant of the headstock. In 1929, the top edge was cut slanted so that the back of the headstock was higher than the front, for a slightly more "streamlined" look.

In the last few years of tricone production, National changed over to a solid headstock, retaining the same outline. Various overlays were used, generally featuring a black-over-white celluloid sandwich, engraved with a few variations of a more modernistic National logo (see illustrations). The first style 97 tricones had this overlay on a slotted headstock. The 1940-41 tricones sometimes had the large, ungainly headstock found on other Nationals of that time. These headstocks had large curving sides, perhaps symbolic of a lyre shape, with a rounded curved top. Usually a metal plate with a modernized National logo was attached to this headstock with two small rivets. This is the same plate found on 1938-1940s National electric lap steels.

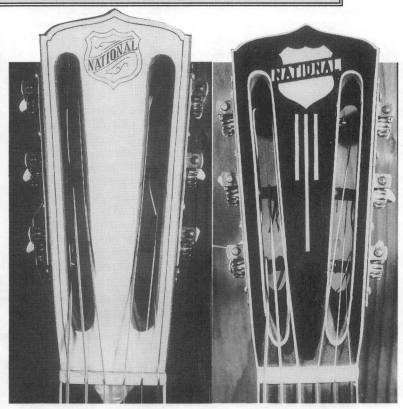

White pearloid style 3 & 4 tricone headstock 1928-1936.

1936 Style 97 tricone headstock.

1938 Style 97 tricone headstock.

1938 Style 35 tricone headstock.

German silver mandolins and ukuleles (style 1, 2, & 3) had similar peaked headstocks to the tricone guitars, while the triolian and style O mandolin and uke headstocks were squared-off in the manner of their guitar counterparts. Style 1 mandolins and ukuleles had the National decal affixed to the maple or mahogany headstocks. Style 2 mandolin and uke headstocks were either like style 1, or featured the decal on an ebony overlay. Style 3 mandolins and ukes had either a mother-of-toilet-seat overlay or a mother-of-pearl shield logo, both engraved. Mandolins utilized four-on- strip tuning gears. Ukuleles used banjo-type friction gears on Style 1 instruments, and miniature planet geared tuners for Style 2 and 3.

German silver (style 1, 2, & 3) tenor and plectrum guitars had their own headstock shape, very similar to a standard "figure eight" banjo headstock, with the top part peaked like a tricone guitar headstock. Overlays followed the same patterns as the mandolins and ukuleles. Planetary banjo tuning gears were used on Silver models, and two-on-a- strip guitar-type gears were used on Triolians and Style O tenor/plectrums.

Style O and Triolian instruments were made with eastern rock maple necks, carved to hefty but comfortable width and thickness. Duolians had maple or low-grade mahogany necks, with later models made of basswood. The headstocks of these three styles were a simple but graceful squared-off shape, with a National decal in front. (Some Duolians are stamped "National Duolian instead.) The 12-fret models (1930-34) and the earliest 14-fret models (1935-36)

had slotted headstocks. The severity of the corner-points of these headstocks varied from a sharp corner to a 3/8 inch radius curve. In keeping with the industry trend of the period, National switched to a solid headstock for the remainder of the 1930s.

Style O and Triolian mandolins, ukuleles and both tenor and plectrum guitars had the squared-off headstocks of their guitar cousins, however they were always solid. The illustrations show the variety of style O headstock shapes and National logos.

In 1930, National experimented briefly with Bakelite composition necks for single-resonator guitars. Apparently at least several hundred Bakelite-necked Triolians were produced, since some have been seen within a serial number range of 1,500. Also, references to dealer problems with these necks is made in the board of directors meeting of July 3, 1930. Apparently, many Bakelite-necked guitars were returned to the factory for replacement wood necks. These strange necks look as if scraps of canvas and cloth were mixed in with mottled brown and black bakelite when poured into the mold. The neck and fingerboard were cast as one piece (a repairman's nightmare) with bar frets installed directly on the neck. One of the main problems with these necks was extreme variability under conditions of heat. Since they expanded and contracted with temperature changes, maintaining tuning proved to be difficult. Since this neck was produced so briefly, Triolians with bakelite necks are somewhat rare today.

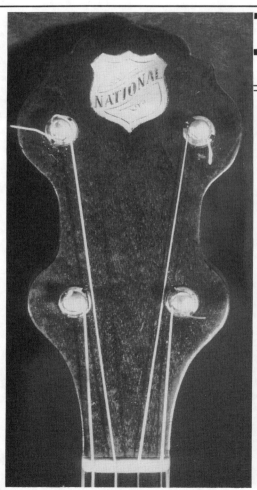

Typical silver tenor-plectrum headstock shape, only Style 3 had this mother-of-pearl shield.

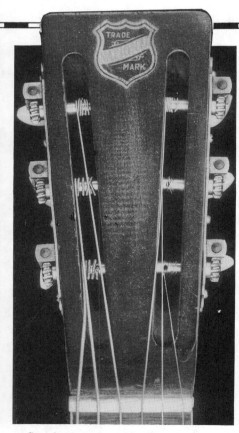

Standard single-cone guitar headstock shape, as seen on Style 0 and Triolians from 1930-1935.

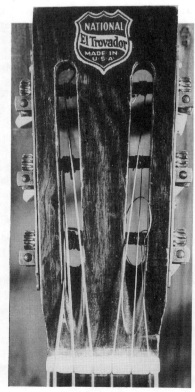

Kay-made El Trovador headstock, cruder than National.

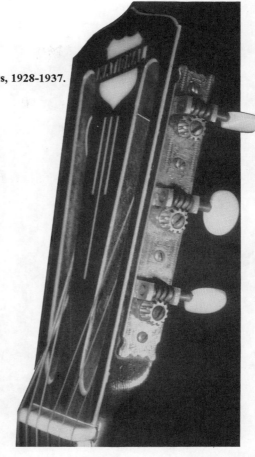

FINGERBOARDS

Several fingerboard woods were used by National throughout the entire production of instruments: Ebony, "ebonized" (dyed black) maple and rosewood or red bean wood on very early tricones (below serial #400).

All of National's high-quality german silver instruments (style 1, 2, 3, 4) generally had ebony fingerboards. The exceptions are very early style 1 and 2 tricones which had rosewood or red bean fingerboards. Styles 3 and 4 had large square pearl inlays angled at 45 degrees for a diamond effect. An additional large triangular pearl inlay decorated the center of the first fret at the nut, a nice Art Deco touch. Some 1929 models had pearl 'arrows' at the 12th fret.

Style 97 and 35 tricones (made from 1935-40) featured ebony fingerboards for the Spanish models and black celluloid fingerboards for the Hawaiian models. These celluloid fingerboards were made by combining a thin black layer over a thicker milky-white layer. The fret-lines and modern roman numeral position markers were engraved through the black layer, showing in white. In addition, these fingerboards extended all the way to the coverplate, ending in a slant to fit the line of the coverplate. The material was advertised as "ebonoid"--an up-to-the-minute miracle of modern science.

As with any professional instrument, all ebony fingerboards on Nationals were bound in ivory celluloid, coined "ivoroid" in the catalogues. Some batches of instruments had the "ivory grain" running lengthwise along the binding strip, while many batches came with the grain running at a right angle to the strip! In addition, many instruments from the mid-1930s on had black side-markers inlayed in the binding strip, a general guitar industry trend of that time.

Generally, all other styles of metal National instruments (style O, Triolian, Duolian) had "ebonized" maple fingerboards, though many later Triolians and Duolians have rosewood boards. These dyed fingerboards retain their black color very well over time under heavy use, though the maple will often become gouged out between the frets at the frequently used positions. Very early Polychrome Triolian fingerboards feature light-finished maple with color highlights. The budget-priced Duolians are the only Nationals with unbound fingerboards. All other models have ivoroid-bound fingerboards, with 1/4" pearl dots inlayed in the standard positions. Style 3 and 4 tricones were inlayed with larger pearl squares, set in diagonally.

"Ebonoid" fingerboard with modern Roman-numeral markers adorned Style 97 and 35 tricones, note extended length.

Production tricone, stamped grating, bass side.

Production tricone, stamped grating, treble side.

Handmade grating (bass). The right-angle perimeter of the opening was hand-beaten with hammers by Rudy.

Handmade grating (treble) on the first several dozen tricones only. Hand-soldered strips of metal are at a slightly sharper angle than on production models.

METAL BODIES

The primary metals used by National for making guitar bodies were German silver, yellow brass, and sheet steel. German silver is also known as white brass, nickel silver, or white copper. It is the same alloy that almost all guitar fretwire is made from, and is typically made from 65% copper, 10-23% zinc, and 10-20% nickel. Yellow brass is a 65/35 blend of copper and zinc. The thickness of National body metals varied from .032" to.034" depending upon raw materials. German silver and yellow brass bodies were heavily nickel-plated to a thick, high-quality polished finish. Steel bodies were painted, in various finishes described elsewhere.

All of the first Nationals from 1927 to 1929 were mad from German silver. This includes all tricone guitars, tenor and plectrum guitars, mandolins, and ukuleles. These bodies were silver-soldered together from three pieces: a back, a top, and a one-piece side tapered from lower to upper bout.The soundwell and resonator platform was soldered to the top.

The nickel plating on these instruments is absolutely beautiful when in good condition; the bevel and finish on the soldered edges is finely crafted. In no way can these German silver instruments be described as crude or cheaply made, and the engraved models are top-notch examples of old-world craftsmanship meeting "modern" production methods.

The very first tricone guitar bodies were handmade (without dies) by John and Rudy Dopyera. The thinking process that went into creating the visual design of the tricone body remains a mystery. This design, with its asymmetrical layout and Art Deco geometric cut-outs, still looks quite modern today. It must have been considered extremely futuristic and radical in its day. The design certainly evokes the optimism of the then-new modern industrial age.

These earliest bodies may be distinguished by some or all of the following features. The backs are flat, rather than with the stamped arch found on production models. The "waffle-grating" soundholes in the upper bouts of the tops are "woven" strips of metal, rather than stamped from one piece as on the production models. Some of these (the earliest) have 7 extra diamond-shaped cut-outs in the body, outside of the coverplate. These holes were soon eliminated because they were uneccessary for obtaining sound, and because they weakened the top.

The earliest production tricones (up to c. serial #380) also have flat backs. These instruments have a wooden internal platform for the cones to sit on, rather than the integral metal platform of all the higher-numbered tricones. Dopyera's 4-9-27 patent application specifies a wooden platform. While collectors may appreciate the lowest numbered instruments, there is no question that the integral metal platform on instruments above c. #380 delivers much more sound from the cones. Hence, we have a rare case when earlier is not necessarily better. The post #380 tricones represent the perfection of the concept, and are the superior instruments for the player.

1930 saw the introduction of steel as a body metal for the budget-priced Triolians and Duolians, and yellow brass for the medium-priced Style O instruments. The first few hundred Style O guitars were steel, rather than the yellow brass used through the rest of its production run. Some brass guitars with steel coverplates and steel guitars with brass coverplates, from the transitional time, have been seen. Steel did not accept the nickel plating as well as brass, hence copper had to be plated on the steel first. It is fairly easy to determine if a style O is steel or brass. First, serial numbers below c. S-1300 are likely to be steel. Second, the plated surface on steel will always look slightly rougher or more rippled than plated brass. Often little rust-spots will appear on steel, where brass, of course, does not rust. Generally, the steel-body guitars are best for blues, while the brass-body guitars are best for ragtime and jazz, having a slightly more "controlled" decay.

Rather than a three-piece construction, the single cone guitars in Style O, Triolian and Duolian models were made from 2 pieces. The 12-fret instruments (1930-34) were made with the top and sides drawn from one piece. On these instruments the top-side edge is rounded, and the back-side edge is soldered and has a small beveled edge. For some reason, this arrangement is reversed on the 14-fret guitars, with the back and sides drawn from one piece, and with the bevel along the top edge.

Single resonator guitars had f-holes stamped through the tops at the upper bouts. This includes Triolians, Duolians, and Style O guitars. The f-holes were a simple cut-out, (often called 'flat-cut') comprised of two long cuts, two 1/2" holes, and two small holes. The design is a modern stylized abstraction of the traditional f-hole.

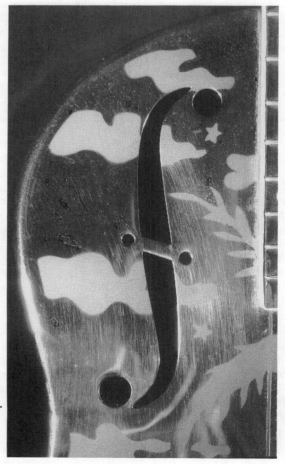

Flat-cut f-hole, 1929-1933.

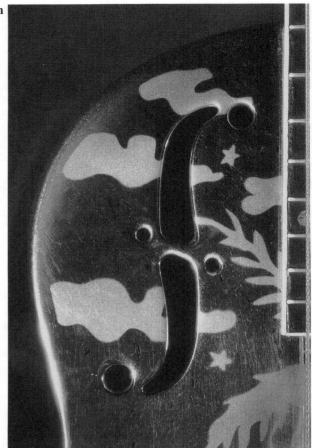

Sometime in 1933, these f-holes were changed to a "rolled-in" design. The number of cuts was the same, but the edges of the cuts were rolled into the body for 1/8" and the overall length of the f-hole was shortened from 5 3/8" to 4 7/8." The change had the effect of modernizing and streamlining the look of the guitars. Comparing photos of both f-holes, we see that the flat-cut design evokes the 1920s, while the rolled-in design suggests the more streamlined look of the 1930s. There are similarities here to design changes occurring in other industries at this time. Additionally, the rolled-in f-hole served to strengthen and stiffen the tops, stifling some extra overtones and yielding a tighter, warmer sound with a more controlled decay. 1933 and 1934 were the only years when 12- fret guitars with rolled-in f-holes were made, and hence they are, generally speaking, the rarest single-cone guitars. All 14-fret guitars have the rolled-in f-hole (1935-41).

The small guitar-shaped single-cone tenor and plectrum guitars had smaller f-holes, which were always flat-cut. The die used for these small f-holes was the only f-hole die around the re-formed Dobro factory of the 1960-70s. It was used on its 6-string guitars, and looked rather clumsy, inapropriate and too small. Only recently has the original large rolled-in f-hole die been found and it has been used since 1987 on Dobro's reproductions.

National's mandolin and ukulele bodies were made without f-holes, so that the only openings in the top are in the coverplate holes. However, in each case, the integral shallow well that the cone sits one is punched with numerous holes to let sound into the main body cavity. Perhaps John Dopyera experimented with extra holes in the top and found them unecessary. As with other models, mandolin and ukulele bodies were made from German silver at first, then yellow brass, and steel for the appropriate models.

National experimented briefly with aluminum as a body material, however none were produced commercially. Dobro did maunfacture an aluminum guitar, but the sound was very weak, and the model was not popular.

TRICONE RESONATOR SYSTEM

Sometime in 1926, John perfected his tricone system, using three 6" aluminum cones. The heart of the system is the resonating cone itself. He experimented with various metals and alloys, deciding that 99% pure aluminum (with trace amounts of chromium, zinc, magnesium, manganese, silicon, and iron) worked best for amplification and strength. When John initially set out to lathe-spin these very thin aluminum cones, all the experienced metal workers of the day said it couldn't be done. Nobody had ever worked aluminum to such hin tolerances before. John's earliest cones were worked as thin as .0045" to .005". Soon he settled on an average of .005" to .007", with the cones graduated in thickness in the manner of a violin top.

One of the most important design features of John's cone concerned the outer rim. He designed a stamping die to create a 6-fold "crimp" around the edge. This rim resembles the perimeter of a loudspeaker cone in that it provides a spring-like flexible base for the entire cone to move up and down freely while vibrating.

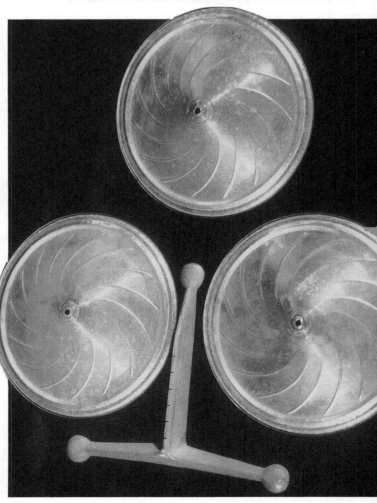

The heart of the tricone: three original cones with T-bar bridge assembly. Note spiral stamping and crimped edges, which provide strength and flexibility.

The New Silver Guitars and Mandolins

Tenor Style Guitar

MANDOLIN AND UKULELE

The Mandolin and Ukulele same size and same type except stringing and tuning

Hawaiian Style Guitar

Early 1928 ad showing the tricones of the day.

A second important improvement to the cone was made very early on. A radiating spiral pattern of embossed lines or grooves was stamped into the cone, providing strength and improving the transmission of tone. Tricone guitars below serial #360 or so will have cones without this spiral. These same low-numbered guitars also have the weaker-sounding wooden cone-rest platform mentioned before. Because of the addition of the spiral and the change to an integral metal cone-rest platform, the instruments improved drastically by 1928. Replacement cones could be bought from National for 90 cents each!

The string vibrations are transferred to the cones by means of a maple bridge-saddle, set into a groove in a sand-cast aluminum "T-bar." At the three ends of the T-bar are little cups designed to sit on the rounded peaks of the cones. In the center of each cup is a short pin made to go through the small hole at the peak of the cone. John Dopyera's patent specifies a bolt and nut arrangement here but production instruments were never built that way. The string-tension is sufficient to hold all the parts in place. A careful reading of the patent application reproduced in this book will make Dopyera's ideas and intentions clearer. John Dopyera said he experimented with many materials for the T-bar, before settling on aluminum.

The six-string guitar T-bar is formed with an inverted V-shaped groove running under the saddle area, to decrease the weight of the casting. The T-bar for the four-string tricone tenor and plectrum guitars is smaller and lighter than for the six-string. It is shaped a little more like a Y, to better accomodate the short four-string saddle, and has no groove cut in it.

The very first few dozen National mandolins employed a tricone resonator system. The illustration shows an early one, which was followed by a tricone mandolin with a single- cone-appearing round coverplate (see Style 2 in Chapter 3). The tricone system proved to be too complicated to manufacture, and too "fussy" in terms of adjustments and set-up. After about 60 instruments, mandolins were changed to a single resonator system. These early tricone mandolins could be purchased with either a mandolin or four-string ukulele neck.

SINGLE RESONATOR SYSTEM

The central issue in all of the fights between John Dopyera and George Beauchamp, and in the lawsuit between Dobro and National is the single-cone resonator concept. The design is simpler than the tricone, and cheaper to manufacture, because it has fewer parts. Instead of three cones attached to the strings by a T-bar, a single 9 1/2" diameter cone is used. The top of the cone is truncated and formed into a little bowl, leaving an annular ring of 2" diameter. A 1/4" thick "biscuit" of maple sits atop the cone, with a saddle inserted in a slot cut into the biscuit. On tenors, plectrums, and mandolins, the top of the cone is truncated at a higher point to make a smaller annular ring for the smaller four-string biscuit.

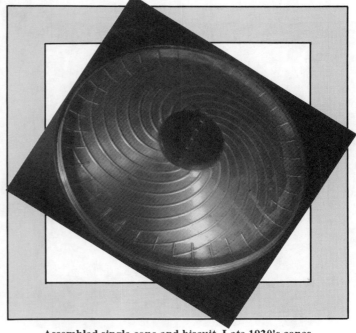

Assembled single cone and biscuit. Late 1930's cones have short radial lines added to the spiral pattern.

This type of resonator proved to be extremely loud and punchy, but with somewhat less sustain than the tricones. These guitars are actually slightly louder than the tricones, but with a less sophisticated tone quality. Hawaiian players primarily stayed with the tricone but blues and country musicians liked the strident sound and affordable price of the single-cones. National sold thousands of these guitars (32,000 by 1937, including many wood-body models) and, in fact, it is the single-cone guitar that really kept National afloat in the rough business waters of the Depression. It is just this success that caused all the dissension and lawsuits.

George Beauchamp applied for a patent on this idea on 3- 11-29, less than one month after John Dopyera left National. However, John Dopyera's original tricone patent (# 1,762,617 filed 10-12-26), while stating that three cones are preferable, says that the single resonator idea may be employed in smaller instruments, such as mandolins, ukuleles, and tenor guitars. This was two and a half years before Beauchamp's application. Furthermore, these smaller single-cone instruments were BUILT AND SOLD before Beauchamp even applied for his patent. The mandolin had a 9 1/2" single cone, and the ukulele had a single truncated 6" tricone resonator. For this writer, that is sufficient information to fully credit John Dopyera for the invention of the single- cone resonator instrument. In this light, it seems quite audacious of Beauchamp to further claim the Dobro spider & upside-down cone as an infringement of his idea. This issue has been covered more fully in the chapter on National's business history.

The 9 1/2" cone was always made with an embossed radiating spiral, similar to the 6" tricone resonator, for strength and tone. There were also the flexible stamped folds around the rim, to provide springiness for the whole cone. Mid to late 1930s cones have additional embossing of 1" long grooves around the rim of the cone, pointing inward. Presumably, they were used to add strength. There is no discernable difference in the sound of these later cones.

The biscuit was often attached rather crudely with hide glue and four small brads, though a screw may easily be used through the hole in the center of the cone and biscuit. It seems odd that a screw was not used, since the center holes in the cone and biscuit are a result of being lathe-spun. With a screw, there is a possibility of slight tone adjustments. Replacement cones of this type could be had in the 1930s for a mere $2.50.

COVERPLATES

Both tricone and single-cone patents make mention of the extreme thinness of the resonating cones. They explain that only a very thinly worked resonator will produce a good tone and amplify that tone. Because of the necessarily fragile nature of the cones, both resonator systems are intended to be removable, rapairable, and replaceable. The removable coverplate makes this possible.

The tricone coverplate, itself a work of Deco style art, remained exactly the same throughout the entire production of tricone instruments (1927-41). The overall shape would be an equilateral triangle, if not for the rounded corners. The

Single cone without biscuit, showing the "bowl" under the biscuit, which contacts the bowl at its perimeter.

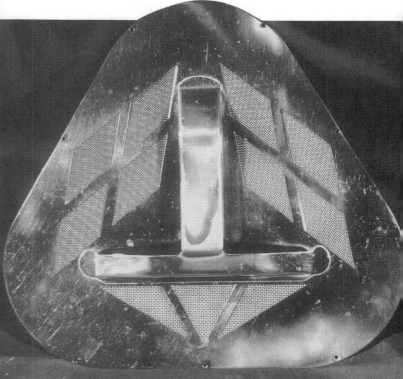

The tricone coverplate--a classic of industrial design.

1932-1935 biscuits had patent stamps on them, others are blank.

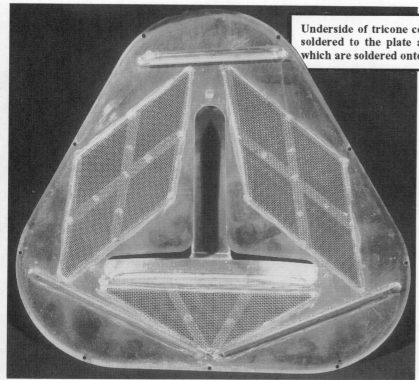

1932-36:

The coverplate remains the same, with the addition of four deeply embossed strengthening grooves radiating from the center. With the neck at "noon," these four grooves point to 10, 2, 5, and 7 o'clock. This coverplate is seen on both 12-fret and 14-fret guitars.

In 1936 or early 1937 the cut-outs on the coverplate were changed to a presumably more modern design. Instead of nine large cut-outs, there are sixteen clusters each composed of four cut-outs. The pyramid shape is still slightly evoked, but is elongated and defined sparsely by these cut-outs, two of which are diamond-shaped and two slanted parallelograms. This coverplate pattern is often referred to by enthusiasts as the "chicken feet" design. The edge of the central 2" hole is rolled in slightly on these later models, though a few have been seen with this edge rolled out.

orientation of the triangle accomodates the two bass cones and the one treble cone. Towards the center of the coverplate are three clusters of cut-outs. The cluster on the bass side is a triangle divided into three smaller triangular sections. There are two clusters of cut-outs on the treble side. They are each cut out in the shape of a diamond, and are each divided into four identically proportioned diamonds. These cutout holes are backed with a plated brass wire screen which is spot-soldered on the underside of the plate. At the center of the coverplate, a T-shaped hole allows the T-bar and saddle to be at the correct height above the plane of the coverplate. This T-shaped hole is covered by a raised T-shaped strap of metal which provides a handrest and protects the cones. This coverplate is identical on tricone tenor, plectrum, Spanish, and Hawaiian guitars.

The single-cone coverplate evolved through four designs from 1929-1941. The basic guitar coverplate unit consists of a 10" diameter slightly convex plate with a round 2" hole in the center to accomodate the biscuit and saddle. This hole is partly covered by a metal strap which functions as a handrest and protects the resonator. The edges of the strap are rounded and rolled down for player comfort. The coverplate is held in place by nine plated brass screws. For a brief period in 1931, National experimented with a hook-and-slot twist-on attachment system, then returned to the use of screws

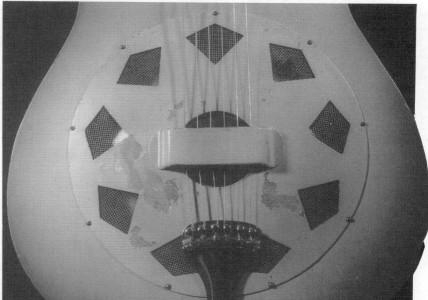

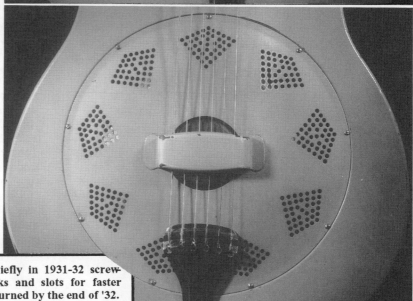

The guitar coverplate variations from 1929-1936 are as follows:

1929:

There are nine cut-outs near the rim. Their shape is suggestive of pyramids and they are centered at each screw. Wire screens are attached beneath the cutouts.

1930-31:

The shape of the cut-outs remains the same, but the wire screens at each cut-out are replaced by 41 small round holes drilled or stamped through the coverplate.

At this time, Triolians and Duolians did not feature the new "chicken feet" coverplate. In fact the coverplates of these 1936-1940 budget models returned to the 1930-31 drilled hole type, without the four "ribs."

Some Duolians, mostly those marketed to Sears and Roebuck, had coverplates with larger pyramid-shaped sections comprised of many small round holes. Both 12-fret and 14-fret guitars have been seen with this coverplate.

Tenor and plectrum guitar coverplates were similar to their six-string cousins. As mentioned above, tricone coverplates were exactly the same for four-string and six- string instruments. Though the cast-aluminum T-bar on the tenor and plectrum is smaller and lighter than the six-string T-bar, the coverplate hole and handrest assembly are identical on both instruments.

The coverplates for the single-cone tenor and plectrums (both pear-shaped and guitar-shaped models) are interchangable with the mandolin coverplates. This coverplate is nearly identical to the single-cone guitar coverplate, but the central hole and handrest are smaller, to better fit the smaller biscuit and saddle assembly. The tenor/ plectrum and mandolin coverplates followed the same evolutionary changes as their guitar counterparts. However, there are two briefly featured items peculiar to the tenor/plectrum/mandolin coverplate:

First, some batches of coverplates from 1929-36 are missing one pyramid-shaped perforated section (or screened cut-out) where a pickguard would be located--the area is simply solid. This was presumably to preclude pick wear. These batches were used intermittently with batches of regular coverplates.

Second, the late 30's "chicken feet" coverplate was slightly different for the tenors, plectrums, and mandolins. The area around the central hole was raised further than the already convex coverplate, in an area the shape and size of a doughnut. This raised area has a thin extension made to fit under the tailpiece. The reason for this raised area is unknown, but perhaps it was done to make a deeper neck set possible in order to increase the downward pressure on the cone. To make matters more confusing, some batches of 1935- 1937 mandolins have this raised central area, but incorporated into the earlier drilled-hole type of coverplate!

Ukuleles, being single-cone instruments, have a miniature version of the standard guitar and tenor/plectrum and mandolin coverplates. As with its larger cousins, the uke coverplate began with wire screens covering pyramid- shaped cut-outs, and changed by the end of 1929 to perforated holes arranged in the same shape. The other changes made to single-cone coverplates after 1931 were not made to the ukulele coverplates--they remained the same from 1931-1941. Though National made ukuleles in two sizes, they both have the same 6" resonator and coverplate. The resonator is the same diameter as a single tricone-type cone.

TAILPIECES

National was very consistent in the design of its tailpieces. All metal guitars used the same tailpiece, a simple one-piece stamping of nickel plated brass. This includes the painted Triolian and Duolian models. The tail- piece had six holes with slots for the strings and string ends. The strings then run over a small ridge on their way to the saddle. It is presumed that National began production of their own tailpiece after using up a batch of about 500 general-purpose "aftermarket" tailpieces, similar to those found on Stella guitars.

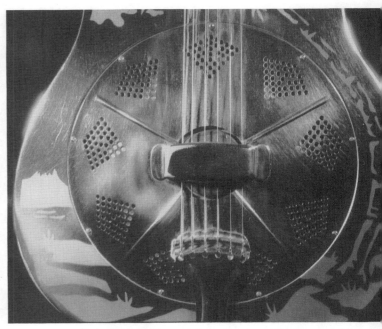

Late 1932-1935 coverplate with four ribs for strength.

These tailpieces differed from the National-produced tailpieces in two ways: There were six "studs" to guide the strings, and there were two small screw holes designed for installation on wood guitars. Tricone guitars below approximately serial #600 generally feature this earlier tailpiece. The standard stamped National tailpiece used an integral ridge rather than the studs. The stamping includes a raised central area running the length of the tailpiece, a simple but effective strengthening device. The endpin screw goes through the tailpiece, fastening it to the endblock inside the guitar.

Tenor and plectrum guitars have a similar tailpiece, only it is half the size of the guitar tailpiece, with a slightly different shape. Instead of holes for ball-end strings, there are four prongs for loop-end strings. The mandolin tailpiece is identical to the tenor/plectrum tailpiece, except that the prongs are doubled to accomodate the eight strings. Unfortunately, this design has not proven to be ideal in terms of durability. Almost half of the National mandolins that turn up have broken tailpieces caused by metal fatigue at the right-angle bend from normal string tension. This is easily repaired by a competent metal restorer.

Four types of ukulele tailpieces have been seen. Three of them are designed to accept gut (or nylon) strings. These three are attached by screws to the coverplate, rather than to the body at the endpin. The earliest ukuleles (large body, screened holes) have a geometrically designed black-painted maple block. Some have this same shaped block only made from plated brass. Later large-body ukes (with perforated hole coverplate) and many small-body ukes have a smoothly curved lozenge-shaped ebony block. For these three types, the strings simply pass under slots in the bottom of the block and are held by knots at the end of the strings. The other type of tailpiece, seen only on late Triolian (wood-grain finish) ukes, is a stamped piece like the guitar tailpiece, only simpler in design and flattened. This tailpiece is designed to accept steel ball-end strings, though gut may be used if a knot is tied in the string-end.

NATIONAL TRICONE PARTS LIST

- Side mounted tuning gears
- Decal
- Bone nut
- Mahogany neck
- Ebony fingerboard (rosewood to #380),   pearl dots or squares
- Screws, nuts, and woodblocks under fingerboard extension
- Mahogany neck extension-through-body
- 2 maple neck-extension supports (5/8" dowel, 1/4" x 2" disc)
- German silver body: back, sides, top, silver-soldered
- German silver coverplate, screens soldered across cut-outs
- 9 brass coverplate screws
- 3 spun aluminum alloy resonating cones,
- 6" diameter
- Cast-aluminum "T-bar" (transmits sound from saddle to cones)
- Maple saddle
- Nickel plated brass tailpiece
- Brass endpin and screw

NATIONAL SINGLE-CONE PARTS LIST

- Side mounted tuning gears
- Decal
- Bone nut
- Maple or mahogany neck
- Generally ebonized maple fingerboard, ebony on "Don" models
- 1/4" pearl position dots
- Screws, nuts, and wood blocks under fingerboard extension
- Maple or mahogany neck extension-through-body
- 2 maple neck-extension supports (5/8" -dowel, 1/4" x 2" disc)
- German silver, brass, or steel body: back, sides, top, silver-soldered together
- German silver, brass, or steel coverplate, with stamped holes.
- 9 brass coverplate screws
- One spun aluminum alloy resonating cone, 9 1/2" diameter
- Maple saddle in slotted 2" x 1/4" maple disc, held to cone by a screw or four tiny brads and glue
- Nickel plated brass tailpiece
- Brass endpin and screw

MEASUREMENTS OF METAL NATIONAL INSTRUMENTS:
(IN INCHES)

	GUITARS ALL 12fr TYPES	PEAR-SHAPE TENOR	GUITAR SHAPE TENOR	MANDO	LARGE UKE	SMALL UKE
OVERALL LENGTH:	38.75 to 39.25*	35.75	35.00	27.5	23.5	22.00
SCALE LENGTH:	24.9	23.00	23.00	15.25	14.875	13.75
BODY LENGTH:	19.75	15.5	15.25	13.25	11.125	9.75
LOWER BOUT:	14.125	14.00	12.75	12.75	7.125	7.00
WAIST:	9.25	N/A	9.00	N/A	5.00	4.875
UPPER BOUT:	10.1875	N/A	9.5	N/A	5.875	5.375
BODY DEPTH AT HEEL:	2.8125	2.75	2.875	2.375	2.25	2.00
BODY DEPTH AT END PIN:	3.25	3.00	3.25	2.75	2.75	2.25
NECK WIDTH AT NUT:	1.875	1.125	1.125	1.25	1.25	1.25

        * Variation is due to differing headstock lengths over the years. Tricone headstocks are generally a bit longer.

        14-fret guitars have the same scale-length as the 12- fret model. The bodies were merely shortened by 1.5 inches to make the neck two more frets clear of the body. Overall length is marginally shorter.

        Plectrum guitars have identical dimensions to the tenors, with the exception of a 26-inch scale length. Note the differences in body thickness taper between both shapes of tenor guitar and both sizes of ukulele.

Sol Hoopii Novelty Trio, early 1927. Sol and his rhythm guitarist hold prototype tricones. Note extra diamond-shaped holes around the perimeter of the body of these guitars.

CHAPTER 6

HAWAIIAN RECORDING ARTISTS USING NATIONALS

SOL HOOPII
KING OF THE HAWAIIAN GUITAR

The creator of instant popularity for Nationals, and perhaps the most well-known National player, Sol Hoopii is without a doubt the most important and musically influential Hawaiian guitarist of this century. In addition to affecting all Hawaiian guitarists, Sol also had great influence on Western swing and country music. He was a great traditional Hawaiian stylist, but was the first to really blend jazz and blues with the Hawaiian steel sound. His particular voice was the Hawaiian guitar, but his fluid bursts of musical ideas, and his relaxed, flawless technical virtuosity made him a great 20th century musician, regardless of instrument. He was also a top-notch Hawaiian falsetto singer.

Sol was born Solomon Hoopii Kaai, in Honolulu in 1902, one of 21 children. He dropped the last part of his name as a professional. The correct pronunciation of the name Hoopii is "Ho-oh-pee-ee" in four syllables. His family was very Hawaiian, and the Hawaiian language was spoken at his home in the Kaka'ako district, an all-Hawaiian part of Honolulu. Sol began playing ukulele at three years of age, and guitar by age six. Sol was interested in music almost to the exclusion of all else. He idolized many of the first-generation Hawaiian guitarists such as David Kaili, Joseph Kekuku (generally recognized as the inventor of Hawaiian guitar), and Pale K. Lua, all artists who were touring and recording on the US mainland by 1912.

Sol reasoned that the fame of these men had something to do with their ventures on the mainland, so at about 17, he stowed away with two friends on a Matson liner heading for San Francisco. It is said that after the boys were discovered stowing away, the passengers were so taken with their music that they paid the fare for the trio. Sol did not stay in San Francisco very long, and in the early 1920s, he moved to Los Angeles. He made his official debut at a chop suey house there. Sol met and formed a trio with Hawaiian musicians Lani McIntire and Glenwood Leslie. This group, the Sol Hoopii Novelty Trio, was to become famous as a recording unit of the late 1920s.

Sol's music really developed during this period, and he enjoyed fame performing in clubs and theatres as well as recording. His most popular numbers were American jazz and blues songs adapted for Hawaiian guitar. Very few other musicians come to mind who were both influenced by American music AND went on to greatly influence American music. In addition, his records of 1926-1938 were issued in many countries worldwide, and his name is still legendary among all Hawaiian steel players all over the world.

It is known that sometime in late 1926, Sol's trio was hired for the then-astronomical sum of five hundred dollars, to play at a party at Ted Kleinmeyer's home. The trio was engaged as part of an effort by Beauchamp to convince Kleinmeyer to finance National. Reportedly, the party went on for three days, with free-flowing bootleg liquor, dancing girls, etc. Sol asked for and received more money by the second day, having gambled the five hundred dollars all away. John Dopyera later gave Sol two tricones; at least one had Sol's name engraved on it. Dopyera was upset when he found that Sol had pawned one of these guitars shortly after getting it, and resolved to give no more away. The current whereabouts of these two guitars is unknown. Sol's ties with the company were not comletely severed; he performed at least once at a NAMM show for National in the late 1920's.

Detail of preceding photo. Note narrow hand soldered metal strips in the upper bouts, and the pre-decal headstock logo. Undoubtedly one of the very first hand-cut tricones.

Sol Hoopii Trio, 1927 The guitar on the left apears to be engraved in an prototype Style 4 pattern. Note diamond holes in the body, the early fingerboard inlays, and the pre-decal headstock logo. The Style 1 roundneck on the right still has the seven extra holes, but has the shield-shaped logo.

Sol changed the personnel in his trio around 1930, taking on Sol K. Bright as rhythm guitarist, with unknown uke player. His 1930-31 recordings feature this trio. By 1933, he changed backup musicians again, because Sol K. Bright was starting his own career. The Hoopii Trio became a quartet with the addition of string bass. Sol's recordings are discussed below.

Sol made appearances in many films in the early 1930s, playing steel in such films as the 1932 Bird of Paradise, several Charlie Chan movies, Waikiki Wedding, Topper, and more. He also recorded a stunning soundtrack for "Betty's Bamboo Isle," an animated Betty Boop film, including versions of Chimes, Dinah, and 12th St. Rag. His tricone was used for all of the above films.

Sol gave up his career as a secular musician in 1938, joining Aimee Semple McPherson's "crusade" and touring the US many times. He was a devout convert and after 1938 performed only religious songs, with occasional presumably harmless marches thrown in. He made his last recordings from 1948-1951, all sacred in nature, featuring still-jazzy electric steel. He died Nov. 16, 1953, after a long battle with diabetes in Seattle, Washington.

SOL'S MUSICAL STYLE

As previously mentioned, Sol Hoopii had a tremendous influence on many styles of music and his records were highly regarded in numerous countries on every continent. He almost single-handedly carried the Hawaiian guitar and most of its players from the ragtime era to the jazz and swing eras. His phonograph records from 1925 to 1951 are a virtual document of the history of the development of Hawaiian guitar-playing. Of course, his records gave a huge boost to the sales of National tricone guitars. After his first 1926 recording session with a National, 90% of Hawaiian recording artists were using Nationals by 1929.

Sol's first recordings were made in 1925 in California on the very small Sunset label. The artist credit is given on the labels as "Waikiki Hawaiian Trio," but there is no question that the steel player is Sol Hoopii. His fiery and highly musical style easily cuts through, even though he is playing a Lyon and Healy flat-top guitar and the records are acoustically recorded. No other Hawaiian or American steel player, up to 1928 or so, approached Sol's 1925 level of speed, accuracy, hot ideas, and general urgency. His playing at this stage consisted mostly of single-string work with rapid picking and frequent "rip" strokes. Twelve songs were cut.

Sol's first nationally distributed records were made for Columbia, in two distinct batches: 1926-29, and 1930-31. The first batch of records, issued on the popular series, was recorded by his Novelty trio consisting of Sol, Lani McIntire, and Glenwood Leslie. Forty four sides were issued, comprised of thirty one Hawaiian titles and thirteen bluesy- jazz titles. These are the records that established Sol's fame and reputation. Playing these blues and jazz titles was revolutionary for a Hawaiian guitarist. One of the most amazing examples of this phenomenon is his version of Bix Beiderbecke's now-famous record, Singing the Blues. Now Bix, in his lifetime, was only known by the most modern and sophisticated musicians, and never sold more than 2,000 copies of any of his records. It is fascinating to speculate how Sol first heard this record, and how he decided to record his version a scant 6 months later. Generally his playing during this period still consisted of single-note work, with blazingly fast, powerful, and clean right hand technique. His playing on the Hawaiian titles was very tasteful and fairly traditional in content, if just a little bit swinging. His playing on the jazz and blues titles was extremely "low- down" in style, with lots of "blue" notes, and very relaxed while still sounding strong.

His second batch of Columbia records from 1930-31, were issued on a special West-coast-only series of mostly traditional Hawaiian material. They are quite rare today, and feature Sol. K. Bright on rhythm guitar. All forty-two titles are Hawaiian songs, mostly traditional; a few hapa- haole songs; and a couple of Hawaiian compositions by Sol. Both Sol's trio and his steel playing are lighter in style than the more urgent sounding 1926-29 sides. All of these records feature excellent singing by the trio. Sol's steel playing became even more precise. It still featured mostly single-string work, but he began to use modern chordal ideas and note-pairs. Most of these sides are somewhat restrained, but it is possible that Columbia requested all-Hawaiian and traditional-sounding music for these sessions.

By 1933, Sol added a bass to his Novelty Trio, making a quartet. From October 1933 to early 1935, the Quartet cut forty eight songs for the Brunswick record company. No restraint here, this batch of Hawaiian, hapa-haole and jazzy numbers represent the pinnacle of musical achievement on the National or any acoustic Hawaiian guitar. Many of the tunes were simply vehicles for great solos by Sol. His playing reached new heights of technical bravado and imagination, with very complex chordal and phrasing ideas. No other players have successfully reproduced Sol's efforts at these Brunswick sessions.

Sol (left) leading one of the largest groups of Nationals ever seen in a photograph. This band never recorded, though one wonders what 15 Nationals would sound like played at once. The four steel players in front (Dick McIntire and brothers) never recorded with acoustic steels, but later had extensive careers as electric players. This was certainly the cream of Hawaiian musicians in L.A. in 1930 or 1931 when this photo was taken. Several ukuleles, tricones and Style O guitars are visible.

The last few Brunswick records of 1935, the eight Decca sides of 1938, and the 26 sacred records made on various labels from 1948-51 all feature electric steel. Sol's first attempts, on a Rickenbacker bakelite model, sound a bit timid, as if he is afraid of the increased volume. However, he soon became quite facile on electric, and all of the above recordings are quite good. To this writer, however, the electric-steel sides are not as exciting as the acoustic steel recordings.

Sol stands alone as the acknowledged king of the Hawaiian steel guitar. The other top players of Nationals were Tau Moe, Sam Ku West, Jim and Bob, Sol K. Bright and Benny Nawahi. They came close to having Sol's abilities and they stand above the rest. However, the surviving players on that list will certainly grant Sol his title. He alone popularized the National more than these other players put together, and forever changed American popular music.

See the discography in Appendix C for available recordings of Sol Hoopii.

A hot platter from 1933 when Sol was at the peak of his powers. The description on the right of the spindle hole is unusual.

Detail of Sol's Style 3 from preceding page. Note his name engraved in a heart in the middle of the back.

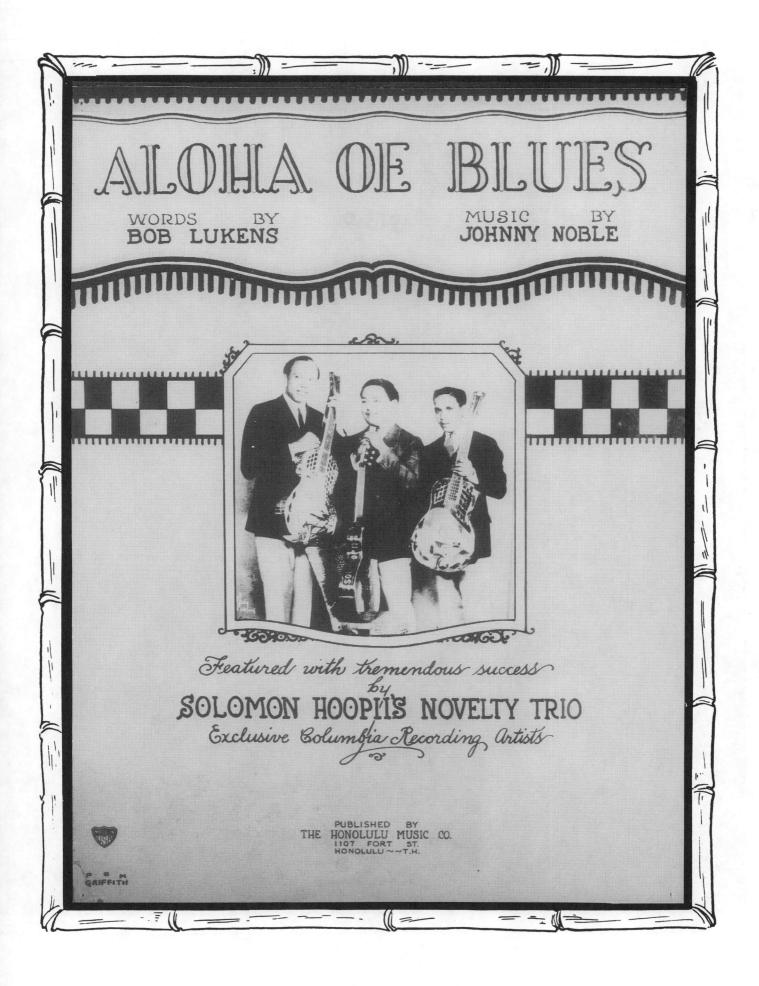

Tau Moe, 1934, with his 1932 Style 2 tricone.

THE TAU MOE FAMILY
LIVING LEGENDS OF HAWAIIAN MUSIC

The story of the Tau Moe Family is a tale that spans almost the entire history of Hawaiian music. Very few careers in any field of show business have been as long-lived and as well-traveled as the Moes'. All four members of the family, Tau, 80 years old, Rose, 80, Lani, 59, and Dorian, 44, are extremely talented musicians, vocalists, and dancers. This close-knit family has been in show business professionally since 1926, and has toured the world many times.

Tau was born in 1908 in Samoa, the son of Chief Savea Moe, and moved to Laie, Hawaii at age 9. Rose was the youngest daughter of the Kaohu family of Kohala, Hawaii. Kohala is the fertile birthplace of many well-known Hawaiian entertainers, including Rose's cousin Winona Love, the great hula dancer. Her childhood was steeped in music and hula.

Tau became interested in music at an early age, inspired by the earliest records of Frank Ferera and Pale K. Lua. He got his first guitar at age 14 from his sister, and immediately converted the action for Hawaiian steel-playing. Tau and his friends would congregate around the outside of the local record store, straining to hear the latest steel guitar melodies so they could rush home and learn them.

Tau and Rose were both involved in music professionally by 1926, working with various local groups including Johnny Almeida. In fact, Tau and Rose met at the music studios of steel-guitarist/teacher M.K. Moke, in 1927. By this time, Tau had joined a show with his uncles Tauivi, Fuifui, and Pulu Moe. This show was organized and managed by Mme. Claude Riviere (whose fascinating life story would require an entire book!). Mme. Riviere was a highly educated French professor who was sent by the French goverment to study the economy of Tahiti. She fell in love with Polynesian music and culture, and obtained a house in Honolulu for her theatre, and engaged the Moe brothers. The show consisted of Hawaiian and Samoan music and traditional dance, and also included films and lecture. This was the first really Polynesian show in existence.

Rose auditioned for Mme. Riviere in 1928, and was easily selected for her incredibly beautiful Hawaiian falsetto singing and graceful hula dancing. She also played Hawaiian guitar, and still plays spanish guitar today. The troupe was known as Mme. Riviere's Royal Samoan Dancers, or Mme. Riviere's Hawaiians.

Tau (seated) with his three uncles (standing, left to right) Fuifui, Pulu, and Tauivi as they appeared in 1929 in the Mme. Riviere show.

The group left Hawaii in December 1928 for an extended tour of Asia lasting until 1934. The tour encompassed Japan, China, Southeast Asia, Philipines, India, Indonesia, Pakistan and Burma, and included many return visits to these countries. In 1929, the troupe recorded 8 songs for Columbia in Toyko. These records were only issued in Japan and on the West coast of the U.S., and are extremely rare today.

Musically, these performances are ethnically pure, with very traditional accompaniment and beautiful vocals led by Rose's falsetto. Stylistically, these records, made in 1929, sound much closer to the earliest Hawaiian recordings made (1905-1915). The rhythm is strongly duple-division, rather than the more modern triple division of the beat as found on every hula record since the late 1920's. There is no jazz influence, and only a slight ragtime influence. These are my favorite recordings of all Hawaiian music of the 1920's. The sound is unearthly and breathtakingly beautiful.

Tau and Rose had their son Lani, in 1929--he was lying on the studio floor when the aforementioned records were made. When in India in 1932, Tau obtained a National Style 2 tri-cone Hawaiian guitar mail-ordered from London. He then purchased a Style O guitar for Rose as well. He says today that he always had wanted a National after seeing Sam Ku West play one in Honolulu in 1928. The tour continued until 1934 when various problems caused the breakup of part of the group. Tau and Rose continued to perform in Asia as a duo, and Lani joined the act in 1934 (at 5 years of age!) dancing, singing, and playing ukulele, to enthusiastic responses.

One of two known copies, this record was cut in Toyko in 1929, and provided much inspiration to the author.

Rose Moe, 1929, from Mme. Riviere's show.

Tau, 1935, from an adverising poster from a Kuala Lampur nightclu

3.
VICTOR
RCA
"HIS MASTER'S VOICE"
CHINA PRESS
OCTOBE 7th 1935
I
Canidrome Hawaiians Make Records
Mr. Tau Moe and Princess Roselani, popular and talented Hawaiian artists now at the Canidrome Garden, were selected by RCA Victor Company of Shanghai for Hawaiian music and songs recordings and, with three other members of Mr. Moe's Hawaiian Troubadours, have just completed four new records which will, it is expected, be released within a few weeks.
The records were made by RCA Victor under the supervision of Mr. Jack Horton. Hal P. Mills, of the Consolidated Amusement Company, Astor House, is agent for the Royal Hawaiians and made the necessary arrangements.
Officials of the local company predict a wide sale of the records, not only in the Far East but in America and Europe. Mr. Moe and Princess Roselani are with Baby Lani a most important part of the current program at the Canidrome Garden. They are singers, dancers and musicians.
Mr. Moe has on several other occasions been chosen for phonograph recordings and many of the records he has made are on the market.
The Royal Hawaiians end their engagement at the Canidrome tonight and shortly after will leave Shanghai on an extended tour which is expected to take them to Australia for a return engagement.

"....These are a few of my favorite things." Page one of Tau Moe's personal scrapbook, including pictures of Nationals that he cut out of a catalog in his youthful enthusiasm.

Tau and Rose hard at work as a duo in Shanghai, 1934. They were entertaining 3,000 people at the Canindrome Club/ Casino/ Dogtrack without microphones.

124

In l934, Tau and Rose, both using Nationals, recorded four songs for Victor in Shanghai. No known copies of these sides exist at this writing, but there does exist an extremely rough tape copy, wherein Tau's National tricone can be heard clearly above the background noise. A few photos exist of the Moes at this period, including the ones you see here.

After several months in India, the Moe Trio set out for Egypt. Arriving late in 1935, Tau soon found work in clubs in Alexandria and Cairo. They were the first Hawaiian act to travel anywhere near the Middle East, and were a sensation. Beginning in 1935, the Moes worked their way into Europe through these countries: Syria, Palestine, Turkey, Greece, Romania, Bulgaria, Yugoslavia, Russia, and Poland, arriving in Germany in 1938. From 1938-39, the Moes worked extensively in Germany, and around Western Europe. Many of these shows featured several acts on one bill. The Moes worked with many others including Alberta Hunter, and Josephine Baker.

A record that has never been found, cut by Tau and Rose in Shanghai. Detail from scrapbook page.

The Moes were advised to leave Europe because of the gathering clouds of World War II, and so slowly worked their way back through Southeastern Europe winding up briefly in Beirut. After working a short time there, Italy declared war, so Tau was again advised to leave. The family boarded a bus for a four-day trip to Bagdhad, to catch a ship back to Hawaii. They arrived in Hawaii right after the bombing of Pearl Harbor and hence decided to return to India. They worked throughout the war years in Calcutta and other principal Indian cities.

In 1941, The Moes made some fantastic records for India HMV that were very swinging and modern, featuring Tau on electric steel with hot accompaniment and vocals by Rose, Lani, and Tau. Tau was leading a 15-piece orchestra at this time, and, in the spirit of Mme. Riviere, presented a tremendous variety of moods and music in one evening's show. Lani, while still a teenager, played several instruments of the saxophone family in this band. Dorian was born in 1945 and, in the family tradition, joined the act by 1950, singing, dancing, and later playing several instruments.

Tau and Rose with son Lani, Rose played a Style 0 guitar to complement Tau's tricone. Taken in Eastern Europe, c 1937.

A poster from Berlin Wintergarden, 1938. Tau really liked the look of Nationals, and emphasized them in most of his promotional materials.

Tau in 1990 in Hawaii with his Style 2 tricone.

The Moes took a brief 1947 trip home to Hawaii where they recorded a few sides for Bell Records, then returned to Europe, which became their base of operations for most of the 1950s, 1960s, and 1970s. Both Lani and Dorian were highly educated in Europe, both academically and artistically. Lani was trained in ballet, and acrobatic dancing, and Dorian was trained in modern dancing as well as hula and acrobatic dance. From the 1960s, Lani created all of the family's show costumes himself--and every show required several costume changes.

The Moes made dozens of records on many European labels during these decades, including some with Felix Mendelson's Hawaiians in England. Tau actually created his own black and white film studio and produced his own Hawaiian films for television. Every element of production and poromotion was carried out by the Moes themselves throughout their career.

In 1980, with plenty of engagements still available to them, the Moes decided to retire, and came back to Laie, Hawaii, Tau's boyhood home. Lani is now director of costumes and wardrobe for B.Y.U. and Dorian is the assistant Theatre manager for the Polynesian Cultural Center. The Moe family continued to perform locally and at the P.C.C. for a few

years. They live together still in Laie. Having seen the world together all these years, they are a very wise, kind, and loving family with a great sense of humor and philosophy of life.

In 1976, this writer found the only known copy of the Moe's 1929 Tokyo recording of Paahana/Mai Kai No Kauai in a basement in San Francisco. This record, with its indescribably beautiful singing and playing, haunted me for years. In 1985, I received a letter from Tau Moe requesting one of my albums. Upon hearing from collector Dirk Vogel that Tau and Rose were the people behind the music on those old 78s credited to "Mme. Riviere's Hawaiians", I had the good fortune of meeting the Moes in May 1988, with Canadian- Hawaiian musician George Keoki Lake.

After an afternoon of playing all the really old tunes from the 1929 Mme. Riviere days, in a session that can only be described as exciting and very deeply moving, the Moes and I decided to make a new album together. The goal of this record was to come as close as possible to re-creating the music, sound and feeling of the original records that Tau and Rose made 60 years ago. Vintage acoustic instruments were used in a live recording made in a 1920s era house near Chinaman's Hat on Oahu. Several Nationals were used for this session, including a style #3 Hawaiian tricone, a style #4 Hawaiian tri-

The Tau Moe Family in Hawaii, 1990. L to R: Dorian, Lani, Rose, and Tau.

cone, a large-size #1 uke and a small #2 uke.

In seven days, thirteen songs were recorded, all in three takes or less. Tau played rhythm guitar in a very old style with authentic bass runs, and also sang bass. Rose sang all of the lead falsetto soprano vocals in a sweet and clear voice absolutely undiminished by 63 years of professional use. Lani supplied authentic old-style ukulele and tenor vocals, while Dorian played rhythm and sang alto. I played National tri-cone Hawaiian guitars in old-style low- bass tuning, as well as Harp-guitar. Tau directed the family and myself to achieve a completely realistic picture of genuine Hawaiian music of days gone by.

Tau and Rose lost their National guitars when they left India after the second World War. Tau began playing electric steel, first using a six-string, then an eight-string. He had long given up hope of being able to find another National to replace his, when, after the recording sessions, for his 80th birthday, it was my pleasure to locate a 1932 Style 2 Tricone for Tau. He is now playing it as well as ever.

See the discography in Appendix C for recordings.

Sam Ku West 1927, with style 2 tricone

SAM KU WEST

Almost nothing is known about the life of this great steel guitarist, who recorded and toured the world from as early as 1914 until his death in Paris sometime in the 1930s. Sam's given name is understood to be Sam Ku. He apparently had 2 steel-playing brothers who lived in Hawaii most of their lives. These two brothers also made a handful of records in the late 1920s under their own names--Dan Ku, and George Ku.

It is assumed by most Hawaiian music enthusiasts that the young Sam was the steel player in an early touring and recording group called Irene West's Royal Hawaiians. It seems that Irene West was another "anthropologist-tour manager" like Mme. Claude Riviere. The group made many big-selling records for the Victor company in the late teens and early 1920s. Though acoustically recorded, the listener can get a pretty good idea of the style of this group. They were among the first generation of travelling Hawaiian performers and their sound is similar to other groups of this generation many of whom performed at the 1915 Worlds Fair in San Francisco. The music consisted of traditional hulas, marches, hapa haole numbers and waltzes.

Sam, who eventually took Irene West's surname, struck out on his own, after touring Europe with Irene West. He was not heard again on records until the period of 1927-1930, when he made several recordings in the U.S. By this time he was using the Style 2 tricone shown in his only known photograph. His first output was recorded by very small companies, such as Gennett, Champion, Challenge and Banner. It seems that company executives were aware of the large sales of Sol Hoopii records, since many of Sam's records from this period are highly imitative of Hoopii's style and song repertoire. It was common practice for record companies to issue other versions of popular selling couplings. It may have been occasionally difficult for Sam to labor under the giant shadow of Sol Hoopii's reputation.

At some point during this period, Sam returned to Honolulu for a concert. Tau Moe (see chapter 6-B) recalls seeing Sam and being extremely impressed with his then-new National tricone. It seems that Sam was doing almost as well as Sol, in terms of touring, recording and reputation.

In 1928, Sam secured a recording contract with Victor records, one of the two largest companies of the day. Victor's rival was Columbia, the label which had Sol Hoopii under contract. As a result, some of Sam's 12 Victor records sound again like Sol, however Sam's individual style comes through quite clearly. His sound is perhaps the warmest of any tricone players, with a beautiful and sensual vibrato on low notes at the ends of phrases. The nuances of his slide style were many, with a wide range of sounds and a well-developed blues sense. He was described by the King of England the "Fritz Kreisler of the Hawaiian guitar." (Kreisler was a well-known violin virtuoso of the day.)

Sam Ku West was probably not the showman that Sol was, judging by the somewhat darker and more pensive sound of his records. His choice of material relied less on novelty and jazz than Sol, and included blues and Hawaiian instrumentals. He sounds like he was a leading stylist of a slightly earlier period who was pushed into more modern playing by the great influence of Sol Hoopii.

One of Sam's great Victor recordings, 1928.

After making a few more records in 1930, for Melotone, Sam apparently went back to Europe where he performed for a few more years before dying at a fairly young age in Paris sometime in the 1930s.

Many of his original recordings are are available on the re-issue albums listed in the discography.

Bennie Nawahi in the early 1920s, before he obtained the wood-body Triolian used in his recordings of 1928-1930. (Nawahi's 1929 recordings still set the standard for hot acoustic steel.)

KING BENNIE NAWAHI

One of the more unusual, original and colorful Hawaiian musicians who performed and recorded with a National was Benjamin Keakahiawa Nawahi (na-va-hee). His style was even more heavily influenced by jazz and blues than Sol Hoopii's, and Nawahi also performed much more often with non-Hawaiian musicians. Though his style may be considered less sophisticated than Sol's, Bennie had a more explosive way of playing, and sounded very much more like a black musician than Sol did.

He was born in Honolulu on July 3, 1899 and had twelve siblings. Like Sol and many other Hawaiian musicians, Nawahi's early family life was steeped in music. He obtained a cheap guitar in his early teens by running grocery errands in exchange for trading stamps which he redeemed for the guitar. Like Tau Moe, Bennie taught himself to play steel in his teens, and entertained on the streets of Honolulu. It is said that he teamed up with the young Sol Hoopii in these street performances, but a disagreement over a tip caused a permanent rift between these two great steel players. One can only dream of what duets between these two young geniuses may have sounded like. Years later, Nawahi correctly categorized Sol's playing as more sweet, and his own playing as more "hot".

At age 20, in 1919, Nawahi got a job on the Matsonia passenger liner with his older brother Joe's group, The Hawaiian Novelty Five. After a few trips between San Francisco and Honolulu, the Novelty Five toured the mainland on the Orpheum vaudeville curcuit. Besides playing steel guitar, Bennie also played mandolin, and exceptionally great ukulele. The ukulele craze that was sweeping the States at this time provided a perfect outlet for Nawahi, and soon he struck out on his own, picking up extra money by winning ukulele contests in many cities. In addition to seemingly impossible numbers, Benny also had a full repertoire of trick-playing techniques for the uke, and was even known to play a novelty tune on the steel--with his feet! Theatre impressario Sid Grauman gave Bennie the title of King of the Ukulele, and so his professional name became King Bennie Nawahi. In 1927, Grauman hired Benny to play a small part in his New York production of The Big Parade. Benny portrayed a ukulele-strumming soldier with a Yiddish accent.

Once in New York, Benny began performing with small groups, and secured some recording contracts. Between 1928 and 1930 he recorded 16 sides for Columbia, 4 sides for Victor, at least 4 for Q.R.S., and at least 14 for the Boston-based Grey Gull group of dime-store labels. There is a strong likelihood that he also made records for the Gennett label, under the name of King, Queen, and Jack, though the steel playing on these sides is a little more subdued. Some of the Grey Gull sessions involved an unknown second steel player, who interweaves his melodies with Bennie with gorgeous results.

Of the approximately forty songs that Nawahi recorded, the breakdown of styles is as follows:

15 Black-jazz or blues numbers, some with black groups
12 Popular songs with hot solos
14 Traditional-type Hawaiian songs

Fortunately for today's interested listener, well over half of these have been re-issued on various LPs listed in Appendix C.

On all of these 1928-31 recordings, Bennie used an early wood-body single cone Triolian guitar with a high nut for Hawaiian playing. This is one of the unusual things about Nawahi's sound--no other recording Hawaiian steel players of this era used a single cone National. It gives his style a very snappy and percussive singnature. No doubt, the acoustic characteristics of a single cone (loud attack, short sustain) helped shape Nawahi's musical style. He attacked his instrument with vigor, played lots of rip-strokes and fast triplets, and also tended to avoid any long slides in his playing. This last was probably due to the lack of sustain typical of single cones. We can only assume that Bennie preferred this sound over the smoother tricone sound, since tricones were readily available at that time. Since he could definitely afford one, at his level in show business, he presumably tried one and liked his Triolian better.

Towards the end of his stay in New York, around 1932, Bennie worked in restaurants and clubs with the Georgia Jumpers, a small hot jazz band consisting of black musicians playing piano, saxophone, violin, percussion and kazoos. The four recordings by this group, issued on the Columbia "Race Records" series only and quite rare today, represent the pinnacle of devil-may-care crazed small-band hot jazz playing!

Like so many other musicians, writers and artists of the early 1930s, Bennie left New York as the Depression curtailed vaudeville, and headed for Los Angeles. Not only was the climate there more like Hawaii, but the financial and psychological lure of Hollywood loomed large in those days. One of his first West coast bands, King Nawahi and the International Cowboys, included a then-obscure Roy Rogers. Bennie apparently made frequent radio appearances in Los Angeles through the 1930s, as there are a few transcription discs in existence, as well as various recollections heard by this writer. In 1935, Nawahi was still doing well in spite of the Depression, when he was suddenly struck blind while driving. He managed to stop the car, but spent the rest of his life in total blindness for which there was no apparent cause. He was able to bounce back shortly and continue working the clubs and restaurants, eventually switching to electric by World War II. In addition to his musical abilities, Bennie was also a long-distance swimmer. In 1946 he swam from San Pedro to Catalina Island, 26 miles, in just over 22 hours. He is still the only blind man to have completed this swim.

In the late 1970s, after remaining musically active all these years, Nawahi suffered a stroke, and gradually his health deteriorated slowly until his death on January 29, 1985. Shortly before his death, musician/artist Robert Armstrong met with Nawahi and gathered the above biographical information and photographs.

Perhaps Bennie Nawahi did not enjoy the amount of fame that Sol Hoopii had, but his records were occasionally issued in Europe and have interested jazz record collectors for years, before collecting Hawaiian became fashionable. He took the single resonator National sound about as far as it could go and his music was a true blend of Hawaiian, Jazz, and Blues.

Jim and Bob in a pensive shot from the eary 1930's. Bob plays his Style 1
tricone while Jim attentively accompanies with a Dyer Harp-guitar.

JIM AND BOB
THE GENIAL HAWAIIANS

As with many other musical artists of the early days of recording, the life stories of these two musicians are unknown today. The music of Jim and Bob was captured on a handful of 78 rpm records made in 1934, for the Bluebird label. According to the 1930 National catalog, this duo worked in the Chicago area, and performed regularly on radio. Their 15 minute show was sponsored by Willard's Stomach Tablets, and broadcast on station WENR, Chicago.

In many cases, artists who only made a few records have a tough time garnering the historical reputation enjoyed by more frequently recorded artists. It is a shame that so few recordings were made by Jim and Bob, because steel guitarist Bob appears to equal Sol Hoopii in musical genius, flawless execution, and perfect intonation. Perhaps Sol was a better showman, and had better luck with recording contracts, managers, etc.

The recorded evidence left by Jim and Bob shows a Hawaiian duo at its best. Both men used tricone guitars, with Jim Holstein playing the rhythm. In songs such as their explosive version of St. Louis Blues, the interplay between the two men shows deep intuition as well as demonstrating the longevity of their partnership. Bob was a master of theatrical restraint on most of his recordings, and by the time he cuts loose at the end of St. Louis Blues, the listener is at the edge of his seat. Bob was also quite capable of wringing the most tender, liquid, and sentimental tones from his tricone, as can be heard on Song of the Range. He was a master of the "cry" note, wherein the steel is quickly moved up and back a whole step from the melody note, evoking the feeling of a tearful catch in the throat of a singer.

Most of the ten original recordings by this group have been re-issued (see the discography). It is quite possible that transcription discs of the WENR radio shows may exist somewhere. Obviously they would be most interesting to hear. It is unknown where or when these two fellows were born and died, how long they continued performing, whether Bob switched to electric steel, etc. We are fortunate to have the few records we have, because they are evidence that Sol was not the only great steel genius of those days.

Jim Holstein posing proudly with his Style 3 tricone. Note extra coverplate engraving. This photo was featured in the 1930 National catalog.

DAVID KANE
OF KANE'S HAWAIIANS

The next musician in our lineup of obscure recording artists is David Kane, shown in this photo from the 1930 National catalog. He is holding a Style 2 tricone with extra coverplate engraving, probably serialized in the 100s. The only known fact about this artist is that he visited the embryonic Oakland, California studios of the Victor record company on April 20, 1927, March 2, 1928, March 23, 1928, and April 3, 1928. Presumably, he and his group were vaudeville performers working on the West Coast when they secured this recording contract. Twenty-one songs were recorded in these sessions, and seventeen of them were released by the company.

The repertoire of these records consisted mostly of well-known Hawaiian songs, with a few more obscure hulas, and a few jazz-tinged numbers. Kane was a competent player, but, perhaps in order to succeed in vaudeville, tended to insert lots of tasteless sound effects and other noises peculiar to the steel. Two of the songs, Kane's Blues, and You Don't Like It Not Much employ these effects almost to the exclusion of any real notes. One can imagine the recording engineer wincing and shaking his head in disbelief. The regular Hawaiian material is performed quite well and the steel playing carries a feeling of sincere emotional intensity. A few records by this group have been re-issued, on albums listed in the discography appendix.

A 1928 recording with designations for title, composer, and artist all sharing the Kane name.

David Kane, c. 1929

The four photographs on the next two pages are of Puerto Rican groups from Kauai, Hawaii, of all places. Two Nationals can be seen in this photo: a 14 fret 1936 Duolian, and a very intriguing c.1938 Triolian tenor, with eight strings, perhaps done at the factory. A small Rickenbacher amp sits in front.

These groups, with their transitional acoustic- electric set-up must have sounded interesting. Unfortunately, no recordings exist of these groups. There are two National tenors here, a 1931-34 Triolian tenor, and a style 1 tenor from the same era. The style 1 appears to have 8 strings, but the extra gears have an added-on look to them.

The Ruiz Rumbadors photo may be slightly older, since there are no electric instruments present. A 1930-32 Style O is on the left and a rare 1932-33 El Trovador is on the right.

This photo shows a rare Bakelite Rickenbacher Tenor guitar, as well as another style 1 National tenor (left), and a 1937-38 Trojan on the right. Any information about these four groups would be most appreciated by the author.

Solomon Uki Makekau, an unrecorded (and therefore, today, unknown) artist in a studio shot from the late 1920's. He is playing an early style 2 tricone with extra coverplate engraving indicating a serial number below 500. Information about this artist is sought by the author for future editions.

John Kahookano, taken in the late 30's, and signed to his friend, Hawaiian musician Johnny Pineapple.

Unknown group from Australia, with the steel player using a style O guitar.

Canadian musician Mel Henderson with his group, from the early 1930's. This artist performed on radio, but never recorded.

Lani McIntire (with Style 3 tricone) accompanies Bing Crosby in this still from the 1937 film, Waikiki Wedding.

Hoot Gibson's Hawaiian Four, in a promotional shot from the 1930 National catalog. Hoot's career as a Hollywood cowboy in the late 1930's and 1940's is fairly well-documented. However little is known about the history or the personnel of his late 1920's Hawaiian group. This group cut four songs on the Okeh label in 1928. It may be that Hoot Gibson sponsored this group only, rather than playing with them. The vocalists on the records definitely sound Hawaiian, and one vocal credit is given to Kaena Silva. These four songs, particularly one titled Mai Givee, feature the most exciting duet steel breaks ever recorded. It is difficult to make two steels sound good together, but these musicians were incredible. The man on the left holds a rare style 3 tricone tenor guitar, the man second from left plays a roundneck style 3 in Hawaiian position. Hoot's tricone appears to have the pre-incorporation (non- shield) logo in the peghead. It is a shame there weren't more recordings made by this quartet.

Photos from the 1930 catalog--CLOCKWISE FROM LEFT: The exotic Betty "Trojo" Kaimano, with a style 4 tricone with her stage name factory engraved on the side. From the 1930 National catalog. By the mid-1930's she switched to a Rickenbacher electric AND bobbed her hair. The Silvertone Melody Boys, radio and vaudeville artists; Russell Thompson Trio, radio artists (note National uke); Irene and Albert Patton in a music store with style 2 Nationals.

Fred Walker's Troubadours, perhaps one of the largest all-National groups ever photographed. It is too bad this radio and vaudeville group never made records— the sound of this many resonator instruments together at once would be downright frightening! A wide variety of Nationals are displayed here, from Triolians, to tricones, mandolins and ukes. The two men standing in front hold very early triplate mandolins.

CHAPTER 7

TAMPA RED

While Sol Hoopii was the first musician to record with a National, Tampa Red was the first black blues player to make records with one. Born Hudson Whittaker in 1903 at Smithville, Georgia, Tampa was to become perhaps the greatest recorded bottleneck guitarist of the 1920s and 30s. He also was one of the first Southern black players to establish a recording career in Chicago. Tampa was one of the first professional black studio guitarists, preceded only by Blind Blake and Lonnie Johnson.

Tampa's pioneering use of a National tricone guitar earned him the nickname of "The Man with the Gold Guitar." His tricone, apparently gold-plated, was a very early Style 4 Spanish guitar, with the separate fronds of chrysanthemums on the coverplate, rather than the later 'flow-through' design. Only one other gold-plated National has been seen, a square-neck Style 4. The location of Tampa Red's gold guitar remains a mystery.

The power and tone of the tricone guitar was very desirable as a means of cutting through the poor recording quality of that time. The flashy visual stage appeal of these shiny nickelled instruments was unbeatable. However, it is more than Tampa's early use of the National that set him apart. His bottleneck technique was considerably more musical and accurate than most of his recording musical contemporaries. He had a strong and very clean sound, due to his early discovery of damping techniques. His music had a relaxed and controlled feeling, somewhat lighter in texture than the heavier Mississippi players. He relied on single- string playing primarily, rarely using full chords. He used his right thumb to provide rhythm--not the every-beat steady Mississippi style, but in a carefully planned but sparse-sounding manner that implied the underlying rhythm.

Tampa's first break in Chicago came when he worked a short time in Ma Rainey's band, and met Georgia Tom Dorsey. While Dorsey was already involved in church activities that would eventually lead to a lifelong career in gospel music, he reluctantly provided a tune for Tampa's "little song" called It's Tight Like That. The recorded song, on Vocalion records, became a huge hit, netting the duo $2,400. on the first royalty check--tremendous money for any musicians of the day, let alone rural black players. Dorsey put off his gospel career for a few years, making records jointly with Tampa as the Hokum Boys, or Tampa Red's Hokum Jug Band. The other group members came and went at various sessions, but Tampa's National was always at the center of the sound.

Many of Tampa Red's 1928-32 recordings (about 90 sides) were duets with Georgia Tom. Most of these records were in novelty-blues style with double-entendre lyrics. Presumably, this style of music, with its mixture of scorn and nostalgia for the old rural South, was meant to appeal to recently urbanized country people. These numbers sold very well and many were copied in some form by almost every blues artist of the day, probably at the behest of the record companies. Many times the duo backed other singers such as Frankie Jaxon, Ma Rainey, Lil Johnson, or Madlyn Davis.

The early type of style 4 tricone with separate clumps of floral engraving on the coverplate, used by Tampa Red.

When Georgia Tom (Dorsey) left the world of blues in 1932 to go into gospel composing and performing, Tampa organzized a quintet for recording more modern blues, securing a contract with Bluebird records. However, he continued to record some guitar solo or duet numbers as late as 1937, still using the National guitar. Like most other players, he eventually switched to electric guitar for the remainder of his career. From the late 1930s until the end of his recording career, Tampa recorded dozens of sides of rather standard-sounding more modern Chicago blues. Tampa had lasting influence on other recording artists, and his use of the National on his very popular records caused many other players to gravitate towards resonator instruments. Many recordings exist today of Tampa Red, but perhaps the best sampling will be found on Yazoo L-1039, which covers the years 1928-1937.

Tampa Red in 1928 with his early type style 4 tricone.
This guitar was reportedly gold plated.

143

Son House with a 1931 Duolian.

SON HOUSE

Eddie "Son" House was one of the main links in the musical chain of development of Mississippi-to-Chicago blues. Directly influenced by the great Charley Patton, Son House was a main influence in the music of Robert Johnson and Muddy Waters. Son's influence is obvious on the records of Robert Johnson, and Muddy Waters once described his musical origins as part himself, part Robert Johnson, and part Son House. Of all of these players, Son was the only one who performed and recorded exclusively with a National guitar. He generally used a single-resonator guitar, either a Triolian, Duolian, or a Style O, playing with an extremely heavy and driving feeling.

House was born in Lyon, a small town near Clarksdale, Mississippi in 1902. He was raised in Louisiana, and moved frequently with his family. As a young man he worked at farming and various odd jobs. At 20, he was employed at a steel plant in East St. Louis. He did not even begin playing guitar until 1926, when he was living back in Mississsppi. He learned some guitar from Willie Wilson and James McCoy (both unrecorded), and was performing at house parties within a few weeks of learning to play. In 1927 or 28, Son was playing in a juke joint when a man went on a shooting rampage, hitting Son in the leg. Son shot the man dead and received a fifteen-year sentence at the notorious Parchman Farm prison. One year later he was released, and moving to Lula, he met Charley Patton, who introduced him to Willie Brown. The three began playing together often, travelling to Wisconsin in 1930 to make their now-legendary recordings for Paramount records. House and Brown became close friends.

At this session, House recorded Dry Spell Blues, My Black Mama, and Preachin' Blues. These recordings easily demonstrate all the power, rhythm, and passion of a classic Delta blues performance. Son played simple repeated phrases on his National in open G ("Spanish") tuning, using stinging bottleneck contrasted with strong punchy bass lines. The chord structures were very primitive: either one-chord songs, or else simple 12-bar structures with only partial allusions to standard blues changes. Son really threw his entire being into his singing and playing, as if it was his last chance each time, leaving the listener positively overwhelmed. Unlike many other bluesmen, he never overstated or exaggerated his importance in blues history, saying "I ain't the best." Son's 1930 records had very small sales, not surprising considering Son's provincial background and brief local performing career. They are impossibly rare today, but have been made available on various re-issue LPs, on Biograph and OJL.

Son's only other 78rpm recordings were made by Alan Lomax of the Library of Congress in 1941, on a farm near Robinsonville. Son still used a National, and his style had not really changed at all. Perhaps due to maturity, Son's overall sound is darker and more controlled. Re-issues of these recordings may be found on the Folklyric label. When musical tastes changed in the 1940s, Son became very discouraged and gave up music. He moved to Rochester, New York in 1943, working at various non-musical jobs. A major personal loss occurred in 1948 when his lifelong friend and playing-partner Willie Brown died. Son always had great ambivalence about the playing of blues ("devil's music") conflicting with his strong religious leanings. This conflict is shown in many of his lyrics, which range from religious to highly cynical comments about the "business" of re-ligion in the rural South, in addition to the standard blues lyrics of love and its abuses.

Son was re-discovered in 1964, when three enthusiastic young white blues fans found him in Rochester. They played him tapes of his old records, told him that audiences were there again for his music, and he re-learned his old material. Son was able to travel, perform, record and receive the recognition he never got in his youth. While he never regained his full strength vocally or instrumentally, thousands of people have been able to enjoy a reasonable facsimile of the authentic Delta Blues of the 1920s. Son's health declined and he retired again, passing away in the early 1980s. The best of the 1960s recordings will be found on Columbia CS 9217, and Blue Goose 2016.

While Son House never really broke new ground with the guitar, his vocals were so strong and emotional as to make his simple guitar parts work well. The primary listening pleasure to be derived from Son's guitar-playing is the intensely driving rhythm and the deeply moving blue notes of his bottleneck playing. He was such a powerful singer that any other guitar besides a National would have been drowned out on the recordings.

Son at work with a 1931 Style O, variation 4.

BUKKA WHITE

The National guitar was absolutely essential to the rough blues sound of Bukka White, born Booker T. Washington White on November 12, 1909 at Houston, Mississippi. An extremely strident and percussive player, White had the following to say about his consistent use of a National (usually single-cone) guitar:

"It is loud! I wouldn't need no mike, and also I play so rough, I would have busted many wood guitars. This one can take rain and punishment--I stomp them; I don't peddle them." Spoken like a true National devotee.

Bukka (he preferred to be called Booker) was one of eight children, and left home early, wandering around the Delta and as far north as Memphis. He was raised about 50 miles east of Dockery's plantation, home to Charley Patton and his blues cronies. While not coming under the direct musical influence of Patton, White certainly admired Patton's reputation as a "great man." Having had some rudimentary musical education from his father, a guitarist and violinist, Bukka began travelling and performing at small joints around the Delta and up to Memphis. He also spent time in St. Louis, where at the age of 14, he would paint on a moustache to look 21 in order to play at clubs there. Booker described his exploits in those days as follows: "I wasn't paying the time no attention--was traveling so fast-- in them days it was easy to get jobs playing--but my main job was looking for pretty girls."

By 1930, at 21 years of age, Bukka was already an accomplished bottleneck blues player. In Itta Bena, Miss. Booker met Ralph Limbo, an informal A & R man for Victor records. Limbo cut a deal with Victor for 8 songs by White, for $800, from which White received $240 and a new National guitar. He made his first records in May 1930 for Victor which resulted in the issue of four sides, including the now-famous train song, The Panama Limited. This number featured nearly every trainlike sound that a National can make, and a storytelling spoken narrative by Booker. He was accompanied on second guitar by Napoleon Hairiston, a very obscure figure. These Victor records did not sell well, being released during the depression on a 75-cent label, and are quite rare today.

Over the next several years, Booker White was engaged in street singing, prize-fighting and ball pitching, among other odd jobs. He travelled extensively through the South during this period and appeared in Chicago on September 2, 1937, where he cut Shake 'Em On Down/ Pinebluff, Arkansas for Vocalion. Total sales for this record exceeded 16,000 copies, making it a relative "hit" in blues recording of those days.

What looked like a promising recording career for Booker was cut short in 1937, when, in a fracas similar to the one Son House was involved in, Bukka drew a gun and killed a man, presumably in self-defense. In his own words,

Booker White with a rare "exploding palm tree" tricone. Though he holds it upright, this guitar is a squareneck.

"I had to burn a guy a little." He was sent to Parchman Farm, where conditions were quite vile for most convicts. According to Booker, his music was so well-liked by the warden that White spent most of his sentence entertaining him rather than doing hard labor. In fact, Vocalion records tried to secure his early release to make more records and was turned down by the warden because he enjoyed Bukka's music so much.

John Lomax visited Parchman Farm on May 24, 1939 with his recording equipment. Lomax, of course, had recorded hundreds of prison and work-farm musicians over the years. He recorded two songs by Booker White at Parchman. Since no money was forthcoming from these recordings, Booker refused to cut more than the first two songs, Sic 'Em Dogs on Me, and Po' Boy Long Way From Home.

Sometime before March 1940, Vocalion was able to secure Booker's release, and at the incredibly low artist fee of $17.50 per song, they recorded 12 more songs by Booker, accompanied by Washboard Sam. This wonderful body of material was well-recorded and the songs almost all dealt with factual and emotional renderings of Booker's prison experiences. For an uneducated black man who barely understood the concept of rhyming blues lyrics, Booker's lyrics are incredibly deep and sensitive, describing the human condition under tough times. There is a slight element of protest in Booker's lyrics, very unusual for recording blues artists of the day. With a sound like older Delta blues and pre-blues styles, these recordings are quite primitive musically for 1940. However, it must be assumed that the thematic content of these songs made them relatively popular among rural black record-buyers. These recordings were made available to the public in the 1960s by Columbia, (number C30036).

Booker's guitar playing on his National was very powerful and exciting, while maintaining a relaxed feeling rhythmically. His bottleneck playing was among the best, and his unusual use of D minor tuning provided a haunting harmonic quality. He was comfortable with alternating-bass fingerpicking as well as what may appear to the uninitiated as wild flailing. His rhythmic sense was steady and flawless, and beautifully complemented his powerful yet sensitive singing.

In 1952, Booker got involved in another scrape which got him six months on a county work farm. Upon his release, he secured a day job which he held until his re-discovery in 1963. His 1940 recording of Aberdeen Mississippi Blues led to his re-discovery by Ed Denson and John Fahey. They located him by sending a letter to Bukka White, old blues singer, General Delivery, Aberdeen Miss. He immediately began touring the States and Europe, and recorded several albums for Takoma, Biograph, and Arhoolie. All of these 1960s recordings are excellent, though his voice had become rougher over the years. His playing had not diminished in any way. The Arhoolie albums contain delightful spoken stories of Booker's childhood and youth, infused with humor and color.

Booker White died in the late 1970s, having left his mark on blues history, and having proved the utility and desirabilty of National resonator guitars. His sound is intimately and inextricably linked to the National.

BO CARTER

National guitars were built to give a lifetime of service, and very few guitars were ever used long enough to actually begin to wear out. Bo Carter's National was thouroughly played-out by the end of his life in the early 1960s, which gives one an idea of how much he used it.

Born to the now-legendary Chatmon family in 1898 on Dr. Dupree's plantation near Bolton, Mississippi, Bo was named Armenter Chatmon at birth. The Chatmon family had musicians in it stretching back to near-slavery times. A racial mixture of black, Indian, and white, this large family entertained in various string band formats at both white and black social functions. Charley Patton reportedly was a half-brother to Bo and his eleven musical brothers including Lonnie and Sam.

Out of this family band, together with brothers Sam and Lonnie, and Walter Jacobs, Bo created the Mississippi Sheiks. The Sheiks were known all over the South from their numerous and popular recordings. Their musical repertoire consisted of blues, country dance tunes, popular and folk songs, and occasional hillbilly numbers. Lonnie and Sam recorded separately, as did Bo--in fact Bo's solo recordings of 1931- 1940 are what he is best remembered for. He was the most successful Sheik in terms of a solo recording career. Almost all of these records feature Bo's single-cone National guitar.

Bo alternately farmed, repaired phonographs, did carpentry and entertained on weekends, from c.1912 through the early 1920's. He moved to Jackson in 1923, and in the late 1920s he served as the personal "minstrel" of the owner of the Drew plantation near Hollandale. By the 1930s, the recording studio had become his main performing venue. Of all the Chatman brothers, Bo had the best business head and was least inclined to drink the liquor provided at sessions to loosen up the musicians. Perhaps these characteristics as well as his snappy double-entendre songs helped him secure a long contract with Bluebird records.

Carter was a rather sophisticated musician for a country bluesman. He played his National in five different tunings, variants of standard, open G, and open D or E. He also reportedly used all five fingers of his right hand in picking, however this cannot be confirmed by listening to his records. His range of musical knowledge and style went beyond blues, probably because of his long musical education playing white dances with his family and with the Sheiks. The changes Bo adds to his songs sound like popular and jazz chord changes. However, he occasionally reveals his down- home roots by accompanying with inappropriate bass notes on open strings. His playing varied a lot during each song, with strummed or picked chords acompanying vocals, and with sharply attacked single-note treble runs in between vocal phrases. These runs were almost all flawlessly played, and demonstrated Bo's familiarity with jazz and popular melodies. Unlike many bluesmen who tailor what they play to the particular tuning they are in, Bo was able to transmit his personal esthetics through any of his tunings--in other words to get similar sounds in different tunings.

Most of Bo's songs were ribald, with such titles as Please Warm My Weiner, Let Me Roll Your Lemon, etc. But even these sexually enthusiastic vocals have a bit of a melancholy shade to them, and his gently swinging guitar playing often approached the sound and sensitivity of Mississippi John Hurt. His output of recordings was quite large, and he apparently could work very fast in the studio. His last two sessions, in 1938 and 1940, each contain an amazing amount of work for a one-day session: eighteen and fourteen titles, respectively. Fourteen Bo Carter recordings may be heard on Yazoo L-1034. They come from his 1931-40 Bluebird sessions, and the originals are beautifully recorded, from a technical standpoint. The sound of Bo's National rings out loud and clear, making it possible for today's listeners to easily enjoy the work of a vintage artist on a factory-fresh National.

Photo courtesy

Bo Carter, 1960, with a well-worn National style N guitar.

148

BLIND BOY FULLER

One of the most famous blues recording artists who used a National on all of his recordings was Fulton Allen, better known as Blind Boy Fuller. He is best known as one of the strongest exponents of the Carolina style of playing, influencing many other recording artists. This bouyant style, as exemplified by other artists such as Blind Blake and Rev. Gary Davis, reflects the easygoing environment of the Southeast. The harsher conditions of the Mississippi Delta produced a more intense musical style. The music from the Carolines, Virginia, and Georgia is often grouped together and referred to as the Piedmont style.

The date of Fuller's birth is not clearly documented, but falls between 1909 and 1913. No information exists on his early days, but apparently he was the only one of his 11 siblings to play guitar. His family moved to Rockingham, North Carolina in the mid 1920s. At some point in his childhood, Fuller had increasing difficulty with his eyesight, and was partially blind by 1927 when he met his wife, Cora Martin. It is said that a Charleston doctor attributed his blindness to ulcers behind his eyes, and according to Cora Martin, he was not totally blind until 1928. This is when he turned seriously to music as a living. Like so many other blind musicians of those days, there were few other career choices to make.

He left Rockingham in 1928 for the more prosperous tobacco town of Winston-Salem. The presence of a large workforce there gave Fuller a ready audience for him to develop his playing and repertoire, as well as the ability to improvise lyrics to fit various situations. He also spent time in the early 1930s in Durham, another large tobacco town.

In the 1920s record companies often engaged local record or furniture (gramophone) store owners as talent scouts for blues and hillbilly performers. Many of the greatest recording artists of these genres were discovered by such talent scouts. In the Carolina area, James Baxter Long was a powerful force in this area. To find good recording prospects, he would rent halls and hold fiddler's contests, gospel and blues auditions, etc. Long was a manager of several stores, and was promoted in 1935 to manage the United Dollar Stores in the tobacco district of Durham. It was only a matter of time before Fuller and Long would meet. In the summer of 1935, Fuller was led to Long's shop, and began a successful recording career which was more prolific than most of other recorded bluesmen.

Between July, 1935 and Fuller's death in June 1940, he had 135 songs released. The quality of the music on all these sessions was consistently high. He used two different National Duolians during his recording career, a 12-fret and a 14-fret. Even though he made plenty of records, Fuller thought of himself primarily as a street musician, never really playing on any stages. Musician Willie Trice recalls being in New York with Fuller for a Decca recording session and noted how impatient Fuller was to get out on the streets of New York to try his luck at entertaining. He seldom went anywhere without someone to lead him, and, other than his visit to New York, usually travelled only in the Carolinas.

Like Robert Johnson in Mississippi, Fuller's records show the influence of other musicians' records. This extension of the oral folk tradition really began taking hold by the mid-1930s. By the time Fuller took up music full-time in 1928, Blind Blake had already been recording for two years.

Many of Fuller's records show similarities to Blake's. Willie Trice and also J.B. Long recall Fuller listening intently to records, and many songs in the later 1930s were borrowed back and forth, with occasional conflicting claims. An additional influence was J.B. Long, who apparently though himself enough of a judge of popular tastes to write, or rewrite songs for Fuller to record. He also spent time rehearsing Fuller for a few days before each session. This type of devotion from a casual talent scout is amazing, and other bluesmen such as Brownie McGhee have spoken very highly of Long. Fuller had many top-selling records and would have continued, no doubt, but for his death in 1941. Long soon retired from his musical activities, after half-heartedly trying to replace Fuller with Brownie McGhee, whom he dubbed "Blind Boy Fuller #2." McGhee chafed under this name, and of course went on to make his own name. Still, the death of Fuller and the retirement of Long signalled the effective end of the Piedmont tradition, until the re-discovery of several Piedmont artists in the 1960s.

Blind Boy Fuller with a 1933 Duolian.

WALTER VINCENT,
aka WALTER JACOBS

Thought known best for his supporting work with the Chatmon brothers, Walter Vincent also made recordings under his own name, with his own songs in the Jackson, Miss. style. Born in Hinds County Mississippi on Feb 2, 1901, he became interested in music at an early age, like so many of his peers. He began entertaining in his ealy teens at local parties and picnics. Living near Crystal Springs in the early twenties, he was one of numerous musicians who were strongly influenced by the two leading stylists of the area--

One of many 1930's recordings of the Sheiks.

Walter Vincent, 1970's.

Tommy Johnson and Ishman Bracey. The Jackson style, as it is known, had many adherents stretching from 1920 to 1950, and the entire Chatmon clan could be said to be included in that group.

Walter Vincent worked occasionally with Johnson and Bracey, until 1928, when he teamed up with fiddler Lonnie Chatmon. The Chatmon brothers, with all their various and versatile perfoming/recording combinations, kept very busy even during the Depression. Notable sessions which include Vincent's string-snapping guitar playing:

1929-30: Mississippi Hot Footers, for Brunswick records
1930: Carter Brothers, for Okeh, San Antonio TX
1930: with Bo Chatmon, for Okeh, Atlanta, GA
1930: Mississippi Sheiks, for Okeh, Shreveport, LA
1930-32: solo sessions for Okeh, Atlanta, GA
1932: Paramount records, Grafton WI
1933: Mississippi Sheiks, for Okeh, NY
1934: Bluebird, San Antonio, TX
1936: Decca, New Orleans, LA

The reader can begin to get a sense of the popularity of the Sheiks and other similar Chatmon groups by looking at the far flung recording locations above. Presumably the boys had no problem finding gigs along the way. The Sheiks broke up in the mid 1930s, and each of them continued recording through the 1930s on their own. Vincent's own records featured strong singing and Jackson-style blues guitar, clearly recorded and demonstrating his rhythmic ease and Delta-style string snaps. He also accompanied other blues singers for various labels until 1941. Like so many other bluesmen caught up in the changing times and economy of the War years, Vincent moved to Chicago and worked outside of music until his re-discovery during the early folk boom of 1961-62.

He played at several large folk festivals throughout the nation in the 1960s, and in 1972, Rounder records included him in a historic re-creation of the Mississippi Sheiks. This highly charged album also featured Sam Chatmon, the only other original Sheik. After several years of illness, Walter Vincent passed away on April 22, 1975

Walter Vincent, 1970's.

151

PEETIE WHEATSTRAW

The photograph shows a proud man with his tricone, presumably a Style 3 or 4, judging by the fretboard inlays. This fellow, William Bunch by birth, was known by his friends and fans as Peetie Wheatstraw. His professional sobriquets were The Devil's Son-in-Law, and the High Sheriff from Hell. Known more for his piano and singing than guitar, Wheatstraw recorded over 160 songs in a recording career which went from 1930 to his death in 1941. He also accompanied several other blues singers on their records as well, most notably guitarist Charley Jordan. Peetie's singing style especially influenced many other concurrent and later recording artists.

Born in Ripley, Tennessee in 1902, Peetie's early whereabouts are unknown, though he apparently had family in Cotton Plant, Arkansas. That is where his body was shipped upon his death in St. Louis from an auto crash, so presumably that is where he lived before his last 12 years which were spent in St. Louis. According to those who knew him, when he arrived in St. Louis in the late 1920s he was primarily playing guitar. However, the St. Louis area was known for its large group of competitive piano players, who no doubt inspired him. By the early 1930s, Wheatstraw was considered to be an equal of the top St. Louis piano men. He stayed close to St. Louis and East St. Louis generally, and lefttown mainly for recording dates.

Due to the hard economic times of the Depression, record companies were regrouping and scaling back their race record catalogs. Several recording careers were ending or slowing down as Peetie entered Vocalion's Chicago studio on August 13, 1930 to begin his recording career. Despite the general effects of the Depression, his records sold well enough for the company to call him back for over a half-dozen more sessions. Peetie's lyrics began to reflect his self-image as the Devil's Son-in-Law, and probably help elevate his popularity. His Vocalion records began to include the Devil's Son-in-Law nickname on the labels. In 1931, he cut a session for Bluebird, including the self-promotingly titled Pete Wheatstraw Blues. Within this song he even tells the listener who wrote it. He later recorded a few more titles of similiar or even more self-conscious bragging--Peetie Wheatstraw Stomp and Peetie Wheatstraw Stomp #2. No shortage of creative titles from this guy.

There was a two-year hiatus until his next recordings in 1934, and by this time Peetie had crystallized his style into an instantly recognizable form. The well-known "oooh well, well" trademark of his vocals has been imitated by many other blues singers. By the time Prohibition was repealed, he had a couple of hits concerning the return of high quality whiskey. One measure of Peetie's widespread popularity was the number of other lesser known blues musicians who used similar nicknames--one fellow named Harmon Ray billed himself as Peetie's Buddy. Ralph Ellison's novel "Invisible Man" has a Peetie Wheatstraw character in it, and as it turns out, Ellison actually knew him and created the character based on Peetie.

Peetie's healthy recording career continued, as a solo artist and in conjuction with Lonnie Johnson, Louis Jordan, Kokomo Arnold, and several others. Some of the later dates inexplicably featured Peetie only as a singer, with rather uninspired accompaniments. This is somewhat strange in view of the fairly high caliber jazz musicians employed at these sessions. It seems as if things were not going as well for Peetie in 1941, because his records began to take on a more gloomy tone. Strangely and prophetically, his last session before his accidental death included titles such as "Hearse Man Blues," and "Bring Me Flowers When I'm Living."

At 11:30 in the morning on December 21, 1941, the car Peetie was riding in failed to make a curve, and crashed into a standing freight train car, less than a block from Peetie's home. His death was noted in articles in several St. Louis area newspapers as well as in Variety, Billboard and Down Beat.

Peetie Wheatstraw with a style 3 tricone.

SCRAPPER BLACKWELL

Scrapper Blackwell, born Feb 21, 1903 in South Carolina, is best known for his supporting role as guitarist with pianist/singer Leroy Carr. Of black and Cherokee Indian heritage, his birth name was Francis Hillman Blackwell. His nickname was given to him in childhood by his grandmother.

His family with 16 children moved to Indianapolis, Indiana in 1906. By 1909, Scrapper demonstrated his early interest in music by making himself a cigar box guitar. Teaching himself music, he worked casually at parties as a teenager, travelling frequently between Indianapolis and Chicago up to the early 1920s. Blackwell often worked outside of music in the mid 1920s, as there was not a lot of work in Indianapolis yet for blues players.

In 1928, he formed a musical partnership with composer, singer, and pianist Leroy Carr which lasted until Carr's death in 1935. The duo made many, many hot-selling records for the Vocalion label from 1928-1932. Probably the most well-known song they recorded was Carr's composition "How Long, How Long." This eight-bar blues was re-interpreted by many other recording artists, with similar structure. Included in this list of similar songs are "The Key To The Highway," "Come on In My Kitchen," "Sliding Delta," "Crow Jane," etc.

As shown in the photograph, Scrapper used a 12-fret (probably walnut sunburst) Triolian guitar. As most guitarists know, it is very easy to be drowned out by the volume of a piano. Considering the primitive recording conditions of the day, Scrapper probably was very happy to discover the availability of the new louder National guitars. In 1929, Scrapper made a few solo records, and also accompanied vocalist Chippie Hill. In 1930, Blackwell visited the Richmond, Indiana Gennett recording studio a number of times, to record solo, and with Carr, Georgia Tom and Teddy Moss. Interestingly, considering his blues background, Blackwell also recorded some Gennetts with the obscure jazz band Robinson's Knights of Rest in 1930-31. These records are impossibly rare today.

Carr and Blackwell worked extensively in clubs and theaters around the midwest through the early 1930s. In 1934, the pair visited Vocalion studios in St. Louis and New York for more recording. Further recordings were made in 1935 for Champion, Bluebird and Decca. Leroy Carr was well-loved by both peers and fans, and his death in 1935 saddened many people. In fact, a recording called "The Death of Leroy Carr" was issued not long after. Scrapper Blackwell became discouraged by the death of his best friend, and left the world of music, working only occasional parties in the immediate area of Indianapolis. By the 1940s and 1950s, Blackwell could again be seen at various Indianapolis clubs, working with Champion Jack Dupree, among others. He actually got to record again for Prestige/Bluesville in the late 1950s. One of his last performances was at the Indianapolis Jazz Club concert series. Like so many other bluesmen, Scrapper Blackwell met with a violent death. He was fatally shot in a back alley in Indianapolis in 1961.

Blackwell was among the most popular recording bluesmen of his time, and his prolific songwriting and musical style had a definite role in shaping the sound of Chicago blues of the 1930s.

Scrapper Blackwell and Leroy Carr. Scrapper holds a walnut sunburst finish Triolian, c. 1931.

BUMBLE BEE SLIM

The given name of the happy guy with a brand new Style O guitar in the photo was Amos Easton. As with many other blues artists, Easton began his life in a rural Southern setting, and migrated to Northern urban centers to follow his career. He was born in the tiny town of Brunswick, Georgia, in 1905. One of six children, he developed an early interest in music, reportedly writing songs from age 10. From 1915 to 1920, Amos worked frequently outside of music, mostly as a barber.

Around 1920, Easton left home to work in a travelling circus that had passed through his area. Through the 1920's he hoboed extensively as an itinerant musician/singer across the U.S. By 1928, he was living in Indianapolis and working in small juke joints in the surrounding area. 1930 saw Easton based in Chicago, with frequent trips to Michigan, Wisconsin, and even Los Angeles. His first recordings were for Paramount, made in Grafton, Wisconsin in 1931. By 1932 he had become an established moderate-selling artist for Vocalion records. He made many sides for them in Chicago and New York from 1932 to 1937. Using variations on his professional name, he also recorded for Bluebird and Decca. Apparently he returned to the Atlanta area in the mid-1930s and performed at a large theater there.

The 1930s style of Bumble Bee Slim was becoming passe by the war years, and the war provided plenty of non-musical employment. Easton dropped out of music during those years, and surfaced for a few sporadic recordings in the 1950s. His whereabouts today are unknown.

Bumble Bee Slim with his shiny new Style O, c. 1931.

154

OSCAR ALEMAN
TRICONE JAZZ MASTER

Oscar Aleman was probably the most musically evolved person that ever played jazz on a National. He is known primarily for his work in the European jazz scene between 1928 and 1939. His work has been frequently compared to that of Django Reinhardt.

Aleman, an Argentinian Indian, was born according to varying reports in 1905 or 1910. He played cavaquinho, a Brazilian ukulele, as a child but by age 12 was touring as a guitarist with the Moriera Sextet. It was when he was working in Brazil with this band that Aleman first heard a jazz record.

At age 20 he formed a duo called Los Lobos with fellow guitarist Gaston Bueno. They traveled to Spain backing dancer Harry Fleming and decided to settle there. After seven years of work together, the duo parted ways and Aleman went to work in Paris for the well established Josephine Baker. His work as the guitarist in her band at Cafe de Paris was his debut in the European jazz world.

Aleman performed and recorded exclusively with a Style 1 National tricone. He was capable of extracting a wide range of timbres from the instrument, swung hard and light like Django, and played effortless florid arpeggios. He recorded with several artists including Sven Asmussen and Danny Polo. It was after hearing a 1939 Aleman recording made with the latter that jazz critic Leonard Feather wrote:

"He plays an all-metal instrument (National); his tone, phrasing, swing, and attack are so grand that if anyone ever mentions Django Reinhardt to me again, I shall stare coldly"

Considering that Django was at the height of his popularity, this is high praise indeed. It seems ironic that Oscar Aleman is not as well remembered today, though this is probably due to the smaller amount of recordings he left to history. He does, however, deserve a place among the pioneers of jazz guitars along with Reinhardt, Eddie Lang, Lonnie Johnson and Teddy Bunn. He is the only recording swing guitarist who used a National. Perhaps he was attracted to it's cutting power in clubs.

In 1941, presumably because of the escalation of World War II, Aleman returned to Buenos Aires. It is rumored that, before his departure, his National was confiscated at a border crossing and melted down by Nazis.

Except for a brief return to Europe, Aleman's international career came to a close at this time. Until his death in 1980, Aleman lived in a modest apartment in Buenos Aires, where he continued to perform and teach guitar.

Oscar Aleman, with his Style 1 Tricone, and saxophonist Frank "Big Boy" Goudie, c. 1935 Inset: Oscar Aleman in 1978.

BLACK ACE

One of the very few black blues players to play his National in the Hawaiian manner (lap-style with slide) was B. K. Turner, known on his records as The Black Ace. Born 7 miles from Louisiana in Hughes Springs, Texas in 1907, Turner's first exposure to music was through his local church choir singing as a child. This stimulated his interest in music, and soon he taught himself guitar on a homemade instrument. Through the 1920's he worked at local parties, dances, and picnics around Hughes Springs. Primarily, he stayed at the family farm, working full-time. By the time he was 22, he was able to buy his own guitar.

The Depression was very bad for small farmers, and soon the family had to break apart in search of other employment. In the early 1930s, he worked for a time with Smokey Hogg in the Greenville, Texas area. He then made his way to Shreveport, Louisiana. It was his good fortune to meet Oscar Buddy Woods, one of the only other black musicians to play guitat Hawaiian style. It was working with Woods that convinced Turner to change his technique to the Hawaiian method. He assimilated Buddy Woods' style, and bought himself a Style 2 National squareneck tricone. At first he tried to play it bottleneck style, but soon saw the greater flexibility in playing lap-style. He developed a few special tunings and techniques to suit his use of a medicine bottle. Sometimes he would use the edge or the corner of the bottle to get single notes sliding against open strings.

Of the three known black blues recording artists who strictly played lap style, Turner's style was in some ways vary similar to Buddy Woods'. Neither Woods or Turner were as sophisticated as Casey Bill Weldon, who adopted simple jazz progressions to his blues repertoire. It is said that Woods decided to play lap-style after seeing a performance by a travelling Hawaiian show in the early 1920s.

Turner and Woods played in open G and in open D tunings. It is difficult to say which of these two men was the better player. Turner did not have quite the grasp of harmonic theory that Woods had, though his tone and technique are equal to Woods. The songs that Turner composed and recorded are well-conceived thematically, with lyrics that show a conscious effort at coherent content. His accompaniments were simple, almost bottleneck blues in style, yet he obtained a fine, liquid tone from his tricone. Obviously, he considered himself a professional artist.

As the Depression slowly began to lift in the mid 1930s, Turner found himself more in demand, and began to travel further afield. His gigs took him through Louisiana, Oklahoma and Texas, where he settled in Ft. Worth. Inevitably, a talent scout heard him play and obtained a recording contract for him for Decca records. He recorded 6 sides, including the song "I Am the Black Ace" , which gave him his professional name. Vocalion also recorded Turner in 1938, but only 2 sides were issued, under the obscure name Buck Turner. Ace frequently appeared on radio station KFJZ in Ft. Worth and other stations between 1936 and 1941. He actually appeared as a performer in the 1937 film, "The Blood of Jesus."

Turner was drafted for World War II in 1943. As he has said, "Uncle Sam told me come on, let's go fight, and that broke up the musical career and I quit then, 1943." After the war, Turner and his wife were reduced to picking cotton to eke out a living. By 1950, he secured a janitorial job at the Ft. Worth Airport. In 1960, he was re-discovered by Chris Strachwitz, and an Arhoolie record was recorded by Black Ace that year. He also appeared in one more film, "The Blues," in 1962. After a ten year retirement, Ace died of cancer in Ft. Worth on Nov. 7, 1972.

Black Ace playing his squareneck tricone, style 2.

"Big" Mike McKendrick with his guitar-shaped National tenor, from a 1932 short film with Louis Armstrong.

THE "MIKE" McKENDRICK BROTHERS

With very few exceptions, guitarists have gotten very little attention from writers and critics of 1920s jazz. The unsung heroes of all the great jazz bands were guitarists who kept the rhythm, but whose sound was often buried on recordings. National was well aware of the limitations of ordinary guitars and the frustration of dance orchestra guitarists who felt drowned out by their bandmates. The early catalogs intentionally targeted orchestra players, though more Hawaiians, hillbilly and blues artists wound up with Nationals than did dance orchestra players. When National brought out its tenor and plectrum guitar models, the Company specifically aimed them at orchestra banjoists. The catalog cited the then-new trend of banjoists switching to guitars and suggested the resophonic tenor and plectrums as a sweet sounding double for banjo players.

The two greatest players of National tenor guitars in a jazz setting were the McKendrick Brothers. To the utter confusion of discographers and jazz writers, both brothers were professionally known as Mike McKendrick! Both of them played tenor Nationals with hot black bands. The brothers were born into a musical family and all five brothers were given the middle name of Michael. The father, Gilbert Michael McKendrick was a trombonist and violinist. The five sons and their instruments: Gilbert Michael, Jr. b. 1903 banjo/tenor guitar/ vocals Reuben Michael b. 1901 banjo/tenor guitar/ vocals Richard Michael, trombone Daniel Michael, violin James Michael, piano

Here we are concerned with Gilbert, Jr. ("Little Mike McKendrick") and Reuben ("Big Mike McKendrick"). Both men participated frequently in some of the greatest jazz records ever made. The family came from Paris, Tennessee, and moved to Chicago, probably by 1920. Chicago, of course, was a hotbed of jazz and recording activity, so it was natural for the McKendricks to gravitate there and find work.

Little Mike's first known job was with the obscure Hughie Swift Orchestra, in the mid-1920s. For a while he was with Doc Cooke and His Fourteen Doctors of Syncopation, and Joe Jordan's Sharps and Flats. He found a great vehicle for his talents as a tenor guitarist for hot violinist Eddie South's small jazz group. He is present with his National tenor (a style 2 tricone, see photo) on the great Victor recordings of Eddie South and his Alabamians. The records afford several brief opportunities for Little Mike to strut his stuff. On most of them, the National cuts through and has that unmistakable tricone tone. He went to Europe with Eddie South in 1928. Around this time he was involved in a shooting incident with musician Sidney Bechet. He left Eddie South in late 1931 and formed his own "International Band" which worked mostly in France and Spain for the next eight years. In 1939, he returned to the U.S. and, after a brief stay in new York, settled back in Chicago where he formed his own "International Trio". He continued working with his own group and as sideman in other bands through the 1950s until his death in Chicago in 1961.

Reuben "Big Mike" McKendrick also found the Chicago area to be ideal for his tenor guitar

talents, and he worked with many bands. He appeared on a lot more recordings than Little Mike. Bands he worked in prior to playing a National were Oscar Young Orch.(mid 1920s), Edgar Hayes Eight Black Pirates (1927), Dave Peyton (1927) and again with Oscar Young (1928- 1929).

The first recordings in which we hear Big Mike playing a National tenor are the fascinating jazz records by Tiny Parham's Musicians. Parham was an unusual recording artist, because his entire output consisted of self-composed and arranged jazz tunes, rather than well-known jazz numbers or Tin Pan Alley tunes. His preferred sound was a very

"Little" Mike McKendrick in 1928, proudly holding his style 2 tricone tenor while posing with Eddie South's band.

sparse bluesy sonority, with plenty of room for solos between the arranged passages. Resophonic tenor solos by Big Mike abound on the 30-odd records made by Parham between 1929 and 1931. McKendrick had very clear phrasing and solid ideas with a good blues foundation on his solos. His single-note playing popped out with confident authority and could cut like a trumpet. He is yet another player whose technique was shaped in part by the tonal characteristics of a resonator instrument.

From early 1931 to 1933, Big Mike joined Louis Armstrong's Orchestra, which was then at its pinnacle, one of the top black bands in the business. He played both banjo and his single-cone National tenor on dozens of records and countless gigs. He also acted as band manager for Louis, no doubt an educational program in itself. McKendrick can been seen with his National in a few short films of Armstrong's band--a Betty Boop cartoon and a short subject from 1932. While the band is swinging hard at a breakneck tempo, Mike seems completely relaxed as he swats out precise rhythms.

Mike led his own band for a while in the mid 1930s, and also worked with Erskine Tate, Zutty Singleton and Cleo Brown. While maintaining his own band, he also worked regularly in a duo with Banjo Ikey Robinson (shown with National Triolian tenor). As jazz music changed and faded in Chicago, McKendrick was able to continue working small clubs intermittently through the 1950s and 1960s. He ended his career after a long stint as a house musician at Jazz, Ltd, Chicago, and died in 1965.

While National did not manufacture a tremendous amount of tenor guitars, it still seems odd that so few of them are heard on records. In all probability, the legions of tenor banjoists who switched to guitar in the late 1920s went directly to six-string guitar, passing the now-obscure tenor and plectrum guitars made by Martin, Gibson, National and others. With the output of both McKendrick brothers, the listener and/or musician of today can get a good idea of the potential and range of these unusual instruments.

"Big" Mike in a group shot with Armstrong c.1933. He is holding a style 1 guitar-shaped tenor.

1927 Style 2 Tricone, very early example, #133, with extra top holes

Spanish Neck Tricones: Left, 1928 Style 3, #0675, and 1928 Style 4, #0769

Hawaiian Tricone Guitars, Left, 1932 Style 3, #2568 and 1929 Style 4, #1173

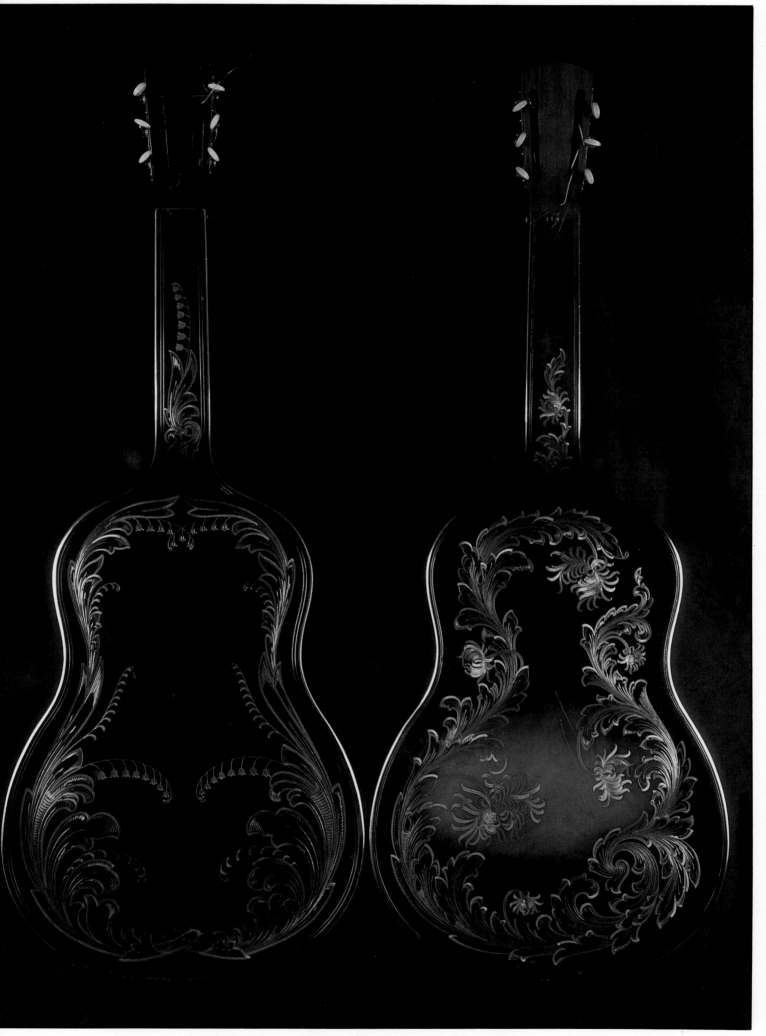

Old world craftsmanship meets modern technology--back of the Tricones on the facing page

1933 Style 4 Spanish Guitar, #S4857

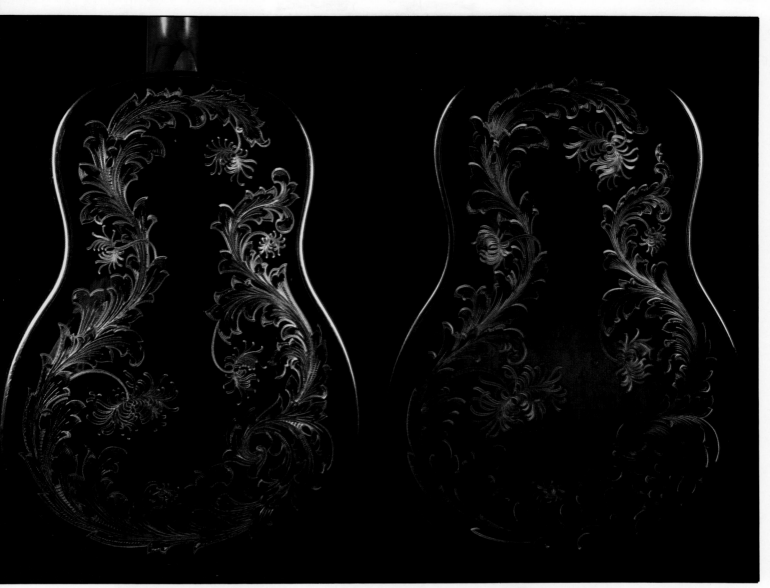

Detail of engraving: 1933 Style 4

Detail of engraving: 1929 Style 4, note the differences in the work of two different men on these two guitars

Side view of 1933 Style 4

Side view of 1929 Style 4, custom engraved at the factory for Chicago music teacher Henry Dixon

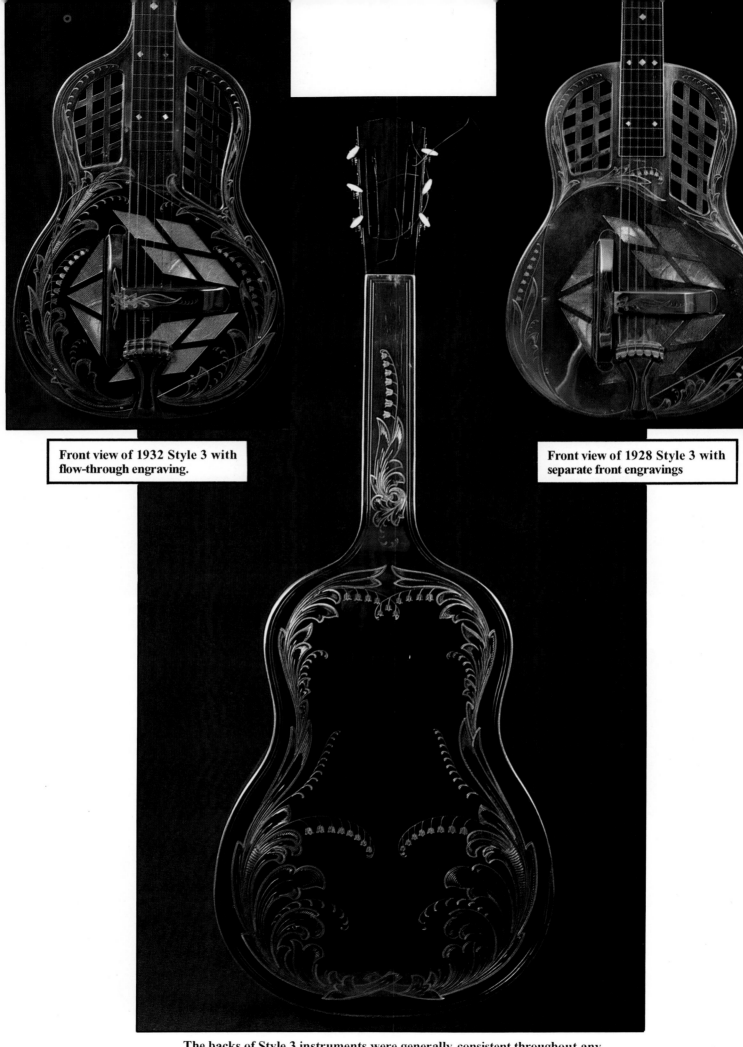

Front view of 1932 Style 3 with flow-through engraving.

Front view of 1928 Style 3 with separate front engravings

The backs of Style 3 instruments were generally consistent throughout any changes in the front pattern

Style 4 examples, with unique 1929 presentation silver mandolin

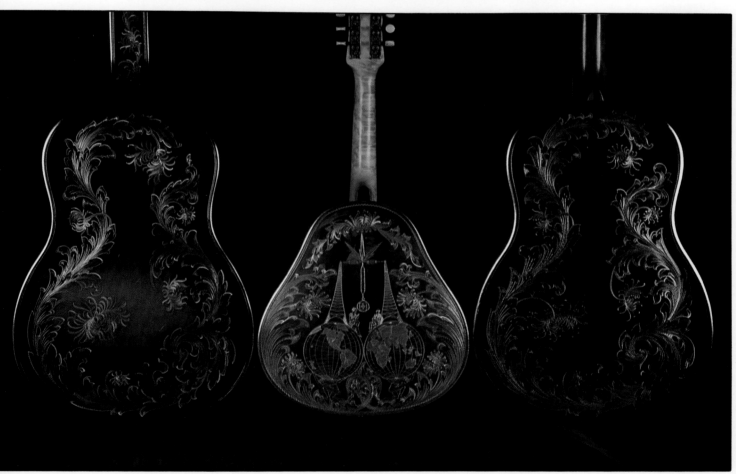

12 fret 1931-32 Style O guitar, #S-3829

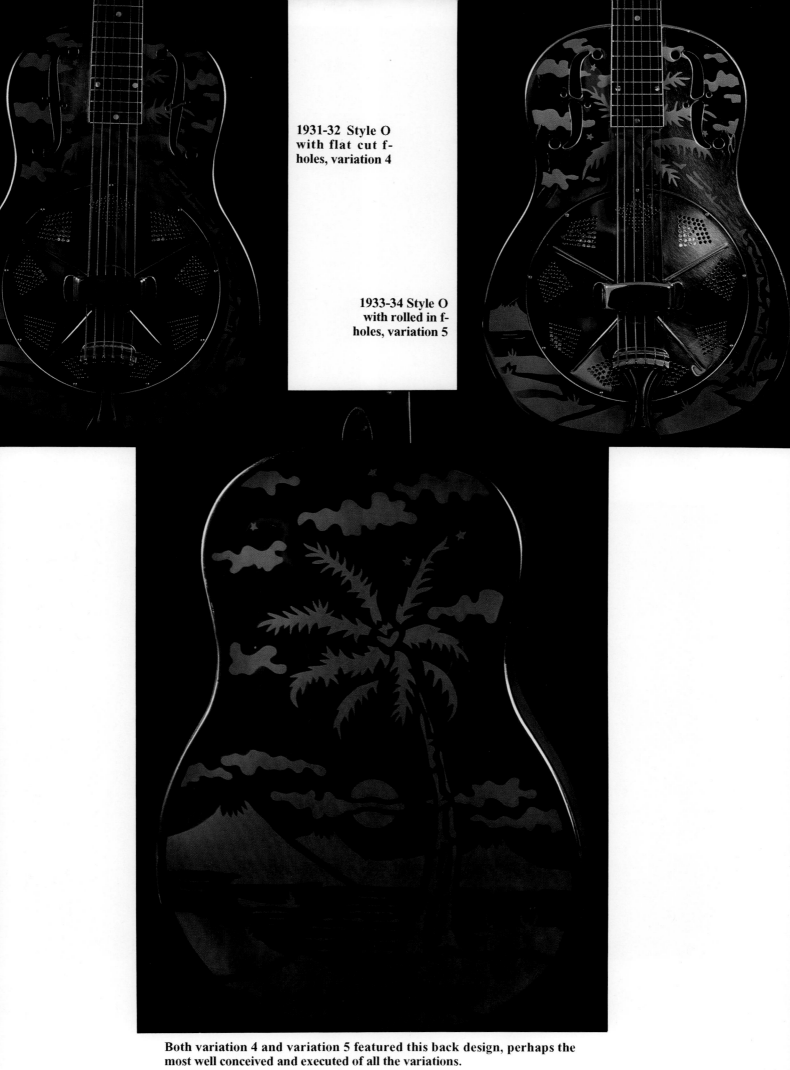

1931-32 Style O with flat cut f-holes, variation 4

1933-34 Style O with rolled in f-holes, variation 5

Both variation 4 and variation 5 featured this back design, perhaps the most well conceived and executed of all the variations.

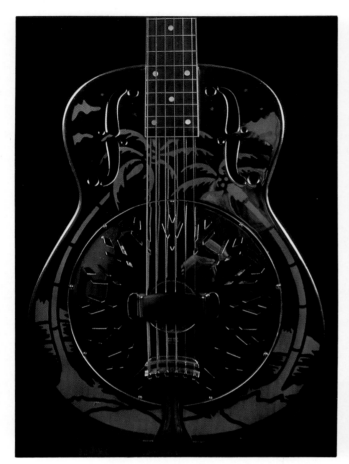

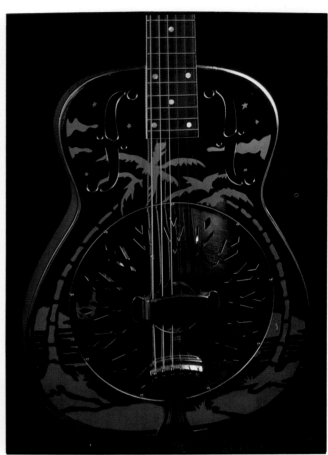

1937 Style O
        1935 Style O, note differences in sandblasted designs

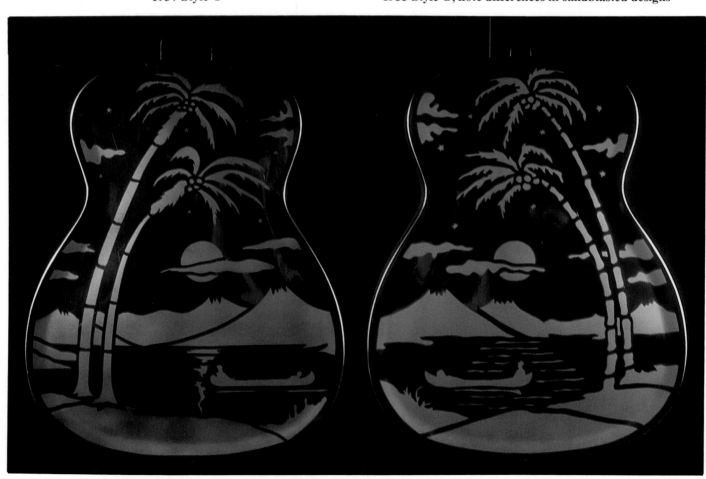

**1937 Style O (left), and 1935 Style O (right).
Little is known about the designer of these sandblasted images**

1935 style O, variation 6, #2344

1937 Style O, variation 7, #A-6228

1934-35 Don model guitar, Style 2

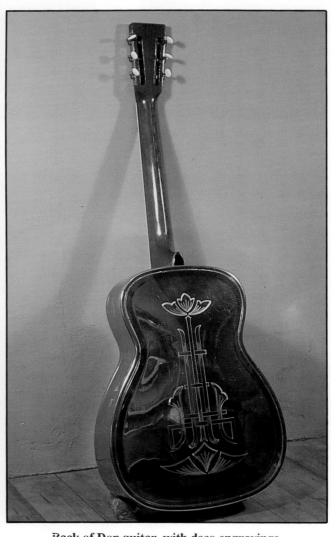

Back of Don guitar, with deco engravings

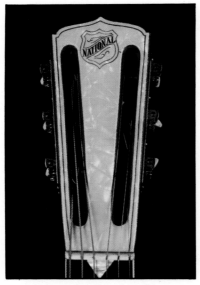

1933 Style 4 Tricone Spanish

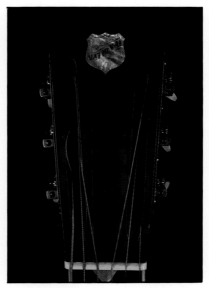

1929 Style 4 Tricone Hawaiian

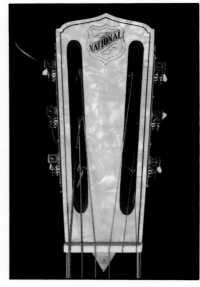

1932 Style 3 Tricone Hawaiian

1935-36 Style 97 Tricone Spanish

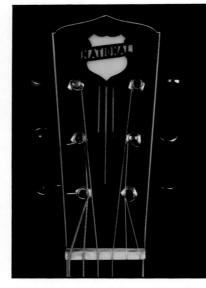

1937-38 Style 97 Tricone Hawaiian

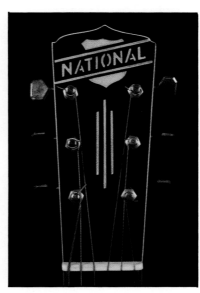

1937-38 Style 35 Tricone Hawaiian

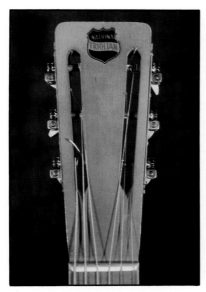

1929 Polychrome Triolian

1930-34 Walnut Sunburst Triolian

1930-35 Style O

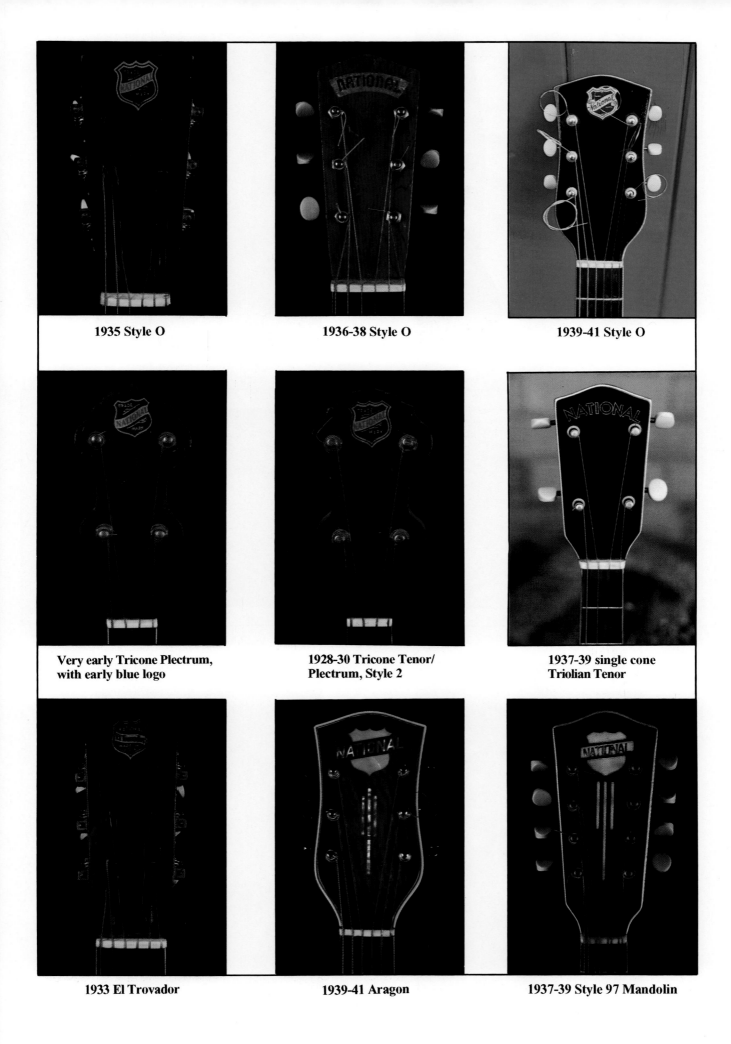

1935 Style O

1936-38 Style O

1939-41 Style O

Very early Tricone Plectrum, with early blue logo

1928-30 Tricone Tenor/ Plectrum, Style 2

1937-39 single cone Triolian Tenor

1933 El Trovador

1939-41 Aragon

1937-39 Style 97 Mandolin

1927 Style 2 Tricone Mandolin

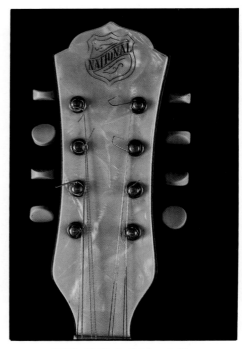

1928-40 Style 3 Mandolin

Stamped logo in white pearloid, 1929-37   **The well-known decal logo of 1930-35**

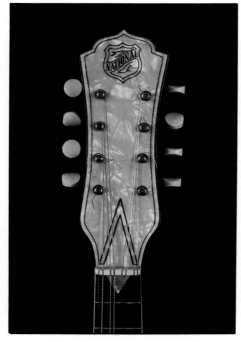

1929 Presentation Mandolin

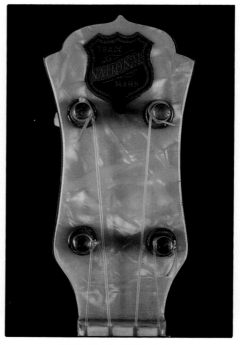

1931 Style 2 Ukulele

1938 Style 35, #A-5740 and 1936 Style 97, #B-1901

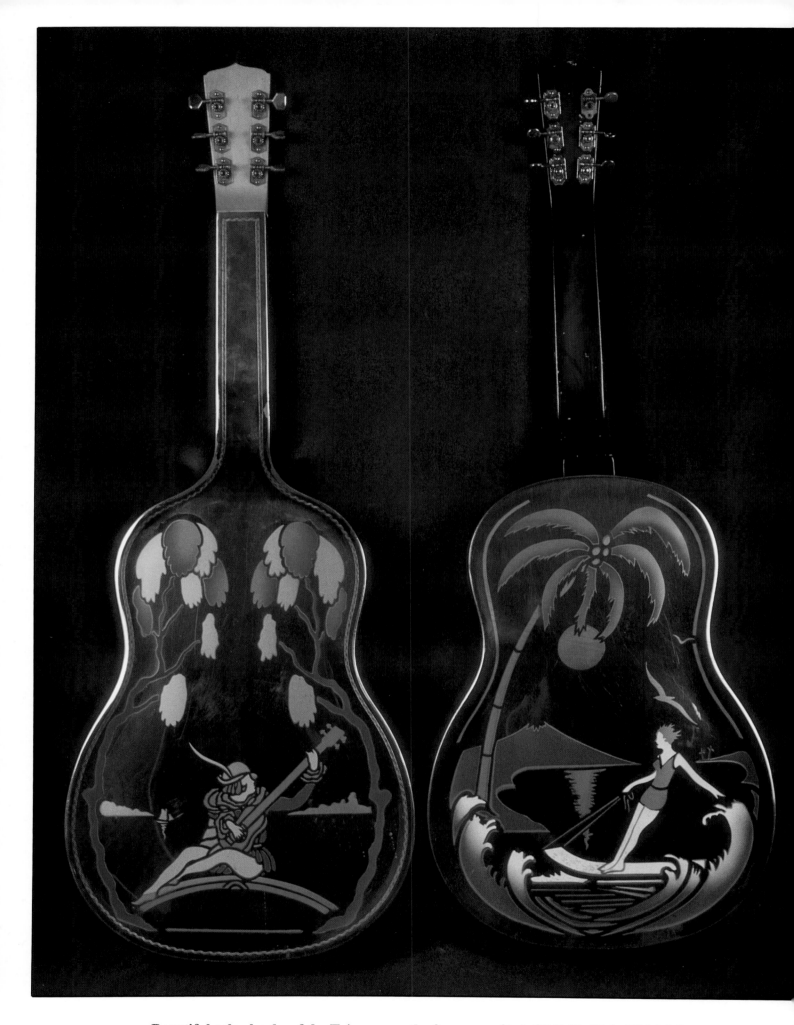

Beautiful color backs of the Tricones on the face page. Style 35 (left), Style 97 (right)

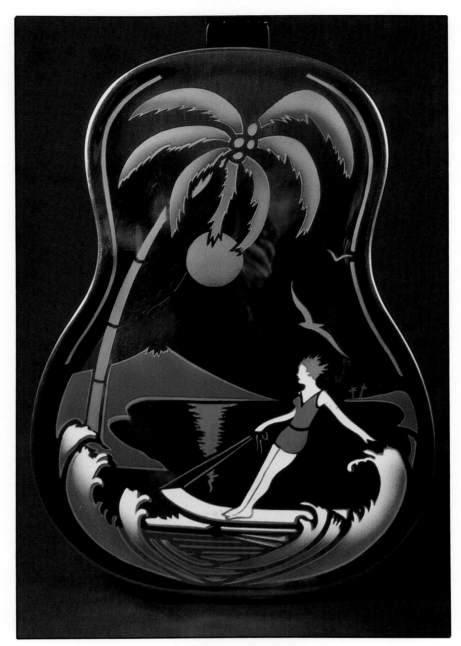

Detail of Style 97 Tricone

Side view of Style 97

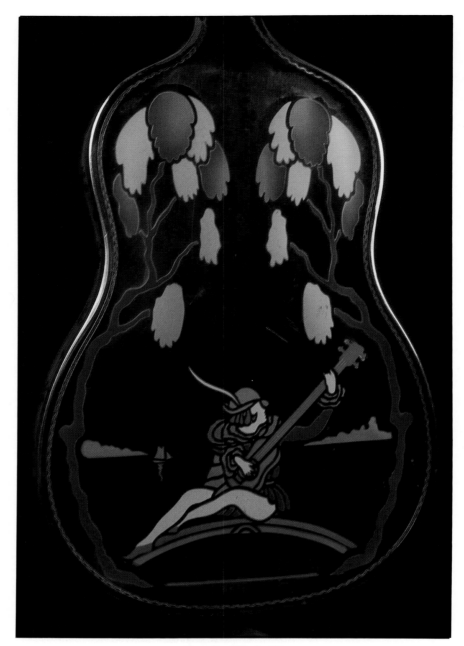

Detail of Style 35

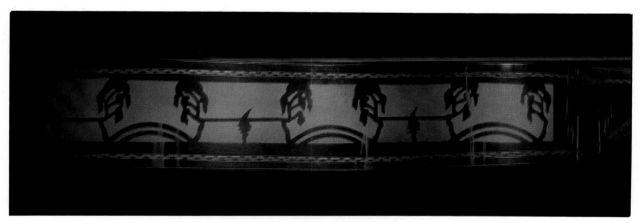

Side view of Style 35

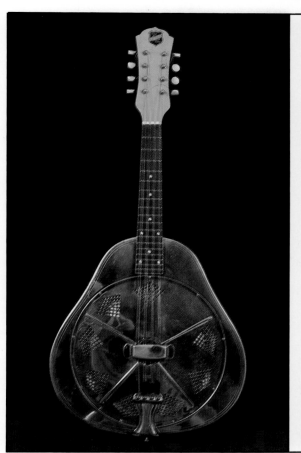 

1931 Style 1 Mandolin, #592   **1927 style 2 Tricone Mandolin, #122**

Detail of the strangely constructed Tricone Mandolin

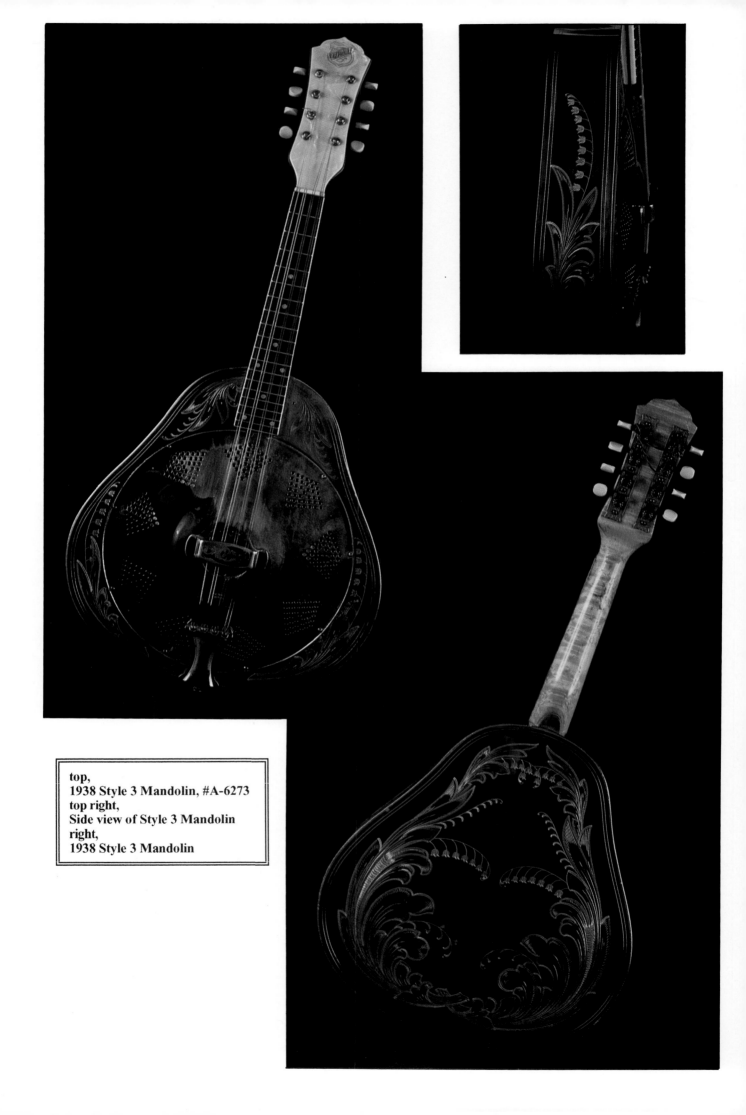

top,
1938 Style 3 Mandolin, #A-6273
top right,
Side view of Style 3 Mandolin
right,
1938 Style 3 Mandolin

Front view of 1929 special presentation silver-plated mandolin, #515. No national instruments except guitars were ever cataloged in Style 4. This one is unique

The back of this mandolin shows engraving with a Style 4 motif, but this design obviously goes beyond the normal Chrysanthemum pattern

Detail of 1929 Special. Note screens soldered under drilled coverplate holes. Neck inlays are also in a Style 4 pattern

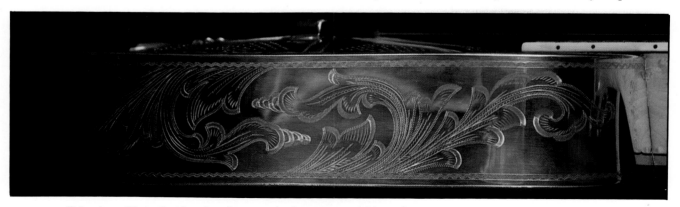

Side view. Note that borders have a wiggle pattern within, a feature not normally found. This side engraving varies considerably from standard Style 4 patterns

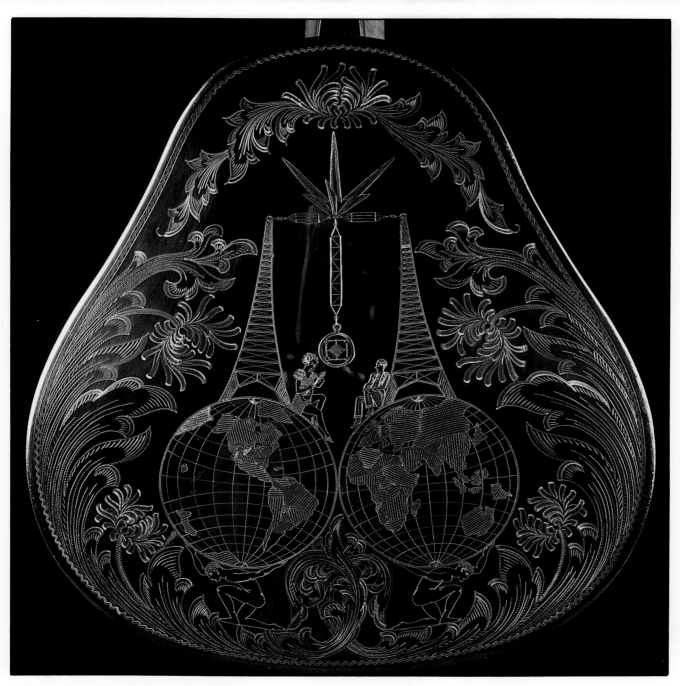

This remarkable design visually evokes some of the same ideas as the optimistic "Scientific" prose in the catalogs. Perhaps this instrument was made for presentation and display at Trade Shows-- it certainly seems to say in metal what National's ad writers were trying to put on paper. Note 1929 political borders on the "Hemispheres"

Detail of the above. The woman seems to be playing a resonator mandolin while the fellow at the base of the radio tower listens

1938 Style 97 Mandolin, #A-5743

The Style 97 design fits well on a mandolin body

Hawaiian scenes grace the sides of the Style 97

Note pattern differences in this side view of
Style 3 Tenor and Mandolin

Comparison of size and designs: Style 3 Mandolin, and 1929 Style 3 pear-shaped single cone tenor.

1929 Style 3 pear-shaped single cone tenor, #633   **1928 Style 1 Tricone plectrum, #26**

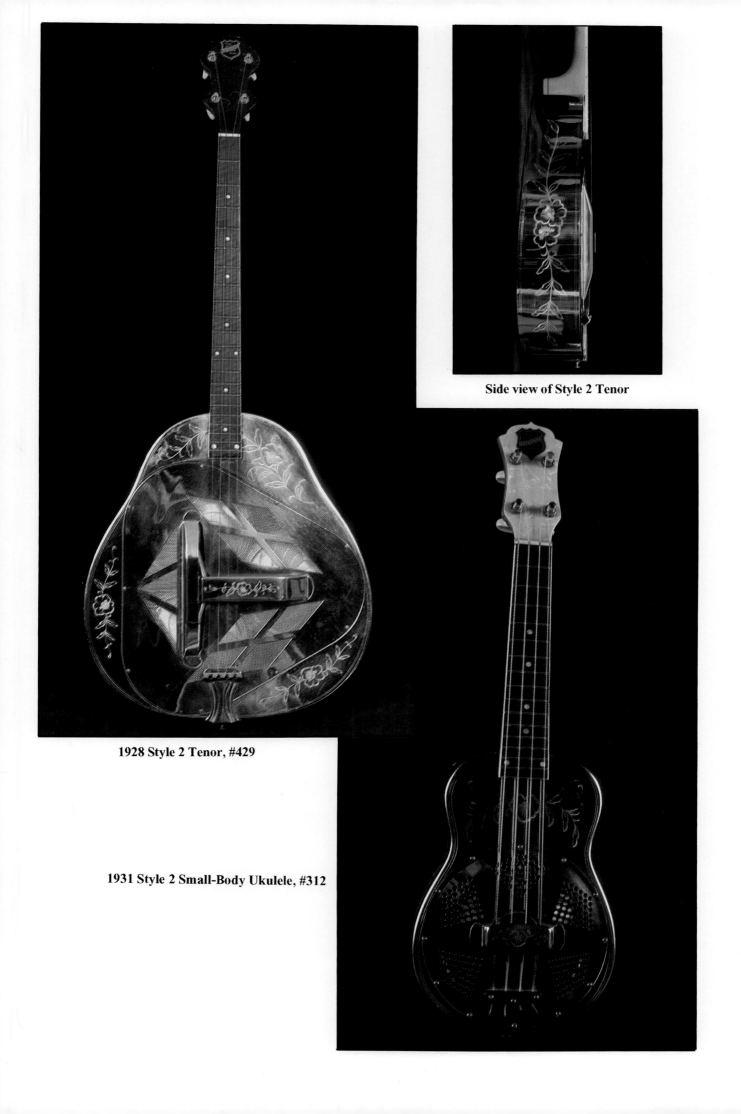

Side view of Style 2 Tenor

1928 Style 2 Tenor, #429

1931 Style 2 Small-Body Ukulele, #312

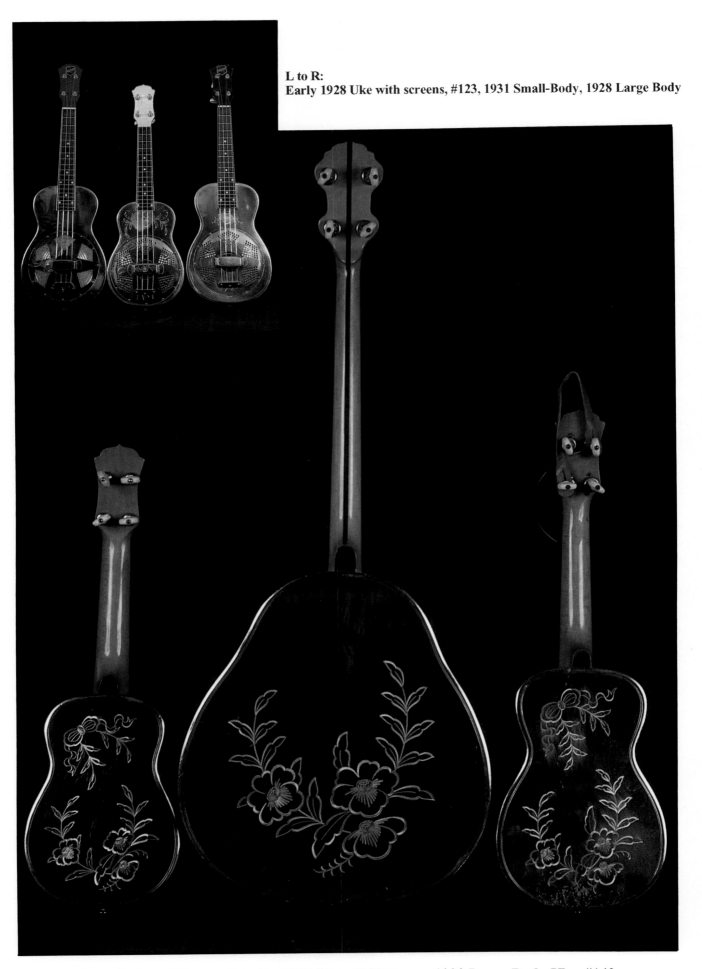

A profusion of Roses: L to R: 1931 Uke, 1928 Tenor, 1928 Large Body Uke, #143

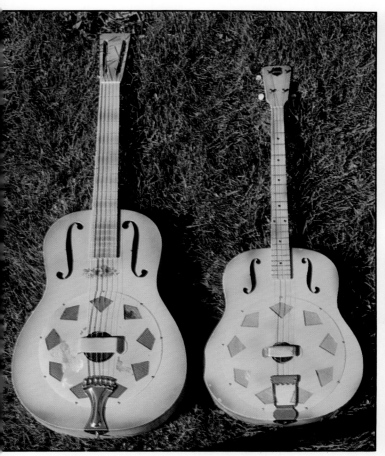

First type of single-cone Nationals: A 1928 wood body Triolian guitar, and a wood body Tenor. Note screens

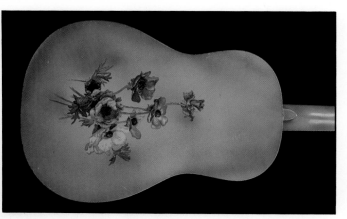

Back of Triolian guitar, with Anemone Bouquet decal

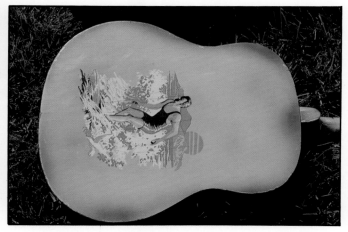

Surf rider adorns the back of this 1928 Triolian Tenor

Slightly later 1928 wood body Triolian

Hula girl decal spices up the back of the wood Triolian

Stenciled scenery adorns the back of the earliest metal polychrome Triolians, this one, #0186, is from 1929

Walnut Sunburst Triolians: 1932 Guitar, Mandolin, and Ukulele. Colors vary slightly over the production run

The last few wood Triolians had stenciled palms, 1929

A polychrome picnic: L to R: 1929 Wood #1626, 1932 Tenor #2028P, 1929 Mandolin #225, 1933 Metal guitar #2266P, 1929 Ukulele unnumbered, and 1929 Metal guitar, #0186. Note different stencils used over the years
Inset: Headstock of 1929 polychrome Ukulele

1939-41 Aragon. One the ugliest resonator Nationals, to be sure, but perhaps the loudest National of all

1933 wood-bodied El Trovador, body by Kay

1938 Triolian with more modern design features, including wood grain paint and pickguard, #C2479

1938-39 Triolian Tenor, with different graining and different pickguard

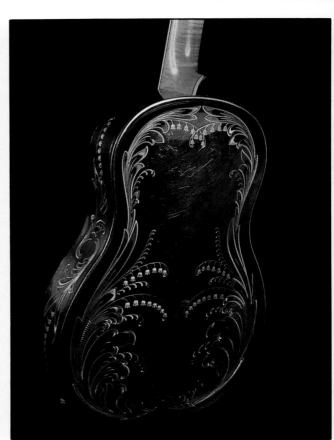

The back of George's guitar, #S2788, is engraved like a Style 3, but with twice as many cuts

The personal presentation guitar of George Beauchamp, given to him in January 1932 by the board of directors. The only such engraved single-cone extant, this guitar sports many unusual features, such as the pearloid fingerboard, with the first use of Roman numeral markers.
Inset: Headstock commemorates the date of George's single cone patent granting

Close-up of the engraving, notice how half of the cuts go through the plating, showing the gold of the brass body

Banjo Ikey Robinson, a prolific and very hot recording artist of the 1920's and 30's, with a Triolian tenor.

Duke Ellington jamming with Cab Calloway in the 1930s. Duke is playing a rare early 14 fret sunburst Triolian.

An unknown but happy owner of a very early 1928 National tricone plectrum guitar.

Maria Valenti, mother of Caterina Valenti, in a 1930's German theatre program photo. She holds a style 1 tricone, and a style 1 uke rests at her feet.

German jazz orchestra, middle 1930's.

1) Paul Tremaine's Orch, a California band, with a style 2 tricone guitar.

2) California Vaudeville group, c. 1929

3) L.A. Biltmore Hotel Trio, 1929. This was the featured vocal and string trio of the Biltmore Hotel Orchestra. Eddie Bush was the steel player, and sounded much like his friend Sol Hoopii. The material performed by this trio, however, consisted of jazz and popular songs. The rhythm guitarist holds an early style 2 tricone with extra engraving.

The Ballard Chefs Jug Band, comprised of members of Earl McDonald's Louisville Jug Band and others. This 1931 photo includes two Nationals: A Bakelite-neck Walnut Triolian guitar, and a pear-shaped Polychrome Triolian Tenor guitar.

A 1932 shot of the Ballard Chefs. A different man is playing the Polychrome Tenor, but it appears to be the same instrument as in the 1931 photo, showing considerable wear put on it's face in the year between these photographs.

NATIONALS ON THE STREET
by Gary Atkinson

When John Dopyera introduced the resonator guitar to the world by way of National and Dobro guitars, two significant things occurred. as illustrated in previous chapters, the invention of these louder instruments, by virtue of unique appearance, volume and tone, was a milestone in guitar manufacturing history.

It is equally significant that these guitars were adopted by musicians of many American musical forms, making the distinctive sound of the instruments a major characteristic of each form. From the beginning of production, Hawaiian and blues musicians were attracted to the National, whereas the Dobro was favored by Cajun, bluegrass and white country guitarists.

Blues musicians were attracted to the National for several reasons. Although the National is recognized as THE country blues slide guitar, with its ability to enhance the technique's sound, the original reasons for its popularity were varied.

Many musicians saw the aesthetic qualities of the National as being of great value in the realms of status and credibility. Son House and Bo Carter both had confidence in the attention-getting qualities of their guitars. Today, stepping in front of an audience with a National will prompt warm comments of recognition--60 years after its invention. The reaction to a musician who appeared with a shiny new National at a Saturday night dance during the late 20s or in the 30s must have been quite sensational. To some, the appeal was the instrument's durability. Bukka White, for one, regarded the National as a lasting, long-term investment. It stood up to his relentless, hard, passionate playing.

The Blues guitarist also recognized the National as the ideal instrument for the common occupation of street playing. When the pioneers of the National company were considering that their resonator guitar would be able to redress the imbalance between guitars and louder instruments of bands and small orchestras, little would they have realized that it would also become the ideal antidote for crowd and traffic noise!

One of the first street musicians to use a National was Oscar 'Buddy' Woods. Born in 1903, he stayed in his native area of Shreveport for most of his life. Referring to himself as a "Street Rustler", he began playing on the city's streets at the age of 22. By 1930 he was already using a National tri-plate; probably a square neck, which he featured on his first recordings. The records, made under the name of 'The Shreveport Home Wreckers' included second guitarist Ed Schaffer and featured some of the finest slide guitar of early blues. 'Fence Breaking Blues' and 'Home Wrecking Blues' were recorded in Memphis on May 21, 1930 and issued on Victor 23275 and Bluebird B5341.

It would seem that Oscar Woods was very well respected among fellow musicians for his unique style of slide playing. He was called upon as an accompianist in 1932 to record with the white country singer Jimmie Davis, famed for 'You Are My Sunshine'. In 1940, John Lomax immortalized Woods as part of the epic Library of Congress field recordings. By that period of his life, the artist was "passing the hat around" in a restaurant on Texas Avenue, Shreveport, playing in the company of guitarist-singers Joe Harris and Kid West.

In 1960, during his 'Conversation With The Blues' project, the English author Paul Oliver went in search of Oscar Woods. His investigations were frustrated by the still segregated facilities of Shreveport and his enquiries repeatedly met with cool receptions. Eventually his search came to an end when he discovered Alex 'Snooks' Jones, a piano player and long time friend of Woods. Jones had been a pall bearer at Oscar Woods' funeral only four years prior to Oliver's visit. Oscar 'Buddy' Woods had died at the age of 53, leaving behind a rare glimpse of some of the finest slide steel guitar Blues recordings ever made.

Oscar Woods was one of only a handful of street players who used a tri-plate. This is not surprising, since the triple resonator system puts out a sound somewhat less strident than that of a single - cone National. Of course, the cheapest tricone cost twice as much as the most expensive single-cone, so economics certainly affected this, too. Those known to have used them were sophisticated and subtle in their styles, as was Woods. Others included Tampa Red, Walter Vincent and Black Ace, who was Woods' pupil and one time musical partner. Enthusiasts must not be taken in by the well known photograph of Bukka White posing with a tri-plate. Closer inspection reveals that this particular guitar is, in fact, a square neck. Bukka holds the guitar in a conventional position, with his left hand holding the neck, appearing to be fretting the strings. Because of the high action on a square neck guitar, It is most doubtful he ever played the instrument as his pose would indicate. For the sake of the photo, he was able to hold the guitar in this manner because the neck had a shallow, thin profile. This model is described in detail as the 'Exploding palm tree design' in chapter 3.

An early 12 fret Duolian was put to good use in the street performances of Babe Stovall. Born on October 4, 1907 in Tylertown, Mississippi, he made his way in 1964 down to New Orleans. Here he worked as a street musician for many years.

Despite his adoption of the Jazz capital, where he would spend the rest of his life, his style was pure Mississippi. Playing a mixture of Blues and religious songs, he was heavily influenced by fellow Mississippian Tommy Johnson. He did not use the National as a slide instrument. His guitar style was sharp and precise. Writer and critic Bruce Cook interviewd Stovall and, because of the instrument's rarity, stated the player "must have been tempted many times to sell his and buy one of the standard wooden sort". I can only guess that Cook did not possess a National, or he would have understood that even in the hardest times, a true National owner would never sell his closest friend. Stovall's answer to Cook's questions about the subject rang true enough: "Oh yeah, that's right. You can't buy them any more. Why do I like it? That's because it gives me a sound 'twixt a guitar and a banjo".

His years of street performing matured Stovall's voice, giving a rich, earthy quality, half singing, half shouting his lyrics to the visitors of Jackson Square. Babe became a popular character of the French Quarter of New Orleans, where he remained until his death in 1974.

A major figure of Black Country music who used a National during part of his career was the legendary 'Harlem Street Singer', the Reverend Gary Davis. Davis' biography has been well documented elsewhere and would not be totally relevant here. However, he was using a single-cone guitar during National's production years of the 30s. The instrument he used for his religious recordings of the mid 1930s was a National, probably a single-cone guitar. By the late 1940s he had replaced his National with a more mellow-sounding wood bodied guitar.

The little-known Doug Quattlebaum combined the occupation of street vending with street performance. I include him because of his unique slant on the business of entertaining. He was born in 1927 in the South Carolina city of Florence and at the age of 14 moved to Philadelphia where he began to take an interest in the guitar. He was taught by his stepfather, who was a brother of the great Mississippi Blues artist Arthur 'Big Boy' Crudup. After his marriage, young Doug learned from his father-in-law as well. Quattlebaum was in good hands. By the age of 26 he had recorded for the blues and spirituals label, Gotham. A National was almost certainly not used at this session.

It is not known how he was earning a living for several years after those recordings were made. Certainly no others were released until the early 1960s. At this time, he drove an ice cream van. Rather than using the usual musical chimes to announce his arrival, Doug would stop the van, step out onto the sidewalk with a National and play to his customers. After treating the small crowd to a short performance, he would serve his ice cream.

In 1961 an album was released on the Bluesville Label entitled 'Mr Softee's Blues'. Shown on the front cover, Doug is standing next to his van posing with his trusty advertising aid - the National.

There are some fine tracks featured on the album including some very nice slide guitar playing. Since then he has slipped back into obscurity and his present whereabouts are unknown.

One of the most well known street singers to have used a National must have been Blind Arvella Grey. A large and powerful man, Arvella made his living playing in the famous Maxwell Street area of Chicago. Summer and Winter alike he would wander up and down the flea market, where stalls offered anything second hand from records and books to household goods. Such artists as Daddy Stovepipe, Maxwell Street Jimmie Davis, Blind James Brewer and John Wrencher offered rich samples of country blues, rhythm and blues and gospel music there. Arvella's high pitched voice was accompanied by his worn and beaten fourteen fret Duolian, made in the late 1930s. He used bottleneck on the treble strings. His playing was harsh and loud. Visitors to the market area would hear him play a mixture of blues, religious and folk songs all sung with great passion and vigor. Listeners would drop coins into the tin mug pinned to his jacket or the full length heavy overcoat he wore to keep out the bitter cold Chicago winter. Often in the winter he would hustle aboard the street cars, earning money from the passengers by playing his guitar.

Grey was born in Texas in 1906. His life, at times, became a catalogue of catastrophic events. When reminiscing, he concluded "I just is proud of my life, 'cause I come through with my skin on". Only just! He was born one of triplets, which brought the total of children in the household to eight. Confronted with the news of the latest arrivals, his father asked Arvella's mother to chose which child she wanted "because I'm gonna drown the other two". Arvella noted in later years "I've been swimming ever since". After being elected into this world by the skin of his gums, he embarked into a life that would bring him hardships from start to finish. At the age of 13 he left home. His father had deserted the family when the mother died while giving birth to twins.

Working on the Dollar Boyd Plantation in the south of Texas, he earned a quarter for a year's work, in addition to having food and basic clothes provided. Not wanting to settle in any particular job for too long his early adulthood became that of a wanderer. He picked up work on plantations, did some sharecropping, construction labor, levee camp work and he worked as a 'gandy dancer' on the B & O Railroad, lining up the track and driving the steel spikes in to hold the rails down.

Traveling the country he took up a job erecting tents for the Ringling Brothers Circus, "They just say a 'roughneck'. I was a roughneck, you know, just put up the tent and the seats and things". The severity of his life made him capable of being an aggressive man, readily prepared to use his physical might to cease prevarication and settle arguments. Several jobs later, he hitched his way north, finally arriving at Detroit, Michigan. Here he took a job as a mechanic. As he tried to establish himself in a city life totally different from what he had known in the south, his early encounters with the people there led down a problematical path. Drawn into the world of drug peddling and gambling, the more dubious side of the hard, fast, city life began to have its effects. Despite his attempts to survive financially,

he was eventually deduced to a state of destitution and desperation. He became involved in crimes of robbery and in January of 1930 he held up a bank in Detroit, escaping with $6000. He stayed in the north keeping on the move between Missouri and Indiana, eventually losing his money in the gambling joints of Kansas City.

Broke and living on handouts, he returned to Illinois, arriving at Peoria. Here he met a woman by the name of Ardella who, it would seem, was a popular girl with the men. Arguments between Arvella and his competitors soon ensued and threats were made. Another boyfriend by the name of Lamar Kilgore, realizing the size and strength of Arvella, suggested that although he would not take a chance fighting him, he would in fact settle the problem with a gun. On the night of September 13, 1930, returning from a gambling trip, Arvella arrived home to find his door locked. Trying his key, the door would not open and upon knocking Ardella told him to 'wait a moment'. While waiting on the outside of the glass panelled door, he took out a cigarette and brought the match up to his face. A gun fired. Arvella had been shot. Inside the room, Lamar had been waiting and had taken advantage of the match illuminating his target. The incident left Arvella with three fingers missing from his left hand and the loss of his sight. Lamar was caught and following his trial was given a 14 year prison sentence.

For some time Arvella wrestled with the problems of his disability. His acute senses of independence and self preservation had been shattered, but he would not be beaten. "I had it pretty rough when I started but I said I'm not gonna let nothin' beat me down". In 1933 he purchased a guitar for $2.50, and under the guidance of another blind musician, he put into an open tuning and began to learn how to play. The loss of his fingers made bottleneck playing an obvious choice of style. Not waiting until he had fully mastered the guitar, he soon began playing on the streets.

In the beginning he earned more money from requests to take his noise further down the street! But of course he had to do something quick. Not only had he embarked upon learning a new skill, he was also teaching himself a new way to survive. His songs often related to his own personal experiences, in particular, his days working on the railroad - such as 'Gandy Dancers Song' and the traditional 'John Henry' and 'Casey Jones'.

At one point he recorded and released 6 songs on his own Grey Label. Produced as 3 45's on Grey 100, Grey 113 and Grey 114, the singles were pressed at a major R & B pressing plant. Despite the importance of the pressing company it is alleged that the records were intentionally pressed poorly, with static, deliberately sabotaging any type of competition with the plant's own pressings. Other recordings have been made including 4 tracks on the long out-of-print Heritage album HLP1004 and a full album titled 'The Singing Drifter' recorded late on the night of September 22, 1972 in Harvey, Illinois and released on Birch 6091. Sadly, he died in the 1970s bringing to a close a tradition of original Black Country music played on the streets using National guitars.

Babe Stovall on the street. . .painting by Gary Atkinson.

CHAPTER 8

Advertisments and Catalogues

E.A. Sutphin Co. – Philadelphia.

The New Silver Musical Instruments

THE GREATEST MUSICAL SENSATION OF THE AGE

The **New National Silver String Instruments** mark a new step in the advancement and progress of string instruments. These new instruments tend to revolutionize the manufacture of fretted musical instruments inasmuch as the new Invention applied to National Silver String Instruments produce a better quality of tone, more power and volume than is possible to get in any other string instruments.

Many letters are received daily from Lovers of Music expressing their appreciation and gratitude for the betterment of string instruments as made possible through the Invention applied to the National Silver String Instruments.

TONE QUALITY

the purity and clearness of which is truly marvelous.

POWER AND VOLUME

of tone that fills the largest auditorium or theatre and always heard even when played with the modern Jazz or Concert orchestra.

APPEARANCE

that is most attractive. The highly polished beautiful hand engraved silver body gives a very flashy appearance which combined with its marvelous tone makes the New National Silver Musical Instruments most valuable for stage or concert work. Without one single exception every musician who has adopted the use of the New National Silver Guitars or Mandolins pronounce them to be the greatest string musical instrument invention of the age and have invariably discarded the use of their wood Instruments for all tim to come.

BANJO, VIOLIN AND MANDOLIN PLAYERS

will be particularly interested in the Silver Tenor Guitar and Silver Mandolin, both of which are built on the same principle as is the National Silver Hawaiian and Spanish Guitars. The Silver Tenor Guitar makes a most valuable double for the Tenor or Plectrum Banjo player, since the scale is the same and tone **more powerful** and of a **more entrancing quality** than the Banjo. Besides this, the attractive and unusual appearance in itself never fails to make a most favorable impression upon an audience. The same may be said of the New National Silver Mandolin to take the place of, or as a double for the ordinary Mandolin or as a double for the Violin.

THE CONSTRUCTION

of the National Silver Instruments embody an entirely new principle resulting in the most beautiful and marvelous instruments, the possibilities of which cannot be realized unless actually heard and played.

SAM KU WEST--Brunswick Recording Artist who was given his title, "Kreisler of the Steel Guitar," by PRINCE GEORGE OF ENGLAND after the Prince heard his Concert in SINGAPORE, Malaya.

THE BODY

is made from selected pure German silver, carefully gauged; will not tarnish, rust or deteriorate in any way and with ordinary care will last a life time.

THE VITAL FACTOR

resulting in the tremendous power and volume of tone is due to the existence of three scientifically constructed diaphragms built within the body of the instrument, they being made from a special metal of our own formula. These diaphragms act as amplifiers, throwing out the tone through the perforated top of the instrument and amplifying the true sweet tone as naturally produced by the strings and giving power and volume scarcely believable in an instrument of this kind.

A 1927 page from the Sutphin wholesale house which describes the principles of the brand new Nationals. The glowing terms that are used convey the optimism of the times and of the Company.

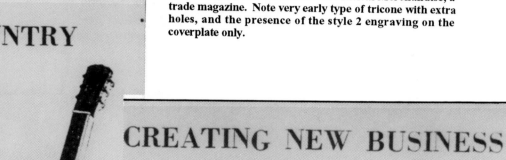

ATTENTION MUSIC DEALERS!!

Send your inquiry for open territory on our SILVER STRING INSTRUMENTS

The Silver Steel Guitar — Spanish Guitar — Tenor Guitar and Mandolin are all ready for distribution — all made under our patented principles.

These instruments are given credit as the greatest Musical Invention of the Age — incomparable in volume and tone — tone that has never been equaled in any String Instrument.

Manufactured by

National String Instrument Co.

1855 West 64th Street   Los Angeles, California

December, 1927 announcement in Musical Merchandise, a trade magazine. Note very early type of tricone with extra holes, and the presence of the style 2 engraving on the coverplate only.

TAKING THE COUNTRY BY STORM!

———

The National
**SILVER
GUITAR**

———

Hawaiian and Spanish models.

———

Immediate
Deliveries

———

Very Attractive Proposition for Dealers. Liberal Discounts.

Exclusive Distributors
Central States

311 So. Wabash Ave.

CHICAGO   **ILL**

November, 1927 ad with standard production tricone.

December, 1927 advertisment in Musical Merchandise.

CREATING NEW BUSINESS

National

SILVER GUITARS

———

The fastest selling "Big" Item since the Saxophone was first popularized.

———

Hawaiian and Spanish Models for immediate delivery.

Tenor Model Soon

———

Very Attractive Proposition for Dealers. Liberal Discounts.

Exclusive Distributors
Central States

311 So. Wabash Ave.,

CHICAGO   **ILL.**

This is the "Metal Age"

Flutes. Piccolos.
Clarinets. Guitars—
and now we announce

The National
Silver Tenor Guitar

Every Tenor
Banjo Player
is a Prospect

Order G...

The Demand is Already C...

Liberal Dealers Discoun...

Chicago Musical Instru...

Exclusive distributors Centra...

311 So. Wabash Ave.

First published announcement of the tricone tenor guitar, March 1928.

May, 1928.

The "Metal Age"
is Paying Dividends

NATIONAL
Silver Guitars,
Tenor Guitars
and Mandolins

P X Laube
Boston Wonder
Silva-Bet
Metal
Clarinets

Bettoney, Boston Wonder, Pan-American Flutes and Piccolos

They're all selling big—

Keep them in stock

Chicago Musical Instrument Co.

311 So. Wabash Ave.   CHICAGO

202

National String Opens Big Advertising Drive

Two of the first cards in the National campaign

Plans for an extensive advertising campaign in national magazines, the professional papers and the leading trade journals have just been concluded by the National String Instrument Corporation, of Los Angeles, manufacturers of silver guitars, mandolins, ukuleles triolian string instruments, etc. The idea behind this widespread advertising program is to extend real co-operation to the jobbers of the National String Instrument line and to create for dealers a genuine market and also to stimulate a constant interest in the company's instruments among the professional and amateur trade.

G. D. Beauchamp, general manager, has so designed the advertising campaign that it will prove to be invaluable in assisting the jobber and dealer. To make this co-operation even more effective, the National String Instrument Co. has issued an attractively colored catalogue and several new window display presentation cards. The two pictures here are reproductions of the window display cards which have been sent to the National String Instrument jobbers for distribution to the dealers.

It will be of interest to the trade to know that Mr. Beauchamp's organization has signally honored *Musical Merchandise* by making this publication its trade medium for the exploitation of their line of instruments to both jobbers and dealers.

The guitars manufactured by National String Instrument Corp. are being sold with excellent results by many leading dealers scattered in all parts of the country. The factory of the company is very busy at this time and is continually confronted with increased demands for the National String product. Orders exceed production, it is said. It is planned by the mangement to increase the factory facilities at an early date to take care of many orders on hand, and to render prompt service to customers.

Mr. Beauchamp has issued the following statement:

"I am very much pleased with the way the trade has taken up our lines of guitars—silver and tenor—and mandolins, ukuleles and other instruments that we manufacture. We wish to assure the trade that our entire organization not only appreciates the co-operation of the members of our industry but is doing everything in its power to offer the best of co-operation to jobber and dealer.

"I personally believe that the guitar is here to stay and that the demand for such goods will continue to increase for several years.

"We are turning out a very excellent line of instruments—second to none. When improved instruments are found necessary to take care of changes in the musical profession, we will make them. National String Instrument Corporation will keep up with the times and will keep in tune with the times."

An article from the May, 1930 issue of Musical Merchandise with interesting comments from George Beauchamp.

Get Your Share
of these
Big Profit Sales

National

SILVER GUITARS

Are Selling Faster
Than They Can
Be Made

They Have
Everything:
Beautiful Tone
Enormous Volume
Flashy Appearance

Order One On Approval Today

Chicago Musical Instrument Co.

Exclusive Central Distributors

311 So. Wabash Ave.   CHICAGO

January 1928 ad appealing to dealers to get in on the popularity of Nationals. The statement "they have everything" still holds true today.

The purple prose in this May, 1930 ad exemplifies the era of American optimism towards an industrial future, even as the depression worsened.

NATIONAL Silver and Triolian Metal Guitars

Every Dealer should have a representative stock of this fast-selling line.

Write for Catalog

The Chicago MUSICAL Instrument CO.

May 1930 ad, show- ing the **early style 4 (separate engraving on coverplate) not produced since 1928.**

A complete orchestra of National String Instruments.

NATIONAL . . . . LEADERS . . .

PRODUCTION DOUBLED AND REDOUBLED IN 1930— AND DEMANDS INCREASING

$45.00

NATIONAL Metal
Triolian Spanish and
Hawaiian Guitars
finished in beautiful
two-tone brown wal-
nut (or polychrome)
are wonderful sell-
ers — "comparable
at any price only
with another
NATIONAL".

WHY has this mass production been made necessary? What has caused the most gifted radio, concert, and motion picture *artists of a nation* to turn wholeheartedly and exclusively to NATIONAL?

There's only one answer: QUALITY. NATIONAL has introduced entirely new ideas in string instruments—progressive, creative and ingenious American ideals stimulating an industry in which you are vitally concerned. Tone quality, volume, durability and beauty have made NATIONAL String Instruments the choice of professional musicians the world over. The same rich, dynamic tone and perfect intonation have made them also ideal for the beginner and the amateur player.

Are you getting your rightful share of the generous NATIONAL profits?

We're launching a national advertising campaign that will mean thousands of dollars of additional business for live dealers who are prepared for it.

Your jobber has the complete line. Place your order for representative items with him now and watch your string instrument department make sales history.

NATIONAL STRING
INSTRUMENT CORP.

LOOK FOR NATIONAL STRING INSTRUMENT
PAGE IN NEXT ISSUE

The figure stated in this November, 1930 ad, if true, would represent the 50 to 70 instruments produced per day, not an unreasonable amount for a 22 man factory.

$55,000 shipments of

NATIONAL
STRING INSTRUMENTS
during September
Did you get yours?

The Best Seller Ever!!!
National Special Style O Silver Guitar
PRICE $62.50

The construction throughout is up to the "National High Standard." Made from a high grade Alloy Metal heavily nickel plated, with a beautiful two-tone Silver Finish, Rock Maple Neck, Ebonized Maple Fingerboard, Pearl Position Dots, etc.

Tone – Quality – Volume and Beauty

an instrument that could easily sell for twice the price—a foolproof product that will stand up for years and regardless of make or price, tone quality and volume, that is comparable at any price only with another "NATIONAL."

By All Means Carry This Instrument in Stock

Wire Your Jobber

Be Prepared for Your Holiday Trade

The Best Seller Ever!!!
National Special Style O Silver Guitar
PRICE $62.50

The construction throughout is up to the "National High Standard." Made from a high grade Alloy Metal heavily nickel plated, with a beautiful two-tone Silver Finish, Rock Maple Neck, Ebonized Maple Fingerboard, Pearl Position Dots, etc.

Tone – Quality – Volume and Beauty

an instrument that could easily sell for twice the price — a foolproof product that will stand up for years and regardless of make or price, tone quality and volume, that is comparable at any price only with another

"NATIONAL."

By All Means You Should Carry This Instrument in Stock

An October, 1930 ad for the Style 0, the model that kept National alive through the depression.

The guitars shown in this 1933 ad are stock models with no special "world's fair" features. Perhaps National sought to increase sales by linking itself to the Century of Progress Fair in Chicago.

NATIONAL
STRING INSTRUMENTS

The next fifteen pages consist of the 1930 National Catalog reprinted here in its entirety. This was perhaps National's most beautiful piece of advertising literature, complete with artist testimonials, factory photos, and an entertaining writing style.

NATIONAL String Instruments are truly "professional" instruments in the fullest sense, being preferred by leading radio and vaudeville artists on all circuits. Six outstanding points that make them so are:

(1) Powerful, rich, dynamic tone.
(2) Unequalled tone quality.
(3) Perfect intonation.
(4) Exquisite finish.
(5) Unaffected by weather, water or temperature.
(6) Will not crack or warp with ordinary care: guaranteed indefinitely.

But they are also ideal for the beginner and the amateur player. It is a great mistake to buy a cheap musical instrument of any kind for a beginner. Not only do the poor tones of a poor instrument tend to lessen the pupil's musical perception but there is no time when inspiration is more needed than while learning to play. To inspire the highest efforts it is essential to provide an instrument worthy of admiration and care.

On the pages following, the reader is introduced to a large variety of instruments covering a wide price range—but all made with the same high regard for quality and performance that has characterized NATIONAL String Instruments since their inception.

Why NATIONAL Excels in Beauty, Tone, Volume, and Durability

Every National String Instrument gives instant, proud response to the lightest touch. And only in these instruments will be found such rare beauty of tone. This and their powerful voicing combine with their attractive and unusual appearance to make them very valuable for stage and concert work —they never fail to impress an audience favorably. The beautiful body, carefully gauged and highly polished, will not tarnish, rust or deteriorate in any way, and with ordinary care will last a lifetime. Every product of the National String Instrument Corporation bears the trade-mark "NATIONAL."

The Heart of the Instrument

Everyone marvels at the tremendous power, the volume and the tone quality of these instruments—little wonder that stage and concert performers are so enthusiastic about them.

The vital feature of construction to which this power may be attributed is found in the diaphragm or resonator illustrated. Just as the modern dynamic radio amplifies every tone from the highest note of the violin to the lowest note of the mighty organ, the dynamic construction of National String Instruments amplifies the true, sweet tones produced by the strings, yielding a quality and volume of tone heretofore considered impossible in a string instrument. This dynamic resonator principle is found only in National String Instruments and is fully protected by our patents.

Constructed for Most Severe Professional Demands

It goes without saying that a valuable instrument of this kind, especially for professional use, must be built not only to withstand the hardest sort of abuse but to give years of service.

The illustration at the right shows the neck construction of National Silver instruments. These are made of selected mahogany reinforced with steel to prevent warping. Fingerboards are correctly fretted, set with pearl position dots, with extra large German silver frets.

And the same care has been devoted to the other parts of every instrument. We have spared no effort in developing construction principles that fully meet the most exacting requirements.

Duke Akina and His Hawaiian Four now en route on world tour, are meeting with wide acclaim and demonstrating that music as produced on NATIONAL String Instruments has power to charm all peoples and all classes, from peasant to royalty.

RARELY indeed have any instruments found such general and hearty acceptance by leading musicians of radio and stage as have NATIONAL Silver Hawaiian and Spanish Guitars.

Each of these two types of guitar is a leader in its field; in no other instruments will be found such rare beauty of tone and astonishing power and volume. They provide the player with a perfect medium for the complete expression of his artistry; and are constructed to give years of service under the most exacting conditions.

Front View
of Hawaiian Guitar
Style No. 1
Price $125.00

Spanish Guitar
Style No. 1
Price $125.00

AS indicated by the price list on the opposite page, each type of instrument (with the exception of the new Style 0) is supplied in four different designs, either plain or beautifully hand engraved. An inspection of these highly attractive NATIONAL instruments will make it easy to understand why NATIONAL owners take such pride in their possession.

Sam Ku West, now touring the world with Irene West's Royal Hawaiians and The Bird of Paradise, so delighted King George of England with his playing that he was titled "Kriesler of the Steel Guitar." He finds that the power and tone of NATIONAL String Instruments are not affected by extreme climatic differences. "Such rare beauty of tone, such power and volume, such dependable performance under all conditions is found only in NATIONAL String Instruments."

NATIONAL
Silver Guitar
Style 0

A Brand New Product

The NATIONAL Silver Guitar Style 0 is sure to win the admiration of everyone because of its beauty of design and marvelous tone quality. It has one 10-inch dynamic resonator providing amazing power and volume while retaining sweetness. May be used for both Hawaiian and Spanish playing.

PRICES

NEW STYLE 0 SILVER GUITAR..........$ 85.00

Furnished in both Spanish & Hawaiian Styles

STYLE 1—German Silver, plain............125.00
STYLE 2—beautiful hand engraved.......145.00
STYLE 3—(De Luxe) Artist's floral design..165.00
STYLE 4—(Artist's model) elaborately
    engraved, fancy pearl, etc.........195.00

Sol Hoopii, considered one of the world's best guitar players, heartily endorses the NATIONAL Guitar as the best ever produced. With his famous Hawaiian Trio, through Columbia records and playing for celebrated motion picture stars to assist them in their roles, Sol is repeatedly demonstrating the superiority of NATIONAL String Instruments.

PRICES

TENOR
Style 1 (plain) ...... $ 75.00
Style 2 .... 95.00
Style 3 .... 115.00

PLECTRUM
Style 1 (plain) 80.00
Style 2 (beautifully
    hand engraved) ... 100.00
Style 3 (artistic floral
    design) 120.00

NATIONAL Silver Plectrum and Tenor Guitars

Through long centuries the Guitar has been one of the most favored of instruments. For somehow, it has the power to express as few other instruments can, the heights and depths of human emotion. . . .

Professionals prefer NATIONAL Silver Plectrum and Tenor Guitars because, for orchestra work, they retain the sweet tone of the guitar while yielding the volume of the ordinary banjo.

Beginners find these instruments surprisingly easy to learn to play.

Out on the lot HOOT GIBSON and his Hawaiian Trio of the Hoot Gibson Productions, Inc., not only render delightful music to assist the players in their portrayals but help to pleasantly pass the time between scenes. They use the new National Silver String Instruments exclusively. The second man from the right in this picture is none other than Mr. Gibson himself.

The NATIONAL Silver Ukulele

Those haunting Hawaiian strains played on the Ukulele . . . how they exalt the emotions!

Thousands of Ukulele players have pronounced the NATIONAL Silver Ukulele an instrument that will delight you. It has the same beautiful German silver finish as our Guitars and Mandolins, and the unique NATIONAL feature of amplifying the volume while retaining all the softness and beauty of tone.

Made in three styles, priced as follows:

Style 1—(plain) each.........................$55.00
Style 2—(beautifully hand engraved)..........70.00
Style 3—(Artistic floral design)..............85.00

Fred Walker's Troubadours are distinguished artists delighting exclusive night club, vaudeville and radio audiences with their marvelous music—produced, of course, on NATIONAL String Instruments.

NATIONAL Silver Mandolins

The very advanced acoustical principles embodied in NATIONAL instruments are keeping fretted instruments in line with the point of progress reached by radio, talking pictures and other such modern inventions. And of course these features, being thoroughly covered by our patents, are found **only** in NATIONAL instruments.

Due to its tremendous power, and volume the new NATIONAL Silver Mandolin may be used to lead the largest orchestra. It makes a wonderful double for the tenor guitar or violin player.

PRICES
Style 1 (plain) each....................$65.00
Style 2 (beautifully hand engraved) each 80.00
Style 3 (artistic floral design) each.....95.00

"Best wishes to the National String Instrument Corporation and the World's Best" is the message from the TRIOLIAN TRIO, popular radio artists broadcasting over stations KFI, KFON, KGER and KPLA. The fact that they have named their trio after the NATIONAL instruments they play is significant of the high regard in which these instruments are held.

Triolian Wood,
Tenor Guitar
Style 0

NATIONAL Triolian Tenor Guitars

like all other NATIONAL instruments, possess great power and volume while sacrificing nothing of tone quality.

These Triolian instruments are all made from an alloy metal (which will not rust) finished in two-tone brown walnut with the exception of our Style 0 Tenor Guitar, which is made from selected 3-ply hardwood finished in two-tone walnut. Latest dynamic principles of amplification in this instrument make it possible to produce more volume than the banjo while retaining the sweet tone of the guitar—an invaluable aid whether playing for dance, concert, records, sound pictures or radio.

PRICES Metal Triolian Tenor Guitar (as pictured) $37.50
Triolian Wood Tenor Guitar (Style 0)... 45.00

214

Solomon Uki Makekau, now en route, is an outstanding artist in the Hawaiian Guitar field. As the illustration indicates, this artist takes a keen delight in playing his NATIONAL instrument.

Triolian Spanish and Hawaiian Guitars

produce a volume and tone quality that is equalled only by other NATIONAL instruments. They are beautifully finished in two-tone walnut, ranking with instruments costing several times the price—a price that is made possible only by exceptional demand and mass production. The bodies of these instruments are made from an alloy metal which will not deteriorate in any way and is not affected by moisture or temperature. With reasonable care these instruments will last a lifetime.

Price (as illustrated below) $45.00

Jim Holstein of the popular "JIM AND BUD" radio team, broadcasting their melodies over station WENR, Chicago, is one of the best known and best liked boys in the business, an artist on the Spanish Guitar, and a NATIONAL enthusiast.

Triolian Mandolins and Ukuleles

In an amazingly short time NATIONAL instruments have become famous in all parts of the world. This has been accomplished not only through personal audiences but through the medium of radio, which demands for perfect reception the ultimate in quality and tone clarity.

Triolian Mandolins and Ukuleles, like the Triolian Guitars, surpass all other instruments of similar price in volume and tone quality. They are made from an alloy metal which will not deteriorate in any way, is not affected by moisture or temperature, and with reasonable care will last a lifetime. Finished in modern two-tone brown walnut.

Triolian Mandolin (as illustrated) $40.00
Triolian Ukulele (not illustrated) 25.00

(1) Trojo, star on Keith-Albee Circuit

(2) Kane's Hawaiians, Victor Recording Artists

(3) Al Meredith and His Boys, Vitaphone, Radio and Record Artists

(4) Russell Thompson and Company, Noted Teacher and Radio Entertainer

(5) Irene and Albert Patton, Eastern Radio Stars

(6) The Silver Tone Melody Boys, Vaudeville Recording and Radio Entertainers

(7) Paul's Hawaiians, Pantages Vaudeville Artists

(8) Geo. D. Fassett of the Fassett "No Note" System of Teaching

Use NATIONAL Strings
Insist on This Package

NATIONAL Strings, noted for their purity of tone, are made to specifications of the National String Instrument Corporation and manufactured by a secret process to a micro specific standard. Every NATIONAL string as well as instrument, is carefully tested before leaving the factory. Make sure you get the best strings for all instruments by insisting on the registered trade mark "NATIONAL" on every package.

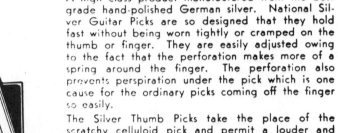

Silver Picks

A high class product manufactured from the best grade hand-polished German silver. National Silver Guitar Picks are so designed that they hold fast without being worn tightly or cramped on the thumb or finger. They are easily adjusted owing to the fact that the perforation makes more of a spring around the finger. The perforation also prevents perspiration under the pick which is one cause for the ordinary picks coming off the finger so easily.

The Silver Thumb Picks take the place of the scratchy celluloid pick and permit a louder and clearer tone than is possible to get with a celluloid or composition pick.

Price 15c

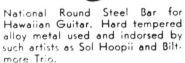

National Round Steel Bar for Hawaiian Guitar. Hard tempered alloy metal used and indorsed by such artists as Sol Hoopii and Biltmore Trio.

Price $1.00

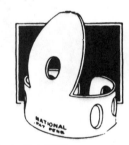

PRICES ON CASES

Side opening, keratol covered three-ply basswood veneer, brass nickel plated lock and catches. String compartment. Strong leather handle. Velvet lined.

For Hawaiian and Spanish Guitars, each....$25.00
Plectrum and Tenor Guitars, each.......... 21.00
Mandolin, each 18.00
Ukulele, each 15.00
Moderately priced composition cases for Triolian instruments, keratol covered, flannel lined, side opening, for
Tenor Guitars, each......................$5.50
Hawaiian and Spanish Guitars, each........ 6.00
Mandolin, each 5.50
Ukulele, each 4.50

Where NATIONAL String Instruments are made

A corner of the assembling room.

The machinist at the right is stamping out metal tops for Silver instruments into which the resonators, being made by the man at the left, are fitted.

Back of NATIONAL String Instruments is not only progressive and inventive American skill but distinguished craftsmanship from the Old World . . . men who have spent half a lifetime in the science of musical instrument making —an art handed down from generation to generation—are whole-heartedly devoted to creating for you instruments possessing a beauty, tone quality and volume never before known.

To insure every instrument being up to high NATIONAL standards of workmanship and performance it must pass the rigid inspection of experts.

TED E. KLEINMEYER
PRESIDENT

PAUL M. BARTH
VICE PRESIDENT

GEORGE D. BEAUCHAMP
SECRETARY-GEN. MANAGER

IN issuing this little booklet it is with a great deal of pride and pleasure that we who are responsible for developing and producing NATIONAL String Instruments wish to thank the many artists—and particularly those whom space has not permitted us to acknowledge—whose exclusive use and hearty recommendations of NATIONAL String Instruments have helped to place these instruments in the paramount position they now occupy.

The realization that NATIONAL String Instruments are bringing greater joy and musical appreciation to countless thousands is one of our most cherished possessions.

Sincerely,

**NATIONAL
STRING INSTRUMENT
CORPORATION**

JACK LEVY
SALES REPRESENTATIVE

C. L. FARR
DIRECTOR

HARRY WATSON
FACTORY SUPERINTENDENT

GLENN E. HARGER
ASST. SECRETARY

A. RICKENBACKER
ENGINEER

The following eight pages are reprinted from a 1935 Chicago Musical Instrument wholesale catalog. The single cone instruments receive more emphasis in this catalog, as tricone sales became a smaller part of National's business. The illustration of the style 4 tricone shows drawn-in engraving designs similar to the very first style 4 guitars. By 1935, of course, style 4 design was of the standard type.

NATIONAL
STRING INSTRUMENTS

NATIONAL
String Instruments

The Duolian
$32.50

The Triolian
$45.00

Constructed along the same lines as the well-known Triolian model but of slightly lighter materials and less expensive finish. Retains the full volume and beautiful tone quality typical of all National Instruments, priced so anyone can afford to own one. Dark black walnut, shaded to light gray, frosted duco finish. Made only in Spanish style but may be had fitted with extension nut for Hawaiian style playing.

The Duolian Guitar. Each $32.50

We believe more of this model guitars have been sold during the past few years than any other high grade guitar made. Its ultra-strong construction, the tremendous power obtained from the large cone amplifier, its ease of playing and sweet tone have built an enviable reputation for this guitar. Made only with Spanish style neck, but may be had with extension nut, if wanted for Hawaiian style playing. Choice of two finishes: Two-tone walnut or polychrome with tropical scene figures.

Triolian Guitar. Each $45.00

Above prices do not include cases. See page 132 for cases.

National String Instruments

NATIONAL
Silver Don
Style No. 1
$85.00

Large Single
Resonator

Style O Silver
Metal Ampli-
fying Guitar
$62.50

Style 1—Genuine mahogany neck, shaped to fit the hand, reinforced with steel, joining the body at the 14th fret; semi-oval fingerboard, black throughout, ivoroid bound; round genuine pearl position dots, pearline scroll. Body is German Silver, nickel plated, with hand engraved border on all sides. Price......................$85.00

Style 2—Same neck and scroll, ivoroid bound fingerboard, with black line inlay; square pearl position dots; body beautifully engraved with modernistic design. Price $110.00

Style 3—Same as Style 2, elaborate conventional engravings; diamond shaped position dots. Price....$125.00

Made of a high grade alloy of metal, heavily nickel plated in a modernistic two-tone effect, fitted with single 10-inch amplifying diaphragm. Fine rock maple neck with celluloid bound, ebonized fingerboard. Pearl position dots, fine brass patent keys. Made in Spanish style only, but can be furnished equipped with metal extension nut for Hawaiian playing at no extra charge.

Style O—Spanish Guitar.......................$62.50

Above prices do not include cases. See page 132 for cases.

National String Instruments

Triolian Tenor Guitar

A wonderful double for the tenor banjo player who doesn't play the six string guitar. The sweet tone of the guitar is retained regardless of the volume produced by the large cone amplifier, making this a perfect orchestra instrument.

Choice of walnut or two-tone polychrome finish. 23-inch scale.

Triolian Tenor Guitar. Each................$37.50

Triolian Plectrum Guitar

The same style and size as the tenor guitar described above and illustrated at the left, except has 27-inch four string plectrum scale.

Walnut or polychrome finish.

Triolian Plectrum Guitar. Each................$42.50

Triolian Mandolin

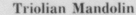

This instrument has done much to bring back the popularity of the mandolin, since it retains the clear, ringing tone typical of a good mandolin, yet the cone amplifier makes possible the volume wanted for ensemble playing. Furnished in either walnut or polychrome duco finish. Eight string style only.

Triolian Mandolin. Each................$40.00

**Triolian
Mandolin**

$40.00

Triolian Ukulele

The Triolian Ukulele surpasses any other instrument of similar price in volume and tone quality. Made of alloy metal which will not deteriorate in any way; not affected by moisture or temperature; it will give a lifetime of highly satisfactory service.

Finished in either two-tone walnut or polychrome duco. Fitted with fine gut strings.

Triolian Ukulele. Each................$25.00

Prices on this page do not include cases. See page 132 for cases.

NATIONAL
SILVER GUITARS

Spanish (Regular) Models

The models of National Silver Guitars shown on this page are built in the Spanish, or regular style, to be played by picking with the fingers. These are ideal accompaniment instruments for the Hawaiian models shown on the preceding page.

Style No. 2
$145.00

Style No. 4
$195.00

[Style 1 and 3
Spanish not
illustrated.]

TRADE NATIONAL MARK

For the accompanist, soloist or orchestral guitarist the Spanish Style National Silver Guitar offers the multiple advantages of beautiful tone, tremendous volume when wanted, and a permanence of construction that only all-metal instruments afford.

Style 1 Spanish—Plain nickel finish..$125.00
Style 2 Spanish—Engraved with neat design............................... 145.00
Style 3 Spanish—More elaborately engraved, ebony fingerboard
    with pearl position dots.. 165.00
Style 4 Spanish—Beautifully engraved all over in especially elab-
    orate design, fine ebony fingerboard with pearl position markers 195.00

Above prices do not include cases. See page 132 for cases.

NATIONAL
SILVER GUITARS

Hawaiian Models

National Silver Guitars are made of German silver, heavily nickel plated. The bridge, a three-armed truss, is supported by three-cone amplifiers, or diaphragms, resting on a sub-frame in the center of the body. The tone is rich and full, and great volume may be had without distortion.

[Style 2 and 4
Hawaiian not
illustrated]

Style No. 1
$125.00

Style No. 3
$165.00

The Hawaiian Models of these new instruments are now being used by practically all of the foremost exponents of this fascinating style of playing. The tone is admirably suited for their purposes and the great volume is especially welcomed by those who play to large audiences.

Style 1 Hawaiian—Plain nickel finish $125.00
Style 2 Hawaiian—Engraved with neat design 145.00
Style 3 Hawaiian—More elaborately engraved, ebony finger-
    board, pearl position dots 165.00
Style 4 Hawaiian—Beautifully engraved all over, especially elab-
    orate design, fine ebony fingerboard with pearl position markers 195.00

Above prices do not include case. See page 132 for cases.

National String Instruments

NATIONAL Silver
Tenor Style No. 1
$75.00

NATIONAL
Silver No. 3
Mandolin
$95.00

National Tenor Guitars

Tenor Style, 4 strings, 23-inch neck, geared pegs, extension fingerboard.

Style 1 Tenor—Plain nickel finish....... $ 75.00

Style 2 Tenor—Engraved with neat design 95.00

Style 3 Tenor—M o r e elaborately engraved, ebony fingerboard with pearl position dots 115.00

National Plectrum Guitars

Plectrum (4-string long neck) style. Fitted with geared pegs, extension fingerboard, 26-inch scale.

Style 1 Plectrum—Plain nickel finish.... $ 80.00

Style 2 Plectrum—Engraved with neat design 100.00

Style 3 Plectrum—More elaborately engraved, ebony fingerboard with pearl position dots 120.00

National Silver Mandolins

The very advanced acoustical principles embodied in National instruments are keeping fretted instruments in line with the point of progress reached by radio, talking pictures and other such modern inventions. These features, being covered by patents, are found only in National instruments.

Due to its tremendous power and volume the new National Silver Mandolin may be used to lead the largest orchestra. It makes a wonderful double for the tenor guitar or violin player.

Eight strings, patent keys, extension fingerboard.

Style 1 Mandolin—Plain nickel finish................$65.00

Style 2 Mandolin—Neatly engraved all over........ 80.00

Style 3 Mandolin—Elaborately engraved, w i t h fine ebony fingerboard and pearl position dots.... 95.00

Above prices do not include case. See page 132 for cases.

National String Instruments

Estralita
$55.00

Estralita
and
Trojan

Wood Body, Amplifying
Guitars

The Trojan
$35.00

New National "ESTRALITA" Guitar

An improved Grand Concert model of larger size and greater beauty, for exacting orchestra playing, with the powerful genuine National amplification, which has won the acclaim of guitarists all over the world.

The body is finely veneered with selected figured mahogany, in a lustrous dark reddish brown hand-rubbed and polished finish. The edges are bound with heavy white celluloid, neatly inlaid with black and white. Inlay to match around the nickel plated cover. The mahogany neck is steel reinforced and the oval fingerboard is nicely inlaid with ornamental position markers on the front, and small markers on the side. 14 frets clear of body.

Powerful amplification of tone, through the time-tested National patented single-cone amplifier, is the feature of this new instrument which will give it a strong appeal to all musicians whose work requires a full volume of tone without loss of the best tone quality.

No. 1245 .... $55.00

Trojan

Maple veneered hardwood body, richly lacquered finish in shaded walnut brown, top bound with white ivoroid purfling. Neck is of selected straight grain mahogany with oval fingerboard having fourteen frets clear, reinforced with steel bar. This model at its low price, with the powerful, perfectly balanced amplification of sound from the large single resonator tone amplifier device represents a truly splendid value in a fine orchestra guitar.

Price $35.00

Above prices do not include case. See page 132 for cases.

"National" Silver Guitars
(3 RESONATOR MODELS)

SPANISH STYLE "NATIONAL" GUITARS
(3 Resonator Models)

All four models of "NATIONAL" Silver Guitars listed below, are the three resonator model. The body is real German silver and highly polished. The neck is genuine mahogany, reinforced with a special steel rod; the fingerboard is genuine ebony, bound with white celluloid and inlaid with neat pearl position markers. Tremendous volume and a sweetness of tone.

Illustration to the left shows "NATIONAL" Spanish style Guitar.

No. 1 S German silver, plain finish, highly polished .... Each $125.00
No. 2 S German silver body, highly polished. Beautifully hand engraved .... Each $145.00
No. 3 S German silver body, highly polished, floral design engraved. De Luxe Artist's model .... Each $165.00
No. 4 S German Silver body, highly polished. Artist's model. Elaborately engraved and exquisitely decorated and finished throughout .... Each $195.00

Spanish Guitar Style No. 1 S

HAWAIIAN STYLE "NATIONAL" GUITARS
(3 resonator models)

National Hawaiian Guitars are identical in construction to the Spanish style, except that they are equipped with a square neck. They are extremely popular and an inspection of these highly attractive "National" instruments will make it easy to understand why owners of "National" Guitars take such pride in their possession.

No. 1 H German silver, plain finish, highly polished. Each $125.00
No. 2 H German silver body, highly polished. Beautifully hand engraved. Each.................... $145.00
No. 3 H German silver body, highly polished; floral design engraved De Luxe Artist's model. Each.... $165.00
No. 4 H German silver body, highly polished. Artist's model. Elaborately engraved and exquisitely decorated and finished throughout. Each....... $195.00

Illustration to the right shows "NATIONAL" Hawaiian style Guitar, with square neck.

1935 Tonk Brothers catalog page with tricones listed.

BRONSON MUSIC & SALES CORPORATION

National Silver Amplifying Guitars

National "Silver" Guitars are the ultimate in metal guitar construction. For the soloist, accompanist, or orchestral guitarist these instruments offer unparalleled advantages. In richness and beauty of tone, in volume, in permanence of construction, in fascinating eye-appeal these "Silver" Guitars cannot be excelled. Made of German Silver, heavily nickel-plated. The bridge, a three-armed truss, is supported by three-cone Amplifier, or diaphragm, resting on a sub-frame in the center of the body. Entire instrument is finished in brilliant, highly polished silver.

Style No. 1 $125.00
Style No. 4 $195.00

Spanish (Reg.) Model Guitars

STYLE 1 — SPANISH GUITAR. Plain German Silver body, heavily nickel-plated neat model. $125.00

STYLE 2 — SPANISH GUITAR. German silver body. Beautifully engraved with neat floral design. $145.00

STYLE 3 — SPANISH GUITAR. Elaborately engraved body with floral designs. Ebony fingerboard with fancy cut pearl position dots. Pearloid covered headpiece. $165.00

STYLE 4 — SPANISH GUITAR. "DeLuxe" Model, artistically engraved with elaborate floral designs all over. Ebony fingerboard with fancy cut pearl position dots. Pearloid covered headpiece. $195.00

Hawaiian Model Guitars

The Choice of the Artist

Style No. 1 $125.00
Style No. 3 $165.00

The Hawaiian hollow-neck Models "Silver" Guitars are now being used by practically all of the foremost exponents of this fascinating style of playing. The tone is admirably suited for their purposes and the great volume is especially welcomed by those who play to large audiences.

Tone — Beauty — Distinction

STYLE 1—HAWAIIAN GUITAR. Plain German Silver body. Heavily nickel-plated neat model. $125.00

STYLE 2—HAWAIIAN GUITAR. German Silver body. Beautifully engraved with neat floral design. $145.00

STYLE 3—HAWAIIAN GUITAR. Elaborately engraved body with floral designs. Ebony fingerboard with fancy cut pearl position dots. Pearloid covered headpiece. $165.00

STYLE 4—HAWAIIAN GUITAR. "DeLuxe" Model, artistically engraved with elaborate floral designs all over. Ebony fingerboard with fancy cut pearl position dots. Pearloid covered headpiece. $195.00

Cases for "National" Guitars Listed on Page 33
"National" Strings and Accessories Page 39

1935 Bronson wholesale catalog illustrating tricones.

PRICE LIST FOR STANDARD REPAIR PARTS

	Name of Model	Resonator Diaphragm Each	Bridge for Strings Each	Top Cover Plate Each	Pick Guard Each	Tail Piece Each	Patent Heads per Set	Finger Board Each	Necks Compl with Finger Boards Each
Spanish and Hawaiian Guitars	Havana	$3.00	$.25	$3.50	$2.50	$.85	$1.00	$4.00	$10.00
	Style "O"	3.00	.25	3.50	2.50	.85	9.50	5.00	12.00
	Marino	1.00	1.00	4.00	2.75	.85	2.50	5.00	12.00
	Artist Model No. 3	1.00	1.00	10.00	2.75	.85	2.50	6.00	14.00
	Aragon No. 5	3.00	.35	10.00	3.95	7.50	2.50	9.00	25.00
	New Yorker Span		1.00		2.75	1.25	2.50	5.00	14.00
	New Yorker Haw		.25			.75	2.50	6.00	
	Sonora		1.00		3.25	7.50	2.50	9.00	25.00
	Grand Console		.25			.75	4.00	7.50	
	Supro Arcadia	2.50	.25	3.50		.85	1.00	1.50	5.00
	Supro Collegian	3.00	.25	3.50	2.50	.85	1.00	2.50	8.50
	Supro Avalon Span		1.00		2.50	1.25	1.00	2.50	8.50
	Supro Avalon Haw		.25			.75	1.00	3.00	
	Supro No. 60		.25			.75	1.00	1.00	
	Supro No. 70		.25			.75	1.00	1.00	
Tenor Guitars	Style "O"	2.50	.25	3.00	2.50	.75	3.60	4.00	11.00
	New Yorker		1.00			.75	2.50	6.00	12.00
	Supro Collegian	2.50	.25	3.00	2.25	.75	1.60	2.50	8.00
Mandolins	Style "O"	2.50	.25	3.00	2.50	.75	1.20	3.50	10.00
	New Yorker		1.00		2.50	.75	1.20	3.50	10.00
	Supro Collegian	2.50	.25	3.00	2.25	.75	1.00	2.50	8.00
Ukes	Style "O"	2.00	.25	2.00		.50	1.50	2.50	6.50
	Supro Collegian	2.00	.25	2.00		.50	1.50	1.50	4.00

	Item	Price Each	Item	Price Each	Item	Price Each
Miscellaneous Prices	National Elec Guitar Cord	$3.50	Hawaiian Steels	$1.00	Frets, per Set	$.50
	Supro Elec Guitar Cord	2.50	Fuses	.10	Cover screws, doz	.15
	Elec Tone Controls	1.00	Pearl Dots	.05	Individual Keys ea	.75
	Elec Vol Controls	1.00	Bone Nuts	.10	Nat'l Haw Hand Rest	3.00
	Control Knobs	.15	Steel Adjuster Nut	.10	Supro Haw Hd Rest	2.00
			Bridge Woods	.15	Finger Picks each	.10
			Tail But with Screws	.15		

1936 National price list for parts.
These amazingly low prices never changed.

NATIONAL "Duolian" Metal Amplifying Guitar

The **"DUOLIAN" Model** is the **single amplifier type.** The steel body is finished in a beautiful two-tone frosted duco; the neck is natural finished mahogany, **steel reinforced** and equipped with a correctly fretted ebonized fingerboard. We will ship instrument adjusted to Spanish style of playing, but can furnish adjusted for Hawaiian playing by special order, at no extra charge. Each $32.50

$32⁵⁰

A 1935 Tonk Brothers wholesale catalog page showing the new 14 fret Duolian, and an older illustration of a 12 fret Triolian.

NATIONAL "Triolian" Metal Amplifying Guitar

The **"TRIOLIAN"** is one of the best known numbers in the National line. It is the **single amplifier type.** Substantially built steel body, finished in a beautifully improved prismatic walnut. The tremendous tone power —the fine adjustments, which assure ease of playing, will convince you immediately that the "TRIOLIAN" is a high-grade instrument, still it is priced within the reach of all. We will ship adjusted for Spanish style of playing, but can be furnished and adjusted for Hawaiian playing by special order at no extra charge. Each..................................... **$45.00**

$45⁰⁰

NATIONAL Style O Silver Metal Amplifying Guitar

Style "O" has been a favorite for many years. Made from a high-grade alloy metal, **heavily nickel-plated with a beautiful two-tone silver finish.** It is the **single resonator type:** the neck is rock maple, reinforced by a steel rod, and equipped with a fine ebony finished fingerboard, which is celluloid bound. Tremendous volume of tone—beautiful finish. We will ship adjusted for Spanish playing but can be furnished adjusted for Hawaiian playing by special order at no extra charge. Each..**$62.50**

$62⁵⁰

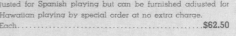

A page from the same catalog, showing the new silver Don model and an older illustration of a 12 fret style O guitar.

NATIONAL Silver Don
Style No. 1

The **"DON"** is one of the latest additions to the NATIONAL line and is of **the large single resonator** The body is **genuine German silver,** highly plated and polished, and decorated with ha graved borders on all sides. The neck is genui hogany, gracefully shaped and reinforced with The fingerboard is ebonized and semi-oval, bou celluloid and joins the body at the 14th fret. A t markable instrument. We will ship adjusted for ish style of playing, but can be furnished and a for Hawaiian playing by special order at no charge. Each ....

$85⁰⁰

NATIONAL Metal Amplifying Mandolins
Tenor Guitars—Plectrum Guitars
and Ukuleles

All instruments listed and illustrated below, are **the single resonator type.**
Irrespective of style or finish, size and model of all instruments are the same.

NATIONAL AMPLIFYING MANDOLINS

"TRIOLIAN" model finished in the new improved prismatic walnut....Each $40.00

Style 1 German silver body, highly polished, plain finish ....Each $65.00

Style 2 German silver body, highly polished and **beautifully hand engraved** ....Each $80.00

Style 3 German silver body, highly polished; **elaborately engraved with artistic floral design** ....Each $95.00

NATIONAL AMPLIFYING TENOR GUITARS

"TRIOLIAN" model finished in the new improved prismatic walnut....Each $37.50

Style 1 German silver body, highly polished, plain finish ....Each $75.00

Style 2 German silver body, highly polished and **beautifully hand engraved** ....Each $95.00

Style 3 German silver body, highly polished; **elaborately engraved with artistic floral design** ....Each $115.00

NATIONAL AMPLIFYING PLECTRUM GUITARS

"TRIOLIAN" model finished in the new improved prismatic walnut....Each $42.50

Style 1 German silver body, highly polished, plain finish ....Each $80.00

Style 2 German silver body, highly polished and **beautifully hand engraved** ....Each $100.00

Style 3 German silver body, highly polished; **elaborately engraved with artistic floral design** ....Each $120.00

NATIONAL AMPLIFYING UKULELES

"TRIOLIAN" model, finished in the new improved prismatic walnut..Each $25.00

Style 1 German silver body, highly polished, plain finish ....Each $55.00

Style 2 German silver body, highly polished and **beautifully hand engraved** ....Each $70.00

Style 3 German silver body, highly polished; **elaborately engraved with artistic floral design** ....Each $85.00

"Triolian" Tenor Guitar

"Triolian" Mandolin

"Triolian" Ukulele

"Style 2" Tenor Guitar

"Style 3" Mandolin

"Style 3" Ukulele

1935 Tonk Bros. page illustrating the triolian line of tenors, mandolin, and uke. Some silver models of the same instruments are also shown.

"DUOLIAN"

"TROJAN"

"TRIOLIAN"

NATIONAL "DUOLIAN" ALL-METAL AMPLIFYING GUITAR

The "Duolian" model with single amplifier, has a durable all-metal body, finished in a beautiful hand-grained walnut. The neck is hardwood, specially strengthened against warping, and finished to match body; fingerboard is hand-fretted to insure ease of action, and is joined to the body at the 14th fret. A genuine favorite at a price everyone can afford.

"Duolian" .... Each $35.00

Also available with square neck for Hawaiian playing. When ordering please specify.

NATIONAL "TROJAN" WOOD BODY AMPLIFYING GUITAR

The "Trojan" model has a combination wood body and metal resonator, giving guitar the fine rounded tone of a wood instrument, plus the volume and power of National amplification. The non-warping neck is of selected mahogany, bound with celluloid; carefully hand-fretted fingerboard joined to the body at the 14th fret; engraved "ebonoid" pick guard. A most striking and popular instrument at a very modest price.

"Trojan" .... Each $37.50

Also available with square neck for Hawaiian playing. When ordering please specify.

NATIONAL "TRIOLIAN" ALL-METAL AMPLIFYING GUITAR

"The "Triolian" is certain to please the critical buyer, and is the most popular of the grained-finished, single amplifier, all-metal guitars. Special heavy gauge metal body finished in natural grain burl mahogany polished to a bright luster. Special carved reinforced hardwood neck makes playing easy. The head piece and pick guard are made of "ebonoid" artistically engraved; rosewood fingerboard, hand fretted, bound with celluloid; pearl position dots; has 14 frets clear of body.

"Triolian" .... Each $47.50

Also available with square neck for Hawaiian playing. When ordering please specify.

CASE

No. 631—Chipboard, covered with waterproof material, flannel lined; fits Duolian, Trojan or Triolian .... Each $4.60

TRADE NATIONAL MARK MADE IN U.S.A.

Amplifying Tenor Guitars

Style 3

NATIONAL

Model 97

1939 catalog illustrations of Style 3 and 97 tenors.

A page from the 1937-38 Wm. Dyer and Brother wholesale catalog with modernized Duolian, Triolian and Trojan guitars, with pickguards and wood-grained finishes.

The Twentieth Century brought about a change and improvements in nearly everything that mankind uses—and so it is today with many new improvements in making of fretted instruments.

With the introduction of the radio and recording in the world of music it required improvement of the old way in making Guitars, Mandolins and other string instruments.

No longer is it necessary to depend upon the acoustics of the hand made wood instruments for quality and response, as the "National" introduced to the profession a RESONATOR TYPE of string instrument developed in the same laboratories that science perfected instruments which give exact measurements of tone resonance and quality—The same scientific laboratory facilities were employed to produce "a heart of an instrument." THE NATIONAL RESONATOR patented in U. S. and foreign countries.

Special alloy metals are employed in making of the bodies of National Instruments to respond sympathetically to the vibration of "the heart of the instrument." The Resonator thereby producing the finest and purest tone which is so desirable for recording as well as radio broadcasting and which is only possible to produce with the "NATIONAL" Instruments.

NATIONAL DOBRO CORPORATION

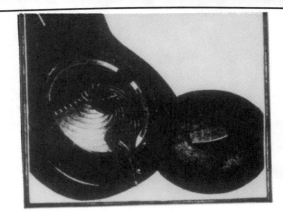

The National Resonator built into the body of the amplifying guitar is the result of developments in laboratories where measurements of its vibratory response were taken with instruments capable of measuring one millionth vibration, for the purpose of determining its responsiveness.

Special gauge and weight aluminum alloy is used in making these Resonators, although they are most sensitive and delicate, they are not subject to easy breakage. However, they are replaceable at a very small cost.

All single plate type instruments have Resonators varying in size approximately from 8" to 11" depending upon the style of the instrument. All 3 plate style instruments have 3-6" Resonator units in one instrument enabling more flexible tone and greater volume.

Model 35 Silver Guitar

MANY an artist gained fame and recognition by using the National Silver Instruments for stage, recording, and radio broadcasting.

The special nickel silver body of the Style 35 model is equipped with 3 Resonator Diaphram scientifically placed to enable a volume and quality of tone possible only when perfect acoustics are employed, such as in the NATIONAL Guitar.

A design etched into the plating in beautiful colors is a work of art in itself. To match the mood and temperament of the artist playing this instrument.

Price $135.00

Available in Hawaiian or Spanish Styles

Finger Picks

Your fingers are never tired when you use National Silver Picks for Hawaiian Guitar playing. They are shaped to fit the thumb and fingers which makes them extremely comfortable to use.

Price ....Each 10c

Available at Your Music Store

Style 97 Tri-Plate Guitar

A NEW addition to [the] world famous National Triple Resona[tor] Guitar. Heretofore obtainable only fr[om] $125.00 and up. This new model, [a] special brass alloy body heavily nic[kel] plated with satin designs in colors etch[ed] into the plating on the front and sid[es]. The back has a design in color of a s[ea] rider with the Hawaiian Islands as [a] background and adds to the atmosph[ere] of this already popular instrument which is appropriate.

All Hawaiian models have squ[are] necks, which not only add to the t[one] but are more convenient to handle w[hen] playing.

Price $97.50

The "Original" Round Stee[l]

The National stainless steel is a favorite of most particular players, designed by artists use of the professional. No rust—no scratch but a compact, smooth steel, which just fits hand and glides easily over the strings.

National Steel..............Each $1.00

The next seventeen illustrations are from the 1936-1937 Chicago catalog. All of the models have been changed since the 1920's. Note the "scientific" prose. Just what IS one-millionth vibration?

"The Triolian" Single Resonator Guitar

THIS special heavy gauge body has a hard baked finish of synthetic mahogany.

The grain pattern was taken from a select piece of mahogany and the result is a high-grade piano finish, depicting a fine mahogany grain which is beautiful as well as lasting.

The powerful single plate National Resonator in this special body enables the reproduction of a tone not possible to obtain with an ordinary guitar.

All Hawaiian models are equipped with a solid hardwood square neck.

Price **$47.50**

National Steels

The weight and size of the Hawaiian Guitar Steels is extremely important.

The National Steel is both shaped correctly and has proper weight because it has been designed by those who play Hawaiian Guitars professionally—and know.

Price . . . . **Each $1.00**

Single Resonator Tenor Guitars

O Style

The Triolian

HEAVILY nickle plated body of Style "O" Tenor Guitars has a satin finish design same as the regular guitar, the rock maple neck with a bound ebony finger board is properly shaped for fast playing.

The head piece and pick guard add to the instrument an air of distinction.

The National single plate Resonator enables the artist to produce a tone not obtainable with ordinary instruments.

Price **$65.00**

THE Triolian Tenor Guitar has a hard baked synthetic mahogany finish on the all metal body, same as the 6 string models.

The modernistic head piece and pick guard are original. The mahogany neck is celluloid bound and shaped to respond to the artist for execution of fast technique.

The single diaphram Resonator produces a tone most desirable for broadcasting performers.

Price **$45.00**

De Luxe Models Amplifying Mandolins

Style 3

THE Style 3 Silver Mandolin is all that an artist can wish for. Its unmatched bell-like tone and tremendous volume makes itself noticeable in the string ensemble.

The hand engraved body is a work of art and will become a treasure to any mandolin player who acquires one.

Price **$115.00**

Model 97

MODEL 97 Mandolin matches the beautiful design of the Model 97 Guitar. A combination of the National Amplifier built into the all nickle silver body provides quality and volume of tone that is appealing and pleasant.

The heavily plated and sand blasted designs filled in with fast coloring makes it so much more desirable and appreciable.

Price **$97.50**

> Use strings that are made for National Mandolins for more Resonance, longer wear, and better tone.
> *Available at Any Dealer*

All Metal Amplifying Mandolins

Style O

The Triolian

STYLE O Mandolin is like the Style O Guitar; it has proven to be particularly adaptable for stage work because of its all nickle plated special brass alloy body with beautiful sand etched designs.

It produces a volume which brings the Mandolin back to its favorite position of a decade ago.

A hard maple neck, celluloid bound and an ebony finger board provide an action for lightning fast technique so desirable by Mandolin players.

Price **$65.00**

THE Triolian Mandolin body is of special alloy metal finished in synthetic mahogany grain which is hard baked and hand polished. It is one of the favorites with the Mandolin players because of its practicability as well as attractiveness in finish and unusual powerful tone.

Price **$45.00**

> All strings made for National Amplifying Instruments are the result of intensive research to produce clear resonant notes without "WOLF" overtones.
> They will improve the tone of any string instrument.
> *Available at Any Dealer*

HAWAIIAN SQUARE NECK

SPANISH NECK

FING. BOARD

PICK GUARD

TAIL PIECE

BRIDGE

PAT. HEADS

RESONATOR DIAPHRAM

RESONATOR COVER PLATE

ELECTRIC GUITAR CORD

Amplifying Ukuleles

Style O

The Triolian

Style 3

MODEL 3 Ukulele is an all nickle Silver instrument, hand engraved to match the style 3 Mandolin, is a favorite with the stage performers. It has flash as well as tone, which is only possible through National Amplification.

Price $85.00

THE Style O is heavily nickle plated with attractive sand blasted designs to match the style "O" Guitar and Mandolin.

A rock maple thin neck and an ebony finger board provides an action for delicate fast fingering.

The National Amplifying Unit is built in to provide volume and quality tone not obtainable with ordinary Ukuleles.

Price $40.00

THE Triolian Ukulele has the same hard baked mahogany finish as the Triolian Guitar and Mandolin.

The all metal bodies have specially designed powerful amplifiers to give volume that is not possible in an ordinary instrument.

Specially adaptable for radio broadcasting and recording.

Price $25.00

Amplifying Tenor Guitars

Style 3

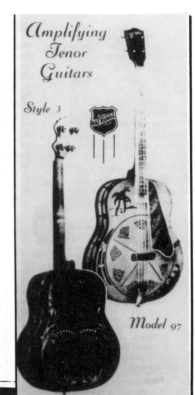

Model 97

STYLE 3 Silver Tenor Guitar is like a fine piece of jewelry. This nickle silver guitar commands attention with its distinctive tone and tremendous volume. It is the answer to the artist that expects—and finds it in the National only.

A select curly maple neck and ebony fingerboard bound with celluloid has an action and response for fast technique.

The nickle silver body is hand engraved which affords a design that is not only artistically beautiful but permanently lasting.

Price $115.00

FOR stage presentation work the Model 97 Tenor Guitar is most ideal. A special brass alloy metal body heavily plated and although modestly it is very tastefully decorated with fast colors in etched designs that are most appealing.

No wood instrument can come up in volume to this National Amplifying Tenor Guitar.

Price $97.50

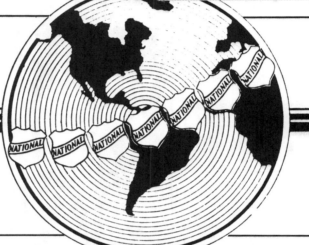

Spanish Electric Guitar

LIKE in the experimental days of the Hawaiian electric guitar—when everyone refused to accept the fact that it was possible to produce an instrument which would answer the requirements of the artist—and not until NATIONAL presented the finished model did all agree that it was no longer a dream, but an actual reality.

And so it is with the National Spanish electric guitar. The most orthodox guitarist will be completely convinced that in the NATIONAL he "can" have volume. . . without sacrificing tonal quality. The conventional arched body, a fine matched two piece maple back and select spruce top is the work of experienced craftsmanship. The seven-ply neck and ebony fingerboard carefully fretted afford an action second to none. Made to meet the requirements of a most particular guitarist.

Price $75.00
Does Not Include Amplifier

Electric Mandolin and Tenor Guitar

THE same precision and workmanship of quality and tone that is being exercised in the National Hawaiian and Spanish Electric Guitars is true with the Tenor Guitar.

The arch top and back, wood body matches the Spanish Guitar, an exceptional fine neck offers no resistance to fast technique, and because of its sensitiveness it requires much less effort to produce a lot more results on the Electric Tenor Guitar than on an ordinary instrument.

Price $75.00
Amplifier Additional

AT last, a Mandolin with a grand piano volume and quality of a harp.

The National Electric Amplification of this beautiful instrument has made it outstanding in the fretted instrument family.

Being a lead instrument in the string ensemble full justice can be given to the mandolin because of its almost unbelievable volume without distortion or sacrificing of tonal qualities.

The wood body matches the Spanish Guitar, has a piano finish and the conventional scale.

National Electric Mandolin, $75.00
Amplifier Not Included

National Hawaiian Electric Guitar

So beautiful in design and yet every inch of it is built to serve the artist playing it and to the listener admiring it.

Only NATIONAL, with the experience of a pioneer can bring to you fingertip control of an instrument which can be played in "whispered" tones or brought up to a volume sufficient to fill an auditorium. It enables an artist to bring out talents and performance never before possible.

Modernistically designed this extraordinary instrument is not only beautiful in appearance but affords special convenience to the player not to be found in any other instrument in the music field today.

A special chamber to accommodate steels and picks is provided in the body of the instrument for the convenience of the player. The face of the instrument is covered with a new type of material that provides a finish that is more lasting than chromium plating. It is hard and has a high lustre. Easily kept clean with little effort.

Six, seven, or eight string models fills the demand for various intricate tunings. The electric pick-up is concealed in the body.

Price for 6 string model .. $75.00
Price for 7 string model .. 82.50
Price for 8 string model .. 90.00

Above Prices Do Not Include Amplifier

National Electric Amplifier

A very useful feature in the National Electric Amplifier is its adaptability as a Hawaiian Guitar stand. When set up it is 27" high and the top is 4½" wide and 15" long.

The National Electric Amplifier is in a cabinet 14¼" high, 9½" wide, and 14" long and is completely enclosed when carrying.

No electric guitar can be better than its amplifier - the NATIONAL is made to the specifications of the strictest requirements of the highest engineering standards—licensed under the A. T. & T., and the electrical research laboratories. It insures maximum in performance and service. The neatly designed fifteen watt chassis and the special heavy duty twelve inch speaker are enclosed in a neat cabinet which is completely enclosed while carrying, or can be set up as a guitar stand while playing.

Will accommodate two instruments, independent of each other or a microphone and an instrument.

Operates only on a 110 volts A. C.—50-60 cycles

Price $75.00

A Universal AC-DC Amplifier for use with various currents and cycles is available.

Prices for Amplifiers to be used for this purpose are furnished upon request.

Specify voltage and cycle current when inquiring.

AND NOW A HIGHLY PERFECTED Electric Violin

THE NEW VIOLECTRIC

Having the background of being the pioneers in developing and perfecting the electrically amplified string instruments. The National engineers produced an electric violin that surpasses the remotest expectations of the old school violin-educated artists—who through their lifetime profession never cease to search for a Violin that will bring them response in fine tone, that is equally satisfying in quality and volume, in all positions of the scale.

The Violectric enables the artist to produce a tone in volume to equal or even surpass other musical instruments, yet, it retains the beauty of tone so traditional with the violin.

The fine ebony finger board and trimmings are of the same quality as in the high-grade expensive Violins. Aluminum and silver wound gut strings used on regular Violins are adaptable on the Violectric.

Model A Outfit
Consisting of a high-grade form-fit plush lined case with a Violectric Amplifier complete.
Price per outfit $175.00

Model B
The National Violectric with the De Luxe Model curly plush lined square case covered with a most attractive ivory Spanish drab to match the powerful and larger Violectric Amplifier which has 3 inputs to accommodate 3 instruments or 2 instruments and a microphone. It is completely enclosed when carrying and is similar to the amplifier description on page 32.
Price De Luxe outfit complete.
$225.00

It is clear that National had adapted to the Depression and other trends of the "moderne" 1930's. The esthetics of these models reflect the economy and consumer wants of the 1930s. The products now resemble those of the modern group of mass-production Chicago-based instrument companies. The transition between old-world guitar makers and modern factory methods was nearly complete by this time. Note the many electric models, the backbone of National's late 1930's business.

NATIONAL

The Worlds

MOST FAMOUS

Electric and Amplifying

String Instruments

STAFFELBACH & DUFFY CO.
ESTABLISHED 1922
ST. LOUIS, MO.

WHOLESALERS MUSICAL ACCESSORIES — WHOLESALERS MUSICAL INSTRUMENTS

THE LINE OF CHAMPIONS

NATIONAL

The World's
MOST FAMOUS

**ELECTRIC AND AMPLIFYING
STRING INSTRUMENTS**

"The Heart" of a National

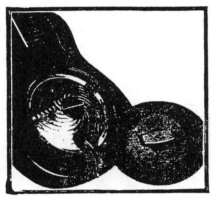

This PATENTED, Super-Sensitive, Virgin Aluminum Cone is the pulsing "Heart" of a National Guitar. From this responsive plate comes the amplified, full, pure tones of the vibrating strings. Its size, gauge, design, weight and vibrating response were not selected by mere chance, but represent the culmination of years of true, scientific experiment. This principle of mechanical sound amplification, made possible and practical the use of metal in the construction of a superior and lasting guitar body.

But this feature of more durable construction was not the greatest achievement, for it was discovered that these amplified tones were more mellow and sweeter even than those of the finest wood instruments. And the smooth volume and penetrating power far surpassed the conventional guitar.

This PATENTED Resonator is not a new and untried principle—but has stood the test of years in the now World Famous Line of NATIONAL Guitars.

**Style 4
Silver Guitar**

Style 4—Silver Guitar

This DeLuxe model, the original and most famous of National Amplified Guitars, played the leading role in popularizing Hawaiian Music in this Country.

The brilliant mirror surface of the beautiful silver body is elaborately **hand engraved** and tops the field for Professional Showmanship.

The Hawaiian model has a hollow square neck of silver, a graceful extension of the body—the super modern black fingerboard is of agate-like "Ebonoid"* with frets and position markings carved into the everlasting surface.

The fine hand shaped neck of the Spanish model is highly polished. The genuine mahogany used in these Spanish necks has been seasoned for over ten years to insure against defect and warpage. The hand fretted fingerboard is of ebony, ivory bound and is inlayed by hand with fancy mother of pearl. The pick guard is crystal clear so as not to obscure the beautiful body design.

The carved headpiece is of jet black "Ebonoid"*. The heavy duty keys are mounted on fancy engraved nickel plates.

These fine instruments are scientifically engineered with three 6" Patented Resonating Plates—giving a flexibility of response and a ll sweetness of tone, unrivaled for perfection of true Hawaiian style music.

Spanish Neck joins the body at the twelfth fret.

Price $195.00

*"Ebonoid"—an exclusive material featured by NATIONAL.

PRICES SUBJECT TO CHANGE WITHOUT NOTICE

1939 Stafflebach and Duffy wholesale catalog page. Note "scientific" language describing the resonator concept, and also the clear plastic pickguard illustrated on the style 4 Hawaiian guitar.

WHOLESALERS MUSICAL ACCESSORIES

STAFFELBACH & DUFFY CO.
ESTABLISHED 1922
ST. LOUIS, MO.

WHOLESALERS MUSICAL INSTRUMENTS

GENUINE NATIONAL GUITARS

**Model 35
Silver Guitar**

Model 35—Silver Guitar

Exquisite as a fine painting, the superb beauty of this elaborate instrument will please any Professional.

The radiant nickel silver body is heavily plated and brilliantly polished. Into the surface is etched a beautiful design, tinted with sparkling, rich, natural colors.

The neck of the Hawaiian model is formed by a flowing extension of the beautiful silver body to the headpiece. The ultra modern fingerboard is of lasting black "Ebonoid"* with the frets and positions engraved into the hard surface.

The neat hand shaped, genuine mahogany neck of the Spanish model is well-seasoned (10 years) and is finished in dark, high polish mahogany. The hand fretted fingerboard is of natural rosewood, neatly bound with celluloid. Neck joins the body at the twelfth fret.

The headpiece is of carved black "Ebonoid"*, Stream-line nickel plates are used on the heavy-duty Patent Heads, adding beauty and form to the Hawaiian models.

The three-plate resonator construction provides that distinctively superior tonal beauty so true of NATIONAL amplification.

Price. $135.00

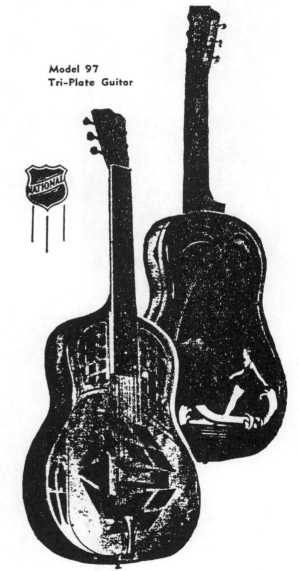

**Model 97
Tri-Plate Guitar**

Model 97 Guitar
Use National Three-Plate Strings

A new popular priced addition to the World Famous Family of National Triple-Resonator Guitars.

The attractive alloy nickeled body is brilliantly polished. Etched into the mirror surface is an inviting design that is finished in bright, natural colors.

The Hawaiian model has a beautiful square, hardwood neck, finished in a rich mahogany. The modernistic fingerboard is of everlasting black "Ebonoid"* with frets and positions engraved into the flint-like surface. Headpiece is of same glossy material.

The Spanish neck is hand shaped from hardwood and is finished in high polish mahogany. The ivory bound fingerboard is of genuine ebony, hand fretted and skillfully arched to allow easy action. Neck joins the body at the twelfth fret.

All gears and working parts of the Patent Heads on the Hawaiian models are enclosed in a nickeled metal shell. The pick guard on the Spanish model is of crystalline transparent, so that all the beautiful body design may be clearly visible.

Has that superior tonal beauty and perfect fidelity that can be produced only by NATIONAL'S famous 3-Plate Resonator Principle.

Price. $97.50

Insist on Square Neck on Hawaiian Models.

Models 97 and 35 displayed and romantically described in the 1939 Stafflebach and Duffy catalog.

1939-40 National catalog with style O guitar and mandolin, and low-priced Havana guitar.

Style "O"

Detail of 1939-40 style O with large headstock, modern inlays, and palm tree side-etching.

1939-40 catalog page with the Aragon and the style 3.

NATIONAL AMPLIFYING INSTRUMENTS

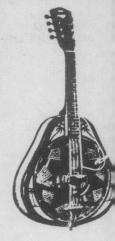

STYLE "O" INSTRUMENTS

The Professional's choice of the Famous Single Plate National Alloy Guitars.

The "life-time" metal body is brightly plated and artistically etched with graceful tropical palms, affording a truly restful island atmosphere. The pick guard is of crystal clear transparent.

Carefully designed, the Style "O" neck offers a new thrill to the Modern Guitar Player. The wood is finished in rich hand rubbed mahogany and ornamented with a lustrous black headpiece.

The neatly bound ebony finger board, carefully hand fretted, is scientifically arched for "feather-touch" action. Positions are marked with beautiful diamond pearl inlays.

Both Spanish and Hawaiian necks join the body at the fourteenth fret. Hawaiian models have famous National non-warping Square Neck.

No. 65 Style "O" Amplifying Spanish
Guitar $65.00

No. 66 Style "O" Amplifying Hawaiian
Guitar 65.00

No. 67 Style "O" Amplifying Tenor
Guitar 65.00

No. 68 Style "O" Amplifying Mandolin. 65.00

No. 69 Style "O" Amplifying Ukulele. 40.00

HAVANA GUITARS

Smooth as a tropical night, the mellow full tone of this beautiful wooden guitar will enchant you. It has all the sharp bark needed for modern swing, but will shade away at a touch to the sweetest of dreamy rhythms.

This grand instrument is constructed with rich maple sides and full arched back finished in a dazzling sunburst. The genuine spruce top glows with a sparkling natural finish. In striking contrast are the radiant nickeled cover plate and bright tail piece.

The slim comfortable lines of the high speed neck are set off by the rich rosewood finger board carefully hand fretted and bound with ivory. Neck joins the body at the 14th fret.

Head piece is of "Ebonoid" with the fancy design engraved into the agate-like surface. The pick guard is shaped from crystal clear transparent.

The Hawaiian Model has the improved square neck which joins the full sized body at the 12 fret.

No. 55 Havana Amplifying (14 Fret Body) Spanish Guitar $50.00

No. 56 Havana Amplifying (12 Fret Body) Hawaiian Guitar 50.00

"ARAGON" No. 5 SPANISH GUITAR

"National" presents a fully arched professional Spanish Guitar that challenge the field—regardless of price! This extraordinary non-electric creation is secor to none for smooth volume and penetrating power. Band playing guitar artist have always wanted a truly beautiful instrument that would also embrace a those features that make the perfect Spanish—the "Aragon" is that instrument

The rich sparkle of the mellow buff sunburst finish and the glow of the elaborat pearl inlays furnish a distinctive appearance. Body edges and head piece a neatly bound with varied fancy block-white-black ivoroid bindings. Gracef scroll openings and the crystal-clear pick guard are also neatly bound. Th scientifically hand carved neck affords the artist that perfect easy action s essential for fast modern technique. The spruce topped maple body is large an commanding—but not too large! Genuine rosewood is used for the finger boar and head piece. The brilliant chrome of the tail piece, guard bracket, keys, an artist key covers, afford a sparkling contrasting trim. The full sweet resonanc of National's famous "weather-free" amplifying principle responds vibrantly t the slightest touch, reproducing the clear rich tone of the pulsing strings.

No. 5 "Aragon" Amplifying Guitar only

$175.00 EACH

All gears and working parts of the heavy duty Patent Heads are neatly enclosed in "stream-line" nickeled key covers.

ARTIST MODEL No. 3 HAWAIIAN GUITAR

This exquisite silver instrument is universally recognized as one of the finest non-electric Hawaiian instruments ever constructed. The famous National tri-plate resonating principle affords a flexibility of response and full sweetness of tone still unrivaled for the true perfection of authentic Hawaiian music. Its amazing sustaining power and smooth sparkling volume were two important reasons why National Silver Hawaiian Guitars played the leading role in popularizing Hawaiian Music in the United States.

The brilliant mirror surface of the beautiful silver body is elaborately hand engraved and has no equal for Professional Showmanship.

The fancy trimmed head piece is of genuine mahogany. The pearl inlaid jet black finger board is of ebony.

This radiant instrument with its graceful sweeping lines and clear sweet tone is truly alive with the throbbing songs of the islands that freely flow from the responsive strings.

Universal ownership and loyalty to these superior and time tested triple-resonator instruments is a sincere tribute to their quality.

No. 3 Artist Model Amplifying Guitar only

$165.00 EACH

CASES FOR ABOVE INSTRUMENTS ON PAGE 141

1941

The last pre-war National catalog was issued in 1941 featured a smaller line of resonator instruments. This page shows the style O instruments available in that year. Note raised-center coverplates on the tenor and mandolin.

STYLE "O" GUITAR FAMILY

The Style "O" National is an established favorite among those professional guitarists who prefer the famous single-plate National alloy guitars. The lifetime metal body is brightly plated and artistically etched with graceful tropical palms. The pick guard is crystal clear and transparent. Carefully designed, the Style "O" neck offers a new thrill to the modern guitar player. The wood is finished in rich hand-rubbed mahogany, ornamented with a lustrous black headpiece. The neatly bound fingerboard is hand-fretted and scientifically arched for feather-touch action. Positions are marked with pearl inlays. The Spanish guitar neck joins the body at the fourteenth fret. Trim nickeled cover plates enclose and protect all gears and working parts of the precision patent heads.

- Perfect neck fast action wide frets
- Brilliant volume sparkling string response
- Streamlined design compact portable
- Rich dynamic tone amazing sustained power
- Modern lifetime metal alloy body
- Guaranteed not to crack or warp
- Genuine National patented amplification
- Craftsmanship by experts

No. 65—Style "O" Spanish Guitar
No. 6-B—Case: two-tone tan, 3-ply, flannel lined
No. 5-K—Case: basket-weave, 3-ply, curly plush

Top—STYLE "O" GUITAR
Center—STYLE "O" TENOR
Bottom—STYLE "O" MANDOLIN

NATIONAL *Amplifying Instruments*

COLLEGIAN GUITAR FAMILY

These sturdy instruments, though popularly priced, embrace those famous features which have established National Guitars as the world's finest. Their tone quality and volume surpass that of any non-electric in this price field, due to the resonator principle—a National exclusive. They possess amazing sustaining power, with bell clear harmonics and smooth, vibrant volume; yet they have really commanding "punch" for the professional. The durable all-metal "lifetime" bodies are not affected by moisture or varying climatic conditions; hence, they will not warp, crack or lose tone. The rich modern design is enhanced by the smart light maple finish and refinements such as the clear, transparent pick guard. The Collegian guitar is equally fine for Hawaiian or Spanish style playing. Collegian Guitar also available with wood body.

COLLEGIAN GUITAR OUTFIT
No. 25—Spanish Body Guitar
No. 6-B—Case: 3-ply, two-tone tan, flannel-lined
No. 5-K—Case: 3-ply, basket weave, plush lined

COLLEGIAN TENOR OUTFIT
No. 27—Tenor Guitar, metal body resonator type
No. 4-D—Case: 1-ply, gray shark Servitex plush-lined
No. 5-E—Case: 3-ply, basket weave, plush-lined

COLLEGIAN MANDOLIN OUTFIT
No. 28—Mandolin, metal body resonator type
No. 4-E—Case: 1-ply, gray shark Servitex plush-lined
No. 5-F—Case: 3-ply, basket weave, plush-lined

HAVANA GUITAR

The full, mellow tone of this beautiful wooden guitar makes it a truly enchanting instrument. The top is of genuine spruce in a soft natural finish, and the arched back is attractively decorated with a dazzling sunburst design. Has the improved square neck which joins the body at the 12th fret; ivory-bound, hand-fretted Rosewood fingerboard; Ebonoid headpiece; nickeled cover plate; transparent pick guard.

No. 56—Havana Hawaiian Guitar, Wood Body
No. 6-B—Case: 3-ply; two-tone tan; flannel-lined
No. 5-K—Case: 3-ply; basket weave; plush-lined

The low-budget Collegian and Havana models, from 1941.

NATIONAL *Amplifying Instruments*

ARAGON DE LUXE

This startling guitar combines a "speed-action" and fully arched professional body with a de luxe amplifying unit. The vibrant resonating construction affords smooth non-electric power that is second to none. Band guitar artists find in the Aragon De Luxe that perfect combination of smart styling, tone and power that makes for a really super Spanish guitar.

- Tonal perfection and balance that are "weather-free"
- Vibrant, pulsating response to the slightest touch
- Exclusive resonator affords greater resonance and timber
- "Feather-touch" action — "cushion-comfort" jumbo frets
- Sleek super-slender neck — guaranteed non-warp.
- DeLuxe bindings on body, headpiece and fingerboard
- Special adjustable action tail piece — crystal clear pick guard
- Precision heavy duty patent heads — special pure tone strings

No. 5 — Professional Amplifying Spanish

No. 6F—Case — 3 Ply — Basket Weave — Curly Plush

Model S-3

Model M-3

S-3 ARTIST MODEL

An exquisite silver guitar, universally recognized as one of the finest non-electric Hawaiian instruments ever created. The famous National tri-plate resonating principle affords a flexibility of response and full sweetness of tone unrivaled for the true perfection of Hawaiian music. Its amazing sustaining power and smooth volume were two important reasons why National Silver Hawaiian Guitars played the leading role in popularizing Hawaiian music in the United States.

- Elaborate hand-engraved silver body
- Genuine mahogany headpiece
- Ebony fingerboard, pearl inlaid
- Gracefully proportioned—durably built
- Clear, sweet tone—full rich volume

No. S-3—Artist Model Amplifying Guitar
No. 6-G—Case, 3-ply, basket weave, plush-lined

M-3 HAWAII MODEL

Sparkling string responsiveness and smooth penetrating volume mark the "Hawaii" as a typically fine National instrument. Equipped with the genuine National three-plate resonating principle, it is outstanding among the non-electric guitars for its sustaining power, clear harmonics and authentic sweet Hawaiian tone. There is commanding showmanship in its radiant, enamel-finished and elaborately tinted body. A splendid instrument for the serious Hawaiian guitarist.

- Lifetime alloy body
- Unaffected by climatic changes
- Accurate tuning pegs
- Compact and portable for strolling work

No. M-3—Hawaii Model Amplifying Guitar
No. 6G—Case, 1-ply, basket weave, plush lined

10

The glowing catalog reference to the startling Aragon De Luxe model—note slotted wood coverplate, soon changed to metal due to structural failure. The model S-3 description fits style 3 guitars, but a model 35 is shown here. The new low-budget M-3 tricone is shown, with wood-grained finish and unbound necK.

CHAPTER 9

SET-UP and
MAINTAINANCE of NATIONALS

NATIONAL REPAIRS and ADJUSTMENTS, BOTH INTERNAL and EXTERNAL, SHOULD ONLY BE DONE BY A COMPETENT PROFESSIONAL!

In fact, due to the relative rarity of Nationals, even many professional repair people have never seen or worked on one. The design and construction of resonator guitars are quite different from the design of ordinary guitars. As a result, the principles of repair and set-up of Nationals follow different rules. The purpose of this chapter is to discuss the optimum SET-UP of these instruments, and to help the reader DIAGNOSE problems only. It will also serve as a guide for the repair professional who has never dealt with the strange complexities of Nationals.

Because of the somewhat mechanical nature of resonator guitars, many seem to have been subjected to crude, homemade "repairs" and modifications. Perhaps since Nationals can be disassembled easily, some owners assumed that automotive repair techniques would work on them. Also, articles have been published in the past advocating radically incorrect procedures. It is the intention of this writer to see as many Nationals as possible in operating condition--without compromising the original specifications of these works of early 20th century industrial art.

John Dopyera often complained of having to undo or correct bad homemade "repairs" on many of the Nationals that came through his shops over the years. Before you disassemble your instrument, make sure you have a good reason. Never modify a National without checking with an experienced repair person. The spirit of John Dopyera lives on through his invention and he may be watching YOU.

STRINGING

Nationals operate on the principle of string tension causing downward pressure on the resonator via the bridge. The best sound is obtained with at least medium gauge, or even heavy gauge strings. Light gauge strings yield a thin, weak, rattle-prone sound because they are not sufficient to drive the resonator system to its full potential. Another consideration is the lowered tension of some strings in open tunings, which must be compensated for with thicker strings. See G tuning below for an example.

Standard: Treble E B G D A E Bass
G Tuning: Treble D B G D G D Bass

Here are some ideal gauges:
Standard Medium: .013 .017 .026 .036 .046 .056
G Tuning Medium: .014 .017 .026 .036 .047 .057
Standard Heavy: .014 .018 .027 .039 .048 .058
G Tuning Heavy: .016 .018 .027 .039 .049 .059

High-Bass G,
or Dobro Tuning: .016 .018 .027 .039 .042 .049
A Tuning Medium: .013 .015 .025 .034 .046 .056
A Tuning Heavy: use G Tuning medium

National string package, 1929. Is a "micro specific standard" similar to the "one-millionth vibration" mentioned in the catalog?

GUITAR 5TH

NATIONAL

The string contained in this envelope has been made to Specifications of the National String Instrument Corporation, and manufactured by a secret process to a micro specific standard.

NATIONAL

strings and string instruments are noted for their purity of tone. Every string, as well as instrument, is carefully tested before leaving factory.

Make sure you get the best strings for all instruments. - - - Insist on the registered trade mark "NATIONAL" on every package.

National String Instrument Corp.

For practical purposes, Standard Heavy and G Tuning Heavy are interchangable. The main point is that slide playing requires a certain amount of string tension--a string that is too slack will make lots of buzzes. Phosphor bronze strings seem to have the best tonal response for resonator guitars, followed by yellow brass and nickel wound strings.

It is important to realize that changing from Standard tuning to A or E tunings is STRONGLY NOT RECOMMENDED--lighter strings must be used for any tunings where strings are raised from standard.

On slotted head Nationals, it is not necessary to put any twists or knots in the string at the tuner. Four or five windings of string are quite sufficient to prevent slippage.

It is important to realize that string-TENSION and string-ACTION are two different, separately adjustable things. TENSION is primarily adjusted by STRING GAUGE, and ACTION is controlled by NECK ANGLE (to the body) and SADDLE HEIGHT (assuming a functional cone).

NOTE: Once a National is set up properly, THE TENSION SHOULD ALWAYS BE KEPT ON THE RESONATOR(S). STRINGS SHOULD BE CHANGED ONE AT A TIME, INSTEAD OF LOOSENING ALL SIX.

BRIDGE SADDLE
SPECIFICATIONS and ADJUSTMENT

On single cone guitars, the saddle is always made of maple, and the biscuit is usually willow or very light maple, usually painted black. Many guitars from c.1932-1936 will have patent numbers stamped on the biscuit, visible on assembled guitars. Quarter-sawn maple is the ideal saddle material for sound. Denser materials, such as rosewood, ebony or bone fail to transmit the warmth of the bass and sound weaker than maple. All have been experimented with and maple clearly delivers the most volume and best tone.

On single cone guitars, the height of the saddle from the surface of the biscuit ranged from 3/32" to 5/16" when manufactured, though most were 1/4" tall. The saddles were designed to have a small range of height (action) adjustment and are also thick enough to provide slight intonation adjustments. However, most of the responsibility for string action lies with the neck angle, discussed below. It is important to make sure the neck angle is correct before adjusting the saddle height. It is even more important to make sure that the resonator has not collapsed, which would cause an incorrect saddle height. If the saddle is too low, there will be insufficient downward pressure on the resonator, causing severe rattles. If it is too high, there is a decrease of volume and tone.

On tricone guitars, the maple saddle fits in a machined groove in the previously described aluminum T-bar bridge. Once again, maple is the correct saddle material, though the earliest tricones utilized orangewood. Many of the original tricone saddles were painted silver. The height of the tricone saddle above the aluminum surface is generally 1/8", or within 1/16" of that. As with single cone guitars, the string action is primarily determined by the neck angle, with only slight adjustment room at the saddle.

On both tricones and single cones, the arrangement of the strings at the saddle differs from regular acoustic guitar bridges. The main difference is that on Nationals the strings must sit in little slots cut into the saddle, instead of just laying across a smooth surface. The way the slots are cut and shaped has a large effect on the tone, particularly on the treble strings.

National string package, 1931, with new single-cone tenor. Perhaps cost-cutting led to the change from "micro specific standard" to a mere "specific standard."

Rather than resting in the slot across the entire width of the saddle, the strings should contact the saddle at a single point in the slot. For better intonation, this point should be at the back edge of the saddle (towards the tailpiece). The remainder of the slot should be V-ed out towards the headstock, to provide clearance for the very end of the vibrating string. This V-shaped slot allows the very highest harmonics to ring, which brightens and clarifies the tone of the string. If the slots are cut too deeply or narrowly the string will sound "choked" and a bit dull. Most Nationals in good unaltered condition require little or no adjustment in this area, though the slots can wear down after many years of use.

NECK ATTACHMENT and
NECK ANGLE CONSIDERATIONS

The way National necks are attached to the body is another main difference between Nationals and other acoustic guitars. The style of construction shows John Dopyera's roots as a banjo maker, since the neck-pole-through-the-body concept of Nationals is similar to banjo construction. This construction is in some ways easier to work with than the dovetail arrangement of regular guitars. However, THE NECK SHOULD ONLY BE REMOVED BY A PROFESSIONAL WHO IS FAMILIAR WITH THE PROCESS. The neck and neck-pole are a single piece of wood in most cases. This unit is attached to the body at the following points: Through the fingerboard with screws under inlays, at the endpin, and at 2 points along the pole. At the fingerboard above the 12th (or 14th) fret, three to five screws go through the metal body-top into nuts set in small wood blocks underneath. At the endpin, there is a small block with shims holding the end of the neck pole. The endpin screw goes through the block and into the neck-pole. There are also screws attaching the neck pole to the cone rest platform or shelf. The neck pole is further secured by two dowel-and-cookie supports which help stiffen the guitar back as well. These supports are nailed into the neck-pole.

The proper neck angle was acheived at the factory on all Nationals by a careful fitting of neck and body at all of the above locations, plus a precise carving of the neck-heel to fit snugly with the body. Years of string tension cause changes to the wood, resulting in two fairly common problems: neck warpage, and change of neck angle to the body. Old National guitars can have either one or both problems. The main symptoms of these problems are high action, and insufficient angle over the saddle. The severity ranges from none, to still-playable, to must-be-repaired.

Diagnosing these problems, and distinguishing between them takes a good eye, and some experience. If the repairman looks at the neck by sighting up the neck by looking from the body, go to another repairman. The proper way to look at a guitar neck is by sighting down it from the headstock. To determine whether the neck has a warp problem, an angle problem, or both you must do the following:

1. Check the straightness of the neck between the 1st fret and the body-joint fret (either 12th or 14th). Looking down the bass side, use your hand toblock the view of frets past the body. Another way is to hold down the low E string at the 1st fret and the body-joint fret, looking for a gap--the string is a staightedge. There shouldn'tbe a gap larger than 1.5 times the diameter of the string.

2. If the neck seems pretty straight, but the action still is high or there is insufficient angle over the saddle, then the whole neck has moved with age. Often you will see a gap between the bottom of the heel and the body--this shows how far the neck has moved. Also if you now sight down the whole neck you will see a change in the slope of the fingerboard beginning at the neck-body joint. Depending on the severity, there are several methods of dealing with the problem. ALL OF THEM SHOULD ONLY BE DONE BY EXPERIENCED PROFESSIONALS. This writer may be contacted for further questions at the address given at the back of this book.

**CAUTION TO REPAIRMEN:
NEVER REMOVE WOOD FROM THE
HEEL WHERE IT MEETS THE BODY–
IT WILL RUIN THE INTONATION.**

TUNING GEARS

Nationals were equipped with open tuning gears, which are of high enough quality to provide a lifetime of service. However, it is essential that the bearing surfaces of the worm and cog gears be lubricated. Tri-Flow spray lubricant is best, since it is made of miscroscopic Teflon balls in an evaporating vehicle. WD-40 is a second choice--it works but is leaves a messy residue. Thick axle grease would be a third alternative. Without lubrication, the gears can easily be stripped eventually. Original gears should be left on the guitar if possible, or at least kept safely for future owners if you feel you absolutely must replace them.

DIAGNOSING RESONATOR and BODY RATTLES

RULE #1: NEVER TAKE THE STRING TENSION OFF THE RESONATOR OR TAKE APART THE COVERPLATE/RESONATOR ASSEMBLY UNLESS THERE IS A VERY GOOD REASON!!

National resonator instruments, particularly those subject to past abuse, often develop slight problems with buzzes and rattles. However, if the instrument is set up properly and the resonator(s) are undamaged, these problems rarely occur. Before attempting to diagnose these annoying buzzes, it is recommended that the reader take another look at Chapter 5 which details the construction and assembly of the resonator systems.

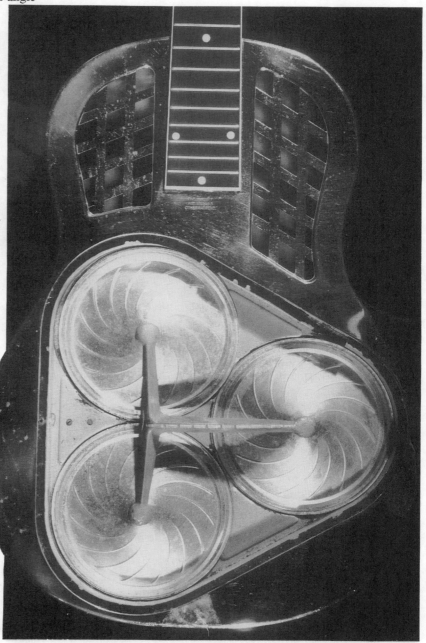

Tricone with coverplate removed, cones and T-bar bridge assembly in place.

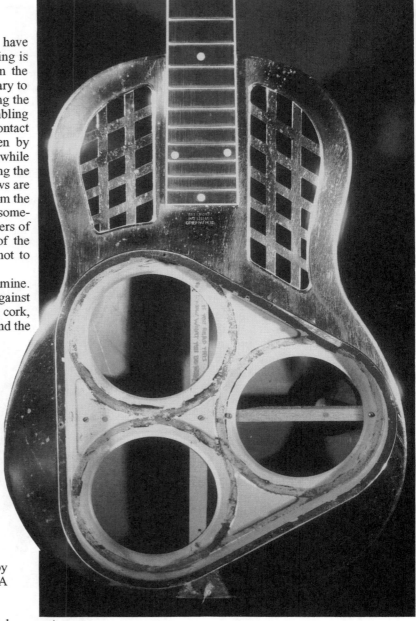

The only way to avoid rattles is to have COMPLETE CONTACT of all surfaces. If something is buzzing, it's because there is a place somewhere in the body where two surfaces are loose. First it is necessary to isolate the location of the rattle. Begin by eliminating the areas which can be examined WITHOUT disassembling the instrument. Check the coverplate-to-body contact first, by making sure the screws are tight and then by pressing gently around the edges of the coverplate while strumming. Keep strumming the strings while holding the coverplate to see if the rattle disappears. If the screws are down, there will rarely be rattle problems coming from the coverplate. On tricone guitars in particular, it is sometimes necessary to take off the coverplate, add 2 layers of masking tape on the little ridge under the edges of the coverplate (where the screw holes are). Be sure not to cover the holes.

The tailpiece is the next area to examine. Sometimes the ball-ends of the strings can buzz against the coverplate under the tailpiece. A bit of felt, thin cork, or even paper wedged between the string ball-ends and the coverplate will take care of this problem.

If taking the above steps does not eliminate the rattle, then it could be emanating from the resonator. Diagnosing this is very tricky and takes experience to pinpoint the problem.

For SINGLE CONE instruments, the first thing to do is look under the handrest in the center of the coverplate. The bridge-saddle and biscuit should be perfectly level, not down on any one side. If it is down, then the resonator has suffered some collapse and must be repaired by an expert or replaced. If it is level, the buzzing can come from one of the following sources:

1. Not enough angle over the bridge, caused by improper neck angle. Neck must be re-set, BY A PROFESSIONAL.

2. Bad contact between biscuit and cone--must be taken apart and reassembled properly--SHOULD ONLY BE DONE BY AN EXPERIENCED PROFESSIONAL!

3. A part of the saddle or biscuit is touching the coverplate, causing a strange buzz--perhaps the saddle was replaced with an oversized piece. There should be no contact between the coverplate and any vibrating parts.

4. Bottom rim of cone is not perfectly flat--this has to be pretty severe to cause problems in single cones.

5. Previous abuse to resonator--repair by professional or re-place with a new one. (Parts are available--see address for National Resophonic in appendix)

Similar problems and solutions exist with the resonator set-up of TRICONE GUITARS. Because there are three cones, these instruments are in many ways more temperamental and trickier to diagnose and adjust.

1. First check the coverplate and tailpiece to insure proper contact and eliminate rattles from these parts.

2. WITHOUT disassembling the guitar, carefully examine the peaks of each cone as much as is possible. They should rise smoothly to meet the little cups at the ends on the T-bar. If they look slightly "pushed in" by the T-bar cups, they need to be repaired. PLEASE TAKE NOTE: A VALUABLE TRICONE CAN BE RUINED IN SECONDS by improperly handling the EXTREMELY DELICATE resonator cones. It is best to have a qualified repair professional WHO HAS EXPERIENCE WITH TRICONES replace the cones and/or work on the originals. The author may be contacted regarding this at the address given in appendix C.

3. The bottom rims of the cones may be warped slightly "out-of-flat" and while this is usually no problem on single cones, it can be a significant cause of persistent rattles in tricones. The pressure of the strings is not always enough to insure complete contact between the cones and their platform if there is warpage. For an explanation of how this is corrected, the author may be contacted at the address in the appendix. Once again, this is NOT something for the inexperienced.

If you wake up one morning, and your National has a buzz, don't panic. Sometimes just a slightly cooler temperature can cause a temporary buzz which will go away once the instrument warms up. Also, as previously mentioned, playing a National, especially a tricone, with bare fingers is almost a guaranteed way to cause rattles. Remember that the general rule with Nationals is that they SHOULD NEVER BE DISASSEMBLED unless there is a real problem. Often a perfect condition instrument can start buzzing just from being taken apart and put back together, without any alterations being made.

MAINTAINING PLATED and PAINTED BODY FINISHES

With proper care, the various finishes on National instruments can retain their beauty for a lifetime or more. Little is involved in caring for these finishes beyond the obvious idea of keeping it clean. On plated finishes especially, it is essential to wipe off the instrument after each use. The perspiration and oils from your hands will begin to corrode the plating after even a few days, making the finish appear clouded and grey. You will notice that the plating on most Nationals will be worn or clouded in the most common areas of hand contact.

Assuming that your instrument's finish is in good condition, whether painted or plated, an annual application of ordinary car wax will help protect it from further wear and make it easier to keep clean. A coat of wax can dramatically improve the look of the painted finishes on Triolians and Duolians. For plated finishes, it may not improve the appearance very much, but will at least prevent further corrosion.

For plated instruments with severe corrosion, dirt, or wear, there is some hope. The SURFACE dirt and corrosion can be removed to some degree without further harm. However, it must be understood that no amount of rubbing or abrasives will get rid of CLOUDINESS, because this cloudiness is a chemical reaction that has occurred in the entire thickness of the plating. If you try to abrade it too much you will only go right through the plating to the less shiny metal below. The best materials for surface dirt removal are metal polishing pastes with a grit so fine that you can barely feel any grit between your fingers. Grittier abrasives will only scratch and dull the plating. FLITZ or Simichrome Polishing Paste is best for severely corroded surfaces, while a smoother silver polish is better for general light cleaning of a fairly good condition surface. The rubbing must be done by hand with a cotton, flannel, or chamois cloth, **NEVER** with an electric buffing tool! **ABSOLUTELY NEVER** use sandpaper or steel wool on the body of a plated National--it will be ruined. This author has seen some very sad cases of abuse, which can not be restored.

Many people have asked about the possibility of re-plating National instruments. Generally, in terms of value of the instrument, it is not a good idea to re-plate. A National in slightly worn original condition will always be worth much more than a re-plated instrument (esthetically as well as monetarily). The art of re-plating previously plated metal is quite a bit more difficult than plating new metal. Plating is like a transparent surface in terms of showing every little scratch, sanding marks, or other defects in the metal under the plating. Therefore the preparation of the metal to be plated is of paramount importance. Furthermore, replating an engraved or sandblasted (style O) instrument will ruin the look of the engraving, and obliterate any sandblasted designs. Nearly every re-plating job seen by this writer has looked obviously re-done, unoriginal, and showing defects in the metal. One re-plated instrument has been seen that looked very well, but the owner spent close to a thousand dollars having it done, and yet still didn't gain close to a thousand dollars increase of value.

The worst cases of re-plating have been done on Nationals that never were plated originally, such as Triolians and Duolians. These instruments are made of steel, a metal which does not accept plating well, which is one reason why these models were manufactured with painted finishes. The earliest Style O guitars were of steel construction, and even though they were plated at the factory, these steel body Style O's always have a rougher, slightly rippled plating surface. Re-plated Triolians and Duolians look worse, and it seems wrong to plate an instrument that was never made that way. While cosmetic condition is very important to collectors of all vintage instruments, ORIGINALITY of condition is far more important.

National guitars—infinitely adaptable....Jane Wisnant, circus entertainer, c. 1936, playing Hawaiian guitar on a c.1931 Triolian which she has adapted for her unique technique.

If you are still hell-bent on replating your instrument, even after considering the above, then it should only be done by a shop specializing in the replating of expensive vintage collectible automotive parts. They must understand that the money is to be spent on careful preparation of the metal--the plating itself is easy. The plating should be nickel. For steel body instruments (really not recommended) there must first be a surface of copper plating for the nickel to adhere to.

PROPER SHIPMENT and CASE STORAGE

The main idea to have in mind when storing, carrying, or shipping a resonator instrument is to KEEP THE COVERPLATE AWAY FROM THE LID OF THE CASE. Just a little banging around loosely in the case while carrying the guitar can damage the resonator. Sometimes, if the case receives a blow, Nationals can suffer internal damage without any visible damage to the case. In the worst situations, the convex single cone coverplate can actually "pop in" to a concave shape, thereby crushing the resonator. The best way to prevent this is to glue in a 1" x 1" or up to 2" x 2" strip of foam rubber around the perimeter of the inside of the case lid over the body. This gently forces the guitar against the back of the case, without putting any pressure on the coverplate/resonator area. You want a slight airspace between the coverplate and the case lid.

It is also a very good idea (with Nationals or any guitar) to provide foam padding in the case under the headstock. The bend in the neck of any guitar is a very weak point, because the grain of the wood stays straight even at this bend. Without this padding, headstocks can snap easily if the case is dropped (or thrown by an airline baggage handler). For airline shipping, more padding can be added around the neck, but NEVER over the coverplate.

Standard 12 and 14-fret National guitars fit perfectly in a standard 00 Martin-sized case. While original National hardshell cases are esthetically more pleasing, they are not strong enough to withstand modern-day shipment unless placed in a cardboard guitar shipping box stuffed with padding. Several manufacturers make 00 size hardshell cases. The best cases have an arched lid and back, and are constructed of 5-ply half-inch plywood. Guitar shipping boxes are available at any music store. These boxes, with padding, are a very safe container for shipping, and essential for any type of case.. Shipping by United Parcel Service has proven to be a fairly reliable and secure method, and is used by most dealers. Be sure to require a recipient's signature when you ship.

THE OWNER'S RESPONSIBILITY

National resophonic instruments were made during an age when things were built to last. The idea of planned obsolesence, begun by General Motors' introduction of annual model changes in the 1920s, did not become a general way of life in America until after World War II. The quality of the materials and workmanship maintained by National resulted in a line of instruments that has withstood the test of time. Many of these instruments are still at work today, and many have been brought back to working condition with only minor repairs.

These instruments have the potential to last a thousand years or more, with proper care. With an object of such durability, it is difficult to claim anything other than temporary ownership. The ownership of such a long-lasting instrument should be thought of more like a guardianship, protecting the instrument from harm, so that it may be enjoyed by future musician-guardians.

CHAPTER 10

THE FUTURE OF NATIONAL

The last tricone guitar was assembled in 1942 from pre-war parts. None have been made since then, except two that have been built by hand in England--one by Alan Timmons and one by W.R. Johnson. The author has examined these two instruments and found them similar but not exactly the same as the old ones or each other. These men are to be commended for their efforts, and it is assumed that each successive instrument will improve upon the last. Editor's note: A West German company in 1993 begins shipping repro Tricones under the name "Continental."

To mass-produce the original tricones is a difficult proposition. Twenty-four separate dies were used in the construction of the original instruments. Six of the original dies were lost sometime around World War II. The other eighteen dies were carefully preserved for the next 30 years by Rudolph Dopyera. Each year, he would inspect them and faithfully apply grease to the metal to prevent rust. Those dies stayed with Rudy as he moved from one shop to another, and he had them in storage at the new Dobro factory which he had started in 1960 with his brothers Emil (Ed) and John. The business was known as Original Musical Instrument Co., or O.M.I.

The Dobro story should be told in another book, but briefly, the brothers resumed production of a fairly good reproduction of the old wood-body Dobros. They also began to make metal guitars with the Dobro-type spider resonator in the late 1960's. These instruments only vaguely resembled Nationals in sound, workmanship and appearance. By 1970, the factory was manufacturing several models each of wooden and metal Dobros, including some metal instruments with an oversized National-type single cone resonator. The resonator was not the same as the original--there was no spiral swirl embossed in the cones, and no "bowl" under the biscuit. The alloy used was stiffer, and offered a rather pinched tone with little "echo." Some were sandblasted with a pattern which roughly approximated the old Style O tropical scene, and some were engraved with patterns loosely based on the original Styles 2, 3 and 4. Sadly, these instruments also failed to come close to the sound and esthetic quality of the original Nationals.

Ron Lazar, a Dopyera nephew, took over the business in the early 1970's. Rudy still had his eighteen tricone dies, in perfect condition. When they moved the Dobro factory from Long Beach to Huntington Beach in 1975, Ron decided to "clean house" and Rudy's dies were placed outside in the yard. Of course, they quickly rusted and were ruined. Sometime later, they were hauled away for scrap. Two pickup trucks full of old dies and shoes were melted down.

To re-create these dies today would cost at least $150,000. It would be difficult to market enough instruments to finance the dies, let alone the huge stamping presses, materials, and labor. The tricone will probably never be built in quantity again, but National Resophonic has one in the works!

There is however, hope for the future. Many musicians who play Nationals are more than a little fanatical about them. A lot of them can vividly recall their first exposure to these memorable instruments. One fellow by the name of Don Young, recalled seeing a tricone in a pawn shop window for $35, in 1961. He was ten years old. This inspired him to learn the guitar. When he was 15, he heard a Black Ace record, and was fascinated by the distinctive sound of Ace's sliding tricone. He began working on repairing instruments in 1969 and got his first resonator guitar, a new Dobro. He needed a job, and so he called the number on the Dobro warranty card to ask for one. Even though he had little experience, he was hired and soon was sanding necks. After a year and a half, he started building Dobros at home with John Quarterman, an independent maker. This only lasted five months, so he returned to Dobro. In 1972, he was fired for "insubordination" resulting from his repeated complaints about frets popping out of fingerboards. Ron Lazar had invested a sizable amount of money in a hydraulic fret press which didn't work well, and didn't take kindly to Don's reluctance to let instruments out of the factory with loose frets. Ron was an accountant turned manufacturer who had a different perspective towards the instruments. Lazar was a good businessman, and the company thrived un-

McGregor Gaines (left) and Don Young (right) 1991. These guys are serious about recreating the National.

der his care, but the quality of the instruments was not his first priority. Don Young spent the next five years as head repairman in a music shop. He states that while he generally got along very well with Ron Lazar, they always disagreed about production. Nevertheless, Don came back to O.M.I. in the early 1980's when asked to be shop foreman. He stayed from 1984 to 1988. Don had always been interested in the vintage Nationals even in his first years of employment at Dobro. In fact, he went to the scrap yard where the tricone dies had been dumped, to try and recover them. Sadly, they had already been fed to the smelter.

Don met McGregor Gaines in 1981. McGregor had been an obsessive model builder as a child. His father had been an inventor, an industrial designer, and a wartime metals industrialist. As a child, McGregor developed an early passion for the artistry and craftsmanship of industrial production. Young McGregor progressed to serious study of graphic arts, drawing, and sculpture. In the 1970's he began at the bottom of the construction industry, working his way up to finish carpentry, cabinetmaking, and ornamental woodworking.

Don and McGregor hit it off immediately, and McGregor was fascinated by the detail and skilled workmanship required to make the guitars Don had built for himself. Soon after, Don got McGregor a job at O.M.I. McGregor worked at several different jobs within the factory, getting his exposure to large scale guitar production. He eventually did a turn as shop foreman. McGregor designed many new woodworking jigs and production-flow ideas for wooden resonator guitars during his tenure at O.M.I.

In 1987, Don telephoned the author to inquire about an endorsement for O.M.I. He particularly wanted to know why the author preferred to perform and record with old Nationals, and if there were any suggestions to improve the O.M.I. metal body instruments. The author replied, "Which end would you like me to start at?" and listed all the changes that would be necessary to make the new instruments sound and feel like the original Nationals. Don made note of the changes, discussing with the author the various costs of making each change. The changes were then ranked in order of importance, the most important, of course, being the resonator.

Don brought a list of production changes and suggestions to the company. Management rejected all of the suggestions because they felt that as long as they were "moving units" it wasn't worth investing any money into improving the instruments. Don felt rather dismayed at working for a guitar company that didn't seem to be concerned with the quality of the product and had no interest in the needs of the working musician. He began to work at home experimenting with improving the resonator. He researched the various aluminum alloys to find the closest alloy to the originals, and began lathe-spinning his own cones. Several prototype cones were sent to the author over a period of time for testing installations in old Nationals. After many gradual changes, Don was able to spin cones which sound identical to old National Style O or Duolian/Triolian cones. He continued to experiment and began a small replacement parts service for old Nationals. He started making both types of cones (large single and small tricones) as replacements, complete with bowl and swirl pattern.

Both McGregor and Don had disagreements with the management at O.M.I. concerning production and quality of the product. They wanted to make a classic vintage-type resonator guitar--one that would be a joy to play for the working musician. By 1988, they left Dobro to start a new company, National Reso-Phonic Guitars, dedicated to bringing back the real National. Their shop is located in San Luis Obispo, California. These men have a strong respect for the design of the original instruments and a well-developed sense of nostalgia for the detail, craftsmanship and style of the Industrial Age of the 1920's.

At this writing several wood-body models have been in production for two years. These models are illustrated here. The resonators, coverplates, body shape and neck profile of

Necks and bodies await finishing at National Reso-Phonic's shop.

Left to right: Reso-lectric guitars before metal parts installation and assembly, an old tricone in for restoration, and the new prototype metal-body National.

248

these instruments are identical to the original hardwood-body Triolians of 1928-1929. These men are not only reproducing old designs, but are also creating new designs and ornamentation that look like they could have been designed by National's somewhat wild estheticians. The models range from a Trojan-styled sunburst model to regular and deluxe Polychrome-finished guitars to a mahogany El Trovador- inspired model. Genuine mother-of-toilet-seat overlays are used on deluxe models, similar to National, and m.o.t.s. bindings are employed as well. The back design on the Islander is all-new, yet McGregor's silkscreened design harks back to the old days. Colors have gradually changed over the first few hundred instruments, making each one fairly unique. McGregor designed and made the jigs for the production of the wood bodies and necks, which are all individually hand built. McGregor also handles the creation of colors and designs for the instruments, and does the finishing work. Both men do the woodworking, while Don does most of the metal work, including spinning resonators, designing dies for coverplates and tailpieces, and stamping the metal parts. Don designed a die and press for re-creating the spiral They have recently expanded their shop to four men. Don and McGregor have also made several fine exact reproduction necks and parts for restoration of original Nationals, and are the best possible source for these repairs and parts. They both love to talk with musicians and are interested in the needs and ideas of players.

The catalog cover, designed by McGregor, for the new company is reminiscent of the 1930's National artwork.

Finished Jazz-Blues bodies drying before final assembly.

Paul Hostetter, a luthier from Santa Cruz, California has begun a cooperative venture with National Reso-phonic to collaborate on wood-body National resonator mandolins. This is a new idea, since all the old ones were of metal. Several have been built at this writing. Those examined by the author have plenty of cutting power, yet retain the sweetness and warmth of wood. Paul makes the necks and bodies, National adds metal parts and finishes the instruments.

The most exciting item on the horizon is the resurrection of the metal body single cone National. The author very recently had the pleasure of playing and adjusting the one-day-old prototype 12 fret metal-body National built by Don Young. Built from galvanized steel-true bluesman's garbage-can model--this instrument sounds wonderful, and responds just like an old National. Don and McGregor plan to reissue an exact reproduction of the Style 0 guitar. All dimensions and materials will be identical to the old models, including the correct Hawaiian scenes on the top and back, which have been carefully transferred from a Variation 5 original. A steel body, single resonator enhanced reproduction of the old Duolian™ called the "Delphi" is now being made. Various other models are planned, such as guitars with engraved designs, and new Triolian paint schemes devised by McGregor. The possibilities for new designs are endless when working with paint and silk-screen. Don has also built a metal National ukulele prototype, and plans are in the works for both metal and wooden resonator ukes.

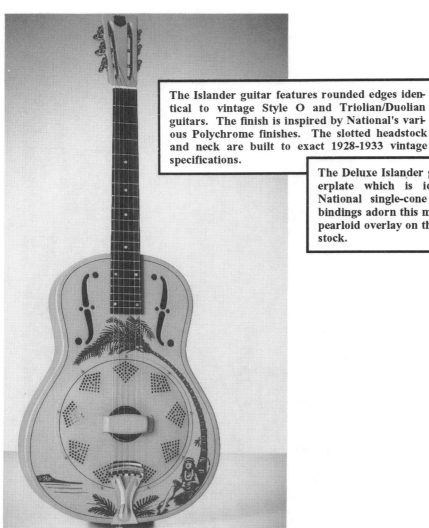

The Islander guitar features rounded edges identical to vintage Style O and Triolian/Duolian guitars. The finish is inspired by National's various Polychrome finishes. The slotted headstock and neck are built to exact 1928-1933 vintage specifications.

The Deluxe Islander guitar features a plated coverplate which is identical to the 1929-1931 National single-cone plate. Multiple pearloid bindings adorn this model, as well as an engraved pearloid overlay on the tricone shaped solid headstock.

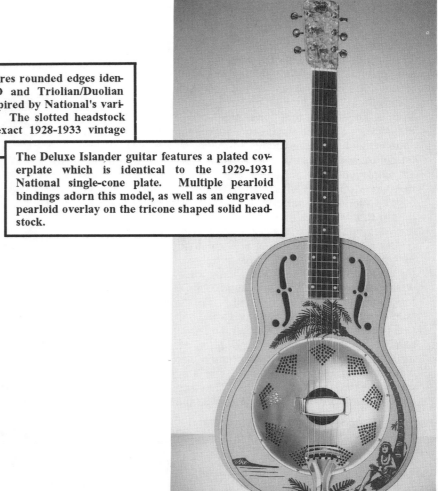

Curly maple is seen under the image on these special custom Islander guitars

Both men feel the heavy passion that surrounds the National. In McGregor's words:

"All of my past work experience in the arts and industry are called upon: from making jigs, organizing the flow of production, detailed woodworking, to artistic design and direction. There is a mystique, an allure about National guitars. None of my senses are left unaltered by doing this work. I am grateful for the opportunity to be a part of National's history."

Don Young states his feelings this way:

"I'm making National reso-phonic guitars because it gives me the opportunity to apply everything I know to something that I love. It is such a unique instrument. I love those old Nationals and we are getting to replicate them as well as create new designs. McGregor and I are creating a solid thing out of something mystical and magical. We are doing every boy's dream."

And so, fifty years after the last metal National was made and ninety-nine years after John Dopyera's birth, the magic of the National begins anew.

The mahogany deluxe model corresponds to the 1933
El Trovador model. The f-holes on these guitars are
transferred from an original El Trovador.

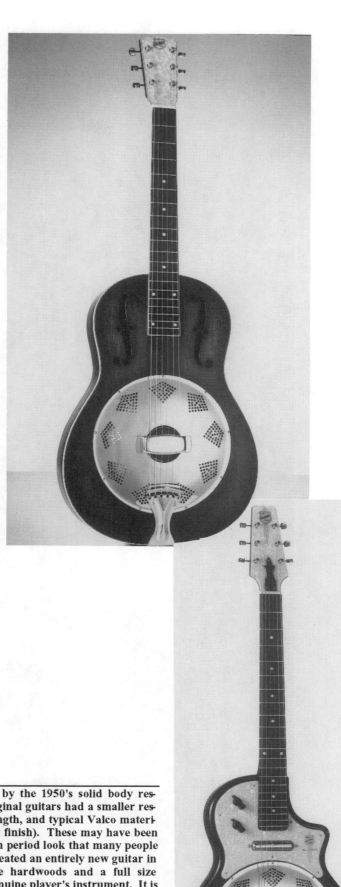

The Jazz-Blues model resembles the
Trojan in materials and finish.

The unique Reso-lectric model is inspired by the 1950's solid body resonator guitars in appearance only. The original guitars had a smaller resonator, no pickups, a three-quarter scale length, and typical Valco materials and quality (i.e. cheap woods and tacky finish). These may have been
poor instruments, but they do have a certain period look that many people
find attractive. Don and McGregor have created an entirely new guitar in
the Reso-lectric. Full scale length, dense hardwoods and a full size
National cone and coverplate make this a genuine player's instrument. It is
quite surprisingly loud acoustically. One lipstick tube type pickup in installed in the pearloid pickguard area, and a transducer is installed under
the saddle. The mix may be blended between these two different sounding
pickups. McGregor has come up with custom colors which evoke the different kind of American optimism that existed in the 1950's, and the overall design is well-integrated artistically. The guitar performs well in the
recording studio, where is is possible to mike the resonator and add it to
the sound of the two pickups.

The very first of the new Generation of Style O guitars. This guitar, Serial #001, was patterned after one of the author's 1933 Style O's and presented to the author by the National Reso-Phonic Company in 1992

NATIONAL SERIAL NUMBERS

FINDING ORDER IN APPARENT CHAOS - <u>THE CODE HAS BEEN CRACKED!</u>

Among the business papers located during the researching of this book, no factory listing of serial numbers has survived. Therefore, the only way that is has been possible to unravel a seemingly random tangle of numbers is by patiently keeping a list of numbers as instruments came up over the years. The following list of serial numbers has been compiled over a period of several years, mostly through the author's visual inspection of many instruments. Many contributions were made also by musicians, dealers and collectors throughout the world. (They are acknowledged at the end of this section.)

The search for more serial numbers continues, and readers are invited and encouraged to submit them for future revisions of this book. PLEASE SEND ALL SERIAL NUMBERS INCLUDING ANY ZEROES AND LETTERS) WITH DESCRIPTIONS TO THE AUTHOR AT THE CENTERSTREAM PUBLISHING CO. ADDRESS GIVEN AT THE FRONT AND BACK OF THIS VOLUME.

Since thousands of National instruments were made, this list of numbers represents a small sample of the total. However, there are enough instruments documented here to enable us to draw some conclusions about totals and relative scarcity of various models. There is also sufficient information here to help the owner determine the age and exact variation of any National instrument. Unfortunately, there are also some slightly unclear issues and a need for more data to answer various questions.

Here are some examples of considerations encountered in assembling this list of numbers:

1. National used many different series of numbers over the years, with different series for each type of instrument, from 1927 through 1935. from 1936 through 1941, all instruments (metal, electric, wood) were issued numbers on five general number series, changed about once a year.
2. Attempts were made to find and verify numbers that confirmed or denied the existence of various separate series.
3. There are a few cases of human error in the number-stamping procedure at the factory, such as two different instruments of the same period with the same number, or numbers double-stamped or stamped too hard.
4. I have double-checked as much as possible on the reporting of numbers and descriptions of instruments by other contributors to this list, to narrow down the human error factor to National's workers only.

An example of double-stamping. Numbers were punched one at a time—in this case the workman picked up the wrong punch, tried to overstamp it, then gave up and stamped the last 4 again. Double-stamping has also been seen on metal bodies.

5. For the earliest numbers, instruments had to be double-checked for the many short-lived design features of that period, in an effort to solve some mysteries of the numbering of the first year of production.
6. Locating exact transition points for design and production changes will always require more serial numbers from readers. However, in many cases, this list shows model/style transitions as close as six instruments apart.

This list of National serial numbers is the largest such list extant. The numbers fall into several groups which bear brief explanations to further clarify this listing as a reference source for musicians, collectors and dealers.

GENERAL GROUPINGS OF NATIONAL SERIAL NUMBERS:

There are many separate series of serial numbers issued by National until the 1935 move to Chicago, after which all instruments, regardless of type, were numbered together. These numbers have letter-prefixes, which changed from year to year. Think of two large groups of numbers: Los Angeles and Chicago.

This serial number list has the following groups of numbers:

1. First series of tricone Hawaiian (squareneck) guitars
   1927-1934   (#100 to c. 3323)

2. First series of tricone Spanish (roundneck) guitars
   1928-1930   (#0100 to c. 01004)

3. S-prefix tricones (numbered in with Style O's)
   SQUARE: 1934-35   ROUND: 1930-1935

4. Silver ukuleles 1928-1935   (#100 to c. 425)

5. Silver mandolins (includes tricone mandolin/uke)
   1928-1935   (#100 to c. 625)

6. Silver tenor and plectrum guitars
   1928-1935   (#1 to c. 1500)

7. Style O guitars, S-prefix (most 12 fret)
   1930-1934   (# S-1 to c. S-6250)

8. Early 14 fret style O guitars,
   1934-1936 (#100 to c. 7050)--this series also
   includes early 14-fret Triolian and Duolian guitars.

9. Silver Don guitars, X-prefix
   1934-1935   (# X-1 to c. X-200)

10. Wood body Triolians
    1928-1929 (no numbers) 1929 (#1000 to c.1650)

11. Early metal Triolians 1929   (# 0100 to c. 0225)

12. Bakelite-neck triolians, A-prefix
    1929-30 (# A-100 to c. A-1850)

13. Polychrome Triolians, P-suffix
    1930-1934   (1-P to c. 2400-P)

14. Walnut sunburst Triolians, W-suffix
    1930-1935   (1-W to c. 3400-W)

15. Other Triolian numbers (Tenors and early 14 fret)

16. Triolian mandolins and ukuleles
    1930-1935   (#100 to c.650)

17. C-prefix Duolians
    1931-1936   (C-1 to c. C9799)

18. 0-prefix Duolians
    1931-1936   (0100 to 09550

19. E-prefix Duolians
    1935-1936   (E-7000 to c. E-7900)

20. No prefix Duolians
    1935-1936   (1000 to 6500)

21. Sears-Roebuck Duolians
    1931-1932   (R-1 to c. R-600)

22. Chicago era all-instruments-together series 1936-1941
    a. A-prefix series: A1 to A8550
    b. B-prefix series   B1 to B3600
    c. C-prefix series   C1000 to C5730
    d. L-prefix series   L9800 to L10200
    e. G-prefix series   G-100 to G-4500

23. Wood models: K, T, N, and Z series

THE TRICONE SERIAL NUMBERS

Understanding the numbering of the tricones from the first year of production requires some attention to details. Referring to the description in Chapter 5 of the early metal body construction, we see early features such as "woven" (hand-soldered) strips in the upper bouts, seven extra holes in the top, wooden platform (or well), and studded tailpieces. In this listing, one will quickly see that the early numbers relate to one or more of these early features. However, it is quite possible that the transitions from one type of construction to another may not have been instant, smooth, or in exact numerical order!

HAWAIIAN (SQUARENECK) TRICONE GUITARS (Style 1,2,3,4)

National squareneck (Hawaiian) tricones, besides a few non-serialized prototypes with pre-standard logo, begin at serial number 100, in June-July 1927. This series continues to at least # 3323, when in 1934-1935 the last few California squareneck tricones were numbered in with the S-series style O guitars. After 1935, tricones were given regular Chicago series numbers, with A, B, C, L, or G prefixes.

Tricones under c.400 exhibit one or more early features. Only the first forty tricones have the seven extra holes cut in the top outside the perimeter of the coverplate, though about another fifty retain the "woven" upper grilles. The first forty instruments are stamped "PAT APPL'D FOR". After that, they are stamped "PAT PEND" until c. #1890 when patents were granted (June 1930) and the stampings reflected this. The metal well replaced the wooden well after about 250-280 instruments (c. #380). Arched backs replaced flat backs about the same time. Studded tailpieces were probably purchased by National in a lot of 500, before the company began making their own non-studded tailpieces. Somewhere between #500 and #600, the tailpieces were changed over.

Totalling these instruments, plus another 100 or so S- prefix tricones, yields a figure of about 3,500 squareneck tricones made from 1927 to 1935. Considering the fact that resonator instruments (particularly expensive ones) became a smaller and smaller part of National's business during the Chicago era, an estimate of a further 2,000 squareneck tricones seems very liberal. This figure will always be an estimate, since all Chicago instruments were numbered together.

Style 4 Hawaiian tricone, 1930.

Typical 1933-1934 tricone patent stamp. Patent numbers are for both tricone patents originally granted to John Dopyera.

Style 4 Spanish tricone, 1928. Two holes in tailpiece indicate stud variety.

SPANISH (ROUNDNECK) TRICONE GUITARS (Style 1,2,3,4)

Roundneck tricones have long been thought of by players and collectors as being far more scarce than square-necks. The serial numbers bear this out, though perhaps not to the extreme degree previously stated in other publications. The roundnecks begin a little later than the squarenecks-- December, 1927 at the earliest, probably January, 1928. They were given their own series, beginning at 0100. The very first few have extra holes in the top, and woven upper grilles continue for a few more, but by number 0137, the bodies are standard. Flat backs were replaced by arched backs at about # 0200. Wood wells change to metal wells in the mid-0200's. These changes of early features occur about 100 numbers earlier on roundnecks than on squarenecks, suggesting that about 100 squarenecks were produced before the first roundneck was. The 0100's continued to c. 01002, which was in 1930. All of these have PAT PEND stamps.

Roundnecks were then numbered in with Style 0 (S-prefix) instruments. The earlier S-prefix tricones retain the PAT PEND stamp until c.# S-2300. To review: 0100-01002 runs from 1928 to 1930. S-prefix tricones run from 1930-1934. Beyond 1935, all Nationals received general Chicago numbers. As with the square necks, we can assume that not many were produced in Chicago. Since S-prefix and Chicago tricones are mixed in with other instruments, the exact number cannot be determined. However, taking the intitial 900 tricones plus a very liberal estimate of 300 S-prefixes and possibly 900 Chicago roundneck tricones, we have a maximum total of 2,100 roundneck tricones made.

SPANISH AND HAWAIIAN TRICONES

In comparing roundneck and squareneck serial numbers, one must keep the production differences in mind. Since less roundnecks were produced, the numbers move more slowly relative to dates. Therefore while squareneck # 999 dates from the end of 1928, roundneck # 0999 would date from the beginning of 1930.

The other thing to remember is that one of the revolutionary aspects of the National idea was that of mass- produced interchangeable parts. In the factory photographs, stacks of separate components can be seen. Workmen were assembling these guitars from large stocks of components. These separate components were made in batches to feed stockpiles. As each instrument was assembled the workmen would gather parts from these stockpiles as required. In National's earliest years modifications occurred at different times to various components. It is therefore safe to assume that the chronological flow of finished products did not always run parallel to evolutionary changes of the components. The last step in production was the stamping of the serial number. For example, it would be possible to find an tricone fitted with a wood well that has a slightly higher serial number than a tricone with a metal well. Presumably during the transition from wooden to metal wells several instruments were made with remaining stocks of wooden wells. Another example is the presence of 12-fret style O guitars with higher numbers than 14 fret models, again produced with extra bodies found in parts stocks. Little did National's employees realize to what extent they were contributing the to the frustration of latter day historians by choosing parts at random from large stocks.

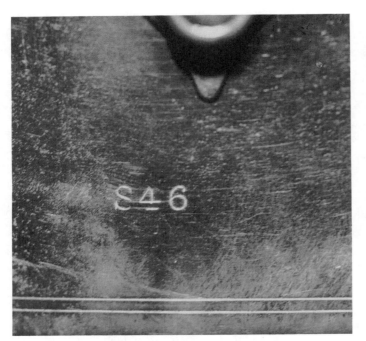

Style 3 Spanish tricone, 1930.

With Nationals, the stamping of patent numbers help in dating, since they roughly correspond with the dates that patents are granted. On Spanish neck tricones, the serial numbers are stamped into the metal just below the endpin. On Hawaiian models, the numbers are stamped in the back of the metal neck, just below the head stock. Sometime around serial number 2400, numbers for both models began to be stamped on the headstock, rather than the body. The two basic roundneck 0100 and squareneck 100 series of tricone numbers were used for all style 1, 2, 3, and 4 instruments until mid-1930. Distribution of styles 1, 2, 3 and 4 among these numbers are what one would expect from their sales prices.

If one includes S- and the post-1935 A-prefix tricones, model 35 and model 97 tricones (A, B, and C prefixed) then the total number of round and square-neck tricone guitars must still be well under 7,500. Even this figure assumes a very liberal amount of model 97 and letter-prefix tricone guitars--about 3,000. With the Chicago letter-prefix system of all instruments numbered together, it is impossible to determine how many A, B, or C-prefix tricones were actually made. Remember that by the late 1930's, very few tricone were made, and most of them were inexpensive models. The early 1930's S- prefix tricones are equally difficult to total, since they were numbered in with batches of Style O's. Remember that the Style 0 was a big seller (half the price of a Style 1), so that almost all S-prefix instruments are Style O guitars. The earliest S-prefix tricones have PAT PEND stamps so they would begin in mid-1930. The later S-prefix instruments have patent numbers, so it is safe to say that S-series tricones continue to about 1935, when the Chicago letter-prefix tricones (A, B and C) begin.

SILVER UKULELES
(Style 1,2,3)

National ukes in silver seem to be fairly scarce. Their numbers start at 100 with large body ukes and change at c.300 to small body ukes. The highest known number in this series is 405, so we can assume that about 500 were made up to 1935 when the letter-prefix numbers begin. There are, of couse, additional silver ukes scattered within the Chicago letter-prefix series, but probably not many. Painted ukes are covered in the Triolian number section. Presumably many more painted ukes were made.

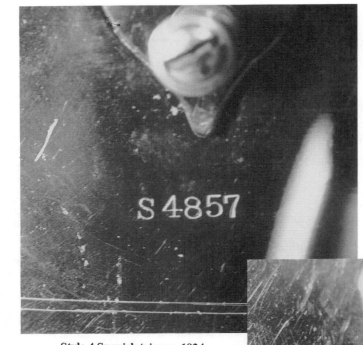

Style 4 Spanish tricone, 1934.

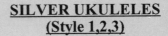

Style 1 large-body ukulele, 1928.

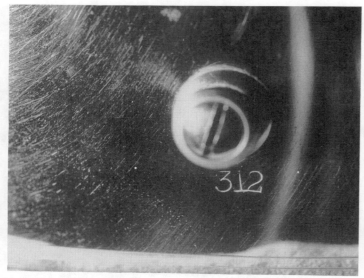

Style 2 small-body ukulele, 1932.

SILVER MANDOLINS
(Style 1,2,3)

National mandolins went through several changes in a short time before becoming standardized. The first batch were actual tricones, with a round coverplate, a raised ring for the plate, and screens. They could be had with a uke neck on request, which indicates the tricone ukulele does precede the regular silver uke. Numbers for mandolins start at 100 and the highest known triplate mandolin number is 148. The next step was a single cone mandolin with a small cone, and a ring-surrounded round coverplate with screens. One example has been seen with a number in the high 100s. #266 is the same, but the screens have been replaced with drilled holes. However, #256 has been seen with a regular-sized coverplate and cone.

The highest known instrument in this regular series of silver mandolins is 602, which has a chicken-feet coverplate. This suggests perhaps 600 to 700 total silver mandolins made from 1927 to the end of 1935. After this, the mandolins are numbered in with the Chicago letter-prefix series, and totals are difficult to determine. Considering the decline of mandolin popularity and the decreasing interest in resonator instruments in the late 1930s, there cannot have been many more silver models made. Painted mandolins are covered in the Triolian number section, and since they were cheaper than silver models, undoubtedly more were produced.

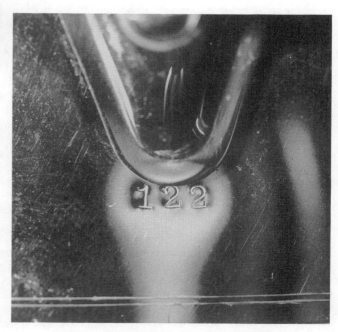

Very early 1928 Style 2 tricone mandolin.

The neck of the tricone mandolin was also stamped.

1929 custom Silver Presentation mandolin.

Style 3 single cone guitar-shaped tenor, 1931-32.

SILVER TENOR AND PLECTRUM GUITARS (Styles 1,2,3)

Unlike the ukuleles and mandolins, the silver tenors and plectrums seem to start at 1, in 1928. The lowest documented instrument on this list is number 12. Both tenors and plectrums of this period are tricones, with pear-shaped bodies and triangular coverplates. The tenors and plectrums share the same number series, since both bodies are identical and numbers were stamped on the bodies, not the necks. Around number 500, the necks were made less ornate. The dark wood central stripe and the carved volute were eliminated. At approximately serial 600, these instruments were changed to a single cone resonator system with round coverplate. However, the bodies on these single cone tenor/plectrums were still pear shaped. Number 633 is the lowest number on the list to exhibit this change. By the time the serial numbers reached into the 800's, the bodies were changed again, to a small guitar shape. The highest number known thus far for the pear-shaped single cone is 876. The first number listed herein of this type of tenor/plectrum is 882. Guitar-shaped tenors and plectrums seem to run up to the 1300's, but there is one numbered 2642. This may be from another series, however.

Total production of silver tenor/plectrums, then, may be derived from this list as follows: about 600 tricone tenor/plectrums, about 250 pear-shaped single cone tenor/plectrums, and either about 550 or 1,750 guitar shaped tenors, depending if one counts 2642 as part of the same series or not.

The totals for tricone and pear-shaped single cones are quite definite. The guitar-shaped tenors continued in production well into the 1930's, so the total is difficult to determine, since the mid-1930's and later instruments were all numbered together.

S-PREFIX STYLE O GUITARS (all 12-fret and earliest 14-fret)

The S-prefix number series was generally assigned only to style O guitars, though an occasional style N or tricone has S-numbers. Beginning at S-1, all 12-fret and the very earliest 14-fret style O guitars are numbered in this series. The variation changeover points are indicated in the number listing. The rarest would be Variation 5, (12 fret with rolled in f-holes) which starts at about S-4500 and ends only 900 guitars later. Sometime around number S-5100, numbers began to be stamped on the headstock instead of on the body. At around S-5400, 14-fret guitars appear. There are, however, a few 12-fret squareneck style O's with higher numbers, probably from leftover 12-fret bodies at the factory. The highest S-prefix number in this listing of the series is S-6205, which brings us to the year 1935.

With the help of more serial number data one could nail down even more exact points of transition from each variation to the next. (As previously mentioned, the author will appreciate any serial number information provided by readers). Still, this list will help owners of Style O guitars to place their instrument in perspective.

Style 1 tricone plectrum guitar, 1928.

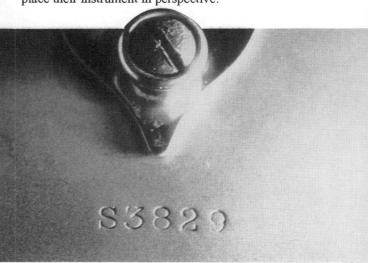

Style O guitar, 12 frets, Variation 4, 1932.
All were body stamped until about S-5100.

Style O guitar, 12 frets, Variation 5, 1934.

EARLY 14 FRET STYLE O GUITARS

The very next batch of Style O numbers after the S-prefix series are found on early 14 fret style O guitars, from 1935 and 1936. The numbers have no prefix, and begin at either 1 or 100. Slotted head guitars run up to c. 5500, and solid head guitars follow, with the highest on the list being 7027. The stamped numbers themselves are larger than previous series stampings, and are located at the top of the peghead. These 7000 numbers may not all represent style O guitars, since some Duolians and Triolians of the late 1934-1935 era have numbers that seem to fit in this series. Assuming that this series is continuous and ONLY represents style O guitars, then adding these to the S-prefix numbers yields a style O guitar production total of about 13,000 instruments prior to the inclusion of subsequent style O's in the Chicago letter-prefix, all-instruments series. 10,000 would be a more probable figure, assuming that some Duolians and Triolians were numbered in with this series.

Style O, of course, was continued as a catalog item for the rest of the decade. A further undetermined number of Style O guitars were produced in Chicago through 1941. Since the Style O was a popular model, perhaps another 2,000 to 3,000 were made from 1936-1941. These all have general series A, B, C, L, or G numbers as do all Nationals of this period.

Style O guitar, 14 frets, solid headstock, 1935-36. Sandblasted design is the same as the previous slotted head guitar. Original Variation 6 body, variation 7 neck—transitional model between the two.

X-SERIES SILVER "DON" GUITARS

Numbering of these instruments is quite simple, since not very many were made, and the model was short-lived. The series probably started at X-1, and the highest number in this listing is X-126, though there are bound to be higher numbered Don guitars in existence. The numbers were stamped on the bodies at the endpin. All Don guitars were made from late 1934 to 1936.

Style O guitar, 14 frets, slotted headstock, 1935. Variation 6. Stamp punches are changed to slightly larger more old-fashioned-looking numbers.

TRIOLIAN GUITARS

The very first wood bodied Triolians had no serial numbers. The remainder of the early wood body Triolians were numbered in a series ranging from 1000 to c.1650. The earliest metal Triolians were Polychrome and numbered from 0100 to somewhere in the low 0200's. When National introduced the new walnut sunburst finish, two new series were created: beginning at 1 W and 1 P. These are two separate series, and the changeover to 14 fret bodies occurred at a different place in each series--2300 P and 3200 W. It would seem from these numbers that the walnut Triolians sold nearly 50 percent better than the Polychrome version. In fact, the polychrome finish was dropped very soon after the change to 14-fret bodies. The highest on the list is 2311 P. It is safe to assume that the rarest Triolians would be 14-fret polychrome finished models. In addition, as with style O guitars, the 12 fret models had rolled-in f-holes only briefly before the change to 14 fret. These 12-fret Triolians with rolled-in f-holes are also among the rarer versions of this model.

In 1930, a large batch of Triolians with experimental Bakelite necks were made. Numbered in a range from A-1 to about A-1825, they were made in both finishes. However, it is known that about half of these were returned to the factory for re-necking with wood necks. Since Triolians were serialized with neck stampings, it is quite possible that many guitars which have wood necks with W or P numbers may have originally been part of this A series of Bakelite neck Triolians.

Polychrome Triolian tenor guitar, 1933. Note patent number (Beauchamp's single-cone patent) and made in USA stamp.

Polychrome Triolian guitar, 12 fret, rolled F-holes, early 1934. One of the last 12 fret Polychromes.

One of the last wood body Triolians, 1929. Stenciled palm scenes on the last few resemble the metal Polychrome guitars.

One of the first metal Polychrome Triolians, 1929. Note PAT APLD FOR stamp.

There was, briefly in 1933, a third series, with a B suffix. Very few were made. The serial numbers range from1 B to 87 B, the highest known. The finish on this version was different from the walnut or polychrome models. The B designated a crystalline finish similar to the Duolian, but with a non-metallic opaque dark green base. Only two tenor guitars and two rolled-f-hole 12 fret guitar have been documented in this edition of the list.

While some Triolian tenor/plectrum guitars have W or P suffixes, there are also some numbered in a range from 794 to 1483. There are also some mid-1930's Triolian guitars with numbers in the 5000's that are likely part of the early 14- fret style O series. Of course there are numerous Triolians numbered in with the general Chicago letter-prefix series. Most, if not all, of these Chicago Triolians will be of the wood-grain finish variety.

Triolian mandolins and ukuleles have their own number series, though some have turned up with regular W or P suffixes. There may be a separate series each for mandolins and ukuleles, but no duplicate numbers have turned up to confirm this. Probably not more than 650 Triolian mandolins and ukuleles were made before their numbers began to be blended in with the Chicago letter-prefix series.

Early 1930 'walnut' sunburst Triolian guitar. PAT APLD FOR stamp.

1932 sunburst Triolian guitar. "Made in USA" stamps were not added until 1933. Only occasionally does the W precede the number. Note double-stamping of the 3.

1933 strange-finish Triolian, 12 fret, rolled F-holes. None have been seen with a higher number.

Duolians, made only as guitars, came with several series of numbers, prior to the mid-1930's blending of serial numbers of all instruments. The major continuous series from the beginning of the model run in 1930 is the C-prefix series. The series begins at C-1 and continues to at least C-9721. It includes 12-fret slotted-head Duolians to approximately C-7700. The remaining 14-fret guitars up to the end of this series all have slotted headstocks. This series represents the production of nearly 10,000 guitars prior to the change to solid headstocks in late 1936. This breaks down to approximately 1600 Duolians per year for this series alone during the six year run. As with Triolians, the 12-fret models will rolled-in F-holes are the scarcest Duolians.

There are also Duolians numbered with an 0-prefix. It seems quite likely that this series ran concurrently with the C-series. The changeover to 14-fret bodies occurs at a similiar place to the C-series. This listing ranges from 0827 to 09564, and therefore seems to represent another quantity of nearly 10,000. All of these are slotted-head models. It is also possible that these two sets of numbers are actually intermingled numerically, with only a prefix difference. Matching numbers with C- and 0-prefixes will have to be found to disprove this. The prefixes could possibly indicate different finishes or different wholesaler's batches. If this were the case, the total would stand at 10,000, not 20,000.

To make matters more confusing, there are also a few Duolians with E-prefixes. All of them, however fall between E-7272 and E-7807. Those that have been examined by the author all have a brown crystalline finish. So again it is possible that these are all part of one production run of 10,000, with different prefixes indicating a color or marketing difference.

There are also some early 14-fret Duolians with non-prefixed serial numbers. They seem to be part of the same series as early 14-fret style O and Triolian guitars, changing from slotted to solid headstocks at c. 5500.

The R-prefix Duolians are from a 1930-32 batch of special cheaper grade models for Sears Roebuck. They have five large drilled areas around the coverplate, instead of the normal National coverplate.

1933 Duolian, 12 fret, rolled F-holes.

1936-1941 LETTER-PREFIX SERIAL NUMBERS

THESE NUMBERS APPLY TO ALL NATIONALS, REGARDLESS OF TYPE OF INSTRUMENT OR MODEL. Determining relative production totals of each model is nearly impossible for two reasons. First, all instruments were lumped together in one series, which started over with a new letter-prefix series about once a year. Second, many of the numbers of these series are for electric National instruments and the production of metal-body resonator instruments declined in proportion to the electrics. Starting dates of new prefixes are accurate within three months and based on catalog dates, patent stamps and known dates of original purchase.

A-PREFIX SERIES (1937): Minor construction details of the headstocks and bodies show that A-prefix instruments are slightly later than B-prefix models. The series covers at least 8,540 instruments (electrics included), an unknown amount of which were metal resonator instruments. Most of the metal body production was of Duolians and Triolians.

B-PREFIX SERIES (1936): This seems to be the first of the Chicago letter series. Headstock shape and other details indicate late 1935 into 1936. The series as listed here only runs up to 3522, but probably goes a little higher.

C-PREFIX SERIES (1938): Construction and design details changed again slightly in 1938, and C-prefix instruments belong to this period. This series is not to be confused with the much earlier C-series Duolians (1930-1935). In fact, this list shows a 1938 14-fret solid head Duolian with the number C-1642. Undoubtedly, there is a 1930 12-fret slot-head Duolian out there somewhere with the same number, but from the earlier series. This Chicago C-series runs at least to C-5730.

The numbers of the above A, B, and C series, when added together, suggest a total of just over 18,000 instruments, including of course, many electrics, from 1936-1939.

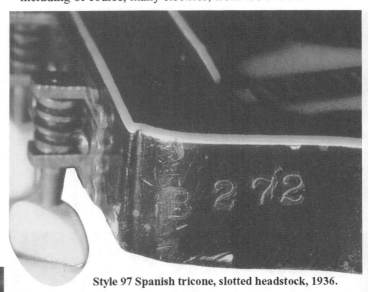

Style 97 Spanish tricone, slotted headstock, 1936.

"Exploding palm tree" etched tricone, 1937.

New Yorker 7-string electric lap steel. All Chicago-made Nationals, regardless of model, shared the letter-prefix series.

Style O guitar, Variation 7, 1937.

Style 97 Hawaiian tricone, solid headstock, late 1936.

L-PREFIX SERIES (1939): This series is another general numbering series for all 1939 era Nationals. All of the L-series instruments documented in this listing come from the narrow range of L-9803 to L-10111. Perhaps this is a continuation of the A-series, which may end higher than the 8500's. Or, it could be a continuation of the Duolian C-series, which may end higher than C-9721.

G-PREFIX SERIES (1940-41): This is the last of the pre-war set of serial numbers. The numbers are often found stamped onto a small metal plate which is attached to the back of the headstock with two small brads. This method of serializing is found on most Valco/National instruments well into the 1960s. However, some G-series Nationals have been seen with the regular headstock stamping. The series seems to end after some 4,500 instruments, bringing the total Chicago-era production to approximately 22,000 Nationals of all types, including all electric models. It is not possible without considerable further documentation to estimate the portion of this total taken up by metal body instruments.

Supro Collegian mandolins received regular Chicago National numbers. This one dates from 1938-39.

WOOD BODY NATIONALS

The Kay-bodied El Trovador guitars of 1933 all have K-prefix numbers. The highest documented number is K-555, which correlates with factory records of about 600 made before the agreement with Kay was terminated.

Harmony-bodied instruments, such as Trojans, Rositas, and Estrallitas, have either T, Z, or N prefixes. The numbers suggest a fairly large quantity of these instruments. Some Trojans were also stamped with regular Chicago C-prefix numbers.

SOME ABBREVIATIONS USED IN THIS SERIAL NUMBER LISTING:

RD= ROUND (SPANISH) NECK
SQ= SQUARE (HAWAIIAN) NECK

EXTRA HOLES= SEVEN DIAMOND HOLES CUT IN TOP OF EARLIEST GTRS.
WOVEN= HAND-SOLDERED STRIPS IN UPPER BOUTS OF TRICONES
STOCK= STAMPED UPPER BOUTS OF TRICONES
STUDS= EARLY TAILPIECE WITH STUDS
WD WELL= EARLY WOODEN PLATFORM FOR CONES, OR "WELL"
MTL WELL= METAL WELL, AFTER DIE WAS OBTAINED, FIRST 1/2 1928.
PAT APPL= "PATENT APPLIED" STAMP, EARLIEST TRICONES ONLY
P.A.F.= "PATENT APPLIED FOR" STAMP
PAT PEND= PATENT PENDING STAMP
PAT #= PATENT NUMBER STAMP
2 PAT#= BOTH PATENT NUMBERS STAMPED
MDUSA= MADE IN USA STAMP

SCREENS= OLDEST STYLE ROUND COVERPLATES WITH SCREENED HOLES
HOLES= LATER DRILLED-HOLE COVERPLATE
RIBS= FOUR RADIATING EMBOSSED STRENGTHENING COVERPLATE RIBS
CHICK.FEET= 1936 AND LATER COVERPLATE PATTERN
RAISED CENTER= VERY LATE COVERPLATE WITH RAISED CENTER
SCREWS= SINGLE CONE COVER ATTACHED WITH SCREWS, NOT HOOKS
HOOKS= BRIEF PERIOD OF COVERPLATE ATTACHMENT BY SMALL HOOKS

FLAT= FLAT-CUT F-HOLES
ROLLED= F-HOLES CUT WITH ROLLED-IN EDGES

OLD CONE= FOR UKES, EARLIEST CONCENTRIC RING STAMPED CONE
REG CONE= FOR UKES, STANDARD SPIRAL CONE
SM CONE= FOR MANDOLINS, SMALLER CONE USED BEFORE SERIAL #260
REG CONE= FOR MANDOLINS, STANDARD 9 1/2 INCH CONE.

LIP= FOR MANDOLINS, SMALL COVERPLATE FOR SM CONE WITH OUTER
RAISED RING ON THE BODY.

DECO= 1936 AND LATER BLACK AND WHITE HEADSTOCK DESIGN
VARIATIONS= REFER TO CHAPTER ON STYLE O INSTRUMENTS
SCENE= POLYCHROME TRIOLIANS WITH STENCILLED SCENE ON THE BACK

NATIONAL SERIAL NUMBERS

SERIAL NUMBERS
TRICONE GUITARS

GERMAN SILVER
S Q U A R E N E C K (HAWAIIAN) TRICONE GUITARS:

XTRA HOLES = 7 DIAMOND HOLES CUT IN TOP OUTSIDE OF COVER.
WOVEN = HANDMADE UPPER HOLES
STOCK = UPPER HOLES DIE-STAMPED
WD WELL = EARLY HANDMADE WOODEN RESONATOR WELL
MTL WELL = STANDARD STAMPED METAL WELL

#102, #106, AND #109 ARE KNOWN TO HAVE ORGINALLY HAD
UNDERSIZE CONES WITH STRANGE T-BARS.

NUMBERS STAMPED ON UPPER BACK OF METAL NECK UNTIL c. 2500

YEAR	SER #	PATENTS	MODEL	DETAILS AND OTHER
6/1927	102	PAT APPL	#1 SQ	WD WELL/ WOVEN, XTRA HOLES
	106	PAT APPL	#1 SQ	WD WELL/ WOVEN, XTRA HOLES
	109	PAT APPL	#1 SQ	WD WELL/ WOVEN, XTRA HOLES
	112	PAT APPL	#1 SQ	WD WELL/ WOVEN, XTRA HOLES
	122	PAT APPL	#1 SQ	WD WELL/ WOVEN, XTRA HOLES
	133	PAT APPL	#2 SQ	WD WELL/ WOVEN, XTRA HOLES
	142	PAT APPL	#1 SQ	?? ??
	145	PAT APPL	#2 SQ	WD WELL/ WOVEN, NO HOLES
	148	?	#1 SQ	WD WELL/ WOVEN, NO HOLES
	183	?	#1 SQ	WD WELL/ WOVEN, NO HOLES
	191	?	#1 SQ	WD WELL/ WOVEN, NO HOLES
	195	?	#1 SQ	WD WELL/ WOVEN? NO HOLES
	227	PAT PEND	#1 SQ	WOOD WELL/STOCK, NO HOLES
	240	" "	#1 SQ	WOOD WELL/STOCK, NO HOLES
	256	" "	#1 SQ	WOOD WELL/STOCK, NO HOLES
	288	" "	#1 SQ	WOOD WELL " " "
	311	" "	#2 SQ	WOOD WELL " " "
	0314	" "	#1 SQ	exception to # system
	0333	" "	#2 SQ	WOOD WELL, exception #
	356	" "	#2 SQ	
	359	" "	#2 SQ	
	363	" "	#2 SQ	WOOD WELL 2 1/2
	364	" "	#1 SQ	?
	373	" "	#1 SQ	METAL WELL STARTS HERE
	388	" "	#1 SQ	
3/1928	393	" "	#1 SQ	FLAT BACK ENDS NEAR HERE
	395	" "	#1 SQ	
	396	" "	#1 SQ	EARLY RSWD BD, STUDS TPC
	404	" "	#1 SQ	
	439	" "	#1 SQ	
	444	" "	#4 SQ	SEPARATE FRONDS ENGRAVED
	454	" "	#1 SQ	
	469	" "	#2 SQ	
	481	" "	#1 SQ	
	488	" "	#1 SQ	
	499	" "	#1 SQ	STUD TPC
	0499	" "	#1 SQ	not confirmed, poss. error
	510	" "	#2 SQ	STUD TPC
	512	" "	#2 SQ	2 1/2 STUD TPC
	535	" "	#1 SQ	
	547	" "	#1 SQ	
	575	" "	#3 SQ	3 SEP. FRONDS ON COVERPLATE
	588	" "	#1 SQ	
	600	" "	#2 SQ	
	639	" "	#1 SQ	
	671	" "	#1 SQ	
	683	" "	#1 RD	
	700	" "	#4 SQ	
	704	" "	#1 SQ	
	717	" "	#1 SQ	
	750	" "	#3 SQ	
	771	" "	#2 SQ	2 1/2
	778	" "	#2 SQ	
	809	" "	#1 SQ	
	812	" "	#4 SQ	
	816	" "	#1 SQ	
	824	" "	#2 SQ	
	828	" "	#2 SQ	
	833	" "	#2 SQ	
	844	" "	#2 SQ	
	847	" "	#2 SQ	
	848	" "	#2 SQ	
	858	" "	#1 SQ	
	0860	" "	#1 SQ	not confirmed, could be 860
	871	" "	#2 SQ	
	876	" "	#1 SQ	
	877	" "	#2 SQ	
	886	" "	#2 SQ	
	892	" "	#2 SQ	
	917	" "	#4 SQ	
	921	" "	#1 SQ	
	962	" "	#1 SQ	
	975	" "	#1 SQ	

980	" "	#1 SQ	
0991	" "	#2 SQ	not confirmed, could be 991
1000	" "	#4 SQ	
1006	" "	#4 SQ	
1009	" "	#1 SQ	
1021	" "	#1 SQ	
1032	" "	#2 SQ	
1034	" "	#2 SQ	
1036	" "	#2 SQ	
1056	" "	#1 SQ	
1070	" "	#1 SQ	
1072	" "	#2 SQ	
1091	" "	#1 SQ	
1093	" "	#2 SQ	DAISY/FREDIE ENGR. + 2 1/2
1098	" "	#4 SQ	
1104	" "	#1 SQ	
1115	" "	#1 SQ	
1127	" "	#1 SQ	
1128	" "	#1 SQ	
1132	" "	#4 SQ	CUSTOM FACTORY INLAYS, DARK
1136	" "	#2 SQ	
c.1929 1139	" "	#1 SQ	
1141	" "	#2 SQ	
1173	" "	#4 SQ	HENRY DIXON ENGRAVED, DARK
1187	" "	#1 SQ	
1199	" "	#1 SQ	
1217	" "	#1 SQ	
1219	" "	#1 SQ	
1243	" "	#1 SQ	
1257	" "	#4 SQ	
1265	" "	#1 RD	# not confirmed
1270	" "	#1 SQ	
1307	" "	#2 SQ	STOLEN CONTACT AUTHOR
1317	" "	#2 SQ	
1330	" "	#4 SQ	DARK HEAD
1336	" "	#3 SQ	DARK HEAD
1346	" "	#4 SQ	
1353	" "	#1 SQ	
1355	" "	#4 SQ	
1365	" "	#1 SQ	
1374	" "	#4 SQ	
1411	" "	#3 SQ	WHITE HEAD
1414	" "	#2 SQ	
1442	" "	#3 SQ	
1445	" "	#3 SQ	WHITE HEAD
1463	" "	#1 SQ	
1467	" "	#1 SQ	
1472	" "	#1 SQ	
1473	" "	#1 SQ	
1478	" "	#3 SQ	
1480	" "	#3 SQ	
1494	" "	#1 SQ	
1498	" "	#2 SQ	
1508	" "	#3 SQ	WHITE
1509	" "	#3 SQ	????
1514	" "	#4 SQ	
1518	" "	#1 SQ	
1524	" "	#1 SQ	
1553	" "	#2 SQ	
1583	" "	#4 SQ	
1593	" "	#2 SQ	
1598	" "	#3 SQ	
1616	" "	#4 SQ	WHITE NO ARROWS
1643	" "	#1 SQ	
1646	" "	#4 SQ	WHITE NO ARROWS
1647	" "	#1 SQ	
1644	" "	#3 SQ	
1651	" "	#3 SQ	ENGR'D "JOSEPH G. BARONET"
1657	" "	#1 SQ	
1673	" "	#1 SQ	
1696	" "	#2 SQ	
1710	" "	#2 SQ	
1714	" "	#1 SQ	
1722	" "	#1 SQ	
1724	" "	#1 SQ	NON-FACTORY ENGRAVED
1760	" "	#1 SQ	
1763	" "	#1 SQ	
1771	" "	#4 SQ	
1778	" "	#4 SQ	DARK HEAD
1786	" "	#1 SQ	
1789	" "	#1 SQ	
1790	" "	#1 SQ	
1808	" "	#1 SQ	
1864	? ?	#1 SQ	
1869	? ?	#1 SQ	
1886	? ?	#2 SQ	
6/1930 1891	2 PAT#S,OPP	#1 SQ	
1909	" "	OPP #1 SQ	GRANTED 12-31-29 & 6-10-30
1916	" "	#1 SQ	
1925	" "	#1 SQ	
1927	" "	#4 SQ	
1933	" "	#1 SQ	
1937	" "	#1 SQ	
1947	" "	#1 SQ	
1958	" "	#1 SQ	
1960	" "	#2 SQ	
1962	" "	#4 SQ	
1971	" "	#1 SQ	
1999	" "	#1 SQ	
2001	" "	#1 SQ	
2010	" "	#4 SQ	
2011	" "	#4 SQ	
2014	" "	#1 SQ	
2032	" "	#1 SQ	
2039	" "	#2 SQ	
2041	" "	#4 SQ	
2047	" "	#3 SQ	
2049	" "	#2 SQ	
2079	" "	#1 SQ	
2090	" "	#1 SQ	
2096	" "	#3 SQ	
2116	" "	#3 SQ	WHITE HEAD, STANDARD ENGR.
2127	" "	#1 SQ	
2170	" "	#1 SQ	
2191	" "	#1 SQ	
2210	" "	#1 SQ	
2222	" "	#2 SQ	
2224	" "	#1 SQ	

Year	Ser #		Details
	2230	#1 SQ	
	2233	#3 SQ	
	2250	#2 SQ	
	2255	#1 SQ	
	2260	#1 SQ	
	2273	#1 SQ	
	2294	#4 SQ	ENGRAVED NAME: ART REED
c.1931	2301	#3 SQ	
	2336	#1 SQ	
	2346	#1 SQ	
	2358	#1 SQ	
	2364	#1 SQ	
	2372	#2 SQ	
	2381	#1 SQ	
	2391	#1 SQ	# STILL STAMPED ON NECK
	2404	#1 SQ	
	2408	#4 SQ	
	2414	#3 SQ	
	2430	#1 SQ	
	2433	#1 SQ	
	2434	#1 SQ	
6/1931	2438	2PAT-MDUSA #3 SQ	PARTIAL FLOW-THRU ENGR.#NEK
	2444	#2 SQ	
	2469	#1 SQ	# ON NECK
	2481	#2 SQ	
	2528	#1 SQ WIGGLE BORDER	# ON HEAD
	2534	#1 SQ WIGGLE BORDER	# ON HEAD
	2543	#1 SQ WIGGLE BORDER	# ON HEAD
	2548	#1 SQ WIGGLE BORDER	# ON HEAD
	2549	#1 SQ WIGGLE BORDER	# ON HEAD
	2551	#1 SQ WIGGLE BORDER	# ON HEAD
	2568	2PAT- USA #3 SQ	FLOW-THRU ENGR # ON WH HEAD
	2571	#1 SQ WIGGLE BORDER	" " "
1932	2601	#4 SQ	
	2615	#3 SQ	WHITE HEAD NO OTHER DETAILS
	FS2626	#4 SQ	FACTORY SECOND, ENGR.ERROR
	2634	#3 SQ	FLOW-THRU ENGR.
	2655	2 PAT # USA #1 SQ	WIGGLE BORDER
	2657	#1 SQ WIGGLE BORDER	
	2666	#2 SQ	
	2671	#1 SQ WIGGLE BORDER	
	2682	2PAT # #4 SQ	
1933	2833	#1 SQ	WIGGLE BORDER
	3315	#1 SQ	WIGGLE BORDER
c.1934	3323	#3 SQ	FLOW-THRU, WHITE HEAD

ODD ONES:

Year	Ser #		Details
1937	A2950	SQ	"EXPLODING PALMS ETCH..PART OF A-SERIES
	A2952	SQ	"EXPLODING PALMS ETCH..PART OF A-SERIES
	A3709	SQ	"EXPLODING PALMS ETCH..PART OF A-SERIES
1936	* 7038	SQ	"EXPLODING PALM TREE" ETCHED TRICONE

*PROBABLY PART OF EARLY 14 FRET STYLE O NUMBER SERIES

S-PREFIX TRICONES--
PART OF STYLE O NUMBERING BATCH 1930-1934

8/1930 S137 PAT PEND   #1 SQ

1934 S4550 2 PAT OTH #1 SQ NO WIGGLE BORDER
VERY FEW SQUARENECKS WERE NUMBERED IN THE
S-SERIES

A-PREFIX SILVER TRICONES--
PART OF 1936 CHICAGO NUMBERING SERIES

Ser #	Patents	Model	Details
A2103	2 PAT	#1 SQ	WIGGLE BORDER
A3599	2PAT	#3 SQ	FLOW-THRU ENGRAVING WHITE
A3600	2PAT	#3 SQ	FLOW-THRU ENGRAVING
A3629		#1 SQ	WIGGLE BORDER SOLID HEAD
A-3686		#1 SQ	WIGGLE BORDER SOLID HEAD

A FEW MORE SILVER TRICONES WILL BE FOUND
SCATTERED THROUGH THE 1939-40 L-SERIES LISTED WITH
THE LATER CHICAGO LETTER PREFIX NUMBERS. EXAMPLE:

L-9853   #1 SQ WIGGLE BORDER SOLID HEAD

SEVERAL NON-SILVER (BRASS-BODY) TRICONES, SUCH AS
STYLE #97, STYLE #35, M-3, ETC. WILL BE FOUND AMONG
THE CHICAGO LETTER- PREFIX SERIES (A-, B-, C-, L-, G-)

OBVIOUSLY THERE ARE MANY OTHERS FOR WHICH SERIAL
NUMBERS HAVE NOT BEEN GATHERED. PLEASE SEND IN
ALL NUMBERS.

GERMAN SILVER R O U N D N E C K TRICONE GUITARS:

WOVEN = HANDMADE UPPER HOLES
STOCK = UPPER HOLES DIE-STAMPED
RSWD. BD. = ROSEWOOD FINGERBOARD
FLAT BACKS TO C.0205

YEAR	SER #	PATENTS	MODEL	DETAILS AND OTHER
	NO #	PAT APPLD	#? RD	WD WELL/WOVEN, UNIQUE ENGR
	0118	PAT PEND	#2 RD	WD WELL/WOVEN, NO HOLES
	0137	PAT PEND	#2 RD	WD WELL/STOCK, NO HOLES
	0141	PAT PEND	#4 RD	WD WELL/SPECIAL EARLY ENGR
1928	0145	PAT PEND	#1 RD	WD WELL/ STOCK/ STUDS TPC
	0156	PAT PEND	#2 RD	WD WELL/STOCK/RSWD BD. 2.5
	0160	PAT PEND	#1 RD	? WELL/ALL STOCK FROM HERE
	0169	PAT PEND	#1 RD	? WELL
	0181	PAT PEND	#1 RD	METAL WELL
	0189	PAT PEND	#4 RD	NOT CONFIRMED
	0194	PAT PEND	#1 RD	METAL WELL/ STOCK/ STUDS
	0204	PAT PEND	#1 RD	METAL WELL/
	0205	" "	#1 RD	METAL WELL ARCHED BACK
	0207	" "	#2 RD	METAL WELL RSWD BD,STUDS
	0212	" "	#1 RD	METAL WELL "
	0213	" "	#1 RD	METAL WELL RSWD BD,STUDS
	0214	" "	#1 RD	METAL WELL STUD
	0224	" "	#1 RD	METAL WELL.NO SPIRAL,STUD

0228	" "	#1 RD	?
0234	" "	#1 RD	
0236	" "	#1 RD	METAL WELL
0241	" "	#1 RD	METAL WELL ROSEWD BD
0243	" "	#1 RD	?
0248	" "	#1 RD	METAL WELL
0260	" "	#4 RD	" STOCK ENGR, FLATBACK,RSW
0264	" "	#1 RD	
0268	" "	#2 RD	WOOD WELL ARCHED BACK
0283	" "	#1 RD	METAL WELL
0291	" "	#1 RD	
0314	" "	#1 SQ	exception to # system
0318	" "	#3 RD	METAL WELL 3 SEP.FRONDS
0320	" "	#3 RD	3 SEP.FRONDS
0325	" "	#1 RD	
0333	" "	#2 SQ	exception to # sys
0338	" "	#3 RD	3 SEP. FRONDS
0339	" "	#1 RD	EARLY T-BAR
0340	" "	#1 RD	
0348	" "	#1 RD	
0363	" "	#1 RD	
0364	" "	#1 RD	EBONY F-BD
0396	" "	#1 RD	
0400	" "	#2 RD	
0420	" "	#1 RD	
0423	" "	#2 RD	2 1/2
0424	" "	#2 RD	2 1/2, EBONY BD., REG TPC
0427	" "	#1 RD	
0434	" "	#4 RD	ARROWS AT 12 FR,DARK HEAD
0442	" "	#4 RD	
0444	" "	#1 RD	ENGR: P.LOWERY 7/31/1928
0483	" "	#1 RD	
0486	" "	#1 RD	
0496	" "	#1 RD	
0499	" "	#1 SQ	
504	" "	#1 RD	number not confirmed
0504	" "	#4 RD	DECAL HEAD, ARROWS AT 12 FR
0514	" "	#3 RD	
0529	" "	#2 RD	
0532	" "	#2 RD	
0534	" "	#1 RD	
0542	" "	#1 RD	
0544	" "	#2 RD	
0547	" "	#1 RD	
0558	" "	#2 RD	
0561	" "	#2 RD	
0595	" "	#1 RD	
0607	" "	#1 RD	
0611	" "	#1 RD	
0615	" "	#1 RD	
0624	" "	#1 RD	
0630	" "	#1 RD	
0632	" "	#2 RD	
0638	" "	#1 RD	
0639	" "	#4 RD	DARK HEAD
0642	" "	#2 RD	
0650	" "	#2 RD	
0666	" "	#1 RD	
0675	" "	#3 RD	PLAIN COVERPLATE

	683	" "	#1 RD	Number not confirmed
	0684	" "	#1 RD	
	0713	" "	#1 RD	
	0731	" "	#1 RD	
	0748	" "	#3 RD	DARK HEAD
1929	0781	" "	#1 RD	
	0814	" "	#1 RD	
	0815	" "	#1 RD	
	0837	" "	#1 RD	
	0847	" "	#1 RD	
	0850	" "	#2 RD	
	0854	" "	#3 RD	
	0860	" "	#1 SQ	possibly 860
	0867	" "	#2 RD	
	0913	" "	#2 RD	
	0919	" "	#1 RD	
	0949	" "	#1 RD	
	0960	" "	#2 RD	
	0977	" "	#3 RD	PLAIN COVERPLATE
	0987	" "	#1 RD	
	0989	" "	#4 RD	CUSTOM FOR HARRY WATSON
	0991	" "	#2 SQ	possibly 991
	0994	" "	#4 RD	
	0998	" "	#4 RD	
	01002	" "	#1 RD	
1930	01004	" "	#1 RD	
	1265	" "	#1 RD	Number not confirmed

S-PREFIX TRICONES--
PART OF STYLE O NUMBERING BATCH 1930-1934

6/1930	S 46	PAT PEND	#3 RD	
	S 96	PAT PEND	#1 RD	
	S153	PAT PEND	#1 RD	
	S166	PAT PEND	#1 RD	
	S194	PAT PEND	#2 RD	
	S282	PAT PEND	#1 RD	
	S295	PAT PEND	#1 RD	
	S300	PAT PEND	#2 RD	
	S408	PAT PEND	#2 RD	
	S759	PAT PEND	#1 RD	
	S769	PAT PEND	#4 RD	
	S1119	PAT PEND	#1 RD	
	S1277	PAT PEND	#1 RD	
	S1341	PAT PEND	#1 RD	
	S1351	PAT PEND	#1 RD	
	S1602	PAT PEND	* RD	CUSTOM SPECIAL ETCHING, BRASS
	S1822	PAT PEND	#1 RD	
	S1834	PAT PEND	#1 RD	
	S2195	PAT PEND	#1 RD	
1931	S2197	PAT PEND	#2 RD	
	S2282	PAT PEND	#1 RD	
6/31	S2286	PAT PEND	#1 RD	
	S2300		#1 RD	
	S2720	2 PAT #	#3 RD	PLAIN COVERPLATE
2/32	S2960	2 PAT #	#1 RD	NO WIGGLE BORDER
	S3293	2 PAT #	#1 RD	
	S3295	2 PAT #	#1 RD	

	S3437	2 PAT #	#4 RD
	S3552	2 PAT #	#1 RD
	S3805	2 PAT #	#1 RD
1933	S4077	2 PAT #	#1 RD
	S4078	2 PAT #	#1 RD
	S4426	2 PAT #	#1 RD
	S4857	2 PAT MDUSA	#4 RD
	S4863	2 PAT MDUSA	#2 RD
1934	S5057	2 PAT MDUSA	#4 RD
	S5632	2 PAT MDUSA	#1 RD WIGGLE BORDER
	S6064		#4 RD
4/1935	A 2	2 PAT	#3 RD
	A 3	2PAT	#1 RD NO WIGGLE
	A 11	2PAT	#1 RD NO WIGGLE
	A 26	?	#1 RD NO WIGGLE
	A 3717		EXPLODING PALM TREE ROUNDNECK
	A 3720		EXPLODING PALM TREE ROUNDENECK

THERE ARE A FEW MORE #4 ROUNDNECKS, SEEN BY THE AUTHOR YEARS AGO, WITH UNCOLLECTED SERIAL NUMBERS.

SEVERAL NON-SILVER (BRASS-BODY) ROUNDNECK TRICONES, SUCH AS STYLE #97, #35, AND M-3 WILL BE FOUND SCATTERED AMONG THE CHICAGO LETTER-PREFIX SERIES (A-, B-, C-, L-, G-).

OBVIOUSLY THERE ARE OTHER ROUNDNECK TRICONES FOR WHICH SERIAL NUMBERS HAVE NOT BEEN GATHERED--PLEASE SEND IN YOUR SERIAL NUMBERS FOR FUTURE EDITIONS.

OTHER GERMAN SILVER INSTRUMENTS
(SEPARATE NUMBER SERIES):

SILVER UKULELES: STARTS WITH 100

1928	118	PAT PEND	#1 OLD CONE, SCREENS, MAHOG,MTL/TP
	123	PAT PEND	#1 OLD CONE, SCREENS, MAHOG,WD/TPC
	125	" "	#1 OLD CONE, SCREENS, MAHOG. "
	128	" "	#2 OLD CONE, SCREENS,
	141	" "	#1 OLD CONE, SCREENS, MAHOG.
	143	" "	#1 OLD CONE, SCREENS, MAHOG. "
	162	" "	#1
	182	" "	#1 OLD CONE, SCREENS, " "
	191	" "	#1 OLD CONE, SCREENS, MAHOG
	200	" "	#1 REG CONE, SCREENS, MAHOG
	212	" "	#1
	213	" "	#1 REG CONE, HOLES
	231	" "	#2
	236	" "	#2 REG CONE, HOLES, MAPLE "
	241	" "	#2 REG CONE, HOLES
1931	258	" "	#1 ? CONE, SCREENS

SMALL BODY UKES BEGIN HERE,
ALL WITH HOLES-TYPE COVERPLATE.

1932	305	" "	#1 SMALL-BODY, MAHOG
	312	" "	#2 SMALL-BODY, MAPLE, PEARLOID "
	342	" "	#1 SMALL-BODY
	358	" "	#1 SMALL BODY
	367	" "	#1 SMALL-BODY
	387	" "	#2 SMALL-BODY, MAPLE ONLY "
1934	405	" "	#2 SMALL-BODY, MAPLE ONLY
			(PAT# ON BISCUIT)

A FEW MORE HAVE BEEN REPORTED TO THE AUTHOR, BUT SERIAL NUMBERS ARE UNAVAILABLE.

ALSO, SEVERAL MORE WILL BE FOUND SCATTERED AMONG THE CHICAGO LETTER-PREFIX NUMBER SERIES.

GERMAN SILVER MANDOLINS:
INCLUDES TRICONES, AND TRICONE UKES.
STARTS AT 100 (1928-1934)

	PROTOTYPE		#2 TRICONE UKE, SM. FLAT SCREEN COVER,LIP
	122	NO PAT STAMP	#2 TRICONE MANDO,SM FLAT SCREEN COV
	127		#2 TRICONE MANDO,SM FLAT SCREEN COVER,LIP
	132	?	#1 TRICONE UKE, SM FLAT SCREEN COVER,LIP
	134		#2 TRICONE MANDO,SM FLAT SCREEN COVER,LIP
	137		#2 TRICONE UKE, SM FLAT SCREEN COVER,LIP
	138		#2 TRICONE MANDO,SM FLAT SCREEN COVER,LIP
	148		#1 TRICONE UKE, SM FLAT SCREEN COVER,LIP
	166		#1 SINGLE CONE MANDO, SAME SM COVER W/LIP
	194		#1 SINGLE CONE MANDO, SAME SM COVER W/LIP
	256	PAT PEND	#1 SINGLE CONE MANDO, SM COVER, HOLES,I
	266		#1 SINGLE CONE MANDO, SM.COVER, HOLES,LIP
1930	343	PAT PEND	#1 NOW LARGE COVERPLATES
	350	PAT PEND	#1 COVERPLATE: NO RIBS, 9 HOLES
	377	PAT PEND	#3 NO RIBS, 9 HOLES
	388	PAT PEND	#1 RIBS, 9 HOLES
	405	PAT PEND	#1 NO RIBS, " "
	406	PAT PEND	#1
	457	PAT PEND	#2
	483	PAT PEND	#1
	515	" "	#4++ CUSTOM: GLOBES ENGR.,RIBS, 9
	522		#1 CHICKEN-FEET COVERPLATE
	537		#2 RIBS 9 HOLES
	567		#1
	571	?	#1 ?
	596	?	#1 2-LINE BORDER, RIBS, 8 HOLES
	602	?	#1 CHICKEN-FEET COVERPLATE

NOTE RANDOM USE OF EARLIER HOLES-COVER AND CHICKEN-FEET COVER IN THE 500-600'S.

MORE SILVER MANDOLINS WILL BE FOUND AMONG THE CHICAGO LETTER- PREFIX NUMBER SERIES.

GERMAN SILVER TENOR AND PLECTRUM GUITARS:

1928	12	?	#4 SPECIAL TENOR TRICONE, DARK NK
	26	PAT PEND	#1 PLECTRUM TRICONE, EARLY LOGO,
			DARK NECK W/ STRIP
	66	PAT PEND	#1 TENOR TRICONE, EARLY LOGO
			DARK NECK, NO STRIP
	71	PAT PEND	#1 PLECTRUM
	81	PAT PEND	#2 TENOR (2 1/2) DARK NECK,SPIRAL
	82	PAT PEND	#1 TENOR, EARLY LOGO, NO SPIRAL
	94	PAT PEND	#1 TENOR TRICONE
	102	" "	#1 TENOR TRICONE
	105	" "	#1 TENOR TRICONE
	111	" "	#1 PLECTRUM TRICONE
	119	" "	#1 TENOR TRICONE
	131	" "	#3 TENOR TRICONE
	156	" "	#1 TENOR TRICONE
	169	" "	#1 TENOR TRICONE
	191	" "	#1 TENOR TRICONE
	198	" "	#3 PLECTRUM TRICONE NECK #L10195
	200	" "	#1 TENOR TRICONE
	220	" "	#3 PLECTRUM TRICONE
	225	" "	#1 TENOR TRICONE

227 " "	#2 PLECTRUM	TRICONE
239 " "	#1 TENOR	TRICONE
242 " "	#3 PLECTRUM	TRICONE
255 " "	#1 TENOR	TRICONE
322 " "	#1 TENOR	TRICONE
335 " "	#1 TENOR	TRICONE
344 " "	#2 TENOR	TRICONE,

MAPLE NECK W/ ROSEWD STRIP

369 " "	#1 PLECTRUM	TRICONE
379 " "	#1 TENOR	TRICONE, AS ABOVE
380 " "	#2 TENOR	TRICONE, AS ABOVE
383 " "	#1 TENOR	TRICONE, AS ABOVE
408 " "	#1 TENOR	TRICONE, AS ABOVE
429 " "	#2 TENOR	TRICONE, AS ABOVE
478 " "	#1 TENOR	TRICONE
507 " "	#1 TENOR	TRICONE
546 " "	#1 TENOR	TRICONE, NO STRIP
633 " "	#3 TENOR	SINGLE-CONE,

BUT BODY STILL PEAR-SHAPED

662	#1 PLECTRUM	SINGLE-CONE, PEAR
667 " "	#? TENOR	SINGLE-CONE, PEAR
707 " "	#1 PLECTRUM	SINGLE-CONE, PEAR
710 " "	#1 PLECTRUM	SINGLE CONE, PEAR
777 " "	#1 TENOR	SNGL CONE NECK #L9975
815 " "	#3 TENOR	SINGLE CONE, GTR SHAPE!
873 " "	#1 TENOR	SINGLE-CONE, GTR?SHAPE
876 " "	#1 TENOR	SINGLE-CONE, BODY IS

STILL PEAR-SHAPED

1931 882 " " #1 TENOR SINGLE CONE, BUT BODY

NOW GUITAR SHAPED

885 " "	#1 TENOR	SINGLE CONE, GTR SHAPE
886 " "	#1 TENOR	SINGLE CONE, GTR SHAPE
888 " "	#3 TENOR	SINGLE CONE, GTR SHAPE
949 " "	#3 TENOR	SINGLE CONE, GTR SHAPE
964 " "	#1 TENOR	SINGLE CONE, GTR SHAPE
995 " "	#1 TENOR	AS ABOVE
1008 " "	#1 TENOR	AS ABOVE

1932 1030 #1 TENOR

1045 ? ?	#1 TENOR	AS ABOVE
1067 " "	#1 TENOR	AS ABOVE NO RIBS
1144 " "	#2 PLECTRUM	AS ABOVE
1248 " "	#2 TENOR	AS ABOVE RIBS
1318	#1 TENOR	
1438	#1 TENOR	

1934 1498 #1 TENOR

1645 #2 TENOR

1298 SILVO ON TENOR BODY,

MAY BE ANOTHER SERIES

2642 " " #3 TENOR SAME SERIES OR REG

TRICONE SERIES?

A FEW MORE SILVER TENOR-PLECTRUM GUITAR-SHAPED INSTRUMENTS WILL BE FOUND SCATTED AMONG THE CHICAGO NUMBER SERIES.

---

12 FRET STYLE O GUITARS:
(ALL SLOTTED HEADSTOCKS)
(SOME 14 FRET BEGINNING c. S5400...)

MOST STYLE O'S BELOW # S1000 ARE MADE OF STEEL, BUT MANY ARE MIXED BRASS AND STEEL PARTS UNTIL #S1750. SUBSEQUENT STYLE O'S ARE CONSTRUCTED OF BRASS.

YEAR	SER #	PATENT	DESIGN ELEMENTS	COVERPL.	F-HOLES
6/1930	no#	P.A.F.	VARIATION 0? LIGHTNING BOLTS		
	S188	?	VARIATION 0? LIGHTNING BOLTS		
	S235	PAT PEND?	VARIATION 1	SCREWS	FLAT
	S238	?	VARIATION 1	"	"
	S240	P.A.F.	VARIATION 1	"	"
	S261	?	VARIATION 1	"	"
	S265	PAT PEND?	VARIATION 1	"	"
	S297	P.A.F.	" " STEEL	"	"
	S306	P.A.F	" "	"	"
	S321	P.A.F	" "	"	"
	S326		" "	"	"
	S342	? ?	" "	"	"
	S399	? ?	" "	"	"
	S477	? ?	" "	"	"
	S525	? ?	" "	"	"
	S534	PAT PEND	" "	"	"
	S557	PAT PEND	" "	"	"
	S583	PAT PEND	VARIATION 2	"	"
	S595	" "	" "	"	"
	S597	" "	" "	"	"
	S625	" " STYLE N-PLAIN SILVER BACK, COPPER TOP			
	S683	" "	STYLE O "	"	"
	S712	" "	STYLE O "	"	"
	S744	" "	" "	"	"
	S788	" "	" "	"	"
	S796	" "	" "	"	"
	S829	" "	VARIATION 2	"	"
	S913	" "	" "	"	"
	S926	" "	" "	"	"
	S934	" " BACK BRASS, " TOP STEEL	"		"
	S971	" "	" "	"	"
	S1004	" "	" "	"	"
	S1031	" "	" "	"	"
	S1032	" "	" "	"	"
	S1039	" "	" "	"	"
	S1050	" "	" "	"	"
	S1083	" "	" "	"	"
	S1096	" "	" "	"	"
	S1167	" "	" "	"	"
	S1221	" "	" "	"	"
	S1289	" "	" "	"	"
	S1311	" " STOLEN! CONTACT AUTHOR	"		"
	S1314	" "	" "	"	"
	S1336	" "	" "	"	"
	S1376	" "	" "	"	"
	S1404	" "	" "	"	"
	S1405	" "	" "	"	"
	S1419	" "	" "	"	"
	S1430	" "	" "	"	"
	S1470	" "	" "	"	"

S1540 " "   " "   " "
S1547 " "   " "
S1621 " "   " "   " "
S1717 " "   " "   " "
S1736 " "   " "   " "
S1754 " "   PLAIN-STYLE N " "
S1772 " "   ? ?   " "
S1865 " "   ? ?   " "
S1922 " "
S1940 " "   ? ?   ?   "
S1953 " "   ? ?   ?   "
S1955 " "   ? ?   ?
S1956 " "   VARIATION 3 HOOKS ON PLATE "
S2024 " "   " "   ?
S2048 " "   " "   ? ? ?
S2112 " "   " " SCREWS
S2114 " "   " "   ?
1931 S2145 " "   " " SCREWS ON PLATE
S2163 " "   " "   ?
S2212 " "   " "   ?
S2260 " "   " "   ?   "
S2275 " "   " "   ?   "
S2330 " "   " " HOOKS ON PLATE "
S2331 " "   " " HOOKS ON PLATE "
S2428 " "   " "
S2434 " "   " "   ?
S2473 " "   " "
S2495 " "   " "   ?
S2498 " "   " "   ?   "
S2512 " "   " "   ?
S2542 " "   " " HOOKS ON PLATE
S2551 " "   " " HOOKS ON PLATE
S2557 " "   " " HOOKS ON PLATE
S2587 " "   " "   ?   "
S2610 " "   " " HOOKS ON PLATE
S2681 " "   PLAIN STYLE N,HOOKS ON PLATE
S2695 " "   STYLE O   HOOKS ON PLATE
S2707 " "   STYLE O   HOOKS ON PLATE
S2779 " "   PLAIN STYLE N,HOOKS ON PLATE
S2785 " "   PLAIN STYLE N,HOOKS ON PLATE
1/32 S2788 CUSTOM FOR BEAUCHAMP ENGRAVED--STYLE #3 PLUS!
S2795   PLAIN-STYLE N HOOKS ON PLATE
S2813 " "   PLAIN-STYLE N HOOKS ON PLATE
S2853 " "   VARIATION 3? HOOKS ON PLATE
S2903 " "   VARIATION 3 HOOKS ON PLATE
S2926 " "   " "   HOOKS ON PLATE "
S2998 " "   " "   ? ? ?
S3020 " "   " "   ? ? ?
S3138 " "   " " SCREWS ON PLATE
S3145 " "   " "   ? ? ?
S3156 " "   " "   ?
S3160 ? ?   " "   ?
S3214 PAT #   " "   RIBS ON COVER
S3244 PAT #   " "   RIBS
S3325 PAT #   " "   RIBS
S3329 " "   " "   RIBS
S3350 " "   " "   RIBS
S3332 " "   " "   RIBS
S3368 " "   " "   RIBS
S3377 " "   " "   RIBS

S3388 " "   " "   RIBS
S3412 " "   VARIATION 3 RIBS
S3421 " "   VARIATION 4 RIBS   " FLAT F-H
S3468 " "   " "   " "   " "
S3492 "   " "   " "   " "
S3532 "   " "   " "   " "
S3532 FACTORY MISTAKE, TWO #S3532 STYLE O GUITARS MAI
S3542 "   " "   " "   " "
S3610 "   " "   " "   " "
S3627 "   " "   " "   " "
S3641 "   " "   " "   " "
S3673 "   " "   " "   " "
S3680 "   " "   " "   " "
S3710 "   " "   " "   " "
S3821 "   " "   " "   " "
S3829 "   " "   " "   " "
S3838 "   " "   " "   " "
S3857 "   " "   " "   " "
S3944 "   " "   " "   " "
S3951 "   " "   " "   " "
S3991 "   " "   " "   " "
1933 S4035 "   " "   " "   " "
S4067 "   " "   " "   " "
S4104 "   " "   " "   " "
S4142 "   " "   " "   " "
S4177 "   " "   " "   " "
S4213 "   " "   " "   " "
S4215 "   " "   " "   " "
S4225 "   " "   " "   " "
S4233 "   " "   " "   " "
S4251 "   " "   " "   " "
S4299 "   " "   " "   " "
S4304 "   " "   " "   " "
S4349 "   " "   " "   " "
S4371 "   " "   "   " FLAT
S4393 "   ? ?   ?   " ?
6/33 S4475 " 12 FRET VARIATION 5 " " ROLLED
S4491 "   " "   "   " ROLLED
S4509 "   " "   "   " ROLLED
S4513 "   " "   "   " ROLLED
S4621 "   " "   "   " ROLLED
S4634 "   " "   "   " "
S4636 "   " "   "   " "
S4716 "   " "   "   " ROLLED
S4732 "   " "   "   " "
S4747 "   " "   "   " ROLLED
S4770 "   " "   " "   "
S4779 "   " "   " "   "
S4895 "   " "   " "   "
S4912 "   " "   " "   "
S4929 "   " "   " "   "
1934 S5037 "   " "   " "   " "
S5050 "   " "   " "   " "
S5051 "   " "   " "   " "
S5076 "   " "   " "   " "
S5079 "   " "   " "   " "
S5108 "   " "   " "   " "
S5144 "   " "   " "   " "
S5152 "   " "   " "   " "
S5162 "   " "   " "   " "

270

	S5173	"	" "	"	"	"	
	S5229	"	" "	"	"	"	
	S5239	"	" "	"	"	"	
	S5256	"	" "	"	"	"	
	S5321	"	12 FRET	"	"	"	"
	S5342	"	12 FRET SQ BUT CHICKEN FEET COVER				
	S5379	"	12 FRET				
9/34	S5401	"	? ? ? ? ? ?				
	S5438		14 FRET VARIATION 6 ALL ROLLED				
	S5463	"	14 FRET " "ALL SLOT HEAD				
	S5466	"	14 FRET " " "				
	S5468	"	14 FRET " " "				
	S5539	"	14 FRET " " "				
	S5563	"	14 FRET " " "				
	S5598	"	14 FRET " " "				
	S5649	"	14 FRET " " "				
	S5650	"	14 FRET " " "				
	S5657	"	14 FRET " " "				
	S5659	"	14 FRET " " "				
	S5669	"	14 FRET " " "				
	S5686	"	14 FRET " " "				
	S5785-2D	"	14 FRET " " "				
	S5732	"	14 FRET " " "				
	S5842	"	12 FRET! SQ "BUT CHICK.FEET COVER				
	S5854	"	12 FRET! SQ BUT CHICK.FEET COVER				
	S5866	"	12 FRET! SQ "BUT CHICK.FEET COVER				
	S5867	"	14 FRET VAR 6 BUT REG COVERPLATE				
	S5914	"	14 FRET VARIATION 6 CHICK.FEET				
	S5919	"	14 FRET " " SLOT HEAD				
	S5949	"	14 FRET " " CHICK/SLOT				
	S5958	"	14 FRET " " CHICK/SLOT				
	S5980	"	14 FRET " " CHICK/SLOT				
	S5997	"	14 FRET " "				
	S6003	"	12 FRET! VARIATION 5 REG COVER				
	S6011	"	14 FRET VARIATION 6 CHICK FEET				
	S6012	"	12 FRET! VARIATION 5 REG COVER				
	S6205	"	12 FRET! VARIATION 5 REG COVER				
	3070		12 FRET SQ CHICK/FT COVER				

PRESUMABLY THE LAST FEW 12 FRET GUITARS SCATTERED
AMONGST THE 14 FRET GUITARS ARE FROM SLIGHTLY OLDER
PARTS STOCKS, BUT LIKE ALL NATIONALS, NUMBERED AT THE
LAST STAGE OF ASSEMBLY.

FOLLOWING NUMBERS ARE CONTINUATION OF EARLY 14-FRET STYLE O:
(ALL HAVE ROLLED-IN F-HOLES)
(ALL HAVE NEW CHICK/FT COVER)

1935	293	VARIATION 6 SLOT HEAD	
	393	" " " "	
	576	" " " "	
	590	" " " "	
	661	" " " "	
	1473	" " " "	
	1757	" " " "	
	2344	" " " "	
	2345	" " " "	
	3070	" SQ " " "	
	3476	" " " "	
	3666	" " " "	
1936	3940	" " " "	
	4605	" SQ " "	
	5453	" " " "	
	5562 SD(?)	" " " "	
	5657	" 6/7 SOLID HEAD	
	5659	" 6/7 SOLID HEAD	
	5705	" 6/7 SOLID	
	6014	" 7 SLOT HEAD	
	6076	" ? ? HEAD	
	6404	" 8 SOLID HEAD	
	6420	" " " "	
	6971	" " " "	
	7019	" 8 " "	
	7025	" " " "	
	7026	" " " "	
	7027	" " " "	

7038 IS THE TRICONE GUITAR WITH EXPLODING
PALM TREE ETCHING LISTED WITH THE TRICONES

THIS SERIES ALSO INCLUDES DUOLIANS AND TRIOLIANS
OF THIS PERIOD--BY NO MEANS DOES IT REPRESENT 7,000
STYLE O GUITARS, RATHER 7,000 OF ALL THREE MODELS

A LARGE NUMBER OF CHICAGO-MADE 14 FRET STYLE O
GUITARS WILL BE FOUND LISTED AMONG THE CHICAGO
LETTER-PREFIX NUMBER SERIES (A-, B-, C-, L-, G-) OF 1936-
1941. THEY ARE VARIATIONS 7, 8, AND 9. THE SCENE ON
THE BACK IS REVERSED AND A DIFFERENT STENCIL THAN
THE PRECEDING SERIES OF 14-FRET STYLE O GUITARS.
ALL HAVE SOLID HEADSTOCKS WITH INCREASINGLY
MODERN DESIGN.

DON MODELS: GERMAN SILVER 14 FRET SINGLE CONES

9/34	X 27	STYLE 1 DON
	X 54	STYLE 1 DON
	X 57	STYLE 3 DON
	X 78	STYLE 2 DON
	X 83	STYLE 2 DON
	X 88	STYLE 1 DON
	X105	STYLE 1 DON TENOR NECK
	X126	STYLE 1 DON WIGGLE INSTEAD OF DON BORDER
	X133	STYLE 1 DON WIGGLE INSTEAD OF DON DORDER

AT LEAST 5 OTHER DONS ARE KNOWN, SERIAL NUMBERS UNKNOWN

WOOD BODY EARLY TRIOLIANS:
ALL POLYCHROME WITH DECAL

FIRST TWO SAMPLES MADE SEPT. 1928,
TRICONE SET-UP, NO NUMBERS

TWELVE TRICONE-SET-UP WOOD TRIOLIANS
MADE AFTER THIS, NO #'S

SINGLE-CONE WOOD TRIOLIANS FOLLOW
BY OCT. 1928

EARLIEST ARE FLOWER BOUQUET DECAL,
SCREEN HOLES, NO NUMBERS VERY EARLIEST
HAVE TRICONE-STYLE HEADSTOCK SHAPE,
THEN SQUARE

NEXT ARE HULA GIRL DECAL,
SCREENED HOLES, NO NUMBERS
AT LEAST 25 POLYCHROME EXAMPLES
WITHOUT NUMBERS EXIST, AND 2
TENORS, BEGINNING C. OCT. 1928

ONE TENOR HAS MALE SURFER

SERIALIZED WOOD TRIOLIANS,
PROBABLY STARTS AT 500.

2/29	729	PAT PEND	HULA GIRL		
	1107	PAT PEND	HULA GIRL	DRILLED HOLES	
	1225		HULA GIRL	"	"
	1287		HULA GIRL	"	"
	1433		HULA GIRL	"	"
8/29	1626		STENCILLED PALM SCENE		

EARLY METAL TRIOLIANS
(PRECEDES P- AND W-SUFFIX GUITARS):

9/29	0139	P.A.F	12 FRET POLYCHROME WITH STENCIL SCENE
	0148	P.A.F.	" " POLYCHROME WITH STENCIL SCENE
	0160	P.A.F.	" " ?
	0181	P.A.F.	" " WALNUT SUNBURST
	0186	P.A.F.	" " POLYCHROME WITH SCENE
	0195	P.A.F.	" " POLYCHROME WITH SCENE
	0197	P.A.F	" " POLYCHROME WITH SCENE
	0202		" " POLYCHROME WITH SCENE
	0209	P.A.F.	" " POLYCHROME WITH SCENE

BAKELITE NECK TRIOLIANS:
(ALL 12 FRET) (METAL BODY)

2/29	A223	BAKELITE NECK (NECK ONLY)
	A227	BAKELITE NECK (REFINISHED BODY)
	A300	BAKELITE NECK
	A364	BAKELITE NECK, BROWN SUNBURST
	A385	" " " "
	A582	" " ?
	A585	" " POLYCHROME, SCENE
	A781	" " ?
	A821	" " POLYCHROME, SCENE
	A1260	" " POLYCHROME, SCENE
	A1270	PAT PEND " " POLYCHROME, SCENE
	A1272	" " POLYCHROME, SCENE
	A1274	" " STRIPPED FINISH
	A1386	" " POLYCHROME, SCENE GRN
	A1413	" " POLYCHROME, SCENE

	A1431	" "	POLYCHROME, SCENE
	A1464	" "	POLYCHROME, SCENE
	A1590	" "	?
7/30	A1658	" "	POLYCHROME, SCENE
	A1814	" "	POLYCHROME, SCENE

4425	P.A.F.	12FRET POLYCHROME, BAKELITE NECK, FL COULD BE A425 AND MISREAD BY REPORTING PERSON

P-SERIES TRIOLIANS:
POLYCHROME (YELLOW-BASED) FINISH
GENERALLY WITH HAWAIIAN SCENE ON BACK.
COLORS VARY, ALSO POSITION OF SUN IMAGE.

1930	26P	12-FRET, POLYCHROME, SCENE FLAT F/H	
	43P	12 FRET, POLYCHROME	"
	65P	" " POLYCHROME	"
	77P	" " POLYCHROME	"
	199P	" " POLYCHROME	"
	231P	" " POLYCHROME	"
	292P	" " POLYCHROME	"
	327P	" " SADLY, RE-PLATED	"
	371P	12 FRET POLYCHROME, SCENE	"
	374P	12 FRET STRIPPED FINISH	"
	399P	? 12 FRET SUNBURST	"
	488P	" " POLYCHROME "	"
	573P	" " POLYCHROME "	"
	647P	" " POLYCHROME, OVER NICKEL PLATE	
	682P	" " POLYCHROME "	"
	705P	" " POLYCHROME, SCENE	"
	871P	12 FRET POLYCHROME, SCENE	"
	891P	" " POLYCHROME, SCENE	"
	902P	" " POLYCHROME, SCENE	"
	911P	" " POLYCHROME, SCENE	"
	1005P	" " POLYCHROME, SCENE	"
	1134P	" " POLYCHROME, SCENE	
	1143P	" " POLYCHROME, SCENE	
	1183P	" " POLYCHROME, SCENE	"
	1189P	" " POLYCHROME, SCENE	"
	1221P	" " POLYCHROME, SCENE	"
	1229P	TENOR-- POLYCHROME, SCENE	"
	1270P	12 FRET POLYCHROME, SCENE	"
	1398P	P.A.F. " " POLYCHROME, SCENE	"
	1448P	" " POLYCHROME, SCENE	"
	1475P	" " POLYCHROME, SCENE	"
	1520P	" " SUNBURST?	"
	1614P	" " POLYCHROME, SCENE	"
	1631P	" " POLYCHROME, SCENE	"
	P1707	" " POLYCHROME, SCENE	"
	1795P	" " POLYCHROME, SCENE	"
	1828P	" " ?	"
	1882P	" " POLYCHROME, SCENE	"
	1913P	" " POLYCHROME, SCENE	"
	1969P	" " POLYCHROME, SCENE	"
	2001P	" " POLYCHROME, SCENE FLAT F-	
	2028P	TENOR POLYCHROME, SCENE	"
	2046P	12 FRET POLYCHROME, SCENE, DARK F-BD	
	2048P	TENOR " "	
	2084P	12 FRET " "	
	2091P	TENOR " " "	
	P2121	12 FRET " " FLAT-CUT F-HOLE	

```
2168P        "  "         "   "          "
2170P        "  " POLYCHROME          "
2194P     12 FRET POLYCHROME, SCENE RIBS, FLAT
2204P     12 FRET POLYCHROME, SCENE, RIBS, ROLL
2242P     12 FRET POLYCHROME, SCENE, RIBS, ROLL
2258P     12 FRET POLYCHROME, SCENE  RIBS, ROLL
2266P     12 FRET POLYCHROME, SCENE, RIBS, ROLL
9/34 2298P   14 FRET POLYCHROME, SCENE,ROLLED F/H
2303P     14 FRET, ?  ?  SLOT,      RIBS ROLL
2311P     14 FRET,POLYCHROME, SCENE,SLOT, RIBS
```

W-SERIES TRIOLIANS:
WALNUT (BROWN) SUNBURST FINISH

```
1930   50W      12 FRET SUNBURST  NO RIB FLAT F-HOLES
       63W      12 FRET   "        "   "   "   "
       71W       "  "     "        "   "   "   "
       98W       "  "     "        "   "   "   "
      135W P.A.F. "  "    "        "   "   "   "
      214W       "  "     "        "   "   "   "
      233W P.A.F. "  "    "        "   "   "   "
      312W       "  "     "        "   "   "   "
      332W P.A.F. "  "    "        "   "   "   "
      368W P.A.F. "  "    "        "   "   "   "
      456W       "  "     "        "   "   "   "
      465W       "  "     "        "   "   "   "
      494W       "  "     "        "   "   "   "
      550W      12 FRET   "        "   "   "   "
      572W P.A.F. 12 FRET "    NO RIB "  "   "
      630W      12 FRET   "        "   "   "
      638W P.A.F. 12 FRET "        "   "   "   "
      644W      12 FRET   "        "   "   "   "
      659W       "  "     "        "   "   "   "
      682W       "  "     "        "   "   "   "
      744W P.A.F. "  "    "        "   "   "   "
      815W   ?  MANDOLIN         RIBS
      820W      MANDOLIN         RIBS
      840W      MANDOLIN         RIBS
      847W P.A.F 12 FRET " BROWN NO RIB "  "   "
      870W P.A.F. "  "    "    NO RIB "  "   "
      928W P.A.F. "  "    "    NO RIB "  "   "
     1027W P.A.F  "  "    " ORANGE   "   "   "   "
     1029W P.A.F. "  "    "        "   "   "   "
     1089W        "  "    "        "   "   "   "
     1104W        "  "    "        "   "   "   "
     1117W        "  "    " BROWN   "   "   "   "
     1122W        "  "    "        "   "   "   "   "
     1125W        "  "    "        "   "   "   "   "
     1139W        "  "    "        "   "   "   "   "
     1162W        "  "    "        "  NO RIB "  "   "
     1182W P.A.F. "  "    "        "   "   "   "   "
     1186W P.A.F. "  "    "        "   "   "   "   "
     1188W P.A.F. "  "    "        "   "   "   "   "
     1207W P.A.F. "  "    "        "   "   "   "   "
     1214W P.A.F. "  "    "        "   "   "   "   "
     1240W   ?    "  "    "        "   "   "   "
     1280W        "  "    "        "   "   "   "
     1357W        "  "    "        "   "   "   "
     1374W        "  "    "        "   "   "   "   "
```

```
1397W     "  "      "   "        "   "   "   "
1481W     "  "      "   "        "   "   "   "
1482W     "  "      "   "        "   "   "   "
1541W     "  "      "  "<<<<<NO RIB"  "   "
1574W     "  "      "  RIBS>>>>> >  "   "   "
1703W     TENOR
1772W          WOOD BODY? NOT CONFIRMED
1798W  P.A F.  12 FRET    "  ALL RIBS>>>> >  "   "
1931 1910W PAT PEND  TENOR  "        "   "   "
     1938W PAT PEND  TENOR  "        "   "   "
     1977W  "  "  12 FRET    "        "   "   "
     2053        "  " NO RIBS, NO W, REPL BAKENECK
     2054        NO RIBS, NO W, REPL BAKENECK
     2071W  "  "  12 FRET    "  ALL RIBS>>>>>   "   "
     2126W  "  "  12 FRET    "        "   "   "
     2134W  "  "  TENOR           "   "   "
     2190W  "  "  TENOR           "   "   "
     2224W  "  "  12 FRET    "        "   "   "
     2237W  "  "  12 FRET    "        "   "   "
     2293W  "  "   "   "        "        "   "   "
     2294W  "  "   "   "       " REGULAR SCREWS "   "   "
     2342W  "  "   "   "       " HOOKS ON PLATE
     2357W  "  "   "   "        HOOKS ON PLATE
     2422W  "  "   "   "       ?             "   "   "
     2438W  "  "   "   "
     2485W  "  "   "   "
     2495W  "  "   "   "
     2532W  "  "   "   "       REFINISHED
1932 2568W  "  "   "   "       HOOKS ON PLATE   "   "   "
     2574W  "  "       " HOOKS ON PLATE   "   "   "
     2637W  PAT #  "  "   " SCREWS          "   "   "
     2710W  "  "       " SCREWS "    "    "   "   "
     2839W  "  "       "   "     "    "   "   "
     2924W  "  "       "   "     "    "   "   "   "
     2993W  "  "       "   "     "    "   "   "   "
     3087W  "  "       "   "     "    "   "   "   "
     3109W  "  "       "  ? ? ?   FLAT F/H
     3174W    12 FRET       "       ROLLED F/H
6/1934 3201W PAT # 14 FRET  SLOT HEAD      ROLLED
     3205W    14 FRET SQ SLOT HEAD      ROLLED
     3223W    14 FRET  SLOT HEAD REFINISHED   ROLL
     3234W PAT # 14 FRET  SLOT HEAD SUNBURST  ROLL
     3242W    14 FRET   SLOT HEAD SUNBURST   ROLL
     3346W   ?  12 FRET!   "    "  SUNBURST   ROLL
     3350W    14 FRET   SLOT HEAD SUNBURST   ROLL
```

TRIOLIAN TENOR SERIAL NUMBERS:
(SEPARATE FROM W-SERIES)

```
           NO NUMBER  WOOD BODY POLYCHROME WITH SURFER
9/29  558             WOOD BODY
      773  P.A.F.     PEAR SHAPED SINGLE CONE POLYCHROME
      794  P.A.F.     ??
      803             ??
1930  823            PEAR SHAPED SINGLE CONE,          W SUNBURST
      824            PEAR SHAPED SINGLE CONE POLYCHROME
      924            PEAR SHAPED SINGLE CONE          W SUNBURST
     1058        ?    ?     "    "         "   SUNBURST
     1160        GUITAR SHAPED SINGLE CONE POLYCHROM
     1176                          "    "           SUNBURST
1931 1247        ?    ?        "       "            SUNBURST
     1266   GUITAR SHAPED         SINGLE CONE, SUNBURST
     1427   GUITAR SHAPED         SINGLE CONE, SUNBURST
     1483   GUITAR SHAPED         SINGLE CONE, SUNBURST
     1550   PLECTRUM  GUITAR-SHAPED  SINGLE CONE, SUNBURST
     1551   PLECTRUM  GUITAR SHAPED   SINGLE CONE, SUNBURST
     1555   TENOR     GUITAR-SHAPED  SINGLE CONE, SUNBURST
1932 1589   PLECTRUM  GUITAR-SHAPED  SINGLE CONE, SUNBURST
```

THE FOLLOWING NUMBERS APPEAR IN 1933 FOR A SHORT-LIVED
TRIOLIAN MODEL WITH A CRYSTALLINE LAQUER FINISH SIMILAR TO
THE DUOLIANS, BUT A NON-METALLIC OPAQUE DARK GREEN.

```
6/33  11B          12 FRET GUITAR OPAQUE FROST
      12B  PAT#    GTR-SHAPED TENOR, FROSTED, DECAL
      18B   "      GTR-SHAPED TENOR, OPAQUE GRN FROST
      39B   "      12 FRET OPAQUE GREEN FROST
      87B   "      12 FRET OPAQUE GREEN FROST, ROLLED
     125B   "      TENOR GTR, OPAQUE GREEN FROST
```

OTHER MID TO LATE 30'S TRIOLIANS: SAME SERIES AS 1935-1936
STYLE O GUITARS, AND DUOLIANS OF THE SAME ERA

```
1935  1088         14 FRET SLOT, SUNBURST
1936  4827         MANDOLIN WOODGRAIN B/W HEAD
      5246         14 FRET WOODGRAIN  SOLID  ROLLED
      5543         14 FRET  ?
      5974         14 FRET, BROWN
     10184 PROB'LY L- TENOR   WOODGRAIN
```

THE FIRST FOUR NUMBERS OF THIS GROUP ARE PART OF THE SAME
SERIES AS THE NO-PREFIX EARLY 14-FRET STYLE O GUITARS.

TRIOLIAN MANDOLINS AND UKULELES:
SEPARATE FROM -W AND -P

```
9/29  no#             UKULELE, POLYCHROME, SCENE
      118  PAT APL.FOR POLYCHROME, SCENE, SM.CONE MANDO
      121  "    "    " MANDOLIN---SUNBURST, SM CONE
      132  "    "    " MANDOLIN---SUNBURST, NO SCENE
      201  "    "    " UKULELE---POLYCHROME
      224  "    "    " UKULELE---POLYCHROME  METAL SHIELD
      225  "    "    " MANDOLIN---POLYCHROME, SMALL CONE
      226  "    "    " MANDOLIN---POLYCHROME, SMALL CONE
      305  "    "    " UKULELE---SUNBURST
      324  "    "    " MANDOLIN---SUNB.,REG CONE NO RIBS
      332  "    "    " MANDOLIN
      338  "    "    " MANDOLIN   ?   ?   ?
      358            UKULELE---REPLATED OVER PAINT
1931  400  "    "    " SUNBURST--MANDOLIN REG CONE,RIBS
```

```
422  "    "    " POLYCHROME---UKULELE SM BODY
512  "    "    " SUNBURST---UKULELE SM BODY
534  "    "    " POLYCHROME---UKULELE SM BODY
609  ?          UKULELE--REFINISHED SMALL BODY
```

THESE INSTRUMENTS BELOW WERE INEXPLICABLY NUMBERED
IN WITH THE -P AND -W SUFFIX GUITAR SERIES:

```
308P          MANDOLIN---POLYCHROME, SCENE
737P          MANDOLIN---POLYCHROME, SCENE

535P  ?       MANDOLIN---SUNBURST
560W  PAT #   MANDOLIN---SUNBURST
616W  ?       MANDOLIN---SUNBURST
642W  PAT #   MANDOLIN---SUNBURST
815W  PAT #   MANDOLIN---SUNBURST
820W          "         "
840W          "         "
```

THESE LAST FEW ARE PART OF REGULAR -P AND -W SERIES, LIKELY,
THOUGH PAT #'S APPEAR AT DIFFERENT PARTS OF THE SERIES THAN
THE GUITARS, SUGGESTING THE POSSIBILITY OF A SEPARATE SERIES
OR A CONTINUATION OF THE NON-W AND NON-P MANDOLIN NUMBER

12 AND 14 FRET DUOLIAN GUITARS:
MORE THAN ONE SERIES FLAT F-HOLES TO c. C6000

```
1/31  C 32  P.A.F.   12 FRET  SLOT HEAD       STAMPED LOGO
      C 38  P.A.F.   12 FRET  SLOT HEAD SHIELD-STAMPEDLOGO
      C 307           "   "    "    "
      C 327  P.A.F.   "   "    "    "
      C 420 - 2       "   "    "    " (FACTORY SECOND)
      C 431           "   "    "    "        STAMPED LOGO
      C 478  P.A.F.   "   "    "    "        STAMPED LOGO
      C 498  P.A.F.  12 FRET  SLOT HEAD STUDS STAMPED LOGO
      C 509    "      "   "    "    "
      C 558    "      "   "    "    "
      C 565    "      "   "    "    "  GREY FROST
      C 597    "      "   "    "    "
      C 605    "      "   "    "    "   "    "
      C 658    "      "   "    "    "  BLACK FROST    "
      C 872    "      "   "    "    "
      C 860    "      "   "    "    "        STAMPED LOGO
      C 886  P.A.F.   "   "    "    "
      C 928    "      "   "    "    "
      C 961  P.A.F.   "   "    "    "
      C1025    "      "   "    "    "  GREY FROST
      C1034    "      "   "    "    "   "   "
      C1054  P.A.F.   "   "    "    " STRIPPED/PLATED
      C1118  P.A.F.   "   "    "    "
      C1132    "      "   "    "    "
      C1171    "      "   "    "    "   "    STAMPED LOGO
      C1204    "      "   "    "    "   "    "       "
      C1365    "      "   "    "    "   "
      C1440    "      "   "    "    "  BROWN FROST
      C1467    "      "   "    "    "
      C1597  ?        "   "    "    "  GREY
      C1673    "      "   "    "    "
      C1914  PAT PEND "   "    "    "   " NO RIBS
      C1963    "      "   "    "    "
      C1968    "      "   "    "    "
      C2007    "      "   "    "    "   " HOOKS IN PLATE
```

	Serial	Fret	Head	Color	Notes
	C2033	" "	" " "		
	C2206	" "	" "	" HOOKS	
	C2214	" "	" " "		
	C2274	" "	" " "		
	C2303	" "	" " "		
	C2316	" "	" " "		
	C2324	" "	" " "		
	C2356	" "	" " "		
	C2380	" "	" "	" STAMPED, HOOKS	
	C2455	" "	" " "		
	C2528	" "	" " "		
	C2577	" "	" " "		
	C2583	" "	" " "		
	C2626	" "	" " "		
	C2832	" "	" "	" SCREWS IN PLATE	
6/31	C2836 PAT #	" "	" " "		
	C2861	" " " "	" " "		
	2869C	" "	" "	" GREEN FROST	
	2915C	" "	" " "		
	C2931	" "	" " "		
	C2935	" "	" " "		
	C2955	" "	" "	DK GREEN FROST	
	C3115	" "	" "	DK GREEN FROST	
	C3159	" "	" "		
	C3244	" "	" "	LT GREEN FROST	
	C3700	" "	" "	RIBS, STAMPED LOGO	
	C3767	" "	" "	RIBS, STAMPED LOGO	
	C3883	" "	" " "	" "	
	C4127	" "	" "		
	C4196	" "	" "	RIBS, STAMPED	
	C4227	" "	" " "	" "	
	C4469	" "	" "	GREY FROST	
	C4553	" "	" " "	" "	
	4597C	" "	" "	RIBS, STAMPED LOGO	
	C4665	" "	" " "		
	C4687	" "	" "	RIBS	
	C4721	" "	" " "		
	C4738	" "	" " "		
	C4844	" "	" " "		
	C4901	" "	" " "		
	C5033	" "	" " "		
	C5037	" "	" " "		
	C5144	" "	" " "		
	C5323	" "	" "	GREY	
	C5353	" "	" "	RIBS, GREEN FROST	
	C5659	" "	" " "	"	
	C5791	" "	" "	FLAT-CUT F-HOLES	
	C5807	" "	" "	FLAT-CUT F-HOLES	
	C5857	" "	" "	FLAT-CUT F-HOLES	
	C5885	" "	" "	FLAT CUT F-HOLES	
1933	C6056	" "	" "	ROLLED F-HOLES	
	C6172	" "	" "	" ROLLED F-HOLES	
	C6342	" "	" "	" ROLLED F-HOLES	
	C6394	" "	" "	" STAMPED LOGO	
	C6438	" "	" " "	" "	
	C6505	12 FRET	SLOT HEAD,RIB,ROLLED F-HOLES		
	C6548	12 FRET	" "	" ROLLED F-HOLES	
	C6559	12 FRET	" " "	ROLLED F-HOLES	
	C6710	12 FRET	" " "	ROLLED F-HOLES	
	C6773	12 FRET	" " "	ROLLED F-HOLES	
	C6778	12 FRET	" "	" ROLLED F-HOLES	
	C6857	12 FRET	" "	" ROLLED F-HOLES	
	C6865	12 FRET	" "	" ROLLED F-HOLES	
	C6872	12 FRET	" "	" ROLLED F-HOLES	
	C6876	12 FRET	" "	" ROLLED F-HOLES	
	C6926	12 FRET	" "	" ROLLED F-HOLES	
	C7005	12 FRET	" "	" ROLLED F-HOLES	
	C7245	12 FRET	" "	" ROLLED F-HOLES	
9/34	C7701	14 FRET	SLOT HEAD	GREY	ALL ROLLED
	C7783	14 FRET	SLOT HEAD	GREY	ALL ROLLED
	C7919	14 FRET	" "	"	" "
	C7967	14 FRET	SLOT HEAD	GREY	
	C8083	14 FRET	SLOT HEAD	GREY	
	C8088	" "	" "	"	
	C8096	" "	" "	"	
	C8184	" "	" "	?	
	C8260	" "	" "	"	
	C8266	" "	" "	"	
	C8376	" "	" "	"	
	C8433	" "	" "	"	
	C8437	" "	" "	"	
	C8477	" "	" "	"	
	C8560	" "	" "	" RIB	
	C8599	" "	" "	"	
	C8659	" "	" "	"	
	C8665	" "	" "	"	
	C8780	" "	" "	" DECAL	
	C8847FS	" "	" "	" "	
	C8893	" "	" "	" "	
	C8916	" "	" "	" "	
	C9053	" "	" "	" "	
	C9148	" "	" "	" "	
	C9192	" "	" "	" "	
	C9195	" "	" "	" "	
	C9231	" "	" "	" "	
	C9257	" "	" "	" "	
	C9323	" "	" "	" "	
	C9449	" "	" "	" "	
	C9453	" "	" "	" "	
	C9454	" "	" "	" "	
	C9458	" "	" "	" "	
	C9500 FS	" "	" "	" "	
	C9568	" "	" "	" "	
	C9667 SQ	" "	" "	" "	
	C9689 SQ	" "	" "	" "	
1936	C9721	" "	SLOT HEAD	"	"

0-PREFIX DUOLIANS:
SEEMS POSSIBLE THAT THEY RUN
CONCURRENTLY WITH C-PREFIX MODELS, SINCE
CHANGES OCCUR AT SIMILAR NUMBERS.....

	Serial	Fret	Head	Color	Notes
8/31	0 509	12 FRET	SLOT HEAD	? ?	
	0 824	12 FRET	SLOT HEAD		
	0 827	12 FRET	SLOT HEAD	GREY FROST	
	01236	12 FRET	SLOT HEAD	GREY FROST	
	01432	" "	" "	" "	
	01446	" "	" "	" "	
	01570	" "	" "	BLACK/GREY FROST	
	01732	" "	" "	" "	

	02294	"	"	"	"		"	"
	03405	"	"	"	"		"	"
	03659	"	"	"	"		"	"
	04202	"	"	"	"	GREEN FROST		
	04204	"	"	"	"	GREY	"	
	04237	"	"	"	"		"	"
	04369	"	"	"	" RIBS	"	"	
	06123	"	"	"	"		"	"
9/34	O6547	14 FRET						
	07919	14 FRET	"			"	"	
	08030	"	"	"	"		"	"
	08165	"	"	"	"		"	"
	08786	"	"	"	"		"	"
	08932	"	"	"	"		"	"
	09114	"	"	"	"		"	"
	09464	"	" SQ	"	"		"	"
1936	09534	"	" SQ SLOT HEAD			"	"

E-PREFIX DUOLIANS:
PROBABLY CONCURRENT WITH C-PREFIX SERIES:

1934	E7272	12 FRET	SLOT HEAD	? FROST
9/34	E7376	14 FRET	SLOT HEAD	BROWN FROST
	E7410	14 FRET	SLOT HEAD	BROWN FROST
	E7571	14 FRET	SLOT HEAD RIBS	BROWN FROST
	E7580	14 FRET	SLOT HEAD	BROWN FROST
	E7646	14 FRET	" " "	
	E7704	14 FRET	" " "	BROWN FROST
	E7747	" "	" "	? "
	E7807	" "	" "	?
	E7821	" "	" "	GREEN FROST

"NO PREFIX" DUOLIANS:
A SEPARATE SERIES.....WHICH IS PART OF
A RANGE SHARED BY EARLY 14 FRET STYLE O
AND EARLY 14 FRET TRIOLIAN GUITARS.

1935	899	14 FRET	SLOT HEAD				
	1277	12 FRET	SLOT HEAD				
	2402	14 FRET	SLOT HEAD	GREY FROST			
	2659	14 FRET	"	"	"	"	
	2718	" "	"	"	"	"	
	3248	" "	"	"	"	"	
	3472	" "	"	"	"	"	
	3482	" "	"	"	"	"	
	3510	" "	"	"	"	"	
	3769	" "	"	"	"	"	
1936	4048	" "	"	"	"	"	
	4106	" "	"	"	"	"	
	4573	" "	"	"	"	"	
	4631	" "	SOLID HEAD	"	"		
	5445	" "	SOLID HEAD	"	"		
	5474	" "	SOLID	"	"	"	
	5478	" "	"	"	"	"	
	6311	" "	"	"	"	"	
	6512	" "	"	"	"	"	
	6529	" "	"	"	"	"	
	?6897	" "	SLOT	"	"	"	

COULD BE REG C- PREFIX AND WOULD FIT WITH THOSE

ALSO: SPECIAL CHEAPER DUOLIANS FOR SEARS ROEBUCK--COVERPLATE HAS FIVE LARGE DRILLED AREAS, INSTEAD OF THE NORMAL NINE.

1931	R63	12 FRET	SLOT	SEARS COVER
	R65	12 FRET	SLOT	" "
	R332	" "	SLOT	" "
	R402 PAT#	" "	SLOT	NORMAL COVERPLATE
	R415	" "	"	NORMAL COVERPLATE
	R422	" "	"	SEARS COVER
	R473	" "	"	
	R563			
	R572	12 FRET	"	GREY FROST

CHICAGO NUMBER SERIES:
EACH ONE INCLUDES VARIOUS INSTRUMENTS

THE A SERIES MAY RUN CONCURRENT WITH THE B SERIES FROM LATE 1936 THROUGH 1937, THOUGH IT INCLUDES MANY MORE INSTRUMENTS, AND CONTINUES WELL INTO 1938

(DO NOT CONFUSE THESE WITH THE A-PREFIXED BAKELITE-NECK TRIOLIANS OF THE 1930 PERIOD.)

	A 2	#3 RD TRICONE	
	A 3	#1 RD TRICONE	
	A 11	#1 RD TRICONE	
	A 26	#1 RD TRICONE	
1936	A 364	#0	14 FRET SOLID HEAD
	A 810	TRIOLIAN 14 FR, WD GRAIN, SOLID	
	A 914	DUOLIAN 14 FRET SOLID HEAD	
1937	A1034	TRIOLIAN TENOR	
	A1402	DUOLIAN " " " " GREY	
	A1678	#0 SQ	14 FRET SOLID
	A1817	DUOLIAN " " " "	
	A1878	#0 RD	14 FRET SOLID
	A1956	DUOLIAN " " " "	
	A1966	#O RD	14 FRET SOLID
	A2103	#1 SQ WIGGLE BORDER	
	A2224 ?	DUOLIAN " " " "	
	A2227	DUOLIAN " " "	
	A2814	#O RD	14 FRET SOLID
	A2843	DUOLIAN	
	A2950 2 PAT	TRICONE SQ, EXPLODNG PALMS ETCHED	
	A2952	TRICONE SQ, EXPLODING PALMS	
	A2970	UKULELE TRIOLIAN SUNBURST SM BODY	
	A2980	#1 MANDOLIN	
	A2994	#0 RD	14 FRET, SOLID
	A3118	#0 RD	14 FRET, SOLID
	A3181	ELECTRIC LAP STEEL CAST ALUMINUM	
	A3599 2 PAT	#3 SQ FLOW-THRU ENGRAVING	
	A3600	#3 SQ FLOW THRU ENGRAVING	
	A3629	#1 SQ WIGGLE BORDER SOLID HEAD	
	A3686	#1 RD WIGGLE BORDER	
	A3696	TRIOLIAN WD-GRAIN	
	A3709	EXPLODING PALMS TRICONE SQ	
	A3717 2 PAT	EXPLODING PALMS TRICONE ROUNDNECK!	
	A3720 2 PAT	EXPLODING PALMS TRICONE ROUNDNECK!	
	A3773	CAST ELECTRIC LAP STEEL	
	A3804 2 PAT	TRIOLIAN MANDOLIN WD GRAIN	
	A4079	ROSITA	
	A4081 "	DUOLIAN	SOLID HEAD

A4096	"	DUOLIAN SQ	SOLID HEAD
A4498	"	#35 SQ	
A4699	"	TRIOLIAN UKULELE SM BODY WD GRAIN	
A4719	"	#0 SQ 14 FRET, VAR.7	SOLIDHEAD
A4744	"	DUOLIAN	" "
A4751	"	DUOLIAN	" "
A4756	"	DUOLIAN	
A4798	"	DUOLIAN	
A4837	"	DUOLIAN	" "
A4977	"	TRIOLIAN UKULELE SM BODY WD GRAIN	
A5272	"	DUOLIAN SQ	
A5300	"	DUOLIAN SQ	
A5388	"	UKULELE TRIOLIAN, SMALL, WOODGRAIN	
A5426	"	#97 SQ	DECO
A5485 FS	"	#0 RD VARIATION 7	
A5488	"	#0 RD VARIATION 7 SOLID HEAD	
A5572	"	#0 RD VARIATION 7 SOLID HEAD	
A5730	"	#0 RD VARIATION 7 SOLID HEAD	
A5740	2PAT-MDUSA	#35 SQ	SOLID DECO
A5743	2PAT-MDUSA	#97 MANDOLIN	RAISED CENTER
A5959		#97 TENOR, NECK HAS G-20 NUMBER	
A6009		#0 RD VARIATION 7	
A6165	2 PAT	#97 MANDOLIN (REPLATED) "	"
A6207		#0 RD	

1938	A6228	2PAT-MDUSA	#0 SQ VARIATION 7	SOLID HEAD
	A6273	2PAT-MDUSA	#3 MANDOLIN	RAISED CENTER
	A6346		TROJAN	
	A6445	2PAT MDUSA	#35 RD SLOT HEAD	DECO
	A6448		#97 RD SLOT HEAD	DECO
	A8540	?	#97 SQ SOLID	DECO

THE B-SERIES SEEMS TO BE PERHAPS ONE YEAR EARLIER THAN THE A-SERIES, BUT MAY ALSO BE CONCURRENT:

1936	B 89		UKULELE TRIOLIAN, SUNBURST, SMALL
	B 168		UKULELE STYLE O SMALL
	B 272	2 PAT	#97 RD B/W DECO SLOT HEAD
	B 253		DUOLIAN SQ
	B 703		DUOLIAN SQ
	B 715		DUOLIAN
	B 734		EARLY NEW YORKER ELECTRIC SPANISH
	B 754		NEW YORKER ELECTRIC LAP STEEL
	B 834		#0 RD (14 FRET) SOLID HEAD
	B 899		#0 SQ (14 FRET)
	B1000		TROJAN, LATE MODEL, DECO SOLID, PKGD
	B1099 FS		#0 TENOR
	B1387		MANDOLIN, TRIOLIAN
	B1418		MANDOLIN, TRIOLIAN, PICKGRD
	B1458		NEW YORKER ELECTRIC SPANISH
	B1470		#0 RD VARIATION 7 SOLID HEAD
	B1471		#0 RD VARIATION 7 SOLID HEAD
1937	B1844	?	#0 RD VARIATION 7 SOLID HEAD
	B1855		NEW YORKER ELECTRIC SPANISH
	B1895		#97 SQ
	B1901	?	#97 SQ B/W DECO SOLID HEAD
	B1970		TROJAN
	B1979 FS		MANDOLIN, SILVO ELECTRIC
	B2209	?	DUOLIAN, 14 SQ, SOLID HEAD, BROWN
	B2268		TRIOLIAN, WD-GRAIN, 14 FR, SOLID

B2274	TRIOLIAN, WD-GRAIN
B2378	DUOLIAN
B2672	TRIOLIAN, AS ABOVE
B3072	TRIOLIAN PLECTRUM
B3235	#0 14 FRET RD
B3522	#0 14 FRET SQ, BLACK SOLID HEAD
B3539	SILVO ELECT. LAP STEEL ON TENOR

THE C- SERIES BELOW SHOULD NOT BE CONFUSED WITH THE THE C-SERIES DUOLIANS---THAT SERIES BEGINS IN 1930 AND THE INSTRUMENTS BELOW ARE MID-TO-LATE 30s.

1937	C 130	SILVO TENOR BODY ELECTRIC LAP STL
	C 229	DUOLIAN 14 FRET SQ WOOD GRAIN FIN
	C 874	MANDOLIN TRIOLIAN, WOOD GRAIN FIN
	C1468	SILVO TENOR BODY ELECTRIC LAP STL
1938	C1556	#97 SQ TRICONE GUITAR
	C1590	TROJAN
	C1642	DUOLIAN 14 FRET
	C1784	NEW YORKER 7-STRING ELECTRIC LAP
	C2025	SILVO TENOR BODY ELECTRIC LAP STL
	C2479	TRIOLIAN, WD-GRAIN, 14 FR, SOLID
	C2603	ESTRALITA
	C2676	#0 14 FR, B/W/ DECO HEADSTOCK
	C2689	#0 TENOR
	C3312	#0 12 FR, MAY BE REPLACED NECK #
	C3326	NEW YORKER ELEC. MANDOLIN
	C3390	SUPRO COLLEGIAN GTR
	C3839	NEW YORKER ELECTRIC SPANISH GTR
	C4187	SUPRO ELECTRIC SPANISH GTR.
	C4404	#97 SQ TRICONE GTR
	C4487	#97 SQ TRICONE GTR
	C4497	#97 SQ TRICONE GTR GREEN SCHEME
	C4593	SUPRO COLLEGIAN MANDOLIN
	C4620	#97 RD TRICONE GTR
1939	C4817	#97 RD TRICONE GTR
	C5542	NEW YORKER ELECTRIC MANDOLIN
	C5564	NEW YORKER ELECTRIC SPANISH
	C5614	NEW YORKER ELECTRIC LAP STEEL
	C5730	HAVANA FLAT-TOP SINGLE CONE

THE L-SERIES INSTRUMENTS DATE FROM 1938-1939: PERHAPS A CONTINUATION OF A-SERIES NUMBERS. POSSIBLY A CONTINUATION OF A DOBRO NUMBER SERIES (A DOBRO UKE # L9208 HAS BEEN SEEN).

6/38	L9803	2 PAT	#0 RD VARIATION 7
	L9838	?	#1 SQ WIGGLE BORDER
	L9848	?	#0 RD VARIATION 7 SOLID HEAD
	L9853		#1 SQ WIGGLE BORDER
	L9854		DUOLIAN FROST FINISH
	L9871		DUOLIAN
	L9908		FACTORY REPLACED NECK OF 1928 STYLE 1 UKE #200
	L9945		FACTORY REPL.NECK OF #3 PLECTRUM GTR #198
	L9975		FACTORY REPL.NECK OF STYLE 1 TENOR GTR #777
	L9957		#2 SQ
	L10004	2 PAT MDUSA	#2 RD
1939	L10074		TROJAN (WOOD)
	L10111	?	#1 MANDOLIN RAISED CENTER
	10184		TRIOLIAN TENOR, WD GRAIN

THE G-SERIES INSTRUMENTS DATE FROM 1940-1941:

G-122	DUOLIAN
G-137	DUOLIAN
G-182	DUOLIAN
212-G	#0 MANDOLIN LATE STYLE
219-G	COLLEGIAN GTR
338-G	NEW YORKER ELECTRIC SPANISH
390-G	FIDDLE-EDGE DOBRO PAINTED MODEL
821-G	#0 MANDOLIN LATE STYLE
822-G	#0 MANDOLIN LATE STYLE
1164-G	COLLEGIAN GTR.
1406-G	#0 RD VARIATION 8
1684-G	DUOLIAN?
1753-G	#0 SQ " " " "
1836-G	M-3 TRICONE (YELLOW WOOD/GR PAINT
1843-G	COLLEGIAN GTR.
2296-G	#35 SQ TRICONE BUT NO COLORS
2301-G	#35 SQ TRICONE BUT NO COLORS
2303-G	#35 SQ TRICONE BUT NO COLORS
2304-G	#35 SQ TRICONE BUT NO COLORS
2308-G	#35 SQ TRICONE BUT NO COLORS
2719-G	M-3 TRICONE
2841-G	M-3 TRICONE
2917-G	M-3 TRICONE
2943-G	M-3 TRICONE
3096-G	ELECTRIC ARCHTOP
3122-G	NEW YORKER LAP STEEL
4084-G	DUOLIAN
4119-G	ARAGON
4198-G	NEW YORKER LAP STEEL
4242-G	DYNAMIC LAP STEEL
4327-G	ARAGON
4449-G	#0 RD VARIATION 8

WOOD BODY NATIONALS:

EL TROVADOR:

8/33	K338	12 FRET
	K387	" "
	K538	" "
	K555	" "

TROJAN: ALL TROJANS ARE 14 FRET

	A786	PART OF A-SERIES
1934-35	D322	
	D348	
1934	T204	ALL 14 FRET
	T236	
	T358	
	T449	
	T629	
	T641	
	T679	
	T682	
	T713	
	T769	
	T788	
	T1108	
	T1259	
	T1546	
	T1906	
	T1915	
	T2011	
	T2025	
	T2030	
	T2116	
	T2248	
	T2481	
	T2623	
	T2628	
	T2972	
	T2978	SUNBURST
1937	T3179	
	1329	14 FRET SQ
	1589	
1934	Z 107	14 FRET
	Z 641	14 FRET DARK SUNBURST
	Z 875	14 FRET
	Z1005	14 FRET
	Z2037	14 FRET
1936	Z2222	14 FRET
	Z2287	14 FRET
1937-38	A6346	PART OF REGULAR GENERAL A-SERIES
1938	C1590	PART OF REGULAR GENERAL C-SERIES
	C1687	
	C3138	
	C3343	
	4243	

ROSITA:

1361	
1575	
3203	SQ
4274	
4703	
6586	FS

ESTRALITA: (ALL 14 FRET?)

N 017	14 FRET	N-SERIES MAINLY ENCOMPASSES
041		CAST ALUMINUM ELECTRIC LAPS
880 N		
C2603	PART OF CHICAGO C SERIES	
H151		

ARAGON:

G4119
G4327

SEVERAL MORE ARAGONS ARE KNOWN, NUMBERS UNREPORTED.

THANKS TO THE FOLLOWING PEOPLE WHO CONTRIBUTED SERIAL NUMBERS TO THIS LISTING:

MARK MAKIN, GARY ATKINSON, DR. JOHN DOPYERA, JR., WALTER CARTER & DENNIS WATKINS OF GRUHN GUITARS, STAN JAY AND LARRY WEXER OF MANDOLIN BROS.,DON YOUNG AND MACGREGOR GAINES OF NATIONAL RESPOHONIC, DAVE CROCKER, LARRY BRIGGS, JOE MACNAMARA, GAYLE WARDLOW, JAY LEVINE, PAUL WARNIK, BUZZ LEVINE, JOHN BERNUNZIO, NORMAN HARRIS, MICHAEL MESSER, STEVE SENERCHIA, DR. DON COUNTS, MARK MOORE, DIRK P. VOGEL, BEVERLY KING, MATT UMANOV, GRYPHON MUSIC, DAVE HULL, FRED WALLECHY, HOGEYE MUSIC, STAN WERBIN, MI$ER MUSIC, DICK BLATTENBERGER, JAMES MACDONALD, STAN WEST, JIMMY BROWN,ROBERT SALOMONE, BOB DASCOULIAS, JACK SUDERMAN, DAVID SHEPPARD, ELBERT L. WALKER, BILL GREGORY, RICHARD L. JACKS, J.C. GRIMSHAW, RUSS NEWELL, CURTIS CRAWFORD, TERRY FRANK, TERRY LEMONDS, TERRY ZWIGOFF, RONNIE CONDON, ARMAND BERTACCHI, ANTHONY HUVARD, RICHARD SMITH, DOCSTEIN, MIKE ESPOSITO, JIM WITT, RON SIMPSON, DOUG SMITH, PEGGY OSWALT, FLIP VAN DOMBERG SCIPIO, DAVID BALL, DAVID & SCOTT MACDOUGAL, SCOTT AINSLIE, ACOUSTIC GUITAR MAGAZINE, VINTAGE GUITAR, 20TH CENTURY GUITAR, DICK LEE, ROBERT TIPTON, ALEX BURNS, BOB EVONIUK, HAL SMITH, JOHN MANLEY, CATFISH KEITH KOZACIK, JOHN LOKKE, BOB TEKIPPE, FUNAO KAZUNORI, JOHN HURLSTON, W.L. BARON CORDELL, ALEX VARTY, BRENDALAWRENCE, SCOTT KERN, ROYAL V.PROUDFIT, RICK LUDWICK, RON LIRA, CULLEN VECKER, BART WITTROCK, BART POTTER, DOUG SUTHER, TIM RYAN, MIKE TEEPE, LARRY SIGLER, LYNN DIEBOLD, BERNARD AYLING, SAM PALMER, ROD PHILLIPS, SONNY BOY LONDON, NEIL SMIMABUKURO, JIM ZADWODNI, LOU REIMULLER, PAUL CARNES, TONY MARCUS, GENE HOLTZMAN, GEOFF GRAY, BLAINE HAMPTON, GULFCOAST GUITARS, CYRIL LEFEBVRE, MIKE COOPER, MICHAEL DREGNI, CRAIG CAMERON, RON KUSHNER, JOE KARAM, GORDON DOW, ROBERT L. ROBINSON, D.K. HERNEY, STEVE CRISAFULLI, JIM MUMM, JEFF SKINKLE, CRAIG CAMERON, JIM PASCH, STEVE SPENCER, CADILLAC BOB, JOHN BATTAGLIA, JAY MOELLER, ARTHUR AUGSPERGER, LIBBY WATSON, JOHN SOWA, BIG MONT, TERRY MITCHELL, AL BRITTEN, TERRY GARLAND, C. VAN VUUREN,JOHN REUTER, DENNIS LUCERA, STEVE SPENCER, JOHN HAWKINS, AND MANY OTHERS.

PLEASE CONTINUE SENDING IN SERIAL NUMBERS FOR
FUTURE EDITIONS AND TO CLARIFY ANY REMAINING
LITTLE MYSTERIES.
SEND ALL DETAILS TO THE AUTHOR IN CARE OF THE PUBLISHER.

-APPENDIX B-

THE NATIONAL COMPANY
A CHRONOLOGY

10-12-26
First tricone patent applied for by J. Dopyera which is for the first attempt at a resonator guitar which he made for Beauchamp. (see Chapter 2 for illustration.)

10-18-26
Sol Hoopii (Hawaiian guitarist) makes first recording using National tricone, Farewell Blues/ Stack O'Lee Blues, Columbia 797-D. He almost singlehandedly popularizes the National tricone overnight.

4-9-27
Refined tricone patent applied for. This is very close to the production version--see Chapter 2.

c. 4-27
Tricone dies made at Rickenbacker's shop.

8-7-27
National guitars announced in Musical Merchandise Magazine.

10-27
Advertising in Musical Merchandise for tricone guitar.

11-27
More advertising in Musical Merchandise, continuing monthly for several months.

1-26-28
National String Instrument Corporation certified by the State of California. Dopyeras sell name to Corp. for stock.

1928
E.A. Sutphin Co./Philadelphia prints earliest known catalog of Nationals showing very early production models, tricones only. Includes the mysterious tricone mandolin/ukulele, perhaps only a prototype.

2-21-28
Rudy Dopyera applies for patent on banjo with 3-piece body.

2-28-28
Organization meeting held, officers elected: Kleinmeyer, president; Dopyera, vice-president; Beauchamp, secretary; Barth, treasurer. Articles of incorporation and by-laws signed.

2-29-28
First National Corp. board of directors meeting. Present are: Beauchamp (sec.), Kleinmeyer, J. Dopyera, and Paul Barth. They offered to sell their previous business of instrument manufacture for $30,000, to execute a license agreement for the product patents for $170,000, and Dopyera offered on behalf of himself and his brothers to sell their trademark, National, to the Corp. for $12,500. It was also proposed to raise an additional $40,000 by selling stock. All of the above was agreed upon, payable in National stock.

3-28
Tricone tenors announced in Musical Mdse. Mag.

3-12-28
Design patent for tricone applied for by J. Dopyera

3-18-28
Resonator harp patent applied for by J. Dopyera

6-20-28
National receives permit to issue stock. National buys the business from the four with 2,799 shares of stock, rather than $30,000 cash.

6-20-28
National enters licensing agreement, giving 6,599 shares to the license holders, and agreement stipulates that 100 instruments a month must be made.

6-21-28
A. Rickenbacher buys National stock.

7-16-28
Board meeting held, Beauchamp voted General Manager, Dopyera voted Factory Superintendent, Barth voted assistant Factory superintendent, at weekly salaries of $55, $50, and $48, respectively.

7-30-28
Beauchamp files National fingerpick patent app.

9-28-28
CMI orders first (wood) Triolians.

1-17-29
Special meeting held to discuss the fact that John Dopyera "left his position and refused to return." Remaining board members give Beauchamp a vote of confidence. NO REASONS GIVEN IN MINUTES.

2-19-29
John Dopyera officially resigns from National. He assigns his stock interest to Kleinmeyer.

3-3-29
Board meeting, Dopyera's board-vacancy filled by Charles Farr, Barth made vice-president, Beauchamp made secretary.

3-11-29
Beauchamp files patent for SINGLE CONE RESONATOR GUITAR. Patent drawings show what became the production model.

3-14-29
Beauchamp asks National to turn over $4,200. in royalties owed him to Kleinmeyer. Perhaps to re-pay a cash advance or loan. The figure suggests the following: His 1/4 share of the 10% royalty suggests approx. 1,600 instruments manufactured to date.

6-29-29
Dobro patent applied for

12-20-29
Board meeting: Beauchamp's salary raised by $10/wk. Six-month advertising budget set at $500.

12-31-29
Dopyera's 4-9-27 application for patent on refined tricone is granted PATENT # 1,741,453. As discussed in the Schierson lawsuit--this patent ALSO INCLUDES MENTION OF SINGLE-CONE IDEA FOR MANDOLIN AND UKULELE ALREADY BEING MADE AND SOLD BEFORE BEAUCHAMP'S SINGLE-CONE PATENT

1930
National's "blue" catalog is published, showing all tricones, tenor/plectrums, single-cone mandolin, and single-cone ukulele. Triolians are shown as wood-construction and also in metal.

1-3-30
Board meeting: First mention of Dobro and Dopyera Bros. threatened $25,000. damage suit (for Beauchamp's rumors about Dobro being an infringment?). Dopyera Bros. barred from viewing National's books. Kleinmeyer's ex-wife appoints Kleinmeyer to be proxy for her half of his shares.

1-12-30
Beauchamp files patent for a second type of single cone. This looks like an attempt to cross a single-cone with a tricone and was not produced at all.

1-13-30
Stockholders meeting: Major share-holders at this time:

Kleinmeyer:	common--1864	preferred--33
Barth:	" --1225	" --66
Beauchamp:	" --1211	" --66
Jack Levy/CMI	" -- 130	" --260

2-12-30
Meeting to discuss reducing costs, due to Depression

3-18-30
Patent # 1,750,881 granted to J. Dopyera

5-30
Tonk Bros. (wholesalers) take the National line

5-30
Plain Style O guitars (single cone--without sandblasted scenes) announced at $85.

6-9-30
National becomes member of NAMM

6-10-30
Patent # 1,762,617 granted to J. Dopyera, for his first tricone patent application, filed 10-12-26

7-3-30
Board meeting: dealer complaints and problems of Bakelite necks discussed. First mention of new Style O guitar, price set at $62.50. Harry Watson resigns as Factory Superintendent. Further cost-cutting measures discussed due to the deepening Depression.

8-8-30
Board meeting: representatives of Central and South America request exclusive sales agreement with National. Beauchamp presents sample of all-aluminum guitar, commended but not approved for manufacture.

8-18-30
Dobro incorporated

9-30
Announcement in Musical Mdse. of changes in Style O: price dropped to $62.50, sandblasted Hawaiian scenes added to body.

11-30
National ad in Musical Mdse. reads: "Over $55,000 shipments in September!"

1-1-31
Announcement in newspaper of Dobro infingement case (Shown in Chapter 2).

1-5-31
Board meeting: National gives a $200. retainer to lawyer for protection againt Dobro suit. Discussion of a new $27. guitar (the Duolian), and sample made to send to sales rep Jack Levy.

1-12-31
Stockholders meeting: Majority stockholders are: Kleinmeyer--1917 shares, Barth--1279 1/2 shares, Beauchamp--1279 shares. Board of directors unchanged.

1-29-31
C.L. Farr, attorney stated that both counts of Dobro's lawsuit had been thrown out of court, but that Dobro was given the right to amend and re-instate the first count.

3-19-31
Board meeting: sample instruments are furnished to Mr. Michael Gluschkin, to determine his worth as an exclusive sales rep to South America. The retail price of the "new cheap guitar" is set at $32.50, with an even cheaper Sears model at $29.00.

3-30-31
DEPOSITION about Beauchamp: unknown writer (presumably a dealer) and associate Mr. Mutchler visit National factory. Beauchamp tells them that Dobro is a direct infringment on National AND that National "won a lawsuit" with Dobro. Writer also hears from other dealers that National has told them this.

4-1-31
DEPOSITION CONTINUES: Writer again visits National, says that he "very quickly found out that Beauchamp was inclined to change his stories very often, in other words, make statements he could not back up." Beauchamp brings in a Dobro, points out the spider & bridge and states especially that this was the PARTICULAR part which Dobro was infringing on. He also claims that he himself had perfected and completed it six months to a year BEFORE the Dopyera brothers left National--"blew up and walked out." Beauchamp offers a letter of assurance attesting to the "truth" of the above "facts."

4-3-31
DEPOSITION CONTINUES: Writer calls at National for the letter. Beauchamp claims he is the "originator of the National, had perfected all the patents, and financed the company." Beauchamp goes to his safe, gets out patent papers, ALL OF WHICH SHOW JOHN DOPYERA'S NAME AS INVENTOR, and the agreement of the sale of all the patents to the National Corp. All of this certainly contradicted Beauchamp's statements. "After seeing who the real inventor was," the writer asks for the letter previously mentioned. He dictates letter to stenographer, Beauchamp objects to statement in letter that Dobro was direct infringement. Writer is perplexed since it was Beauchamp who first made that very claim, saying that "Dobro would give $10,000 for a letter of this nature." Next day Beauchamp says it will take two weeks to get the letter, so writer attempts to write letter then and there. Beauchamp and Levy will not commit themselves to their claims, and the matter is dropped.

4-6-31
DEPOSITION CONTINUES: Writer phones Jack Levy, who admits that he thinks the litigation concerns the SINGLE CONE PATENT that National "bought" from Dopyera. He "was very much surprised that the litigation pertained the the SPIDER construction, and not the single-cone."

4-7-31
DEPOSITION CONTINUES: Writer and E.H. Kelly go to Paul Barth's home, find out from Barth that "the spider bridge was NEVER MADE OR WORKED ON AT NATIONAL". Draws single-cone diagram, acts surprised that the litigation is about the spider-bridge, and again states that the spider was never planned, worked on, or made while the Dopyeras were at National.

> (THIS DEPOSITION IS MOST ENLIGHTENING REGARDING BEAUCHAMP'S
> PERSONAL AND BUSINESS STYLE. I FEEL SOME REFERENCE SHOULD
> BE MADE TO THIS, IF ONLY TO VINDICATE JOHN DOPYERA.)

4-23-31
Board meeting: Because of Dobro's $225,000 damage suit, National officially resolves to refuse to allow Louis Dopyera to review National's books.

6-1931
Dobro/National in court

6-9-31
Beauchamp's 3-11-29 patent application for his first single-cone design is granted PATENT# 1,808,756.

6-9-31
Beauchamp's 1-21-30 patent application for his second single-cone design (never produced) is granted PATENT #1,808,757

6-15-31
Board meeting: License agreement made in connection with the SINGLE CONE (pat# 1,808,756-7) between patent holders Beauchamp, Kleinmeyer, & Barth, and the National Corp., for 10% of sales price.

8-14-31
Board meeting: Discussion of new wooden model using new single-cone concept.

9-17-31
Board meeting: First mention of possible move back East. Barth sent there to explore conditions. Further discussion on wood guitars. Beauchamp presents a sample "slide saxophone" for possible manufacture--not approved by board.

10-6-31

Board meeting: Beauchamp states that other offers had been made for the single-cone patent, and because of its apparent value, offered an exclusive license to National for $3000 cash AND the same 10% royalty, on behalf of himself and the other patent holders Barth, and Kleinmeyer.

10-13-31

Board meeting: Tentative new license agreement read and discussed, but no action taken.

10-14-31

Paul Barth resigns from the board of Directors.

10-15-31

Board meeting: Barth's resignation accepted--no reasons given for resignation. Glenn Harger elected to the board.

10-15-31

Ro-Pat-In papers filed to become a California corporation. (eventually becomes Rickenbacker)

10-20-31

Board meeting: problems of Depression getting worse, salaries discussed. License agreement changed to $2,400 cash, and accepted.

11-10-31

Board meeting: Discussion of other makers making wood bodies for National to install cones. Discussion of Schierson Bros. instruments as patent infringements. Much discussion of cost-cutting. Beauchamp and Barth fired from National management, but inexplicably remain in attendance at directors meetings.

11-18-31

Board meeting: Sample wood single-cone guitars made by Harmony are examined. Factory lease reduced from $150 to $125 per month. Discussion of Dobro vs Beauchamp suit.

1-1932

Technical drawing of Beauchamp electro.

1-4-32

Board meeting: Jack Levy's sales contract renewed for 2 years. Beauchamp is given a style O guitar engraved like a #3 and chromium plated. The headstock is pearloid as is the entire fingerboard. The body is double-engraved, with half the lines cutting through the plating, for a gold and silver effect. The headstock has special engraving commemorating the granting of Beauchamp's single-cone patent, given as June 1, MCMXXXI. Though the date on the granted patent papers is given as June 9, perhaps the Company received the notice about it on June 1. This gift seems a bit strange in light of the fact that he was fired. However, Beauchamp did make undeniable and valuable contributions to the National, as he was well-liked by most of his associates.

1-11-32

Annual Stockholders Meeting: Major shareholders are now: Kleinmeyer--1917, Barth--1278, Beauchamp--1273, Louis Dopyera--1218 Dopyera had been quietly accumulating shares. Louis Dopyera signs minutes of this meeting as President of National board of Directors. Beauchamp assigns all of his rights to his wife (ex-wife?)

It is not fully understood how Dopyera went from not being let into the books to owning this first large chunk of stock. This remains a mystery.

1-11-32

Later that night, Kleinmeyer is re-elected President, Beauchamp is elected Vice-president. Also very strange considering past events.

2-8-32

National sends letter to Schierson Bros., attempting to collect royalties on patents. Also sends letters asking patent holders to act in protecting National. WAGES ARE CUT AGAIN for factory employees.

2-9-32

Jack Levy is prepared to order 500 wooden Nationals, and jobbers are enthusiastic.

2-10-32

The new wooden National is to be made by Kaykraft, at a cost of $7 each, National provides metal parts, guitar to sell at $50. National pressures Levy to order metal guitars as well.

3-7-32
Patent holders were again admonished to do something about the infringment problems. Tentative contract be-tween National and Kaykraft is read--no action taken. Guitars to be called El Trovador.

3-22-32
Plans and specifications for wood Nationals are blueprinted, to become part of contract with Kay. New cheaper shipping boxes are discussed, and authorization to order them is given. Budget is also provided for new string packages and boxes.

3-31-32
C.L. Farr resigns as a member of the board of Directors of National.

4-32
Open letter to Musical Mdse written by Ed Dopyera on behalf of Dobro, to supress rumors started by National concerning patent infringements.

4-11-32
Paul Barth elected to the board to replace Farr. Contract with Kay for the El Trovador guitar is signed by the Board. Harmony makes proposition to make cheaper wood guitars for National, with proposed name "Violian." This would eventually become the Trojan model.

5-14-32
Kleinmeyer's ex-wife assigns Beauchamp to be her proxy for her 227 shares of common and 33 preferred.

6-8-32
Beauchamp files first patent app. for Frying Pan.

6-13-32
Kleinmeyer resigns from National, assigning his stock and share of patents to Louis Dopyera. Apparently Kleinmeyer drove up to Taft, Calif. to sell his shares to Dopyera. One wonders what went through the minds of these people at this time. Dopyera places Martin Barth on the board, and Dopyera is elected President. National quits NAMM.

7-11-32
Jack Levy replaces Ferguson on the board--apparently there were disagreements about the merits of CMI having a representative on National's board.

7-16-32
All salaried employees take another 20% pay cut.

8-8-32
El Trovador tenor guitar discussed, to be made by Kay. Paul Barth is made General Manager.

8-1932
Ro-Pat-In starts production.

9-12-32
Dobro writes letter to distributor regarding patents--Jack Levy admonished to respond, patent holders admonished again to protect National. Jack Levy requests permission to represent ELECTRO STRING INSTRUMENT CO. and is given permission on condition that it does not prove to be competetive. Paul Barth presents a sample Triolian walnut finish guitar--WITH A 14-FRET body. Levy instructed to get "complete information regarding public demand for this 14-fret type of guitar, especially the El Trovador" (wood).

10-13-32
Much discussion of Schierson resonator guitars,made by Globe, and Regal-made Dobros both from Chicago, as stated in a letter from Harmony. The board moved to purchase one each of these guitars to examine.

10-13-32
Barth and Beauchamp, the patent holders, are told to assist Levy in responding to distributors. Beauchamp claims to be unable to find a copy of the patents, but would investigate whether or not there was infringement. Both agree to have $25 each held back from royalties to cover legal costs. Public demand for a 14-fret guitar is discussed further, and the idea is tabled for now.

11-21-32
Beauchamp still has no news on patent. Jack Levy letters still to be written. Rent for factory now is $100.

12-19-32
Still no action from Beauchamp and Levy on patent problems. However, all employees of National to be presented with turkeys "averaging 10 pounds" for Christmas.

1-1933
Regal announces in Music Merchandise a new line of ampliphonic guitars using Dobro amplification.

1-9-33
Annual stockholders meeting: Louis Dopyera now owns 4,502 shares of stock, more than 2/3 of the National. Alton L. Beauchamp holds 1,357 shares, voted to Beauchamp, and CMI holds 600 shares, voted to Jack Levy. There are 10 other shareholders, none with more than 30 shares. Board now is: L. Dopyera, M. Barth, Beauchamp, Levy, Harger.

1-9-33
Board meeting: Factory now leased for 2 more years at a Depression-priced $85 per month. Levy still hasn't responded to letters about patent problems. Levy motions to remove National's listing in the L.A. directory. Motion seconded by Barth and carried. Strange, indeed, unless this was a subtle maneuver by Levy to position CMI for a takeover.. Wood resonator guitars discussed, patent holders take a cut to 75 cents net on each guitar sold.

Sample Harmony instruments are examined, and the Board specifies certain quality improvements. Contract planned with Harmony for Trojan (wood) guitars, not over 100 guitars--National to furnish trademark and metal parts. Levy to receive 40 cents commission on each guitar.

What was to become the Sears-Roebuck version of the Duolian is discussed, and it is decided to leave off the National name, and to make a different-looking coverplate for it. (The large 5-hole version shown in Chapter 4)

2-20-33
Harmony contract executed. Including a telegram regarding the improvements required by the Board. A nameless wood Harmony-made National to sell for $22.75 from Sears is also discussed. National retains full-time company lawyer. New brochure discussed. Barth authorizes Levy and Harger to find a deal on 75,000 brochures at less than $300.

3-20-33
Barth amends advertising budget to $450 from $300. Advertising again in Musical Merchandise is discussed. Beauchamp proposes $100 for a full-page ad in the next issue. Approved.

4-17-33
Board meeting: Barth orders two new dies for "centering and turning up the edges, which strengthens and perfects the resonator." Levy reads letter from Canadian manufacturer R. S. Williams Company requesting the use of National parts for its own guitars. Kay Company asks for similar situation in order to make guitars for Montgomery Ward.

5-6-33
Glenn Harger leaves National, unclear as to whether fired or quit. Hurried motion carried to remove his name (as secretary of National) at the bank. Jack Levy appointed temporary secretary.

5-15-33
Board meeting: discussion of "apparent shortages in the accounts of former secretary Harger." Notice sent to Harger demanding explanation of financial irregularities. Barth and Levy instructed by Dopyera to get an accountant to close the books each month. It is hard to believe it took so long to make what seems like a very basic business decision.

6-16-33
A Mr. Kirkoff and Mr. Hoter demonstrate an electric pickup for a guitar to board members. Martin Barth appointed as a delegate of National to create a better feeling between National and Dobro, and to try to make a settlement arrangement. Harger is sent a letter from the Board giving him ten days to make restitution for his shortages.

7-3-33
Rickenbacker sells his National stock to Jack Levy.

7-17-33
Barth reports failure in his mission to Dobro. Beauchamp moves, seconded by Levy, that L. Dopyera be appointed to try the same thing--with a goal of eliminating the litigation.

8-1-33

Special stockholders meeting called by Dopyera (by letter dated 7/24/33) based upon the allegations that "certain rumors and mis-statements were made to various stockholders by a certain group of men for the purpose of obtaining options to purchase their stock." Apparently the only conclusion made was the the corporation should not have paid preferred-stock dividend out of capital assets when there was no earned profit.

8-2-33

Letter to stockholders calling special meeting to remove all directors on the board of National and to replace Martin Barth, who resigned. Meeting called for the 7th.

8-7-33

Special stockholders meeting: Dopyera, M. Barth, P. Barth, Levy, Beauchamp, Hughett,and CL Farr present. Farr objects to impropriety of meeting-calling procedure and much discussion ensues over laws concerning same. Roll call of stock shares follows:

Dopyera	4,808
Beauchamp	1,020
Levy	288
small owners total	63

Proxies accepted:

Levy	600	for CMI
Beauchamp	317	for Alton Beauchamp
Levy	51	for Rickenbacker
Dopyera	30	for Jas. Kylionek
Larabee (lawyer)	20	for Geo. Beauchamp

Fights over Mrs. Kleinmeyer's 310 shares

More fighting over legality of the meeting, due to not all directors being notified. Farr states that since some of the stock is involved in court cases (presumably Ted K.'s shares to Dopyera, and Cynthia K.'s shares to Beauchamp) and there might be litigation if the stock was voted, moves to adjourn meeting. Dopyera tries again to get a motion to remove the directors, no motion made, meeting adjourned. This all occurs between 8:30 and 9:45pm.

8-7-33

Board meeting begins at 9:45pm, where stockholders meeting left off. Discussion reveals that M. Barth resigned at L. Dopyera's request. Barth no longer holds stock, probably went to Dopyera. Barth given vote of confidence for past performance. Stockholder's meeting to attempt removal and re-election of Board called for 8-23-33.

8-23-33

Stockholders meeting: After brief argument over a few small lots of shares between Levy and L. Dopyera, it is discovered that there are discrepancies between the Stock Ledger book and the stock certificate book. This makes an accurate stock-vote-count impossible and the group decides to retain a CPA to straighten it out, and bring it up to 8-18-33. Meeting adjourned until 8-30-33.

8-30-33

Meeting recessed until 8-31-33, with plenty of arguments. Stock audit ready but unread.

8-31-33

Meeting finally occurs--present are Dopyera, Beauchamp, Barth, Farr, Levy, Larrabee, 3 others. Levy immediately moves to adjourn sine die (without setting future date). Meeting adjourned. It is difficult to know what really happened in that room, because of the dry style of the minutes. There are no documents of any meetings until the 9-13-33 minutes.

9-13-33

Regular Board meeting: Dopyera, Beauchamp, Hughett, Levy present. Minutes of 7-17 read/approved. National re-joins NAMM. Dopyera reports his mission to create harmony with Dobro was favorable. Minutes of 8-7 read and approved. Minutes of 8-18 read and approved. Minutes of 8-21 read and approved. The minutes give the impression of business-as-usual with no mention of the previous stormy meeting. Mention of lawyer to defend National against Dobro in court on 9-25.

(Possible gap in the documents until 11-6-33)

11-6-33

Stockholders meeting: Major players are now:

L. Dopyera........4868.5 shares (incl. 54 proxy)
Jack Levy ....2323 (incl: 1040 Beauchamp proxy 600 CMI proxy)
P. Barth, Auble, Shumaker, Hughett......5 each

Long-awaited re-election of board is held with new board comprised of Shumaker, Auble, Levy, Dopyera, & Hughett. Board meeting follows, with Dopyera elected President, Auble vice-president, Hughett secy./treasurer. Treasury balance $11,312.

11-7-33

Meeting continues: Barth resigns as General Manager, becomes shop (factory) superindendent, with shop wages left to his discretion. Hughett appointed General Manager, at a $234 monthly salary.

11-8-33

Meeting continues: Dobro agrees to settle for $5000 cash. National board resolves to settle with Dobro, and give them $2000 and 900 newly-issued shares of stock (giving the Dopyeras a majority interest in National and setting the stage for the merger).

11-23-33

National values the settlement at $11,000, giving $9000 value to the 900 shares of stock, actually worth about $1800 at this date, obviously preferable to $5000 cash.

12-4-33

Board meeting: Lengthy discussion on settlement with Dobro--no details, though. Board decides to order 14-FRET GUITAR dies from Rickenbacker. Kay discontinues making El Trovador guitars. Employees to receive either a turkey or a $2.50 Christmas bonus.

12-8-33

Dobro drops suit against National, agrees to settlement.

12-21-33

Permit granted for issue of 900 new shares of National stock, to Dobro Corporation. Jack Levy objects, in writing, to the entire settlement agreement. He feels that the settlement is unjustified and detrimental to National and its minority stockholders. There seems to be some animosity between Jack Levy, who wanted National become a part of CMI, and Louis Dopyera, who obviously wanted to merge the two companies, giving control back to the Dopyera family. Board orders 900 shares to be delivered to Dobro Corp. Levy reads letter from Harmony describing "experimental work" on 14-fret guitars. Harmony to make El Trovadors for the present.

Discussion of renewal of Jack Levy's sales contract--Dopyera calls for a motion that Levy's services be dispensed with at 1-1-34. Levy objects on the grounds that the present board has "not been acting long enough to know just how things are handled". No motion made, carried to 1-4-34.

1-8-34

Annual shareholders meeting at National. Last mention of Beauchamp. Litigation note in the minutes where Paul Barth is in a Superior Court dispute with Louis Dopyera. Jack Levy still objects to issue of stock to settle the lawsuit with Dobro. New board consists of: Levy, Auble, L. Dopyera, Hughett, and Edith Schumaker.

2-5-34

National's attorney Penprase put in charge of lawsuit against Schierson Bros. infringement. Case was started by Larabee.

4-34

National announces 14-fret German Silver "Don" guitars--models 1, 2, & 3.

4-12-34

Rudolph Dopyera assigns his Dobro-related patents to the Dobro Corp.

4-16-34

Board meeting: suggests that National get a guarantee on prices from Rickenbacker on stampings for bodies.

5-34

Advert. in Musical Mdse. describing the Don models.

5-21-34

Board meeting: Hughett presents Rickenbacker Co.'s proposition that National pay a 10% royalty for the manufacturing rights to make the Electro guitar. The matter is set aside.

5-29-34
Shumaker resigns from the Board (accepted AUG 6, 34). Martin Barth returns to the Board to fill the vacancy.

8-6-34
Board meeting: Levy brings up subject of Rickenbacker making dies for a new instrument being made by the Dobro Corp. (the new all-metal job, of next entry, presumably) Hughett is asked to speak to Rickenbacker about this.

9-1934
Dobro announces new line of all-metal silver guitars with mahogany necks--known today as 'fiddle-edge'.

9-26-34
National's lawyers gathering evidence against Schierson.

c. 9-34
Single-cone guitars are shortened to 14-fret bodies.

12-22-34
Resignations of Board members Hughett and Auble are accepted. EMIL (Ed) E. DOPYERA added to board, also Maurice Sparling. E.E. Dopyera made sec. and Sparling made Vice-president.

> (THIS SEEMS TO MAKE THE MERGER A DE FACTO ITEM, SINCE EMIL IS ALSO ON THE BOARD OF DOBRO AT THIS TIME.)

3-1935
National and Dobro announce moving to 6920 McKinley Ave, L.A. to operate under one roof.

7-1-35
National/Dobro name-change is completed, and Dobro is dissolved.

1936
Electric instruments become a significant part of National's catalog and sales.

1-1936
National/Dobro begins move to Chicago

3-1937
National/Dobro wins case against Schierson. All Schierson dies and parts become property of National.

4-10-37
Disclaimer of Beauchamp's first single-cone (production version) patent, filed by "assignees of an interest," Louis and Emil Dopyera.

4-10-37
Disclaimer of Beauchamp's first single-cone patent, filed by "assignee of one-third interest," Paul Barth.

8-1937
Regal granted rights to produce complete Regal line and Dobro line of ampliphonic instruments.

8-10-37
Rickenbacker Frying Pan patent granted to Beauchamp.

1937-8
Triolian and Duolians now finished in woodgrain enamel, and shown with pickguards in Stafflebach and Duffy wholesale catalog.

1939
Aragon and Havana wood body resonator guitars listed, bodies mfg. by Kay. Style O guitars changed to have large ungainly headstocks. Electric instruments represent the majority of production.

1940-41
Resonator line reduced to Styles 1, 3, 97, O, and Aragon. Budget priced "M-3 Hawaii" tricone is catalogued, with cheap square neck and painted finish.

1941-42
All production of metal body instruments ceases. National re-organized into Valco by Al Frost and Victor Smith.

> THESE HAWAIIAN RE-ISSUE ALBUMS FEATURE ALL OF THE MAJOR ARTISTS
> IN CHAPTER 6 PLUS MORE MUSICIANS USING NATIONAL INSTRUMENTS THE
> WAY THEY WERE MEANT TO BE USED. THESE RECORDS, TAPES, AND CD'S
> MAY BE FOUND AT STORES WHICH SELL ETHNIC/BLUES/FOLK MUSIC.

VINTAGE HAWAIIAN: Steel Guitar Masters '28-'34 Rounder 1052

VINTAGE HAWAIIAN: The Great Singers 1928-34 Rounder 1053
(Includes 1929 Tau Moe recordings)

SOL HOOPII   Vol. 1 1926-1929   Rounder 1024

SOL HOOPII   Vol. 2 1927-1934   Rounder 1025

HAWAIIAN STEEL GUITAR Vol. 1   Folklyric 9009

HAWAIIAN STEEL GUITAR Vol. 2   Folklyric 9027

KALAMA'S QUARTET (2 STEELS)   Folklyric 9022

KING BENNIE NAWAHI Hot Hawaiian Guitar   Yazoo 1074

HAWAIIAN GUITAR HOTSHOTS   Yazoo 1055

THE AUTHOR HAS RECORDED SEVERAL ALBUMS OF BLUES, JAZZ, HAWAIIAN AND CALYPSO MUSIC FEATURING NATIONALS PRIMARILY:

BOB BROZMAN ALBUMS (1981-1991):

1981: BLUE HULA STOMP   Kicking Mule 173

1983: SNAPPING THE STRINGS   Kicking Mule 322

1985: HELLO, CENTRAL, GIVE ME DR. JAZZ   Rounder 3086

1988: DEVIL'S SLIDE (Hawaiian/calypso)   Rounder 3112

1989: TAU MOE FAMILY W/ BOB   Rounder 6028

1991: A TRUCKLOAD OF BLUES   Sky Ranch/Rounder

CONTACT ADDRESSES:
TO OBTAIN PARTS, OR RESTORATIONS OF OLD NATIONALS:
WRITE TO:
NATIONAL RESO-PHONIC GUITARS
871 VIA ESTEBAN, UNIT C
SAN LUIS OBISPO, CA 94301

TO CONTACT THE AUTHOR REGARDING FURTHER INFORMATION
ON VINTAGE NATIONAL INSTRUMENTS, PLEASE WRITE TO THE PUBLISHER:
BOB BROZMAN c/o
CENTERSTREAM PUBLICATIONS
P.O. BOX 5450
FULLERTON, CA 92635

PLEASE SEND ALL SERIAL NUMBERS
(FOR THE NEXT EDITION) TO THE SAME ADDRESS.

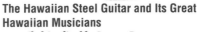

Guitar

The Gibson L5
ITS HISTORY AND ITS PLAYERS
by Adrian Ingram
foreword by Bob Benedetto

Introduced in 1922, the Gibson L5 is the precursor of the modern archtop guitar. It was the first archtop to feature f-holes, which allowed it to project through the horn-dominated bands of the day. Its strong, full, warm sound was an immediate and overwhelming success that turned the heads of makers, players and listeners alike. This book takes a look at its history and most famous players, from its creation, through the Norlin years, to its standing today as the world's most popular jazz guitar. With its stunning 16-page full-color photo section, this book is a must for every guitar enthusiast's collection!
00000216 112 pages $29.95

Gretsch – The Guitars of the Fred Gretsch Co.
by Jay Scott

This comprehensive manual uncovers the history of Gretsch guitars through 32 pages of color photos, hundreds of black & white photos, and forewords by Fred Gretsch, George Harrison, Randy Bachman, Brian Setzer, and Duane Eddy. It covers each model in depth, including patent numbers and drawings for collectors. 286 pages.
00000142 Softcover.......................................$35.00

Guitar Legends
THE EVOLUTION OF THE GUITAR FROM FENDER TO G&L
by George Fullerton

The work of Leo Fender revolutionized the guitar and has influenced nearly every modern guitarist. This book by Leo's best friend and partner in G&L examines the life of the man behind these instruments. It features photos (including 16 pages of color!) never before published.
00000156 112 pages $24.95

The Hawaiian Steel Guitar and Its Great Hawaiian Musicians
compiled & edited by Lorene Ruymar

This fascinating book takes a look at Hawaiian music; the origin of the steel guitar and its spread throughout the world; Hawaiian playing styles, techniques and tunings; and more. Includes hundreds of photos, a foreword by Jerry Byrd, and a bibliography and suggested reading list.
00000192 208 pages $29.95

The History & Artistry of National Resonator Instruments
by Bob Brozman

This book is a history book, source book and owner's manual for players and fans which covers the facts and figures necessary for serious collectors. In addition to many black and white historical photos, there is also a 32-page color section, and appendixes with serial numbers for all instruments, a company chronology, and a Hawaiian Artist Discography.
00000154 296 pages $35.00

Making an Archtop Guitar
by Robert Benedetto

The definitive work on the design and construction of an acoustic archtop guitar by one of the most talented luthiers of the twentieth century. Benedetto shows all aspects of construction through to marketing your finished work. Includes a list of suppliers; a list of serial numbers for Benedetto guitars; full-color plates; photos from the author's personal scrapbook; and fold-out templates.
00000174 260 pages $39.95

The Ultimate Musician's Reference Handbook
THE MOST COMPLETE GUIDE TO WHO'S WHO IN POPULAR MUSIC
by Brent E. Kick

This complete handbook will enlighten readers with many details about their favorite artists. Includes historical listings for over 3,500 musicians; a breakdown of over 500 bands, including personnel changes; a chronological listing of all in-print albums; listings of unusual or little-known session work with other performers; notations for Grammy Awards and movie appearances; and much more. All information is cross-indexed to make the book easy to use. 8-1/2" x 11"
00000190 256 pages $24.95

Banjo

Ring the Banjar!
THE BANJO IN AMERICA FROM FOLKLORE TO FACTORY
by Robert Lloyd Webb

This is a second edition of a publication originally published to coincide with an exhibition of the same name at the Massachusetts Institute of Technology Museum. Includes information on the banjo's enduring popularity, the banjo makers of Boston, instruments from the exhibition, a glossary and bibliography of the banjo, and more. 6" x 12"
00000087 102 pages $24.95

The Larsons' Creations - Guitars and Mandolins
by Robert Hartman

Swedish immigrants Carl and August Larson made instruments under the brand names of Maurer, Prairie State, Euphonon, W.J. Dyer & Bros. and Wm. C. Stahl, and their highly-collectible creations are considered today to be some of the finest ever made. Lovingly researched and written by Robert Hartman, grandson of Carl Larson, *The Larsons' Creations* contains many beautiful color photos of the artful instruments, classic advertisements, and catalog reprints and a CD featuring guitarist Muriel Anderson playing 11 songs on 11 Larson instruments.   00000180   (208pages,9"x12")................$39.95

Rickenbacker
by Richard Smith

A complete and illustrated history of the development of Rickenbacker instruments from 1931 to the present, complete with information and full-color photos of the many Rickenbacker artists.
00000098 256 pages $29.95

Sunburst Alley
A PICTORIAL GALLERY OF THE
LES PAUL SUNBURST 1958-1960
by Vic DaPra

These guitars have been responsible for some of the best rock & roll ever recorded, and this book pays them tribute. "Pharaoh of the Flame" Vic DaPra, a collector for over 25 years, has put together 80 full-color pages showing over 200 of the world's finest Gibson Les Paul Sunburst guitars. Features beautiful photography and captions on each of the instruments.
00000208 80 pages $24.95

Drums

Gretsch Drums
THE LEGACY OF THAT GREAT GRETSCH SOUND
by Chet Falzerano

This tribute to Gretsch kits features full-color photos and interviews with sensational players.
00000176 144 pages $34.95

History of the Ludwig Drum Company
by Paul William Schmidt

This book uses extensive interviews with the Ludwigs and photos from their personal collections to recall the origins, development and tools of crafting drums. You'll also discover why the best drummers use Ludwigs. Over 150 photos and illustrations make this an invaluable reference source for all drummers.
00000132 172 pages $29.95

Guide to Vintage Drums
by John Aldridge

Written by John Aldridge, publisher of *Not So Modern Drummer*, this in an essential guide for collectors-to-be that want to shop around, or for current collectors to discover drums outside of their area of interest. Includes many photos.
00000167.......................................$24.95